D1616913

Studies in the English Renaissance

John T. Shawcross, General Editor

WORLDMAKING SPENSER

Explorations
in the
Early Modern Age

Edited by

Patrick Cheney and Lauren Silberman

THE UNIVERSITY PRESS OF KENTUCKY

Publication of this volume was made possible in part
by grants from the National Endowment for the Humanities
and Professional Staff Congress of the City University of
New York Research Foundation.

Scholarly publisher for the Commonwealth,
serving Bellarmine College, Berea College, Centre
College of Kentucky, Eastern Kentucky University,
The Filson Club Historical Society, Georgetown College,
Kentucky Historical Society, Kentucky State University,
Morehead State University, Murray State University,
Northern Kentucky University, Transylvania University,
University of Kentucky, University of Louisville,
and Western Kentucky University.

Editorial and Sales Offices: The University Press of Kentucky
663 South Limestone Street, Lexington, Kentucky 40508–4008

04 03 02 01 00   5 4 3 2 1

Library of Congress Cataloging-in-Publication Data

Worldmaking Spenser : explorations in the early modern age /
    edited by Patrick Cheney and Lauren Silberman.
        p.   cm.
    Includes bibliographical references (p.   ) and index.
    ISBN 0-8131-2126-4 (alk. paper)
    1. Spenser, Edmund, 1552?-1599—Criticism and interpretation.
    2. Literature and society—England—History—16th century.
    3. Literature and society—History—16th century. I. Cheney,
    Patrick Gerard, 1949-   . II. Silberman, Lauren.
    PR2364.W67   1999
    821'.3—dc21   99-13690

Manufactured in the United States of America

CONTENTS

ACKNOWLEDGMENTS

This volume originated in papers presented at "*The Faerie Queene* in the World, 1596-1996: Spenser among the Disciplines," an international conference dedicated to the memory of A. Bartlett Giamatti and held at Yale University between September 26-28, 1996. We would like to thank the Yale University organizers, Elizabeth Fowler, Jennifer Klein Morrison, and Matthew Greenfield, for making our volume possible. We are also grateful to the many patrons who contributed funding: the James M. and Marie-Louise Osborn Collection, the Beinecke Rare Book and Manuscript Library, the Yale Center for British Art, Richard C. Levin (president of Yale University), Major League Baseball, Inc., the International Spenser Society, the Elizabethan Club of Yale University, the Jeffrey White family, the Department of English at Yale University, and the Pennsylvania State University. Individuals from Penn State who helped with the conference include Don Bialostosky, Beth Catherman, Donna Harpster, Robert A. Secor, and Wilma Stern.

Special gratitude for the volume goes to Robert R. Edwards, director and fellow of the Institute for the Arts and Humanistic Studies at Penn State, who kindly contributed encouragement and scholarly advice. Also at Penn State, Amy Barber and Todd Preston served as enthusiastic and expert research assistants, helping with the computer assembly of the manuscript, initial copyediting, compiling of the works cited list, and correspondence with the contributors. Chad Hayton provided valuable computer support, and Sandra Stelts of the rare books room helped with the volume jacket. Thanks also go to Laura Lunger Knoppers and Garrett Sullivan for their collegial conversation.

Some of the work on this volume was facilitated by course remissions granted by Baruch College. For this, thanks go to Alexandra Logue, dean of the Baruch School of Arts and Science, and Professor John Todd, chairman of the Baruch College English department.

At the University Press of Kentucky, we would like to thank Professor John Shawcross, who is the ostensive definition of collegiality, for his support and advice from the early stages of this project. We are also grateful to Professor Noel J. Kinnamon of Mars Hill College for copyediting the manuscript with a superb scholarly eye and to Grant Hackett for compiling an excellent index.

Special thanks go to Roland Greene, who directed us to the illustration appearing on the volume jacket.

Finally, we would like to thank the colleagues who contributed essays to this collection: for their superb professional expertise, their personal patience, and their general good will.

For James A. Carcallen
and in memory of Millar MacLure and Northrop Frye
Victoria College, University of Toronto

P.C.

For Harold L. Skulsky and in memory of Richard B. Young

L.S.

INTRODUCTION

Recent literary criticism has usefully directed our attention to what we have known all along: that works of literature exist in the world, that they respond to social and political forces operant at the time of their writing, that they take part in forming the systems of beliefs upon which people act, individually and collectively, and that those belief systems continue to have an effect long after the time of their initial construction. In keeping with the focus of much recent literary criticism, many Spenser scholars have been undertaking to remind those in Spenser studies, as well as a much wider scholarly community, of what has been nominally acknowledged but never fully registered: that the writings of Edmund Spenser occupy a substantial place in a crucially important era of English history and European culture.

The essays in this collection attest not only to the important place of Spenser's works in English history and European culture but also to the richness and complexity of the notion of place through which Spenser's work may be located. Although the historical itinerary of belief systems and the genealogical unfolding of literary history are mutually influential, each proceeds according to a logic or to logics of its own. Literary works, especially those as eclectic and allusive as *The Faerie Queene,* need to be understood in relationship to a variety of cultural phenomena and to multiple traditions, the preeminently literary as well as the political, economic, or ideological. Spenser's writings reflect the preoccupations and disseminate the beliefs of his time, but, as times change, his work has been appropriated by writers with very different concerns, sometimes for purposes antithetical to those of their Spenserian source.

In the opening essay of this volume, Roland Greene reflects on the place of *The Faerie Queene* in the world. By giving full scope to the global and geographic ramifications of the term "place," he attempts to lead *The Faerie Queene* out of a nationally oriented, if not nationalist, scholarship to a broader interdisciplinary one that includes such fields as human geography. Complementing Greene, David Quint demonstrates the extent to which the place Spenser's text assumes in the world is determined by and mediated through its function as literature. Quint shows how the image-making of

Spenser's major figure and dark double Archimago allegorizes in advance the logic of doubles that the entire *Faerie Queene* both resists as it affirms unitary truth and depends on as it purports to represent a social and political reality outside itself. Thus, in this first unit on "the World" Greene and Quint together centralize topics, terms, and methods for the volume as a whole, including Spenser's role in the Western literary and cultural traditions and the need to approach his texts through a fusion of formalism and history, poetics and environment.

Spenser's work positions itself in the world by literary means, and by its literary processes registers and responds to the world. Complex imitations and subtle rewritings by Spenser of precursor texts and of Spenser by subsequent literature reflect and are shaped by shifting attitudes to ownership, to literary property, to marriage bonds, to reciprocal claims of monarchs and subjects, to the myriad concerns of early modern Europe. In the next unit on "the Continental other," broad issues of negotiating literary history and shaping literary careers thus emerge. Sharing with Quint an interest in literary genre, in the structure of *The Faerie Queene*, and in the poem's commitment to eros, William J. Kennedy shows Spenser reflecting on his position in literary and cultural history, as Kennedy considers an author's proprietary rights over a literary text in the course of reworking the treatment of male proprietary rights over a bride in such precursors as Virgil, Ovid, Chaucer, Petrarch, and Ariosto. Assimilating multiple sources in a kind of literary exogamy allows Spenser to mediate a complex interaction of values and ideals in European culture. Accordingly, Anne Lake Prescott witnesses the migration of Spenser, the author of eros, genre, poetic architecture, even Rome and Italy, across the Alps to France in order to introduce a form of criticism she calls "intercareerism." Prescott demonstrates how the fortunes of Ronsard, as he constructed a long and successful career from the sometimes conflicting needs to please his patron, to express an ideal image of his nation, and to satisfy his own artistic inclinations, provide a model for Spenser's own career in England.

The interplay of literary texts in Spenser's writing extends from worldly concerns of careerism to the most fundamental issues of gender and identity formation. Thus the next unit on "the English other" roots Spenser's interest in literary traditions in his native soil, showing first how that interest reaches back from the written to the oral and then how subsequent writers inherited and appropriated his interests for their own (quite different) purposes. Mary Ellen Lamb reveals how the interaction of traditional fairy tale material with the matter of epic in *The Faerie Queene* allows Spenser to make accessible the conflicts of maternal culture and paternal culture in the formation of early modern male identity. If Lamb joins essayists from earlier units in looking back across traditions, the remaining essays in this unit look ahead. Susanne Woods, Jacqueline T. Miller, and Shannon Miller all present women writers of the seventeenth century empowered by Spenser as they find authority for their own writing by responding to Spenser's works. Woods explores how Aemilia Lanyer found in Spenser's writing a model for giving centrality to the conventionally marginal. Just as Spenser shows Una, seemingly the damsel-in-distress, giving crucial instruction and aid to the Redcrosse Knight, so in *Salve Deus Rex Judaeorum* Lanyer represents women such as Pilate's wife, the Daughters of Jerusalem, the Virgin Mary, and Lanyer's own patron, the Countess of Cumberland, as the source of understanding lost to the male figures of the poem, who are mostly wicked or misguided. Jacqueline Miller traces Lady Mary Wroth's multiple revisions of Spenser's House of Busirane, as Wroth's repeated attempts to figure the relationship of male and female achieve their most productive version in her own engagement with Spenser's text. Shannon Miller shows how Spenser's influence on both Wroth and Lanyer is determined by the needs of each; the aristocratic Wroth borrows romance motifs from *The Faerie Queene,* and the middle-class Lanyer models her addresses to patrons on Spenser's invocations of Elizabeth. Not only do seventeenth-century women writers find Spenser indispensable to the construction of their voices; so do men. John N. King shows Milton using Spenser as a source of ecclesiastical satire directed against seventeenth-century targets. Milton patterns Sin after Spenser's Error, as she reflects the evil motherhood and false feeding ascribed by seventeenth-century Protestant polemicists to the Church of Rome and the Roman Mass. Extending King's interest in theology and intertextuality, John Watkins explores how Spenser's complex positioning of the "classicism" of *The Faerie Queene* with respect to apocalyptic constructions of history in the sixteenth century allows the appropriation of the text for very different political agendas in the seventeenth century—by writers such as those commemorating the death of Queen Elizabeth, as well as by Dekker and Milton. In arguing that Spenser "incorporat[es] multiple models of poets and political authorship in a single vision," Watkins helps explain why such diverse writers as Milton and Dekker, Wroth and Lanyer, discover Spenser to be so valuable.

Spenser's work engages political and cultural questions still at issue in the late twentieth century. Thus the unit on "the Colonial and the Criminal" extends the time frame of the volume considerably: from classical, medieval, Continental, and seventeenth-century English culture to the global present. Elizabeth Jane Bellamy examines how the contemporary question of postcolonialism can be traced through figurations of India in *The Faerie Queene;* she argues that we can "reconfigure *The Faerie Queene* as a meaningful critique of imperialism" by discovering its careful embedding of India/America, and that by doing so we read a poem that is "'postcolonial' *avant la lettre*." As David J. Baker shows, present-day debate over the place of England in what is now called British studies has been prefigured in Spenser's *View of the Present State of Ireland,* as Spenser meditates on the historical and genealogical instability of British identity and contemplates the newly aggressive assertion of English power over the British Isles in the late sixteenth century. While, as Heather Dubrow demonstrates, Elizabethan constructions of the thief as the prototypical criminal inform the villainous brigands of *Faerie Queene* 6 and energize generic romance concerns with loss and recovery, the tendency to project anxieties about predatory neighbors onto the exotic Other recorded in "The Legend of Courtesy" remains a strategy for coping with a threatening world to the present day.

The last unit on "the self" internalizes Spenser in two quite different yet equally vital ways—by looking at Spenser's representation of inwardness itself, and by probing the vehicle for all of his representations: language. Although Spenser plays an important role in the formation of political matters still at issue, Judith H. Anderson reminds us of how thoroughly even Spenser's prose tract *A View of the Present State of Ireland* is informed by a sensibility alive to the ambiguity of language, and how complexly linguistic construction shaped the "saying self" of early modern England. In his essay on the House of Alma and Elizabethan physiology and faculty psychology, Michael Schoenfeldt demonstrates just how different Elizabethan ways of looking at things can be from our own in the late twentieth century, how important it is in reading Spenser to allow for Elizabethan ways of thinking, and how important it can be to read Spenser in order to historicize late-twentieth-century ways of thinking (particularly as embodied in New Historicism and psychoanalysis).

Despite a productive engagement with major concerns of early modern England, as well as of our own time, Spenser has become, in David Lee Miller's succinct phrase, "the most marginalized major author in the canon." In his afterword, Miller reminds us of the discrepancy between the canon that literary artists make and the history of literary reputation. Not only does Spenser's poetry inform the work of indisputably major figures such as Milton, but seventeenth-century women writers such as Wroth and Lanyer, whose authorial position was necessarily marginal, felt impelled to engage Spenser's work both because they found that his strategies could empower female voices, and because they felt the need to contend with his authority. Spenser has enjoyed an influence and authority with readers who are authors not adequately reflected by his reputation with the reading public at large.

In sum, the volume includes a considerable critical scope. The worldly relations here set forth include Spenser in relation to previous literary texts and traditions, future literary texts and traditions, such cultural figures as sovereigns, patrons, and thieves, and such cultural formations as the nation and the empire—even "language and digestion." The essays spread widely over the Spenser canon: both longer and shorter poetry; poetry as well as prose. They concentrate on the six books of *The Faerie Queene* (a consequence of their origin, the 1996 Yale conference on the 400th anniversary publication of the 1596 *Faerie Queene*), but they address such poems as *Amoretti*, while two essays focus specifically on *A View of the Present State of Ireland*. The essays also spread widely over the Western literary tradition, from classical Rome to medieval England, to Renaissance Europe, to both sixteenth- and seventeenth-century England, and onward to twentieth-century America. They examine extra-Spenserian texts and traditions that are both written and oral, in verse and in prose, by men and by women.

The collective picture of Spenser that emerges is of a poet who is central to the formation of early modern Europe and to the continuing expansion of Western Europe. In this "postcolonial" age aggressively bent on "de-canonizing" Spenser for what Louis Montrose memorably terms Spenser's "racist\misogynist\elitist\imperialist biases" ("Spenser's Domestic Domain" 122), our picture may be more than controversial; it is worldmaking. In an essay published recently, "Spenser's Lives, Spenser's Careers," Richard Rambuss surveys twentieth-century criticism to discover two different portraits of Spenser—what he calls "Spenser . . . the new poet, the prince of poets, the poet's poet" (16) and "Spenser . . . [the] frontier poet or . . . poet\bureaucrat" (12): in other words, the Poetical Spenser and the Colonial Spenser. Rambuss finds these two principal "Spensers" in both earlier and current criticism, and he calls for a "de-canonization" of the Poetical Spenser and a recontextualization of the Colonial Spenser, producing "new or alternative 'Spensers'" (15) that include "Spenser, an early modern anglophone poet" (17). Although we do not emphasize Spenser's role as a bureaucrat or secretary and spend considerable time with Spenser's role as a poet, nonetheless, our alternative Spenser may join others in what is now emerging as a goodly gallery.

The Spenser we portray is a Worldmaking Spenser. The phrase is resonant enough to include Spenser the maker of poetic worlds, Spenser the maker of the Elizabethan world, and Spenser the maker of the modern world, as later writers remake him. The Worldmaking Spenser suggests "Spenser" as both a subject and an object, a self and an other. This Spenser is important, we venture, because by its very formulation it authorizes its underlying assertion. If we de-canonize Spenser, we do so at our peril, through the erasure of history. We need Spenser—our students need Spenser—because he has made so much of the world and so much of the world has been made of him. To be the poet's poet is not to be a slender thing; it just might be a splendid thing. It is to be *present as a poet* throughout the world, then and now, in between, and for the future. The Worldmaking Spenser occupies a central place in the expansion of Western culture; his still "goodly frame" remains strategically lodged along an ever expanding trajectory, from the classical and medieval periods to the modern and postmodern. The Worldmaking Spenser fuses the Poetical and the Colonial Spenser, refusing bifurcation; it insists on what emerges here as a salient feature of Western literary history and culture: not merely that Spenser self-consciously authored himself into the world, but also that the world self-consciously authored him into it.

The volume testifies to the multifaceted nature of the Worldmaking Spenser. His own commitments emerge as extraordinarily wide: from the word to the world, from inwardness to India, from the "colon to colonialism" (Schoenfeldt). Our Spenser is fascinated with and exquisitely skilled in the structure of language, the structure of a poem, the structure of a literary career. He can make a word or a nation. He can build bodies—or souls. He is fascinated with the other; the other is fascinated with him. The Spenser portrayed here is thus at once comparatist and interdisciplinary, political and sexual, postcolonial and pre-Freudian, still always proto-feminist, "British" rather than "English" or anti-Irish—even playfully, performatively "Fool-ish," a "corruptor of words,'" to re-voice Feste (and David Miller). Precisely for that corruption and the rest, we may wish to enter a world that is wondrous for being more than literally in the making.

That an author's work exists in the world, then, means that it coexists with us, and, for readers of this volume that "us" probably means those who study sixteenth- and seventeenth-century English literature and, to a large extent, those who teach it as well. We are part of the world in which the writings of Edmund Spenser occupy a place, and, for good or ill, it largely falls to us to describe the contours of that place and make it part of the intellectual landscape of this and future generations of readers.

I. Spenser and the World

A PRIMER OF SPENSER'S WORLDMAKING

Alterity in the Bower of Bliss

Roland Greene

What is a world in *The Faerie Queene*? The answers to this question inform nearly everything we experience in Spenser's epic, not to mention in epic itself. This essay considers how Spenser's poem participates in one of the constitutive elements of the early modern mentality, namely the realization of multiple worlds, and the expanding evocation of "world" itself. *The Faerie Queene* occurs squarely within an era of developing awareness that the concept "world" no longer names something singular and unitary. Accordingly, emerging disciplines such as philosophy, legal and political theory, and theology, not to mention aesthetics and the theory of fiction, are obliged to come to terms with this plurality of worlds and worldviews: poets, explorers, jurists, and others contend over the protocols between worlds as well as the practical and epistemological stakes in the concept itself. In fiction, the period's two principal models of crossing between worlds might be called the ambassadorial and the immanentist, and these models are loosely connected to stands in politics, society, and culture. There are many sixteenth-century writers, for instance, who see the worlds of fiction as emphatically plural and joined in a poetics of embassy because they subscribe to an early modern reality that cannot be represented otherwise: think of the exuberant proliferation of worlds in More, Nashe, Sidney, Ralegh, and Shakespeare, three of whom are literally ambassadors. Then there are others, including Spenser, who give priority to maintaining the unity and singularity of "the world" in fiction, sometimes in counterpoint to an assumed plurality of metaphysical worlds, sometimes in defiance of the "new" worlds of exploration, philosophy, and science (Roche 7–17; Blumenberg). Spenser is implicated in this play of contested worlds, and *The Faerie Queene* intervenes decisively in it, speaking to a conservative strategy by which plural worlds are contained within the agency of the letter. His participation in this debate gives us much of *The Faerie Queene* as we know it, and can be recovered only by collating accounts that might seem otherwise to be incompatible, or even to describe different poems—for example, Paul Alpers's emphasis on the dynamic and Rosemond Tuve's on the static, or Thomas P. Roche, Jr.'s sense of how truth is maintained and Jonathan Goldberg's sense of how it is undermined. In terms of worldmaking, I will suggest, they describe the same *Faerie Queene*.

My argument draws on the understanding of worlds and worldmaking proposed by Nelson Goodman and adapted by several recent theorists of fiction. According to this view, a world is a symbolic construction that exists in statements about it and responses to it. Every world is made out of extant, alternative worlds—"the making is a remaking," in Goodman's motto—and works of art are prominent among the sites in which world-versions, as well as the conditions of worldmaking itself, are posited and discussed (6). Gunter Gebauer and Christoph Wulf have recently inflected Goodman's approach with a careful attention to the ways in which worldmaking responds to the social: "literary mimesis," they argue, "consists of a confrontation with the power of social institutions and the holders of power, with traditional codification systems, stylistic models, and the worldviews that come to expression through them" (19). Spenser's worldmaking demands such a historically informed discussion. For one thing, while a certain school of thought about epic represented by M.M. Bakhtin insists that its world horizon is unitary, *The Faerie Queene* everywhere displays multiple, partial, and emergent worlds. Despite the poet's efforts to make it seem integral and singular, "the world" is finally an untenable concept here. A historical approach to the poem ought to have something to say about this recurrent fact. Moreover, Spenser's worldmaking is a function of the poem's social, religious, national, and psychic dimensions, demanding a criticism that can address several of these together. David Lee Miller has argued, for example, that the allegory of *The Faerie Queene* posits "the anticipated-but-deferred wholeness of an ideal body." This body, Miller writes, "is an ideological formation derived from the religious myth of the *corpus mysticum* and its imperial counterpart, the notion of the monarch as incarnating an ideal and unchanging political body" (*Poem's Two Bodies* 4), and accordingly his approach counterposes political, psychic, and theological perspectives to get at the several ways in which the poem's ideal body is figured but left incomplete. It might be said that the same logic of anticipation and deferral applies to Spenser's depiction of the unitary world of the poem; it might be insisted that the ideal body is a version of that world, the two joined by immanence. In any case, I believe that the most useful approaches to Spenserian worldmaking will draw on not only history and psychoanalysis but constructivist philosophy, human geography, and social theory, three disciplines that have much to say about the making of ideal and actual worlds. In the pages that follow, I will sometimes adapt freely from these fields to arrive at a provisional account of Spenserian worlds—their dynamisms, their confrontations, their illegibilities. Cognate with allegory and narrative in *The Faerie Queene,* worldmaking nonetheless entails a somewhat different set of problems.

Embassy and immanence, I have argued in detail elsewhere, are the ground plans of two models of worldmaking in the early modern period, two kinds of negotiation between worlds (176–202). The ambassadorial position holds that worlds are multiple, are largely independent of and parallel to each other, and that we move from one to another as ambassadors travel between societies in the geopolitical world, namely by recognizing their differences and adopting a "worldly"—or "transworldly"—outlook. The immanentist view, on the other hand, maintains that worlds are situated within each other, and that to travel between them is to move inward along a thread of identity rather than difference. This view is often closely associated with an emphasis on the ritual and material properties of language, and it envisions the agent who moves between worlds as a kind of adept. One position recognizes alterity where the other emphasizes envelopment; one puts worlds along a horizontal axis while the other describes a vertical relation. One generally pertains to forensic discourse and diplomacy, while the other is allied with prophecy and magic. Together, these two views posit a unique role for the cultural agents who move between worlds, and they invite literary and other artists, if not to take sides, then to locate themselves in an overdetermined, often ad hoc relation to them.

This conceptual duality is played out across early modern poetry, where invocations of "the world" often stand in for strategic endorsements of one view or the other. In love poetry, for instance, one might ask where love is located for any given poet—whether in a world external and other to that of the speaker's own standpoint, or in a world immanent to that standpoint—and the alternatives seem clear. When Philip Sidney's Astrophil gives a list of geopolitical flashpoints and the questions of policy they raise, then concludes, "These questions busie wits to me do frame; / I, cumbred with good maners, answer do, / But know not how, for still I thinke of you" (*Poems* 180), he situates the "world" of love as outside but parallel to—perhaps superior to—that of current affairs. Likewise, when Samuel Daniel writes that "*Delia* her selfe, and all the world may viewe / Best in my face, how cares hath tild deepe forrowes" (12) he situates his love on a stage accessible to the larger world, and implies that his face represents him in each of these settings: "Delia and all the world may view care in my face." But when in the third edition of Daniel's poems the adverb is altered, "*Delia* her selfe, and all the world may viewe / Best in my face, where cares hath tild deepe forrowes" (172), the meaning widens—now including the sense "Delia may view herself and all the world in my face, where care has made furrows"—and a poetics of immanence emerges alongside that of embassy, to propose that amatory experience as registered in the face is the only "world" that matters. Is "all the world" within or without love? The difference may seem inconsequential, but the poetics of embassy sees the exchange of perspectives across worlds as the template for fiction as well as a constructivist reality, while the poetics of immanence claims to recover what is inward, authentic, and real; the former allows for friction and perhaps incommensurability between worlds, while the latter tends to posit a close correspondence between them as well as the poet's necromantic capacity to move from one to another. Of course in these works and elsewhere the two positions are seldom final, and often acknowledge each other's power: every reader remembers that *Astrophil and Stella*, while it generally evokes a poetics of embassy, begins with an immanentist flourish ("'Foole,' said my Muse to me, 'looke in thy heart and write'" [Sidney, *Poems* 165]). And when Michael Drayton concludes his *Idea* (1594) with these lines, "Goe you my lynes, Embassadors of love / . . . / And tell the world, that in the world there is / A heaven on earth, on earth no heaven but this" (1: 124), he is plainly exploiting the capacities of both poetics at once, adapting embassy to tell of immanence. These positions tend to be realized more or less heuristically in a given work, however, and to strike alliances with other elements—with its religion, its style, or its international, cultural, or gender politics, for instance— to become inseparable from how "the world" is figured there.

I might undertake to locate Spenser in this argument by addressing the part of *The Faerie Queene* that will concern me for the rest of this essay, namely book 2, and by moving straight into the proem of the book:

> Right well I wote most mighty Soueraine,
> That all this famous antique history,
> Of some th'aboundance of an idle braine
> Will iudged be, and painted forgery,
> Rather then matter of iust memory,
> Sith none, that breatheth liuing aire, does know,
> Where is that happy land of Faery,
> Which I so much do vaunt, yet no where show,
> But vouch antiquities, which no body can know.

But let that man with better sence aduize,
That of the world least part to vs is red:
And dayly how through hardy enterprize,
Many great Regions are discouered,
Which to late age were neuer mentioned.
Who euer heard of th'Indian *Peru*?
Or who in venturous vessell measured
The *Amazons* huge riuer now found trew?
Or fruitfullest *Virginia* who did euer vew?

Yet all these were, when no man did them know;
Yet haue from wisest ages hidden beene:
And later times things more vnknowne shall show.
Why then should witlesse man so much misweene
That nothing is, but that which he hath seene?
What if within the Moones faire shining spheare?
What if in euery other starre vnseene
Of other worldes he happily should heare?
He wonder would much more: yet such to some appeare.

Of Faerie lond yet if he more inquire,
By certaine signes here set in sundry place
He may it find; ne let him then admire,
But yield his sence to be too blunt and bace,
That no'te without an hound fine footing trace.
And thou, O fairest Princesse vnder sky,
In this faire mirrhour maist behold thy face,
And thine owne realmes in lond of Faery,
And in this antique Image thy great auncestry.

The which O pardon me thus to enfold
In couert vele, and wrap in shadowes light,
That feeble eyes your glory may behold,
Which else could not endure those beames bright,
But would be dazled with exceeding light.
(proem 1–5)

Much more than an advertisement for the Book of Temperance to follow, these stanzas decisively make a place for *The Faerie Queene* in the larger discussion of worldmaking in Elizabethan and early modern culture. Spenser's argument here begins by acknowledging the kind of argument against fictionality that had been current ten years earlier: that its authors and readers are "idle," and that it treats "painted forgery" (Fraser; Herman). In fact, that debate conditioned the late-century emergence of the positions I have described as broadly characteristic of the early modern period, prompting Sidney's *Apology for Poetry* and George Puttenham's *Arte of English Poesie* as lengthy defenses of their respective poetics of embassy and immanence. This proem injects Spenser into the debate, and makes his poem a document with its own, synthetic contribution—what Goodman would call its own "version" of world-relations as a model of how to leverage plurality in the service of the dominant values of *The Faerie Queene.*

Spenser's intervention in stanza 2 frames the issue in his own terms. He insists here as nearly everywhere that there is a single "world," and poses the significance of new lands, polities, and worldviews in terms of "Regions" of that larger world. What then is a "region" in relation to a "world"? In the sixteenth century as now, the term "region" has a studied kind of vagueness to it. Although its etymology follows from the Latin *regere* (to rule) as well as *regio* (boundary or direction, region or province), the early modern "region" tends to describe not self-contained political states but problematic divisions of larger societies; or places that inflect and perhaps defy the social and historical character of the contexts to which they belong; or even spaces not yet translated into the order of maps and governments, not yet rendered into places. In spite of the term, ruled is often exactly what such regions are not. In all its indefiniteness, the concept seems to exist to throw doubt on what might otherwise be taken for territorial integrity: as Anthony Giddens puts it in present-day social theory, "regionalization is best understood not as a wholly spatial concept but as one expressing the clustering of contexts in time-space. As such it is a phenomenon of quite decisive significance. No concept helps more to counter the assumption that a 'society' is always a clear-cut unity with precisely defined boundaries" (*Constitution of Society* 376). Or, we might add, that a world is such a unity either. Spenser's resort to the term here stands for the unruly element in his own worldmaking, in which "many great Regions [will be] discovered" as though to equivocate the unity of the Spenserian world.

What Spenser calls "Regions" are, of course, identical with what in many quarters of the early modern imaginary are called "worlds," starting from the doggerel that was placed over Columbus's tomb at his death—"A Castilla y a León / Nuevo Mundo dió Colón" (To Castile and to Leon / Columbus gave a New World) (Colón 349, my translation)—and continuing through a line of early modern explorers and observers that includes Rabelais, Montaigne, Galileo, Donne, Bacon, and Margaret Cavendish. Each of these figures understands "world" as a plural concept owing to the same proliferation of contexts that Spenser is at pains to remark: we know the least part of what exists, he agrees, and more is discovered to us almost daily. In the third stanza, then, he lets the rhetorical questions pile up—all in the spirit of "how much more must there be than what men have seen?"—and reaches this extravagant conclusion: "What if in euery other starre vnseene / Of other worldes he happily should heare?" Indeed, what if the abundance of contexts amounts not simply to regions but to worlds? Since this section of the proem began with the assertion of the unity of a single "world," the question gathers up all the force of the accumulating instances as though struggling against the designation of "region," bringing under scrutiny the provisional frame that was set around this topic and asking: what if there are multiple worlds? For many Spenserians, the traditional way of interpreting this latter question is to distill it entirely into the matter of whether there was a world in the moon (Kocher 85–86; Nicolson). Doubtless that is the topical referent, but I would aver that Spenser is also posing a more abstract problem in terms that his generation would immediately recognize. Is the reality disclosed by Columbus and Copernicus—not to mention the theorists of other orders of discovery, such as selfhood and inwardness—properly held within "the world," or within plural "worlds"?

The answer comes immediately, and in a fashion that will prove to be critical to this poet and his ambitious epic. As quickly as the question can be raised, Spenser explicitly introduces "Faerie lond" as the poem's locus of worlds and worldmaking. Without quite deciding the question of the plurality of worlds, that is, he invokes the fictional world at hand as containing its own regions, its own multiplicity: entering Faeryland we step out of the welter of innumerable adjacent worlds, the confusion of alterity and diplomacy, and into a unity that will set up its own approximations of these values. The way in is through "certaine signes here set in sundry place," an entrance that is unmistakably immanentist in its emphasis on the material character of language and the vertical passage it allows, through signification treated as spatial event. The fourth and fifth stanzas of the proem go on to preview the epideictic and prudential aspects of the epic, but they also promise the emotional relief of envelopment or "enfold[ing]" in a coherent worldview.

Thus Spenser's conceptual program here has several phases, all vital to how he defines the project of *The Faerie Queene*—for these phases will be enacted again and again. First the "worldness" of the epic's horizons is articulated, as though to set a single context around a given episode; then as though resisting that context or bringing it into question, the episode manifests alterity or diversity, or seems to qualify as a fictional world unto itself; and finally a unitary "worldness" is reasserted, this time with a recognition that Spenser and his complicit readers have rendered singular what in other hands could have been multifarious. This process, by which the reality of the poem is delimited, expanded to test those limits, and then delimited again, might be called narrative subduction: through it *The Faerie Queene* allows for but then subsumes a poetics of embassy, acknowledging its imaginative power before defeating it, as though to make the epic's own power that much greater. (The proem of book 2 makes this process especially vivid by fracturing "the world" of the second stanza into the "worldes" of the third before reinstalling Faeryland as, in effect, that first world again; in a telling indication of Spenser's outlook, the third stanza is one of only two instances in all of *The Faerie Queene* in which he uses "world" in the plural, versus hundreds of singular forms that almost all appear with the definite article [compare Fletcher 94n47]). Narrative subduction occurs not only here in the proem and elsewhere in book 2, but throughout the epic in different registers and guises. On the level of worldmaking, Spenserian subduction contributes to what Jonathan Goldberg has anatomized as the "frustration" of *The Faerie Queene,* in which—Goldberg writes of book 3— "the reader is being asked to take as the pleasure of the text [a] moment of doubled loss, [and] fulfillment through want"; "failed pleasures," he rightly observes, "*are* the pleasures of this text" (3). Alterity and the differentiation of worlds are continually being offered us, and continually taken away; the poem is both fascinated and threatened by those features of early modern reality that are insistently celebrated in many other contemporaneous works. Some of the most vivid episodes in *The Faerie Queene* enact this process of subduction, and several continuing debates among readers implicitly describe subduction as the process to which we respond, often viscerally. In the rest of this essay I wish to make the case that Spenser's disposition of worlds and his recoverable theory of worldmaking is a knowing intervention into the early modern discussion of this problem, and that what we call Spenserian poetics is in some measure the visible result of this intervention. My argument will address the last canto of book 2 as an epitome of the poem at large. If my treatment of the canto will not always apply precisely to other episodes, it will still, I hope, indicate the prevalence of what I call subduction as a narrative process and the import of worldmaking in *The Faerie Queene.*

The most notorious instance of what I am calling subduction, of course, is the episode of the Bower of Bliss at the end of book 2, in which Guyon encounters, and proceeds to destroy, a site of sensual delights that appeals viscerally to every reader. As Stephen Greenblatt sees it in the most acute reading of the episode to date, "in Guyon's destructive act we are invited to experience the ontogeny of our culture's violent resistance to a sensuous release for which it nevertheless yearns with a new intensity." In

Greenblatt's view, selfhood is at stake in the Bower of Bliss, both Guyon's and the reader's: "we can secure that self only through a restraint that involves the destruction of something intensely beautiful; to succumb to that beauty is to lose the shape of manhood and be transformed into a beast" (*Renaissance Self-Fashioning* 175). Throughout the episode, however, there is another term in play alongside "self" and "culture," and that term is "world." The perception of world properties, boundaries, and slippages is fundamental to the process of self-fashioning that Greenblatt rightly sees front and center in *The Faerie Queene*. For one thing, "the world" is often the setting of the necessary "Other" that makes selfhood possible; and for another, "world" as a factor in the drama of self-making flouts the sense of order and scale implicit in much of Greenblatt's argument. A world may be larger than the self defined against it, but just as plausibly it may be smaller, so that the same self that stands out before the backdrop of one world may contain or envelop others. "Self" and "world," it seems important to stipulate, are mutually dependent constructions and are often measured against one another—it is all but impossible to follow the "fashioning" of the former without attending the latter—but their relations are highly fluid. Moreover, they call on complementary disciplinary frameworks; they may tell the same story from alternative standpoints. We cannot afford to keep one construction static and unexamined in favor of the other.

At the opening of canto 12, Guyon and the Palmer have left the Castle of Alma, a site of temperance achieved, on their way to the Bower of Bliss, the destination they have anticipated since canto 1. The Boatman provided by Alma warns them of the dangers they will face:

> Said then the Boteman, Palmer stere aright,
> And keepe an euen course; for yonder way
> We needes must passe (God do vs well acquight,)
> That is the *Gulf of Greedinesse,* they say,
> That deepe engorgeth all this worldes pray:
> Which hauing swallowd vp excessiuely,
> He soone in vomit vp againe doth lay,
> And belcheth forth his superfluity,
> That all the seas for feare do seeme away to fly.
> (12.3)

This preamble frames the episode as the Gulf surrounds the Bower, and its horror has to do with the possibility of distortion around the idea of "the world": not only might "all this worldes pray" be swallowed in the gulf, but then it—that is, everything, according to the usual idea of "this world"—

might prove to be merely a discard, a "superfluity," within an unspecified larger horizon. What if "the world" (in the sense of the entirety of our perception) were not "the world" (in the sense of everything there is)? What if the humanist notion of scale, along which the self is a microcosm of the world, turns out to be only an inversion of a superintending order in which the world is a microego of a larger self? This is a potential terror of the poetics of immanence: if worlds exist within other worlds, who will say which is within which? Who will warrant that we are where we wish to be in an orderly protocol of creation? Cervantes addresses the same question for comic effect in his book of worldmaking, the second part of *Don Quixote*. Quixote and Sancho Panza are blindfolded, made to mount a wooden horse named Clavileño, and persuaded—after being singed by matches and blown at by bellows—that they have flown as high as the region of fire that encircles the earth. Once the experience is over, Sancho claims to have seen a totality ("the whole of it") in which men the size of hazel nuts walk on an earth the size of a mustard seed:

> At which the Duchess remarked: "Sancho my friend, reflect what you are saying. For seemingly you did not see the earth but the men going about on it, since it is clear that if the earth appeared to you like a grain of mustard seed and each man like a hazel nut, one man alone would have covered the whole earth."
> "That's true," replied Sancho, "but, all the same, I looked through one little corner and saw the whole of it."
> "Mind, Sancho," said the Duchess, "for we do not see the whole of what we look at from one little corner."
> "I don't understand these lookings," answered Sancho. "I only know that your ladyship would do well to realize that as we flew by enchantment, by enchantment I could see the whole earth and all men on it from wherever I looked." (Cervantes 2: 835–36; trans. Cohen 733–34)

For Guyon and the Palmer, the same prospect, including the idea that enchantment makes what we call the world, inspires an ontological dread that colors the rest of canto 12.

Moreover, if the "griesly mouth" of the Gulf of Greedinesse represents an unruly immanence, the Rock of Reproach stands for a dangerous embassy:

> On th'other side, they saw that perilous Rocke,
> Threatning it selfe on them to ruinate,

On whose sharpe clifts the ribs of vessels broke,
And shiuered ships, which had bene wrecked late,
Yet stuck, with carkasses exanimate
Of such, as hauing all their substance spent
In wanton ioyes, and lusts intemperate,
Did afterwards make shipwracke violent,
Both of their life, and fame for euer fowly blent.
(12.7)

The tableau of "shiuered ships" embodies what happens when one goes out of oneself and reaches for alterity—in sex, in commerce, in cross-cultural exchange. The same prospect that seems irresistible, and ineluctably humanist, to an ambassadorial thinker such as More or Sidney, threatens the values of Spenser; the same kinds of encounters that make for substantive understanding of "the world" according to a poetics of embassy lead to "substance spent" for Guyon and the Palmer.

In fact, the last word of the seventh stanza represents all of the anxiety of this position. "Blent" is an uncommonly charged word even in Spenser's overloaded and sometimes factitious lexicon. On its face he often seems to use "blent" for the past tense of "blind," as in Thenot's comment on Colin Clout in "Aprill": "Ah foolish boy, that is with loue yblent" (*Works* 7: 41). On closer examination, however, Spenser also uses "blind" and "blinded" in the physical sense, while "blent" includes being defaced to the sight but extends to a destruction as much moral as physical (and thus A.C. Hamilton glosses "blent" in the passage above as "despoiled"). Moreover, this sense of "blent" tends to appear where the boundaries between individuals or worlds are at issue—where substance is at risk of being exchanged, mixed, or "blended" through intercourse. (Spenser scarcely uses the latter verb in its material sense, absent an overtone of moral infection; especially in this Book of Temperance, he uses "mix" chiefly to connote extremes unreconciled into a mean, and therefore a source of weakness.) In effect, while some annotators struggle to maintain a clear division of senses (*Poetical Works* 668), the poet conflates an antique form of "blinded" with a contemporary form of "blended," to produce a word that conveys defilement through intercourse, not only sexual but intellectual and cultural. As Harry Berger observed more than forty years ago, in the Bower of Bliss "all nature and art are directed toward intercourse . . . they are denied any other meaning, deprived of their natural function" (*Allegorical Temper* 226). In the passage at hand, the evocation of the word "blent" suggests that those who travel on ships to distant lands risk that their names, and the substance of their lives, will be blended with and degraded by the others who inhabit those places. In some degree this is the same concern that Spenser—in contrast with many of his famous contemporaries, not a man of "the world"—broaches politely in his elegy for Sidney:

> Besides, in hunting such felicitie,
> Or rather infelicitie he found:
> That euery field and forest far away,
> He sought, where saluage beasts do most abound. . . .
>
> Such skill matcht with such courage as he had,
> Did prick him foorth with proud desire of praise:
> To seek abroad, of daunger nought y'drad,
> His mistresse name, and his owne fame to raise.
> What needeth perill to be sought abroad,
> Since round about vs, it doth make aboad?
> (*Works* 7: 181)

But "blent" with its proximity to "blended" also implies a nativist dread particular to this historical moment, namely that identity will be dispersed through encounter, mixture, and miscegenation of all sorts.

Spenser's general views on racial and other cross-peoplings were likely those of his nation and time—that is, he seems to have regarded the prospect with horror except where it might be used strategically, for example to render heathens into Christians. In *A View of the Present State of Ireland* Irenius first comments scornfully on Spanish and Irish claims of racial purity,

> These the mores and Barbarians breakinge over out of Africa did finallye possesse all spaine or the moste parte theareof And treade downe vnder theire foule heathenishe fete what euer litle they founde theare yeat standinge the which thoughe afterwardes they weare beaten out by *fferdinando of Arraggon* and Elizabeth his wiffe yeat they weare not so clensed but that thorogh the mariages which they had made and mixture with the people of the lande duringe theire longe Continvance theare they had lefte no pure dropp of Spannishe blodd no nor of Romayne nor Scithian So that of all nacions vnder heaven I suppose the Spaniarde is the moste mingled moste vncertaine and moste bastardlie, wherefore moste foolishelye do the Irishe thinke to enoble themselues by wrestinge theire ancestrye from the Spaniarde whoe is vnhable to derive him selfe from any Certeine

then with prompting by Eudoxus admits that

theare is no nacion now in Christendome nor muche farther but is mingled and Compounded with others, for it was a singuler providence of god and a moste admirable purpose of his wisdome to drawe those Northerne heathen nacions downe into these Cristian partes wheare they mighte receaue Christianitye and to mingle nacions so remote so miraculouslye to make as it weare one kindred and bloud of all people and eache to haue knowledge of him. (*Works* 10: 91–92)

In Guyon's adventure, however, the mingling of nations, peoples, and races is one dimension of the krasis—this hero's battle to realize temperance—at the center of book 2. Recall some of the terms that Berger adapts from the Greek as the implicit lexicon of the book:

> *krasis*—a mixing, compounding, blending; climate.
> *kratos*—strength, might, prowess; force, violence; sway, rule, mastery.
> *akratos*—unmixed, pure; untempered, unrestrained, excessive; intemperate, violent. (*Allegorical Temper* 66)

Much of the urgency of book 2 turns on the distinction between good and bad krasis. While temperance is properly an exercise of good krasis, it follows that Guyon is at risk from other versions of mixture that find him out of virtue and out of place. The danger of imbalance or incontinence is not exclusively a matter of received psychology, metaphysics, and cosmology— the levels of krasis with which Berger is concerned—but also reaches as far as the late-century realities that gave new momentum to old doctrines, as far as the weighings of "pure" and "blent" identities that Spenser remarks in Spain, Ireland, America, and elsewhere. In other words, alterity is the condition of a krasis of the present—and in Spenser's view, a danger to Christian temperance. The interval between the passage of the "shiuered ships" and Guyon's arrival at the Bower of Bliss elaborates on this danger: in stanzas 14 to 17 Phaedria reappears from canto 6, embodying the allure of sensuality; at stanza 19 we see "a goodly Ship" laden with merchandise, as though the narrative rewinds to show the ship of stanza 6 in process of "desauenture" and misprision; and after stanza 22, there comes the symbolic outcome of exploration and lust, "trauell" and wantonness:

> Eftsoones they saw an hideous hoast arrayd,
> Of huge Sea monsters, such as liuing sence dismayd.

Most vgly shapes, and horrible aspects,
Such as Dame Nature selfe mote feare to see,
Or shame, that euer should so fowle defects
From her most cunning hand escaped bee;
All dreadfull pourtraicts of deformitee. . . .

All these, and thousand thousands many more,
And more deformed Monsters thousand fold . . .
(12.22–23, 25)

While these are literally sea monsters, figuratively they complete an equation
in which embassy and sensuality produces mixture, miscegenation, or—to
invoke the word coined in this period to identify a new phenomenon—
mestizaje.

In the view of many of Spenser's contemporaries, these outcomes of
otherness are immediate examples of akrasis, incontinence, "the surrender to
lower nature," "the perverter of climate, of the blending of elements, of the
seasonal ebb and flow which characterizes becoming" (Berger, *Allegorical
Temper* 68). It ought to be no surprise to see Spenser implicating
symbolically, through metaphysics, a contemporaneous form of alterity such
as racial and cultural mixture. In 1590, Spenser's contemporary the Inca
Garcilaso de la Vega, himself a *mestizo* humanist, translated the *Dialoghi
d'amore* of León Hebreo into Castilian in part to stage a rethinking of the
conditions of his own mixed races and cultures through the literal words of
a canonical neoplatonist. "Love is of two kinds," the male speaker Philón
tells his female counterpart Sophía in the Inca's version. "Of these, one is
engendered by desire or sensual appetite. Such love is imperfect, deriving as
it does from a source both inconstant and vicious: for it is a child born of
desire. . . . With the cessation by fulfillment and satiety, of carnal desire or
appetite, all love totally ceases." As such a "child born of desire," both
personal and political, the Inca Garcilaso occupies a profoundly colonized
position at the outcome of a vicious and breakable cycle. But "el otro amor"
'the other love,' founded on possession and knowledge, "is that which
generates desire of the beloved, instead of being generated by that desire or
appetite: in fact we first love perfectly, and then the strength of that love
makes us desire spiritual and bodily union with the beloved." Philón's
conclusion describes the shift in roles envisioned by the *mestizo* translator for
himself: "as the first kind of love is the child of desire, so this kind is the father
and true begetter" (1: 103). León Hebreo's insistence on the spirituality of
heterosexual desire in a context of mutual alterity, and his interest in the
several kinds of *mescolanza* or mixing that generate love, make his text

intriguing to the Inca Garcilaso and his transatlantic readership. The involvement between the *mestizo*'s mother and father can perhaps be brought out from under the contemporary European rubric of concubinage and rehabilitated in impeccably neoplatonic theory, as a type of something higher than mere cupidity; *mestizaje* can perhaps be figured as better than bestiality or monstrosity. In the Inca Garcilaso's struggle to refashion these values, however, we can see what in the early modern imaginary he was struggling against. Some years later, in 1609, the Inca Garcilaso writes that

> These two races [the Spanish and the Africans] have mingled [with the Indians] in various ways to form others which are distinguished by the use of different names. . . . The child of a Negro by an Indian woman or of an Indian and a Negro woman is called *mulato* or *mulata*. Their children are called *cholos*, a word from the Windward Islands: it means a dog, but is not used for a thoroughbred dog, but only for a mongrel cur: the Spaniards use the word in a pejorative and vituperative sense.
>
> The children of Spaniards by Indians are called mestizos, meaning that we are a mixture of the two races. The word was applied by the first Spaniards who had children by Indian women, and because it was used by our fathers, as well as on account of its meaning, I call myself by it in public and am proud of it, though in the Indies, if a person is told: "You're a mestizo," or "He's a mestizo," it is taken as an insult. (Garcilaso, *Comentarios* 2: 266, trans. Livermore 607)

Even the *Tesoro de la lengua castellana* of Covarrubias (1611) still treats "mestizo" as an entirely animal phenomenon (802).

Spenser and the Inca Garcilaso alike belong to perhaps the first generation in European history that had to ponder the reality of worldwide race mixture and to confront the prevailing myths of miscegenation and monstrosity in light of the present. In Spenser's feverish imagination, therefore, these creatures produced by embassy and its search for alterity are not only unnatural and misshapen but horribly numerous, like the human products of racial and cultural mixture: introduced within the boundaries of a region or place, they overpopulate, stretch, and uncode that place until it becomes virtually unrecognizable, the rule or program under which it was introduced becomes attenuated and its energies potentially available for redistribution, and what was a region of Spenser's singular world is—to adapt a term that will be useful in worldmaking—deterritorialized (Deleuze and Guattari 130–271; Holland 241–42). In one sense this transposition plays out a humanist nightmare that the author of *A View of the Present State of Ireland* would have felt acutely, namely that a civilized place can be rendered abstract, hypothetical, and ungovernable—in other words, can become open for reterritorialization. In another sense, however, this is a nightmare Spenser intends for us to experience recurrently, as the pattern of this episode will be stamped on canto 2 again and again. As a fairy region or place is redefined by its accumulated manifestations of otherness and becomes unthinkable in its original terms, it becomes less a region and more a world before the reader's eyes—alternative and often oppositional to the unitary fictional world from which it departs. And to the degree that it turns into such a world, it becomes subject to the violent exercise of Spenser's narrative authority, which subducts the emergent world back into the universe of the poem with a few reductive or assimilative gestures. In the case of this episode, the subduction is less striking than many:

> Feare nought, (then said the Palmer well auiz'd;)
> For these same Monsters are not these in deed,
> But are into these fearefull shapes disguiz'd
> By that same wicked witch, to worke vs dreed,
> And draw from on this iourney to proceede.
> Tho lifting vp his vertuous staffe on hye,
> He smote the sea, which calmed was with speed,
> And all that dreadfull Armie fast gan flye
> Into great *Tethys* bosome, where they hidden lye.
> (12.26)

What was an unforeseen world of horrors is naturalized and territorialized again—back into an illusion, an "armie," and a body part. But the ghostly traces of such episodes do much to fashion the experience of *The Faerie Queene,* where worlds continually emerge and vanish, where the contradiction between the observable plurality of worlds and Spenser's universalist ideology colors every episode, and where alterity—the principle at odds with the immanentist credo of the poem—is often visible and just as often out of reach.

The segment of the canto from stanza 27 through the arrival at the Bower of Bliss in stanza 42 presents a surplus of topographical specifications meant to obscure the boundaries between one place and the next, and to delude us into the sense that Guyon and the Palmer have finally reached their "sacred soile, where all our perils grow." A weeping maiden draws Guyon toward her "Island," but the Palmer resists, and the place melts away from the narrative; a crew of mermaids, located at a different "sted" in the "watry wildernesse," entice them toward the "still / And calmy bay" where they dwell, and again the Palmer resists; Guyon and the Palmer reach "the land," and it immediately becomes undefined and deterritorialized for them, "That all things one, and one as nothing was, / And this great Vniuerse seemd one confused mas" (37, 27–31, 34).

Each of these sites mimics and confuses the nature of a world according the alternatives of immanence and embassy: the mermaids, for instance, occupy a port that evokes cross-cultural encounter and otherness ("there those fiue sisters had continuall trade"), but explicitly promise a refuge within the singular world:

> O turne thy rudder hither-ward a while:
> Here may thy storme-bet vessell safely ride;
> This is the Port of rest from troublous toyle,
> The worlds sweet In, from paine and wearisome turmoyle.
> (12.32)

A hypogram for the seductions of immanence, "The worlds sweet In" as epithet conflates the values—sexual, nativist, introspective—that immanentist thought counterposes to embassy. (When the Bower of Bliss is introduced shortly after, its first description—"In which what euer in this worldly state / Is sweet"—is made from these words again.) The mermaids themselves are grotesque hybrids pretending to be familiar, "th'vpper halfe their hew retained still." Their stead and the other sites alike represent illegible worlds, where not only the content but the terms of worldmaking will be mistaken by Guyon. What virtue, including temperance, can triumph in a setting where the protocols are unknown or (perhaps worse) misunderstood, where values are distorted? The interlude clears the way for the Bower itself, a theme park of early modern immanentist fantasies that redeploys the properties of these preliminary worlds while bringing their menace, and the stakes of worldmaking, to a new level. For the essential character of the Bower crosses the illusion of immanence with the reality of embassy— confronting its visitors with a climate of unmasterable rules that falsely promises accessibility and legibility, a new world under the shadow of the old, and alterity disguised as a version, albeit brought up from the depths of the interior, of the self.

Within the Bower, of course, the boundaries between self and other, immanence and embassy, can scarcely be discriminated, and thus Guyon will react in a destructive fashion that would be inappropriate and bizarre in any other setting but that makes sense here; what he will tear down is not so much the Bower as a site of pleasure but the promiscuity of a "world" in which the choices that constitute "worldness" for Spenser and his audience cannot be made. But before we arrive at the climactic scene of destruction, I wish to look briefly at two or three episodes that foreground the stakes and the dangers as Spenser sees them.

Perhaps the first such episode, following hard on the description of the Bower of Bliss itself, is the introduction of a figure about whom readers notoriously disagree:

> . . . in the Porch there sate
> A comely personage of stature tall,
> And semblaunce pleasing, more then naturall,
> That trauellers to him seemd to entize;
> His looser garment to the ground did fall,
> And flew about his heeles in wanton wize,
> Not fit for speedy pace, or manly exercize.
>
> They in that place him *Genius* did call:
> Not that celestial powre, to whom the care
> Of life, and generation of all
> That liues, pertaines in charge particulare,
> Who wondrous things concerning our welfare,
> And straunge phantomes doth let vs oft forsee,
> And oft of secret ill bids vs beware:
> That is our Selfe, whom though we do not see,
> Yet each doth in him selfe it well perceiue to bee.
>
> Therefore a God him sage Antiquity
> Did wisely make, and good *Agdistes* call:
> But this same was to that quite contrary . . .
> (12.46–48)

By consensus the difficulty here is that Spenser conflates different usages of the term "genius," such as the god of generation, the *genius loci* or presiding spirit of any place, and the particular genius within each self that prompts human beings toward good. C.S. Lewis calls the passage "baffling," and decides that it confuses because "Spenser was, in fact, confused" (363). Where the pedantic distinction between *genii* is concerned, that may be true. But when we take the passage as commencing with stanza 46 as I do here, the outlines of this evil genius's deception come clearer: he is a hythlodaeic figure of otherness, a genius of this place, who stretches the limits of the natural— witness his interest to curious sightseers—but confounds them into believing him concurrently the good self who speaks from within. He represents an alterity that makes itself legible as identity. As Spenser knows, the motif of the others who are ourselves, who are sometimes more ourselves than we are, is a commonplace in cross-cultural narratives of this period, from Utopia to Ralegh's Guiana and beyond (M.B. Campbell 177–78). Those figures who seem to embody identity and otherness at once—not only savages but ancestors, counterparts, namesakes, facsimiles, and cultural hybrids—can be the objects of intense fascination. Still, the threat of this counter-Agdistes is that, far from our rendering his otherness as identity, he does so himself—he comes to us already trading on the illusion that he springs from our interiority, to confuse what is familiar with what is "straunge." This brief episode offers a significant preview of what will be Guyon's approach to the Bower in large: refusing to read the figure's appearance as self or other or both, Guyon simply overturns his bowl and breaks his staff. He refuses to commit himself in a world that will change the terms of its worldness on him. The salient fact that is often overlooked in conventional accounts of the canto is that the Bower of Bliss is not exactly beauty embodied, but a variety of beauty that depends on the confusion of worlds and worldviews, that invites us to relax the discriminatory faculty and surrender to a pleasure that overruns the straits of self and other, here and there, inside and outside. The prevalence of racial and other human mixtures in this period testifies to the consequences of such a relaxation, while Spenser's thought everywhere shows him to be its determined enemy. For him and for many of his readers, there is no beauty where these categories are obscured.

The considerable description of the Bower of Bliss that follows is one of the handful of unforgettable set pieces in *The Faerie Queene*, not simply because it is beautiful but because it situates the interlocking questions of selfhood and worldmaking in an irresolvable relation to each other. It is a paradigm for the worldmaking procedure of the entire epic, which is to bring a site into view, develop it into an emergent world that vies with the originary world of the poem, pose directly or not the matter of how one world relates to the other—and then subduct the second world back into that singular world, making unitary what was plural and evanescent what was concrete. In the thirty stanzas from 50 to 80, Spenser first describes and delimits the Bower of Bliss, "A large and spacious plaine, on euery side / Strowed with pleasauns," then expands it through an array of strategies including favorable comparison with received fictional worlds,

> More sweet and holesome, then the pleasaunt hill
> Of *Rhodope*, on which the Nimphe, that bore
> A gyaunt babe, her selfe for griefe did kill;

unexpected adjustments of scale,

> Infinit streames continually did well
> Out of this fountaine, sweet and faire to see,
> The which into an ample lauer fell,
> And shortly grew to so great quantitie,
> That like a little lake it seemd to bee;

enticing gestures toward what remains hidden,

> The wanton Maidens him espying, stood
> Gazing a while at his vnwonted guise;
> Then th'one her selfe low ducked in the flood,
> Abasht, that her a straunger did a vise:
> But th'other rather higher did arise,
> And her two lilly paps aloft displayd,
> And all, that might his melting hart entise
> To her delights, she vnto him bewrayed:
> The rest hid vnderneath, him more desirous made.

and intimations of completeness:

> For all that pleasing is to liuing eare,
> Was there consorted in one harmonee,
> Birdes, voyces, instruments, windes, waters, all agree.
> (12.52, 62, 66, 70)

Taken together, these strategies amount to a primer of early modern worldmaking: they show how the phenomenological and fictional idea of a world is elaborated out of what might otherwise be merely an attitude, an anecdote, or a convention. For the narrative experience of *The Faerie Queene*, this and other episodes of expansion convey something otherwise lacking in Spenser's epic, namely the sense that, as in any fully conceived fictional world, something happens outside the frame of the immediate moment, an implication Spenser will not foster directly—it goes against the announced intention of the poem—but cannot quite do without. However disorderly it seems, Spenserian subduction is a sort of pressure valve that makes possible the epic's immanentist outlook in a society for which the plurality of worlds is becoming ever more commonplace. Moreover, such expansions mean that a poetics of embassy is continually threatening to break out in *The Faerie*

Queene, one of the era's most ambitious manifesti of immanentist thought, and must be defeated again and again. At the abstract level of poetics where alternatives confront each other, this process stamps *The Faerie Queene* as a product of its moment, where equivalent confrontations occur often: between Sidney's *Apology for Poetry* and Puttenham's *Arte of English Poesie,* for example, or between parts 1 and 2 of *Don Quixote.* Subduction is one type of these confrontations, a virtual violence that overcomes an emergent world in the name of an extant one.

The climax of the canto, therefore, comes with the disclosure of Acrasia in the Bower proper, and Guyon's violent reaction to that tableau. It is worth noting that Acrasia is first presented as anything but the intelligence of the Bower, since she and her "new Louer" are found "a slombering, / In secret shade, after long wanton ioyes" (12.72). She is scarcely able to govern herself: how little likely does she seem to be a worldmaker? In her repose in a corner of the Bower, she seems to have turned her back on the world around her, retreated into private experience, and yet once again Spenser will depict a region becoming a world before us. It turns out that the partial, pleasure-driven mode of stanzas 74 and 75—"Gather therefore the Rose, whilest yet is prime, / For soone comes age, that will her pride deflowre"— is the collective outlook of this place, and privacy becomes public as the very notion of a world is turned inside out. Carpe diem is an anthem here (D. Cheney 99–101). Hence anyone who is absorbed into the Bower, like Acrasia's lover Verdant, is disabled from the alternative worlds of negotium, glory, achievement. Within a few years in a number of beguiling lyrics, a young John Donne will consider how to render private experience into a world: "Shine here to us, and thou art every where; / This bed thy center is, these walls, thy sphaere" (1: 12)

But Donne's feat of worldmaking, from the standpoint of the lovers themselves, evades the implications of Spenser's deadly serious survey of sites that intemperately and promiscuously become worlds of their own. In fact it makes sense that Acrasia, seemingly heedless of anything but her own pleasure, presides over all the emergent worlds represented in the episode of the Bower of Bliss, and that her solipsism is the basis for perhaps the most threatening of the alternative worldmakings explored, and challenged, in *The Faerie Queene.* Divulged in their postcoital repose, "Acrasia and Verdant are the revealed centre of the ambiguous relationships which Spenser has played over throughout the book, and which are to become more complex in the books which follow: strength and weakness, aggression and submission, effort and pleasure, love and war" (Williams 77). All of the disasters of the canto can be traced to their incontinence, which opens the way to otherness, monstrosity, and proliferation. In this spirit the word that occupies the most acute position at the end of this description of Verdant is a familiar one in Spenser's moral register:

> ne for honour cared hee,
> Ne ought, that did to his aduauncement tend,
> But in lewd loues, and wastfull luxuree,
> His dayes, his goods, his bodie he did spend:
> O horrible enchantment, that him so did blend.
> (12.80)

As Berger relates it, "what sharply confronts Guyon, there in the heart of the garden of Shame, is a ruined apparition of himself. He sees a knight whose excellence should have been guaranteed by 'native influence,' who can yet feel lust, who in fact has fallen. Perhaps an unsettling thought flashed across Guyon's consciousness: Can this happen to me? The discovery of the noble victim is virtually a projection of the weakness stumbled upon in the center of the hero's excellent garden" (*Allegorical Temper* 217). Guyon and the Palmer then literally enact the process of subduction that occurs everywhere in the epic: they subdue Acrasia and her lover in a net—a gesture that symbolizes the cancellation of her autonomy and her recovery into the unitary world of the protagonists—before Guyon destroys the Bower itself, in the action for which book 2 is unforgettable.

The inexhaustible controversy around this passage might have less to do with the action itself, which can be explained easily enough, than with Guyon's standing in for narrative subduction, which touches every reader's experience of *The Faerie Queene*. When Alpers argues that "it is only in [stanza 83], when moral awareness manifests itself as action, that we find something disturbing in Spenser's evaluation of the Bower of Bliss," he is perhaps observing that an intrinsic feature of the poem breaks out here into purposeful, explicit action (*Poetry* 306). And when Berger characterizes the demolition as "a Puritan frenzy" (*Allegorical Temper* 218), more than taking Spenser's hero out of context he might be acknowledging that contemporaneous Puritans—the Stephen Gossons, Arthur Goldings, and Henry Loks—are often implacably opposed to the poetics of embassy and to the plurality of worlds in any guise. Guyon's action accepts the burden of world-unmaking that is inseparable from the equation at the center of *The Faerie Queene*, where the fashioning of a gentleman takes place only against the backdrop of a singular, civilized, territorialized world. The reader's uneasiness with Guyon's destructive frenzy might be a symptom of another uneasiness with the tendency to make and then destroy worlds that is coextensive with our experience of Spenser's poem. The tug of immediate imaginative experience, where worlds are continually emerging out of one another, against the poem's moral imperative by which such emergences must be neutralized, means that every reader, willingly or not, is a proxy for Guyon for much of *The Faerie Queene,* and that Guyon in turn stands in for us when he renders the emergent world of the Bower back into "the fowlest place." Insofar as Spenser here gives dramatic agency to what is otherwise carried out by the impersonal narrative itself, and all but invites reactions not precisely to this action but, implicitly, to the process of narrative subduction itself, book 2 is perhaps the capital of the poem's worldmaking. Other chapters of the epic may fashion, unfashion, and refashion worlds relentlessly and self-critically, but there is probably none that foregrounds in this way the properties of Spenser's worldmaking itself. Readers have always recognized this fact, although their tendency has been to transpose an issue both constructivist and ideological—how Spenser makes and unmakes worlds, and why—into one simply moral and experiential. Attention to his worldmaking does not cancel such idealist and visceral considerations, but locates them in a wider cultural and aesthetic setting and recovers one of the intractable problems of his time with which I began this essay: what is a world in *The Faerie Queene?* In early modern Europe? In the early modern "world"?

As a worldmaker, then, Spenser is on the front line of those thinkers who are obliged to confront imaginatively the changes undergone by the concept of "world" in his time. He and many of his contemporaries may develop different programs in relation to these changes, but the ubiquity of the term across the range of late Elizabethan writing and the evident markers of assumptions about it—such as Spenser's avoidance of the plural—attest to the pressures at hand. *The Faerie Queene* is principally a document of immanence, but also a contested ground on which the alternative poetics of Spenser's time play out their sometimes subtle, often violent confrontations. And while Spenser builds his worlds out of the available materials of his time, and enacts his version of worldly relations, inevitably he also gives us much we ought to recognize of early modern culture and society. He leaves us a term he has transformed, that tells its own story in *The Faerie Queene,* that will always witness the tensions and tactics of his peculiar moment.

ARCHIMAGO AND AMORET

The Poem and Its Doubles

David Quint

When Archimago uses his infernal spirits to abuse the senses of first the dreaming, then the awakened Redcrosse in the first two cantos of *The Faerie Queene*, he seems to have read the rest of the poem in advance. The series of tableaux that cross the vision of Redcrosse possess both a parodic and prophetic relationship to the poem's subsequent narrative. We might see in this relationship evidence to support Josephine Waters Bennett's thesis that book 1 was written after the originary materials of books 3 and 4. The beginning of *The Faerie Queene* points especially to its center and to its allegorized version of the career of Spenser's patron, Sir Walter Ralegh, whose rise and fall in the favor of Queen Elizabeth shapes the two 1590 and 1596 installments of the poem. In fact, the split that Archimago introduces between Una and her eroticized, demonic double at the opening of the poem is subsequently felt in the relationships of Una to Belphoebe, the personification of the queen; of the chaste Belphoebe herself to her twin or doubling alternative Amoret; of the poem's first part to the second. Archimago, that is, has already invented the structure and method of Spenser's poem.

Archimago's foresight seems to stretch very far indeed in the first of the illusions he sends Redcrosse, the erotic dream in which the knight sees Una brought to his bed in the company of Venus and the Graces (1.1.47–48). The enchanter sees as far across the course of the poem as Mount Acidale and the pipe dream of the personified poet Colin Clout who envisions his damsel as another Grace of Venus (6.10.11–16). Redcrosse wakes up only to be confronted by Archimago's second illusion, a spirit in the shape of Una apparently ready to kiss him (1.1.49–54); the poem meanwhile looks forward some eight cantos to Arthur's telling of his dream of Gloriana's condescending to lie down beside and blandish him (1.9.13–14).[1]

Finally, Redcrosse rides away in amazement and disdain after he has viewed Archimago's third illusion: two spirits copulating, the one as Una, the other in the shape of a young and unwarlike Squire (1.2.3–8).

This is the most interesting illusion of all for reasons that are more and less obvious. The shocked reaction of Redcrosse suggests his own lack of sexual experience. He has read about it in books, presumably in those same sexy pagan classics that provide the mythological materials of his initial dream and leave open the question about how much of that dream comes from Archimago's spirit, how much from the young knight's own literature-soaked fantasy. His glimpse of the false Una and the squire assumes the contours of a primal scene, the child's experience of exclusion as it watches or imagines its beloved mother in the embrace of another—perhaps the more so because, as we later learn in canto 10 (65–66), the changeling Redcrosse has never seen his mother.[2] Archimago defames the true Una who indeed shares both erotic and maternal associations in Spenser's religious allegory: a "pure vnspotted Maid" (1.6.46.8), Una recalls the bride without spot of the Song of Songs (4.7) and the woman with child pursued into the wilderness of Revelation 12, both scriptural sources for the doctrine and iconography of Mary as the Immaculate Conception, the spotless virgin spouse and mother who is, in turn, a figure of the True Church, Mater Ecclesia.[3] But this nice Protestant girl who Redcrosse thought was saving herself for him turns into a whore before his eyes, thanks to Archimago's art—and the enchanter thereby implies that there is no pure religion, that all churches are profane. Only then can Archimago interest Redcrosse in Duessa, the Catholic merry widow.[4]

Like the other two scenes presented to Redcrosse, this final one that slanders Una by appearing to place her in the arms of a lowly lover projects a later narrative in *The Faerie Queene,* in this case a whole series of related narratives concerning amorous squires. Redcrosse is particularly galled to see his Una surrendering her favors to one "[l]ike a young Squire, in loues and lusty-hed. / His wanton dayes that euer loosely led, / Without regard of armes and dreaded fight"[5] (1.2.3.4–6). Out of the sexual need that she has already disclosed to Redcrosse, the false Una has apparently loved beneath her, taking on a squire who is good for nothing except for lovemaking. The question of class is repeated in book 2, though transposed another step down the social hierarchy, when the squire (2.4.162) Phedon will fall for exactly the same trick that Archimago plays on Redcrosse. His treacherous friend and fellow squire (2.4.18.1), Philemon, makes Phedon believe that he is seeing his beloved Claribell in the embrace of a "groome of base degree" (2.4.24.3; 27.8)—really Philemon himself making love to Claribell's handmaid Pryene dressed up in Claribell's clothes. Unlike Redcrosse,

Phedon cannot be restrained from killing his innocent lady. Phedon ends his story by boasting that he comes from an honorable and famous ancestry (2.4.36), and thereby suggests that Philemon knew exactly which buttons to push in order to drive his friend into the hands of Furor, exploiting his class anxiety as much as his jealousy. This anxiety seems to be writ large in the poem in the exploits of the handsome Squire of Dames, who cuts a swathe through womankind in book 3 (7.53f.), and in the career of Amyas, the Squire of Low Degree, in book 4.7–9, who apparently succeeds, together with his fellow squire Placidas, in marrying up into the nobility.[6]

These two episodes, in turn, are carefully interlaced with the poem's central love story of squire and social superior: the meeting, subsequent misunderstanding, and eventual reconciliation between Timias and Belphoebe (3.5; 4.7–8.18). Here the anxieties of *The Faerie Queene* extend from the social to the political, since Belphoebe, according to Spenser's prefatory letter to Ralegh, is the poem's representation of Queen Elizabeth as woman rather than monarch, a "most vertuous and beautifull Lady," and her relationship to Timias, the squire who enjoys the status of a major character of the poem, thinly allegorizes Ralegh's rise to royal favor and his subsequent disgrace after his secret marriage to Elizabeth Throckmorton came to light.

In the Belphoebe-Timias episode, Spenser's poem also reaches its Ariostesque core in its imitation of the enamorment of Princess Angelica with the lowly footsoldier Medoro in the *Orlando furioso*. In the false Una and her squire not only has Archimago anticipated the story of Belphoebe and *her* squire, but Spenser has exploited Ariosto's own first anticipation of the Angelica-Medoro plot. Both the trick that the enchanter plays on Redcrosse and the subsequent trick that Philemon plays on the hapless Phedon are based on the episode of Polinesso, Ginevra, and Ariodante early in the *Orlando furioso* (4.56–6.16)—what will also become the basis for the Don John-Hero-Claudio subplot of *Much Ado about Nothing*. Polinesso persuades Ariodante to stand by and watch while he makes love to Ginevra's maid Dalinda, who is disguised in Ginevra's clothes; convinced that Ginevra has played him false, Ariodante twice unsuccessfully attempts suicide. In his despair he is the poem's first anticipation of the love-madness that will overtake Orlando when he learns that *his* Angelica has given herself to Medoro. What begins, however, in the *Orlando furioso* as the slander of the innocent Ginevra has become all too true in the story of Angelica and Medoro; with its celebrated irony, Ariosto's poem defends women and alternately suggests that they cannot be slandered enough. Spenser's fiction picks up Ariosto's cheerful sexual realism, if not downright cynicism, in the Squire of Dames, the most Ariostesque figure in *The Faerie Queene*. The

Squire laughs (4.5.18) at the tournament of book 4, when the girdle of chastity falls off the false Florimell, herself a second version in the poem of the demonic *eidolon* that Archimago manufactures in the false Una at its beginning, and just before the false Florimell chooses Braggadocchio as her champion and lover (4.5.26). This choice repeats Ariosto's own secondary reflection of the Angelica-Medoro story, the choice that Doralice—later said to be the most beautiful woman in Europe after Angelica's departure (30.17)—makes of her secret sexual partner Mandricardo over the supposedly more deserving Rodomonte (*OF* 27.107). The career of the "losell" Braggadocchio (2.3.4.1)—the character of lowest degree in the poem—is, as James Nohrnberg has pointed out (597–98), systematically interlaced and contrasted with that of Squire Timias—and, behind him in the topical allegory, with the social climber Ralegh.[7] Archimago has already, at the very opening of *The Faerie Queene*, presented his own take on the subsequent plot of Timias and Belphoebe, and he did so by adopting the realist perspective of Ariosto's poem: he presented a version of Angelica and Medoro to the stunned Redcrosse in the tableau of Una enjoying the exertions of her lusty squire. As the maker of the poem's first, if distorting images, Archimago takes on the guise of the predecessor poet whom Spenser, according to Gabriel Harvey's letter, had attempted to overgo.

As critics have long pointed out, Spenser's "Legend of Chastity" in book 3 rewrites the love story at the center of the *Orlando furioso* precisely to counter such Ariostesque realism, especially to deflect it away from the womanly personification of his queen.[8] Whereas Angelica solicits the love of Medoro, here it is Timias who falls in love, not Belphoebe, who is meanwhile intent on cultivating the flower of her virginity (3.5.51–54). Moreover Timias, aware of the social gulf that separates him from Belphoebe, dares not speak his desire: his devotion to Belphoebe is entirely selfless. All appears as it should be and yet *The Faerie Queene* surrounds this innocent couple with amorously successful, social-climbing squires. For her part, Belphoebe does seem to like to have the young squire around and is capable of jealousy when he apparently turns to another. In the social coding of the poem's allegory, Belphoebe indicates that Elizabeth is susceptible to the goodly person of Ralegh, the upstart from the lower nobility, to whom she grants the favor of her presence. She appears, as Archimago's false Una does to Redcrosse, to prefer and accord power and place to a lovemaking squire—that is, a courtier—rather than to a warrior knight, one of the great peers of the land. Redcrosse will eventually earn Una's hand by his knightly prowess, even if the battle he wins over the dragon is a spiritual one; Timias is but the passive recipient of Belphoebe's grace. For all that he tries, Spenser cannot quite dispel the disreputable aura that surrounded the rise of his patron Ralegh and that made him "the best hated man of the world, in Court, city, and country," the sense that he had displaced better men in the affections of Elizabeth by his skill at courtiership, what amounted to making himself lovable to the queen.[9]

For others longed to be in the position of Ralegh-Timias—as close as one could hope to get to Elizabeth short of actually conquering her bed. That further step was something her politically ambitious male subject might dream for himself—witness the dream of Simon Foreman that Louis Montrose has brought to critical attention[10]—and desperately feared that another, whether the Duke of Alençon or a native English rival like Ralegh, might accomplish.[11] Archimago places the false Una in the arms of her lusty squire in order to summon into view a forbidden wish barely hidden in the Elizabethan unconscious—the same wish that Jonson looks back on in *The Alchemist*, when Face tells the law clerk Dapper of a "Queen of Faery," a maiden aunt who is "a lone woman / And very rich, and if she take a fancy / She will do strange things" (1.2.155–57), especially if Dapper, as his name implies, can cut a figure like the well-dressed Ralegh: "You do not know / What grace her Grace may do you in clean linen," Face tells him (174–75).[12] Redcrosse is of course upset to see a squire making love to Una because he, too, dreams of Una, and in some sense both he and later Arthur as well have been dreaming Simon Foreman's dream. Belphoebe's treatment of the "lovely boy" (4.7.23.6) Timias-Ralegh has maternal associations, and Belphoebe too, like Una, bears the Marian attributes of the Immaculate Conception: she is born "[p]ure and vnspotted from all loathly crime" (3.6.52.4). Elizabeth was both figurative mother of her nation and identified with the mothering English church of which she was the head (Hackett 50–52, 77–78, 124, and passim). Insofar as it is she whom Archimago has in mind when he couples the false Una with her squire, the primal scene he invokes is a national one, the traumatic view of *lèse majesté*.

The sequence of abusive images that Archimago presents to Redcrosse—the epithalamic dream, the blandishing Una, Una and the squire—discloses the allegorical homologies among Una herself, the Gloriana dreamt of by Arthur, and Belphoebe. It also suggests the sequence of the three books of the first installment of *The Faerie Queene*: Redcrosse will marry Una at the end of book 1; Gloriana's identity will be revealed in book 2, if only in the book, the *Antiquitie of Faerie Lond* (2.9.60; 2.10.76); Timias will meet Belphoebe in book 3. As Spenser's poem unfolds, we may realize that there is a lot of Una—true religion and church—invested in Elizabeth and her double personifications in the poem. But Archimago also exploits the slippages among the allegorical levels in this sequence in order to suggest a recursive, desacralizing logic. When the supposed whorishness of Una he discloses to Redcrosse also takes the form of a slanderous version of Belphoebe and Timias, he suggests how skepticism about the historical Queen as woman and political player can be turned back upon the poem's allegory of Holiness. Belphoebe herself risks being exposed as a false Una or—Archimago would have us believe—exposing the falseness of Una. The suspicion of temporal and carnal motives in the adoration of Elizabeth reflects upon her Protestantism, and a temporal or carnal Protestant church is no different from its Catholic counterpart. Una or Duessa: *così fan tutte*. Religion and politics, Archimago literally demonstrates, make strange bedfellows.

Archimago conjures up an image of the not-so-secret desire—the desire that Timias must nonetheless keep secret beneath an outward show of deference—shared by Ralegh and other subjects of Elizabeth. Imagine, this prime mover of the imagination suggests, an alternative version of or alternative to Elizabeth. In place of the Queen who, in the words of Francis Bacon, "allows of amorous admiration, but prohibits desire," and thus from the beginning condemns those who court her to frustration, Archimago proposes a proper love object, a woman who can desire in her own right, and can be wooed openly and self-interestedly with the expectation of a return on the lover's erotic investment, whether in the form of royal or sexual favor.[13] Once again Archimago peers far into *The Faerie Queene* or indeed seems to write it in advance. For Spenser's poem itself invents an eroticized double for Belphoebe, her twin sister Amoret. Spenser's letter to Ralegh does not explain to us why Belphoebe-Elizabeth should have a lovable twin, herself twinned with Pleasure when she is raised by Venus and Psyche (3.6.51), but it is not hard to understand that Amoret is the pleasure of the erotic life and the reward denied to the suitors of Belphoebe-Elizabeth. The mutual pleasure into which Amoret melts in the arms of Sir Scudamore, turning the two of them into the figure of a hermaphrodite, marked the goal of the first 1590 installment of *The Faerie Queene*. Notwithstanding its historical basis, Scudamore's name may faintly suggest the Italian "scudiere," the squire who is shield-bearer, and thus spells out his role as foil for Timias, the Timias who earns the favor of Belphoebe while Scudamore gets the girl. It also makes Scudamore's embrace of Amoret one more projection, a climactic one, of Archimago's "false couple," Una and her squire in their "lewd embracement" (1.2.5.4–5), at the poem's beginning.

Amoret is doubly related to that false Una. Either she represents the fantasy—equally hoped for and dreaded—of an attainable Elizabeth: Elizabeth, that is, as an Angelica for some lucky Medoro. Or she is, like the demonic eidolon, an eroticized substitute twin for an Elizabeth who cannot, in fact, be wooed and won. Thus it is Amoret who, in the subsequent allegory of Ralegh's disgrace in book 4, stands in for Elizabeth Throckmorton, who, as one of Elizabeth's maids of honor, had herself stood in for the queen in Ralegh's affections. In order to play this role, Amoret is no longer reunited with Sir Scudamore at the revised end of book 3 in the poem's 1596 edition. Yet she has merely gone from representing one of Elizabeth's maids of honor to representing another, for in the poem's first installment of 1590 Amoret's story had alluded to an earlier secret marriage between the queen's maid of honor, Mary Shelton, and James Scudamore in 1574; Queen Elizabeth had been angered on that occasion, too, so much so that she had broken Mary Shelton's finger. Spenser's poem had thus already invented the precedent and pattern for Ralegh's marriage before the marriage took place in 1591.[14] In book 4, Timias-Ralegh tends the wounds of Amoret who lies "in swoune" (4.7.35.4) just as Belphoebe herself had bowed down over him when he "lay in deadly swound" in book 3: this too, the poem suggests, is an innocent version of Angelica's seeking to revive the wounded Medoro. But it also unmistakably suggests, given that Amoret has been wounded by the monster Lust and by Timias's "owne rash hand" (4.7.35.9), that Ralegh had to marry Elizabeth Throckmorton, whom he had made pregnant. Innocent misunderstanding or not, Belphoebe's disfavor and her jealous claim on Timias—"Is this the faith," she asks him when he has, according to the poem, been unable openly to pledge his faith to her—suggest the very need for an Amoret, an erotic outlet or safety valve in a world where the Virgin-Queen appears to demand exclusive rights on the love of her servants.

One of these servants was Edmund Spenser, personified in his poem as Colin Clout, who on Mount Acidale in book 6 celebrates the elevation of his own "country lasse" (10.25.8) as a fourth Grace. To do so, he has to beg pardon from "Great *Gloriana*" for leaving her momentarily aside "[t]o make one minime of thy poore handmayd / And vnderneath thy feete to place her prayse" (10.28.6–7). Spenser's lady-love is his own Amoret, who is promoted here not only to a Grace, but, like Elizabeth Throckmorton, to a "handmayd" of Elizabeth: in her, the poet loves a substitute version of her mistress. More specifically, Colin's Lasse and Spenser's Amoret are the *Amoretti*, Spenser's private love poems to his wife Elizabeth Boyle that he wrote side by side with his epic and published in 1595 between its two parts. On Acidale Sir Calidore stumbles onto the scene of Spenser taking a break from the poem in which he, Calidore, is a character in order to write his sonnet sequence. In Sonnet 80 of the *Amoretti*, in turn, Spenser announces the completion of the first six books of *The Faerie Queene* and, in a passage that echoes this moment on Acidale, takes time out for love:

Till then giue leaue to me in pleasant mew,
  to sport my muse and sing my loues sweet praise:
the contemplation of whose heauenly hew,
  my spirit to an higher pitch will rayse.
But let her prayses yet be low and meane,
  fit for the handmayd of the Faery Queene.
(*Amoretti* 80.9–14)

Both the *Amoretti* and the poet's lady that they celebrate are subservient handmaids to—but also pleasurable alternatives and vacations from—*The Faerie Queene*, poem and monarch. Like his patron Ralegh, Spenser finds a second Elizabeth to love and marry, breaking the queen's monopoly on his devotion—and on his literary energy. The poet asks for pardon as Timias-Ralegh sues to be restored to favor for these lapses into private pleasure with the lady of the *Amoretti* and with Amoret. Their excuse in part is that Amoret and indeed any woman whom they may love is a twin of the unapproachable Belphoebe-Elizabeth: that they are always loving some form of the queen herself, being true to her in their own way. But by the same logic, Belphoebe's off-limits nature virtually produces her twin Amoret or so many twin Amoretti for her servants to love.

Accept no substitutes. The "country lasse" of Mount Acidale brings us back to the false dream imposed on Redcrosse in which Una appears to him amid Venus and the Graces, and we are forced to remind ourselves that this logic of doubles and twins is Archimago's. Yet it is at this point that the Archimago who seems to dictate the terms of the poem at its beginning—and perhaps behind Archimago the sexual realism of the *Orlando furioso* as well—may be seen to be the accomplice, witting or not, of the poet of *The Faerie Queene*. If Archimago invents the false Una, the carnal imagination's vision of truth that leads to Duessa, he also, as if by way of compensation, gives Spenser the cue to invent Amoret, the imagination of the carnal, erotic life that appears to return through marriage to the true Una. The Amoret who melts in pleasure in the arms of Scudamore at the end of the 1590 book 3 recalls Redcrosse at the end of "The Legend of Holinesse" gazing into the eyes of his betrothed Una—"His heart did seem to melt in pleasures manifold" (1.12.40.9)—and the holiday spirit of the 1590 ending—"to morrow is an holy day" (3.12.47.9)—suggests a recovery of holiness in love. The love and marriage that Amoret represents are a way back to Eden in *The Faerie Queene*, and Archimago's sexual cynicism in this instance seems only to further the poem's ends. The first half of the poem in 1590 begins with Una and ends with Amoret, and on Mount Acidale it may reach a similar conclusion. Still, Archimago's powers to disillusion seem to have taken greater hold by the second installment of the poem in 1596. For while Timias may return to the good graces of Belphoebe in the poem's fiction, Elizabeth had still not restored Ralegh to favor when the second part of the poem appeared, and with the disgrace of his patron went Spenser's own hopes for further advancement to royal favor. In the last three books of the poem, there may be no choice *but* to accept and make do with substitutes (as if these books were themselves the poem's own substitution or doubling replication of its first part). The climactic reunion of Amoret and Scudamore has now disappeared; the corresponding visionary moment at the end of the new sixth book seems to be in another poem altogether, in Spenser's holiday from his epic, a vision not of Amoret herself, but of the love poetry that bears her name.

NOTES

1. These homologies between Archimago's first two temptations and the rest of the poem are also noted by D.L. Miller, "Spenser and the Gaze of Glory" 763.

2. For Freud, in his discussion of the primal scene in *From the History of an Infantile Neurosis* (the "Wolfman"), the child witnessing parental intercourse can confusedly think that its mother is suffering violence; see Strachey 17: 45. The 1590 three-book installment of *The Faerie Queene* ends with another apparent revelation of sexual secrets engineered by an enchanter: Busirane's Masque of Cupid which seems to insist on the sadistic nature of sexual penetration and in which Amoret is the unwilling victim. The parallel might support the larger argument of this essay about the relationship between Archimago's creation of the false Una and Spenser's invention of Amoret.

3. For the classic account of the ecclesiastical imagery of book 1, see Hankins. Nohrnberg has elaborated the biblical contexts of the identification of Una with the True Church and of Archimago's creation of the false Una. See also Waters; Hackett. Una's mothering attributes and relationship to Redcrosse seem to be institutionalized in the House of Holiness in canto 10 with its various presiding female figures—Caelia, Charissa, Mercie—where the knight is spiritually reborn and christened as St. George.

4. "I sit being a quene, and am no widowe, and shal se no mourning," proclaims the Whore of Babylon in the Geneva Bible (Rev. 18.7). In a slightly different vein careless Phrygius in Donne's *Satire 3* abhors all religions, "because all cannot be good, as one / Knowing some women whores, dares marry none" (63–64).

5. All citations from Spenser's works are taken from Spenser, *Poetical Works*, ed. Smith and de Sélincourt.

6. The question of who is marrying whom arises because of the discrepancy, possibly intended by Spenser, between the rubric that opens canto 9 and the expectations of the narrative that Amyas will wed Aemylia and

Placidas Poeana. See Nohrnberg 624. On the interlacing of the Aemylia story with the Belphoebe-Timias plot, see Wofford, *The Choice of Achilles* 314–23.

7. On Braggadocchio and Timias-Ralegh, see also Quint, "Bragging Rights" 391–430, 414f.

8. On Spenser and Ariosto's Medoro episode, see Alpers, *The Poetry of the Faerie Queene* 185–94; and Bennett 138–53. Roche suggests the importance for Spenser's fiction of Harington's allegorization of Ariosto's episode (143–56). On Belphoebe and Timias, see also O'Connell 107–24; and P. Cheney, *Spenser's Famous Flight* 111–48.

9. On Ralegh's unpopularity, see Thompson 33. It *could* be argued that Timias earns the grace of Belphoebe by his defeat of the three villainous foresters (3.5.13–25)—Spenser may wish to make us think so. But Belphoebe herself seems unaware of the Squire's feat.

10. Foreman dreamed that the Queen had begun to make love to him before he woke up—rather as Redcrosse is awakened by an internal censor from the erotic dream that Archimago sends him. See Montrose, "'Shaping Fantasies.'"

11. Rumors and slanders abounded. Mary, Queen of Scots wrote but apparently did not send to Elizabeth a letter in which she accused Bess of Hardwick of having retailed to her stories about Elizabeth's supposed affairs with Leicester, with the Duke of Alençon, with Alençon's ambassador Simier, with Christopher Hatton upon whom Elizabeth was said to have forced herself. See Rawson 271–76. Catholic and foreign accounts about the sex life of the English Jezabel were even more lurid; see Hackett 130–32. Archimago's slander of Una-Elizabeth at the opening of Spenser's poem is thus the counterpart of the calumny of the Blatant Beast at its end, who spares neither "Kesars . . . nor Kings" (6.12.28). The whole *Faerie Queene* can be read as a battle, perhaps finally a losing one, against slander.

12. On Ralegh as dresser, see Quint, "Bragging Rights" 75.

13. The passage from Bacon's *In Felicem Memoriam* is cited by Montrose in "'Shaping Fantasies'" 49.

14. Did Spenser in 1590 already have some inkling or advance knowledge of Ralegh's love for Elizabeth Throckmorton? On the Scudamore marriage, see V. Wilson 107. Lady Scudamore would herself try to mediate between the Queen and another of her maids of honor, Elizabeth Vernon, when the latter secretly married the Earl of Southampton in 1598; see 238 and, on Ralegh and Elizabeth Throckmorton, 170–75. See also the entry by Galyon under *Scudamore family;* Galyon errs, I believe, in identifying Mary Shelton's husband as John, instead of James, Scudamore, but she points out that Spenser "may be cunningly doubling Ralegh's Elizabeth with Mary Scudamore." Scudamore's retrospective narrative in 4.10 of his removal of Amoret from the Temple of Venus would thus refer to an episode some twenty years earlier—James Scudamore's marriage to Mary Shelton—that is intended by Spenser to serve as an exculpatory model for Ralegh and Elizabeth Throckmorton. Scudamore keeps looking at the Goddesse, "for feare of her offence / Whom when I saw with amiable grace / To laugh at me, and favour my pretense, / I was emboldned

with more confidence" (4.10.56.2–5). The goddess in question is as much Queen Elizabeth as Venus, an Elizabeth whose grace and favor Ralegh and his poet hope once again to find. My thinking on these issues is indebted to conversations with James Nohrnberg.

II. Spenser
and the
Continental Other

SPENSER'S SQUIRE'S LITERARY HISTORY

William J. Kennedy

In books 3 and 4 of Spenser's *The Faerie Queene* a minor character identified as the Squire of Dames plays a functionally important role as a transitional figure between the poem's two extant halves. In 3.8.44–3.9.18 he introduces Satyrane, Paridell, and Britomart to Hellenore and Malbecco, and in 4.2.20–31 he introduces Blandamour and Paridell to Cambell, Canacee, Triamond, and Cambina. Chaucerian associations dominate his entrance in 3.7.37 where he is pursued by a giantess named Argante, the twin sister of Ollyphant, a figure derived from *The Tale of Sir Thopas,* and likewise his exit from 4.5.18 after he has identified Cambell and Canacee, the protagonists of Chaucer's unfinished *Squire's Tale.*[1] In these matters the Squire of Dames updates the courtly preferences and ideological leanings, if not the actual person of Chaucer's Squire, in effect showing what the latter might have been or become in sixteenth-century England. But Spenser also complicates this effect by incorporating other models beyond Chaucer, ones drawn from Virgil, Ovid, Petrarch, and above all Ariosto. In each instance Spenser focuses upon concerns registered in sixteenth-century commentaries on these authors. Beginning with humanist editions of the ancient classics and continuing in commercial editions of Ariosto for a proto-bourgeois Italian readership, these commentaries explore issues about dynasty and destiny relevant to the "Legend of Chastity" and the "Legend of Friendship." Responding to matrimony as a contractual agreement designed to secure the continuity of male bloodlines guaranteed only by a wife's chastity, they pose important questions about who owns the bride in this agreement. These questions are replicated in the domain of a dichotomous literary history by the question of who owns a literary text.

The Squire's narrative about his own misadventures in 3.7.37–61 implicates him in these matters as a figure drawn from earlier literary history.[2] Not only does his ancestry reach back to Chaucer's Squire and *The*

Tale of Sir Thopas, but it also evokes the protagonists of Ariosto's scabrous Innkeeper's Tale in canto 28 of the *Orlando furioso.* Here two cuckolded husbands set out to discover whether any faithful women exist in western Europe. Upon finding none, they agree jointly to possess one woman hoping to satisfy her desires. When she manages to elude their constant surveillance, they conclude that no lover or husband ever fully owns his mistress or wife. Spenser's tale takes a distinctive turn when the Squire encounters one woman whose virtue is unconditional, a "Damzell of low degree" (3.7.59) whose lack of patrimonial title or estate affords little economic motivation to protect her family's bloodlines with her chastity. Her absolute virtue heightens by contrast the Squire's depravity, but its exaggerated circumstances also call into question the conditions of its possibility.

The concept subtending the Damzell's absolute virtue clashes with the idea of virtue as a mean between extremes as "Aristotle hath deuised" in Spenser's letter to Ralegh.[3] Aristotle's subdivisions of moral philosophy into ethics, economics (the management of a household), politics, rhetoric, and poetics nonetheless portend conflicts within his system, since what may seem just or good for a single individual may not be so for an entire household in economic or domestic terms, for the state in political terms, for a speaker in rhetorical terms, or for a poet in representational terms.[4] An individual's virtuous self-sufficiency, for example, may deprive his or her family of needed support, or it may allow others less virtuous to seize control, distort rational arguments, or skew its poetic representation. Amid such conflicts the question of ownership and possession figures prominently, as one party may gain what another might lose. In books 3 and 4 of *The Faerie Queene* the institution of marriage proves an exemplary case. Those who enter into it surrender their individual sexual freedoms, including ownership of one's body, in order to form a domestic unit. Society compensates by recognizing their offspring as legal heirs.

Ownership of the bride proves particularly problematic in this contract.[5] Because "pater semper incertus est, mater certissima" [the identity of the father is always uncertain, but that of the mother is unambiguous], she must surrender her sexual freedom absolutely in order to guarantee her husband's paternity.[6] From an ethical perspective she becomes the property of her husband who may retain his own sexual freedom without jeopardizing the legitimacy of their offspring. From the domestic or economic perspective she becomes the property of her and her husband's families, past and present, who certify the continuity of their bloodlines through her chastity. From a political perspective she becomes the property of a cultural system designed to safeguard the titles and estates of its propertied classes. From a rhetorical or poetic perspective she becomes the property of a discourse that may either challenge or uphold the working of this system. In these terms books 3 and 4 of *The Faerie Queene* pursue various narratives about marital consent concerning Britomart, Florimell, Amoret, Hellenore, and Canacee. The Squire of Dames episode provides a transition among these narratives, but it also questions their status by exposing gaps amid their personal and political, ethical and domestic claims. Such gaps record the discordant responses of an earlier literary history to questions of who owns the bride. Chaucer, for example, dramatizes conflicts between individual freedom and domination, mastery and consent, in the marriage cycle of his *Canterbury Tales,* proposing self-mastery as a prerequisite to effective consent. Virgil dramatizes conflicts between demands of the individual and those of the state, interrogating an ethos of submission to law and the binding power of superordinate institutions. Ariosto dramatizes a political conflict between needs of families, friends, allies, and associates, resolving them amid the give and take of various contractual arrangements.

Embedded in Spenser's references to these texts are analogous questions about who owns a literary text. Commentaries appended to early printed editions of the ancient and early modern classics project a host of different understandings about their moral, philosophical, philological, and historical meanings. In the light of such interpretive practices and diverse inquiry, we might ask how any text could invite a universal, univocal, ownership. Allusive poets such as Spenser can only question what constraints govern the possession of a literary past, its continuity with the present and beyond, its preservation and empowerment for the future, and its contribution to a sense of cultural identity for an emergent community.

Spenser's Squire's literary history begins with his entrance in the clutches of Argante, identified in 3.7.48 as the twin sister of "*Ollyphant,* that wrought / Great wreake to many errant knights of yore." Spenser underscores the Chaucerian connection in his 1590 edition with "Till him Child Thopas to confusion brought," but he curiously diminishes this connection in 1596 by emending the line to "And many hath to foule confusion brought." This erasure of Sir Thopas flouts the immense popularity of Chaucer's tale among fifteenth- and sixteenth-century poets who sought to resume it for a literate gentry keen on reimagining the courtly worlds of Chaucer's fiction.[7] Spenser instead heightens Argante's classical ancestry by naming her a daughter of the rebellious Titans, fathered by Typhoeus in incest with his mother Earth (3.7.47). Such a monstrous birth figures in the domestic order as a threat to patriarchal authority, a disruption of familial economy, while in the political order ruled by Jove it figures as a dissolution of contractual bonds that unite households and communities.

Ancient and early modern commentaries on Virgil's Typhoeus in book

1 of the *Aeneid* reinforce this association. There, when Venus addresses Cupid "nate, patris summi qui tela Typhoea temnis" [O son, who scornest the mighty father's Typhoean darts] (665), the son obeys his mother's command to wound Dido with passion: "paret Amor dictis carae genetricis" [Love obeys his dear mother's words] (689).[8] As commentators so diverse as the Latin grammarian Servius (c. 400), the Florentine humanist Cristoforo Landino (1488), the Venetian editor Antonio Mancinello (1490), and the Parisian professor-turned-printer Jodicus Badius Ascensius (1500) explain, this exchange dramatizes the optimum consequences of family relations in a well-managed household. Thus Badius explains: "Vendicat ubi necessitudo parentum, quidquid liberi possunt. Et docet inter filios, & parentes, tale debere esse uolendi, & nolendi studium" [Family relations here require children to do what they can for their parents, and it teaches parents and children what ought to be required and forbidden].[9] Cupid is not only honoring his mother's request to assist his half-brother Aeneas, but he is also helping to ensure a safe transmission of the latter's Trojan patrimony to Italy. Yet another commentary upon Typhoeus in Ovid's *Metamorphoses* makes a similar point. In his influential edition of Ovid's poem (1555) Georgius Sabinus, Rector of the Konigsberg Academy and a disciple of Melanchthon, critiques the cultural relevance of arranged marriages. The story of Typhoeus befits the arrogance of its teller in the *Metamorphoses,* a proud daughter of Pierus who challenges the muses with her song, "falsoque in honore gigantas / ponit et extenuat magnorum facta deorum" [and ascribes undeserved honor to the giants and belittles the deeds of the mighty gods] (5.319–20).[10] Calliope responds to the song with her own story of Proserpina and the contractual agreement struck by her father Jupiter in marrying her to Pluto. Sabinus's commentary links these stories by showing how the moral lessons of the second invert those of the first. Proserpina's marriage to Pluto exemplifies secure domestic arrangements that reinstate a social order previously destroyed by Typhoeus's rebellious misdeeds: "Alterum quod diuino beneficio ciuilis hominum vita exculta sit victu & legibus: alterum, quod hostes nominis diuini aeterno supplicio constringantur" [First, because by divine favor the civil life of humankind is improved; and second, because its enemies are restrained through an eternal supplication of the divine name] (169).[11]

To reach this conclusion Sabinus's commentary must condone the incestuous implications of Ovid's text, where Jupiter and Pluto are brothers and Proserpina, Jupiter's daughter by his sister Ceres, is Pluto's niece. The gods' attempt to channel their inheritance through narrow exogamy finds its apotheosis in incest. For Spenser, the Squire's account of Argante's incestuous origin projects this impulse not just once in Typhoeus's relations with his mother Earth, but twice in Argante's relations with her twin brother.[12] The incest is double as Argante, whose name suggests the Greek *argos* 'bright, swift' or antithetically 'lazy, idle,' mates in the womb with Ollyphant, whose name in Spenser's text suggests the Greek *ollymi* 'to destroy, ruin' and *phantasma* 'appearance, image' that according to the 1596 edition "many hath to foule confusion brought" (3.7.48).[13]

If the Hellenized spelling of "Ollyphant" replaces Chaucer's "Olifaunt" and further diminishes Chaucer's presence in book 3, why then does Spenser reinstate his predecessor so conspicuously in book 4? Here, after the Squire of Dames arrests Blandamour's dispute with Paridell for mastery of the Snowy Florimell, he notes the arrival of two stranger knights and their ladies. After "viewing them more neare," the Squire "returned readie newes" that they include Cambell and Canacee (4.2.31). He apparently knows these Chaucerian figures well enough to recount their adventures, but Spenser does not allow him to speak directly. Instead the poet takes possession of the tale in his own narrative voice, framing it with his direct praise of "Dan Chaucer, well of English undefyled" (4.2.32). Spenser's displacement of his Squire amounts to a displacement of his Chaucerian prototype in *The Canterbury Tales,* the pilgrim storyteller who, through his concern with rhetorical technique (5.36, 67, 105, 383, 401–05, 580, and 589), competes with his fictional father the Knight (5.325, 479, and 593 echo 1.1089, 1761, and 3041) for mastery of narrative form. Chaucer's Squire serves in turn as a parodic analogue of the youthful Chaucer who "koude songes make and wel endite" (195) and also of the mature Chaucer who, like his character, tries to outdo his own literary models until, as in *The Squire's Tale* and *The Tale of Sir Thopas,* they get the better of him and force him to a stop.[14]

Spenser foregrounds this complex interaction between Chaucer's Squire and his own, and between Chaucer's self-representation and his own narrator, author and creation, story and source, by situating his version of the tale within a *dichotomous* model of literary history that separates past from present, "Though now their acts be no where to be found, / As that renowmed Poet them compyled, / With warlike numbers and Heroicke sound" (4.2.32). The interruption of Chaucer's tale throws open the question of its patrimonial focus and its link with Spenser's continuation. The circumstances of this continuation also expose the vulnerability of Chaucer's textual ownership in early printed editions of *The Canterbury Tales.* In modern editions the agent who interrupts Chaucer's Squire is the Franklin, an upwardly mobile man of substance who commends the Squire's "gentilesse" and wit while comparing him to his son who lacks such qualities (5.694).[15] The edition of Chaucer that Spenser most likely used, however, was John Stowe's 1561 reprint of William Thynne's 1532 folio. Here it is the Merchant who interrupts the Squire and with his graphically ugly tale of adultery initiates a newly positioned—and in fact more coherent—Marriage Group that culminates with *The Franklin's Tale*.[16] The latter now provides a climax rather than a beginning for the Marriage Group with its story about a different squire. Here Aurelius pressures the married heroine, Dorigen, to examine her own "trouthe" (5.759) in relation to spousal "maistrie" (5.747, 764–65) and her husband Arveragus's "soveraynetee" (5.751). For Spenser these issues would come to inform Britomart's pronouncement about "maisterie" at Malecasta's castle in 3.1.25 and Duessa's challenge to Scudamour's "maisterdome" in 4.1.46. The implications all point toward Spenser's heightened emphasis on the domestic question of who owns the bride as it intersects with the literary question of who owns the text. From *The Squire's Tale* Spenser inherits several unfinished motifs about marriage and spousal possession that beg him to take literary possession of its textual remnants. According to the Squire's outline in 5.656–68, Algarsif, the brother of Cambell and Canacee, will marry Theodora and be aided by a horse of brass, while Cambell and Canacee will help a falcon to reunite with her tercelet. Spenser slights these motifs for a more problematic one in which "Cambalo . . . faught in lystes with the bretheren two / For Canacee er that he myghte hire wynne" (5.668–69). One scenario might entail Canacee's abduction by two brothers and Cambalo's heroic efforts to rescue her. Another might interpret Cambell's attempt to "wynne" Canacee in a sexual sense with incestuous overtones.[17] A third might introduce yet another character called "Cambalo" as an outsider whose name magically echoes Cambell's, suggesting a sublimation of the incestuous conclusion.

Spenser pursues the second possibility with its focus on the domestic virtue of household management.[18] Cambell's overzealous protection of his sister against her three suitors hints at the family's aversion to cross-cultural exogamic marriage. Carrying the principle of inbred aristocratic endogamy so far as to border on incest, it ignites tribal rivalries that Cambell "perceiu'd would breede great mischiefe" in the larger communal realm (4.2.37). In an outcome not implied by Chaucer, Spenser associates exogamic marriage with the strengthening of political virtue. Thus Triamond's sister, retrospectively named Cambina from Italian *cambiare* 'change' (4.3.51), restores order by inducing a radical, abrupt, dichotomous change. Cambell and Triamond notably ignore her rhetorical plea to stop fighting, but they respond immediately when she strikes them with a rod of peace and ministers a magical Nepenthe (4.3.47–48).[19]

At exactly this point Spenser's narrator supplements the authority of Chaucer, who does not seem especially concerned with the dynamics of patriarchal transmission through exogamic marriage, with that of Ariosto, who was so concerned with this topic that it dominates his dynastic epic. Thus Spenser compares Nepenthe to the spring that transforms love to hate in the *Orlando furioso:*

> The which *Rinaldo* drunck in happie howre,
> Described by that famous Tuscane penne:
> For that had might to change the hearts of men
> Fro loue to hate, a change of euill choice:
> But this doth hatred make in loue to brenne.
> (4.3.45)

Curiously, however, the narrator's homage misreads the *Orlando furioso* by inverting the Ariostan topos. "Thuscan penne," for example, is a false metonymy for the Ferrarese poet who claimed no social or political ties with Tuscany, though it does define the Tuscan lexicon that Ariosto adopted in his 1532 revision of the poem. With regard to plot, Spenser's reference to the magic waters misidentifies their initial effect on Rinaldo.[20] Instead of diminishing his sexual desire for Angelica, they intensify it.

Spenser consequently records this action as "a change of euill choice" while Ariosto and his Italian commentators record it as a victory for Angelica's virtue. Thus Girolamo Ruscelli, editor of the most widely circulated sixteenth-century edition of the *Orlando furioso*, published at Venice in 1556, allegorizes Angelica's refusal to submit to Rinaldo or Sacripante: "Una valorosa donna . . . à niuno se mostra cortese, se non quanto il debito dell'onesta la concede" [A virtuous woman appears receptive to no man, unless as the debt of honor allows it] (1). This "debito d'onesta" is of course the marriage bond, a legal contract that in Spenser provides the basis for a social and economic order that links domestic virtue to the public realm. In "The Legend of Friendship," the "mutuall couplement" of a brother and his sister with a sister and her brother (4.3.52) transforms discord into harmony, just as in "The Legend of Chastity" Britomart moves toward her political destiny through marriage with her appointed spouse. The answer to the question of who owns the bride is that the spouses' families exercise prior ownership over each partner as the couple becomes the guarantor of an extended posterity.

Spenser's incorporation of Ariosto into his version of *The Squire's Tale* in book 4 deepens the question about who owns the tale. On the one hand the narrator explains his compulsion to complete Chaucer's text as an altruistic effort to defend it against "wicked Time that all good thoughts doth waste, / And workes of noblest wits to nought out weare" (4.2.33). On the other hand he implies his own temporal vulnerability, so that his motivation seems almost selfish: "How may these rimes, so rude as doth appeare, / Hope to endure, sith workes of heauenly wits / Are quite deuourd, and brought to nought by little bits?" (4.2.33). If the metrical accent falls on "may" and "rimes" as it should in Spenser's pentameter line, the question is a general response to the fate that awaits all human production. But if it falls on "these" in counterpoint to the regular iambic beat, then the line is not only metrically "rude" and amiss, but it also projects the speaker's concern about the fate of his verse. His effort to revive Chaucer's tale might seem a totemic act to honor the memory of a dead ancestor, if only so that this act might certify his own status as an heir. By paying tribute to Chaucer, Spenser is projecting upon current and future generations a bond of common ancestry, making it difficult for both to ignore his particular contribution. The tale's continuation functions as a magic talisman enabling Spenser to overcome the tyranny of Chaucer by annexing foreign resources from Ariosto. The turn to Italian epic-romance henceforth represents Spenser's deep covenant with his poetic father who himself had shown the way with his own acquisitions from French and Italian texts.[21]

Far from representing an organic view of literary history, Spenser's turn to Italian epic-romance implies what I had termed a dichotomous view. Whereas the former assumes a porousness among literary forms that invites their appropriation, the latter insists upon rhetorical particulars that resist it. The organic theory finds its provenance in an Augustinian hermeneutics that dominated medieval rhetoric, according to which any understanding or use of a sacred or secular text is legitimate as long as it illuminates the lesson of charity in it. The dichotomous theory finds its provenance in the hermeneutics of fifteenth- and sixteenth-century Italian humanists who sought a precise understanding of classical texts through philological research, archaeological reconstruction, and historical inquiry into radical differences between past and present. By calling attention to matters that need explication in local or contemporary terms, humanist commentators on Virgil and Ovid attempt to explain the strangeness of the ancient world. Following their lead, commentators on more recent vernacular authors such as Ariosto try to clarify the sometimes opaque practices of a courtly and aristocratic world inscribed in this poetry. Their target is an emergent and diverse readership, a new and upwardly mobile book-buying public drawn from the mercantile and professional population of the urban middle class.

Ariosto's sixteenth-century readers consequently approached the *Orlando furioso* through editions larded with commentaries that reinforce the practical, earthbound, antiaristocratic values of this clientele.[22] Girolamo Ruscelli, for example, designs his text explicitly "à i mediocri" [for average readers,] to be read "da persona senza lettere, da principiante, da mezanamente, e ancor da sopra il mediocre & il molto, intendente, & dotta" [by someone without Latin or Greek, a beginner, an average reader, and yet by someone above the average mob, intelligent and learned] (**2ᵛ). To the question of who owns the women in Ariosto's narrative, Ruscelli and others respond with sometimes startling pronouncements on a domestic economy that acknowledges but also limits middle-class female autonomy, just as to the question of who owns Ariosto's text they respond with elaborate catalogues of the poet's immense debts to ancient classical and modern vernacular authors. If Ariosto can be shown to possess the classics, then those who draw upon his poem can be thought to inherit its cultural capital and the authority that accrues from it.

The Innkeeper's Tale in canto 28 of the *Orlando furioso* anticipates, as I have mentioned, the narrative outcome of the Squire's venereal adventure. Ariosto's tale attracted from sixteenth-century editors a rich body of commentary with a sociological emphasis on domestic economy. The Innkeeper is a French commoner whose establishment stands beside the Saone near Lyon (27.128). He anachronistically attributes the tale's origin to a Venetian cleric and friend of Ariosto, Gian Francesco Valerio (27.137). One of its listeners takes care to exculpate Valerio of misogyny by shifting the tale's critical weight back to the foreign Innkeeper: "E se 'l Valerio tuo disse altrimente, / Disse per ira, e non per quel che sente" [And if this Valerio of yours said otherwise, he spoke in anger and did not express his true feelings] (28.78). Ariosto's Italian commentators reinforce this point by associating the tale's scurrility with the Innkeeper's lower-class French perspective. Ruscelli, for example, provides an elaborate philological note about the plebeian spelling of Iocondo's name, arguing that an elite speaker would have avoided this form: "I nobili, & le persone di conto parlano in bella, & in buona lingua, la qual se non è toscana pura, nella strettezza di tutta la lingua, e tuttavia molto conforme seco" [The nobility and persons of wealth speak in a fine and correct style, which, if not exactly pure Tuscan, conforms largely to it in the strictness of its usage] (349). Ruscelli's stress on Tuscan usage as the absolute standard of vernacular style embraced by Ariosto in 1532 explains why Spenser associates the poet with a "Thuscan penne." The commentators had represented this usage as normative in the *Orlando furioso,* so that any deviations from it signal social misconduct. Thus the Innkeeper's lexical choices link his tale "allo volgare, & plebea, & non alla nobile, & cortigianna guisa" [to the vulgar, plebeian, and not noble or courtly style] (350), betraying his ignorance of domestic refinement and upper-class values. The tale projects a vulgar sexual economy because its teller is vulgar.

Antonio Toscanella, a commercial publisher who in 1574 abridged the poem with an edifying commentary on it for a newly prosperous middle-class clientele apparently too busy to read the entire text, likewise associates the tale with its teller's social standing. Ariosto maintains stylistic decorum despite the lewdness of his topic: "Non è maraviglia se questo Poema è mirabile; perche mirabilmente il decoro in esso è serbato" [No wonder this poem is admirable, because in it decorum is admirably preserved] (*Bellezze del Furioso* 217). The tale defames adulterous spouses who aspire to exalted rank: "La moglie di Giocondo, che manca di fede al marito, e la Reina che si mescola col Nano di danno ad intendere, che quelle donne, lequali sono d'animo contaminato; fanno poco onore a i mariti, siano di che grado, e condicione si vogliano" [Iocondo's wife who is unfaithful to her husband, and the queen who involves herself with a dwarf represent women of corrupted spirit; they bring little honor to their husbands, no matter what rank or class they aspire to] (216). The words *vile* and *indegni* used to describe the narrator also describe the action of his tale as it distorts marital relationships: "Quest biasimi delle donne siano narrati da persona vile" [The faults of these women are narrated by a mean-spirited low-life] (217). Its meaning nonetheless reaches persons of a worthier sort who can interpret the tale from a wiser perspective, "che gli huomini degni, sogliono dir cose degne" [since men of worth usually speak about matters of worth] (217). For Spenser the tale might well instantiate different conceptions about the marriage bond held by persons of different social standing. Sexual licence allowable to women in the lower classes could only horrify those in the upper classes with patrimonies to transmit to legitimate offspring.

Tommaso Porcacchi, a Tuscan born near Arezzo who edited an inexpensive, widely popular octavo edition of the *Orlando furioso* in 1577, situates the tale in an explicitly commercial context. Here the French Innkeeper not only takes delight in his narrative, but he also uses it to please his customers and boost his business: "Nell'hoste, che per sodisfare all'humor di Rodomonte dice tanto mal delle Donne; si vede che questa qualità d'huomini è sempre dedita ad adulare a'forestieri, che gli portano utile" [In the character of the host who says so many bad things about women to satisfy Rodomonte's humor, we can see that this kind of man is always inclined to indulge strangers who increase his profit] *(Orlando Furioso di Messer Lodovico Ariosto* 139). For Porcacchi as for Ruscelli and Toscanella, the tale has nothing to do with an abstract morality but everything to do with a particular sociocultural perspective. It links gendered attitudes about sexual licence and male ownership of women to social attitudes about market enterprise and profit management. The promiscuity of its characters corresponds broadly to that of the venture economy engaged in by the

French Innkeeper and by his Spanish counterpart in the tale, the father of Fiammetta who trades her to Astolfo and Iocondo in his own interest. The bourgeois readership that Porcacchi anticipates might sympathize with the business motives of the French Innkeeper, but would abhor those of Fiammetta's father despite their mutual affinity for seeking profit.

The readership that Ponsonby expected for the first *Faerie Queene* might have shared similarly conflicted attitudes towards venture economy. To all intents marketed for an urbanized commercial and professional population of London as well as the courtly and gentry elites that gathered there, it aimed at a readership beyond the landholding, knightly, and administrative elites that Chaucer's poetry had earlier attracted.[23] For such upwardly mobile households Spenser redirects Chaucer's *Squire's Tale* to a resolution of the Marriage Question in a pair of exogamic unions that subvert incestuous potentials. The brides belong to their fathers' and their husbands' families as guarantors of lineage and direct inheritance. In this way, too, Spenser resolves the situation that introduces his own Squire in the grip of an incestuous giantess with a literary history that echoes Ariosto's Innkeeper's Tale. It would seem that Spenser is already using Ariostan materials to update the Chaucerian motif for an expanded readership drawn from city, court, and country.

The challenge and rewards of this expanded readership become apparent if we contrast them with the more narrowly defined courtly interests of Spenser's contemporary John Harington, the translator of Ariosto's *Orlando furioso*. Harington famously began this translation in the 1580s with a rendering of the Innkeeper's tale out of context as an entertainment for Queen Elizabeth's ladies.[24] By the time its printer Richard Field entered it in the Stationers' Register in February 1591, fourteen months after Ponsonby's first *Faerie Queene,* Harington had added paratextual apparatus modelled upon Francesco de Franceschi's 1584 deluxe edition of the *Orlando furioso* with Alberto Lavezola's "Osservationi" on Ariosto's classical sources and Gioseffo Bononome's "Allegoria" extrapolated from Ruscelli's annotations.[25] These commentaries lost no opportunity to disparage lower-class mores by favoring the pretensions of its wealthy clientele.

Even in its decontextualized version, Harington's translation of the Innkeeper's Tale may have stung its early audience less for its free-spirited ribaldry than for its palpable emphasis upon class differences. After all, one of the tale's fictive listeners, "un uom d'età, ch'avea più retta / opinion degli altri" [an old man more right-minded than the others,] or, in Harington's words, "Of riper years and judgement more discreet" (28.76), commends the relative virtue of most women by contrast with the absolute lubricity of all men, "che continente non si trova un solo" [for not a single chaste man is to be found] (28.83).[26] Harington nonetheless omits from his translation the intervening stanza (Ariosto's 28.78, quoted above for its reference to Valerio as its original source) that problematizes the uncouth Innkeeper's ownership of his tale. As a result Harington locates chasteness as a categorical mandate for propertied women whose men—whether husbands, fathers, brothers, or sons—have important assets to protect. His translation does not so much offend the refined sensibilities of his hearers as it admonishes those hearers to a limiting code of chastity.

In both his translation and commentary Harington satirizes the behavior and the practices of commoners from the exalted vantage of court. Interpolating economic concerns of Fiammetta's father upon accepting Astolfo's and Iocondo's proposal in a line that has no precise equivalent in the original text, "Because the father money wants to marrie her," Harington puts a specific and aggressive price tag on the deal that Ariosto had simply described as leaving the father with one less mouth to feed: "Poi che promesso avean di ben trattarla" [For they had promised to treat her kindly] (28.53). Offering a "Moral" endnote on the ethics of chastity that holds every woman suspect for "the fraud and frailtie of some of that sexe" (323), he suggests that aristocratic women need to exercise special discretion since "no state nor degree is privileged from shame and slaunder except virtue and grace from above do keepe them from such enormous offences" (324). The very notion that an elite class seems vulnerable to the disruptive urging of the flesh as commoners might be, especially if commoners share the former's economic impulses to secure property and inheritance, could only vex the elite's sense of social and political decorum.

Harington, a gentleman educated at Cambridge and a seeker of rank and fortune who was eventually knighted by Essex in Ireland in 1599, construes this action from a courtly perspective. Spenser, a "poor scholar" who rose to the status of gentleman without arms by virtue of his university education, displays greater sensitivity to socially differentiated nuances when he makes the point in his Squire of Dames episode that a country "damzell" has retained her virtue without ulterior economic pressue to do so. Such attitudes inform the Squire's account of his "seruice" and "vow" to Columbell, a conventional "seruice" with regard to sexual favors, but an exceptional "vow" requiring him to seduce as many women as he can and then to find an equal number who resist him (3.7.51–56). The Squire takes pains to emphasize that the women who relent are "gentle Dames" (3.7.54), members of a propertied class if not titled nobility, whence the sociological significance of his name, "The *Squire of Dames*." The question of ownership in his tale pertains not to patrimony or inheritance passed on through marriage, but rather to the "gentle Dames' enjoyment" (in the erotic sense of ownership) of the Squire's unreclaimed sexual prowess.

The Squire's accent on "proffred curtesie" and "fashions" (3.7.57) suggests that, unlike Ariosto's libertines who explore all ranks and strata of society, Spenser's gallant traffics largely in the privileged realm of courtly love. The three women who resist him are located outside that realm. They include a "common Courtisane," where "common" and her demand for payment identify her as a baseborn prostitute ("Yet flat refusd to haue a do with mee, / Because I could not giue her many a Iane," 3.7.58); a nun who flinches at his breach of confidence ("Because she knew, she said, I would disclose / Her counsell," 3.7.58); and the "Damzell of low degree" in a "countrey cottage" who alone refuses on virtuous grounds: "Safe her, I neuer any woman found, / That chastity did for it selfe embrace, / But were for other causes firme and sound" (3.7.59–60). In a single stroke this Damzell inverts the values of both the nun and the prostitute in a rural setting as yet unaffected by a money economy.[27]

Spenser's designation of a rural commoner as the sole agent of resistance to a noble Squire provokes a vexing response. It can be measured by dramatic laughter generated within the episode. There the Squire's account of his vow to Columbell prompts Sir Satyrane to chortle at the small number of women who have declined his invitation (3.7.57), at the motives of the "common Courtisane" who expected payment for her favors (3.7.58), and at the forced literary comparison of the Squire's efforts to a heroic act "[t]hat may emonsgst *Alcides* labours stand" (3.7.61). Appropriately the Squire himself exits from the poem in a fit of laughter that later recalls Sir Satyrane's ridicule. Thus he can only guffaw when the False Florimell proves unable to keep her girdle fastened at Sir Satyrane's tournament: "He lowdly gan to laugh, and thus to iest. . . . / Fie on the man, that did it first inuent" (4.5.18). Coming on the heels of a literary history inscribed in the Squire's narrative, the rhetorical underpinnings of the word "inuent" resonate strongly. Both the Squire and the knight are responding to a debasement of cultural artifacts as the Squire with privileged origins directs his hilarity toward the effete Petrarchism of the False Florimell and the knight with beastly origins directs his toward the Squire's courtly predicament. Sex has become not just a part of his life—a mass of diversions neither especially pleasurable nor fulfilling—but the very ground of his textually circumscribed, socially limited reality. The Squire's problem is not just more exposure to a degraded environment, but his acceptance of it in a way that devalues everything—a shadow world where he performs his rituals without hope of escape.

The Squire's laughter masks his own weakness as a figure divided between his literary origins in Chaucer and his emergence into a post-Petrarchan world of fatuous lovers. Caught between these literary models, Spenser's Squire falls into the dead weight of a literary construction. His courtly devotion to Columbell and his submission to her command have brought him into the clutches of Argante, who discards him when she "threw her lode aside" (3.7.38). The quaintly archaic spelling of *lode* here points to its etymological double meaning as "leader, guide" (OE *lad* "leader," cf. lodestone) as well as "load, burden" (ME *lode* "weight"), a play on words that recalls Chaucer's punning usage in Troilus's addresses to Criseyde, "my righte lode-sterre" (*Troilus* 5.323, 1392). The man who might serve his woman as a protector and guide becomes a thrall to her and hence her "load" or burden as she becomes his Petrarchan *donna*.

Concerns about title, marriage, family, and sexual ownership that Spenser and the Italian commentators address would ramify throughout English culture in the century after 1596. Near the troubled end of the Stuart monarchy, for example, Sir Robert Filmer formulated his *Patriarchia* (1640s, but first published in 1680) with its archetypal expression of the nucleated family and the corporate polity as analogous institutions dominated by fatherly rule.[28] The royalist Filmer was trying to justify political obligations to the crown by representing its authority as a form of paternal ownership writ large. Spenser, like other Elizabethans, could not represent political obligations in such terms without compromising Elizabeth's female monarchy. He instead represents it as deriving from an elaborated structure of contract and consent negotiated on domestic and economic levels between men and women as in "The Legend of Chastity" and on social and political levels between families and among men as in "The Legend of Friendship."

Spenser's contemporary Richard Hooker likewise projects a provisional, not yet fully articulated sense of contract and consent that distinguishes between the public rule of a monarchy and the private management of a household: "To Fathers, within their private families, Nature hath given a supreme power. . . . Howbeit, over a whole grand multitude, . . . impossible it is that any should have complete lawful power but by consent of men" (1: 252). A more fully articulated expression would appear in John Locke's *Two Treatises of Government*.[29] *The Faerie Queene* sets in motion a possible analogy between social relations predicated on the legal form of a marriage contract and those predicated on the larger idea of a social contract. The poem barely suggests the merits or even the feasibility of a specifically contractual society or consensual government, but its representations of women such as Britomart in transit between a domestic household and the public world dramatize tensions and strains in the interface between these two systems. Unlike such figures as the virile but unmanly Squire drawn from a now dichotomized literary history, Britomart challenges the obsolete ethos of a courtly and chivalric patriarchalist culture.

Spenser found models for this analogy in the *Orlando furioso* as it was presented by Ariosto's Italian commentators, and he used it to displace the authority of a direct but now outmoded patrilineal literary succession from Chaucer in his own cultural history. By moving outside the tribe, as it were, he averts an incestuous possession of the past while managing to widen the pool of poetic inspiration for future literary production. In this turn to alien forms, whether of such ancient classics as Virgil or Ovid or of such later Italians as Ariosto and Petrarch, commentaries play a mediating role in the ownership of texts. It is not a question of how the commentaries shaped or determined Spenser's interpretive understanding in a passive or applied manner, and still less how they prompted or influenced his own composition in a more creative manner. It is rather a question of how they inscribe values and ideals in sometimes complicit, sometimes contestatory ways, variously reinforcing and undermining conventional values and ideals, and occasionally promoting the emergence of new ones. In this sense literary commentary may have some impact on public discourse, even when it comes from scholars and critics who are concerned not that Caesar conquered Gaul, but that he wrote *commentarii* about it.[30] Spenser approached the ancient and modern classics through commentaries rich in cultural insight, not at all monolithic in their interpretive stances, and sensitive to disjunctions among individual ethical, economic, political, rhetorical, and representational positions inscribed in the texts. His own literary history is richer for it.

Notes

1. Bennett interpreted the Chaucerian echoes in 3.7.37–61 as Spenser's earliest work on *The Faerie Queene*, the urtext that he sent to Harvey in 1580 and that, after continuing the story of Cambell and Canacee from *The Squire's Tale* (now in book 4), he abandoned for the models of Ariosto and Virgil (18–23, 159, 166–67, 231–39).

2. For Spenser's general debt to Chaucer, see Giamatti, *The Play of Double Senses* 47–52. For the particular relation of Spenser's Squire to Chaucer's, see Hieatt 75–94; for his relation to Spenser's other squires, see Dasenbrock 52–69. For Sir Thopas as a figure of poetic vulnerability, see Berry, "Borrowed Armor/ Free Grace." For comparisons between Chaucer's "Augustinian" career pattern and Spenser's "Orphic" pattern, see P. Cheney, *Spenser's Famous Flight* 57–62.

3. Quotations from Edmund Spenser, *The Faerie Queene*, ed. Roche.

4. *Nicomachaean Ethics* 1094a25–1096a4, 1159b25–1161a9; *Politics*

1252a24–1274a22; *Rhetoric* 1365b12–1368a23; *Poetics* 1448a1–1448b2. For such conflicts, see Wilkes 341–57; Irwin 133–42; and Swanson. For Spenser, see C.V. Kaske, "Spenser's Pluralistic Universe"; and E. Fowler.

5. See Tuana; Sherman; Orkin; Spelman; and Elshtain ch. 1.

6. Freud cites this legal tag in "Family Romances," *Standard Edition* 9: 239.

7. For the fortunes of Chaucer's Squire in the fifteenth century, see Lerer 57–84.

8. Virgil, *Works*. For Spenser's figure, see Prescott, "Titans."

9. *Opera virgiliana cvm decem commentis . . . et Badii Ascensii elucidatione* 79. For Virgilian allegoresis, see Whitman; Grafton 23–46; and Baswell; for relevance to Spenser, see Murrin, *The Allegorical Epic* 27–50; A. Patterson, *Pastonal and Ideology* 21–42; and Watkins 30–61.

10. All quotations are from Ovid, *Metamorphoses*, ed. and trans. F.J. Miller.

11. *P. Ouidii Metamorphosis seu fabvlae poeticae: earvmque interpretatio ethica, physica et historica Georgii Sabini* 169; for Ovidian allegoresis, see Allen 163–200; Barkan 94–137; and Hexter 1–25.

12. See Boehrer 78–85; and McCabe 30–63.

13. In "Arthur, Argante, and the Ideal Vision" (193–203), J. Anderson acknowledges this etymology but also cites "Argant" as a variant of Morgan in Lyamon's *Brut*. For other variations in Chaucer, see J. Anderson, "The 'Couert Vele'" and "Prudence and Her Silence."

14. Quotations from *The Riverside Chaucer*, ed. Benson. For the association of Chaucer with his Squire, see Pearsall, *The Life of Geoffrey Chaucer* 34–68; and Howard 58. For the Squire's comic insensitivity toward his audience, see Berger, "The F-Fragment of *The Canterbury Tales*"; for his diffidence, see Pearsall, "The Squire as Story-Teller"; for principles underlying such interruptions, see R. Kaske; for narrative self-representations, see L. Patterson, "What Man Artow?"

15. For "gentilesse" as a redemptive power of culture found wanting in *The Squire's Tale*, see L. Patterson, *Chaucer and the Subject of History* 71–73; for parallels between the Franklin and the Squire, see Leicester 394–97; for the social basis of their generic preferences, see Strohm.

16. Hieatt 19–25, 68–69, 76–77; and Miskimin 226–61.

17. Certainly Gower associates the name of Canacee with incest in *Confessio Amantis* 3.143–307, derived from Ovid's *Heroides* 11, where the heroine is impregnated by her brother Machaire (Macareus); thus Chaucer's Man of Law refers to "[t]hilke wikke ensample oof Canacee" (78).

18. Focusing quite differently on political virtue, Spenser's later contemporary, John Lane, a friend of Milton's father, has Canacee marry a wholly new character named Akafir in his continuation, licensed 16 March 1615, left unfinished in two manuscripts now in the Bodleian Library. Lane narrates Algarsif's rebellion against his father (3.187), Cambuscan's death and resuscitation (9.401, 10.369), and Algarsif's repentance (10.149). Akafir, Cambuscan's admiral, flights against Algarsif and Cambell (9.301) to win

Canacee's hand: "And so hee plied them for his little time, / as the last liver sweares, 'all wilbee mine'" (12.329–30).

19. For the episode's treatment of private virtue and public institutions, see Silberman 87–98; for Spenser's encounter with his Chaucerian roots, see Berry, "Sundrie Doubts"; and P. Cheney, "Spenser's Completion of *The Squire's Tale*."

20. It is worth noting another model in cantos 42–43, where Rinaldo refuses a Mantuan knight's offer of a potion that will verify his wife's fidelity. In his "morall" commentary on this episode, John Harington refers to Spenser's Squire as an improvement upon Ariosto's characters: "This tale of the Mantuan knight is simply the worst against women in all the booke, or rather indeed that was ever written. The hosts tale in the xxviii book of this worke is a bad one, *M. Spencers* tale of the squire of Dames in his excellent Poem of the Faery Queene . . . is to the like effect, sharp and well conceyted" (*Ludovico Ariosto's "Orlando Furioso" Translated into English Heroical Verse*, ed. McNulty 513). For strategies of reading implied in Harington's commentary, see Kintgen 87–98.

21. In *Totem and Taboo*, to which these remarks broadly refer, Freud concludes that in this way the dead father becomes stronger than the living one had been (*Standard Edition* 13:122). In "Spenser (Re)Reading du Bellay," Prescott notes also Du Bellay's presence in the quoted stanza (137).

22. For Ariosto's readership, see B. Richardson 109–39; and Bec. Grendler 275–99 finds curricula in vernacular schools that included Ariosto, Pulci, and Boiardo.

23. See Manley 168–211.

24. The legend, probably apocryphal, was first recounted in Thomas Park's 1804 edition of family letters selected by Henry Harington in 1775. See McNulty, ed. xxiv-xxv.

25. *Orlando Furioso di M. Lodovico Ariosto con Allegoria di Gioseffo Bononome;* see Javitch 134–57.

26. Lodovico Ariosto, *Orlando Furioso*, ed. Segre. For Ariosto's irreverent wit, see Giamatti, *Exile and Change* 33–75; for the attitudes of Rodomonte, the Innkeeper, and the old man, see Benson 101–09; for Rodomonte's aggressive masculinism, see Finucci 172–97, 287; for Ariosto's epic emphasis on individual responsibility, see Pavlock 147–86; for his ambivalence about these matters, see Biow, *Mirabile Dictu* 95–122.

27. The prostitute's "many a Iane" refers to silver coins minted in "Genoa"; see in *The Tale of Sir Thopas* the hero's robe "that coste many a jane" (7: 735). For the "Damzell of low degree," the word "damzell" could signify some claim to noble or gentle birth, as the *OED* describes its twelfth-century origins, but it routinely extends to those of lower rank; archaic by the seventeenth century, it was used slightly to refer to country maidens. "Dame" by contrast retained its designation as a name or title for a woman of rank. For competition between court and country with the latter as a defender of traditional virtues, see Heal and Holmes 201–14; for the growing obsession of the gentry and bourgeois families with the continuity of their lineage, see Anthony Fletcher 126–53.

28. See Schochet 37–53, with modifications by Shanley; K. Sharpe 3–71; and Jordan.

29. See Pateman 77–115; for a remarkable application to developments in the Massachusetts and Chesapeake Bay Colonies, see Norton 281–322.

30. This Caesarean section comes from Philippe Monnier (1888) as quoted in Arnold Hauser 2: 83. With insight relevant to later decades Hauser adds, "This is the real '*trahison des clercs*,' the betrayal of intellectual values by the intelligentsia, not the politicization of the spirit for which is has been blamed in recent times" (2: 83).

THE LAUREL AND THE MYRTLE

Spenser and Ronsard

Anne Lake Prescott

De Myrte et de Laurier fueille à fueille enserrez
Helene entrelassant une belle Couronne,
M'appella par mon nom: "Voyla que je vous donne:
De moy seule, Ronsard, l'escrivain vous serez."
Pierre de Ronsard, *Les Amours de Helene* 2.57

Happy ye leaves when as those lilly hands,
which hold my life in their dead doing might
shall handle you and hold in loves soft bands,
lyke captives trembling at the victors sight.
Edmund Spenser, *Amoretti* 1

It is a scholarly commonplace to say that even as he masked in lowly shepherds' weeds for the 1579 *Shepheardes Calender* Spenser was gesturing at a laureate Virgilian career. Had Virgil not begun as a pastoral poet? Virgil was not, though, the only poet whose career Spenser would have traced with interest. For sheer worldly glamour at court, or for what seemed such to others, he would have known that there was no contemporary writer to equal Pierre de Ronsard (1524–85). As he thought about French writers, Spenser's heart may have gone out more warmly to Clément Marot, two of whose eclogues he adapted for the *Calender,* and to Joachim Du Bellay, whose imagination in some regards resembled and perhaps helped shape his own and some of whose sonnets he would translate in the 1591 *Complaints* as "The Ruines of Rome." Evidently, too, he admired the biblical poetry of Guillaume Du Bartas (and perhaps envied that aristocratic poet's friendships with the kings of Scotland and Navarre). But it was Ronsard who, more than any other modern author of approximately his own generation, wrote in almost all culturally available poetic genres, including sonnet sequences, masques, formal odes, Anacreontics, neo-Homeric or Orphic hymns, elegies, epitaphs, epistles, and such erotica as a remarkable sonnet on the vagina. He was, as he put it, the first in France to "Pindarize"; even when he was young, some of his love poetry was printed with admiring commentary by the up-and-coming humanist Marc-Antoine Muret, and not, like the similar notes in the *Calender,* by a mere set of initials; and, a genuine gentleman from the minor nobility with a "de" in his name, he mingled with great lords and exchanged verses with monarchs. To Spenser's Piers, asking in the *October* eclogue if poetry's place is not in princes' palaces, Ronsard could have answered literally that, yes, for a while he had lived in the Louvre.[1] In sum, as Thomas Smith wrote to William Cecil from Paris, Ronsard was the "Archipoete of fraunce."[2]

True, by 1596, as Spenser was seeing to the new edition of *The Faerie Queene,* he would have known of a number of recent European poets whose careers he could ponder. Few of these, however, had quite Ronsard's ability to tend and shape a career. Unlike Petrarch, Ariosto, and Tasso, moreover, Ronsard wrote in a large nation with the first serious stirrings of imperial hopes, not in a small dukedom or city-state, and he served kings wanting to read about their descent from a conquering race of Trojans, a descent that had become (whatever most sensible people's actual beliefs about history) a way of demonstrating that the neighboring Habsburgs were not the only rulers with a claim to have translated Rome's ancient *imperium* to their own realms.[3] Even Ronsard's periodic grumbles that he was seriously underfunded, insufficiently rewarded by the great, revolted by the corruptions at court, and odiously slandered by Huguenots could have added to his attraction to Spenser, although the latter doubtless sympathized with Protestant assaults on a Catholic poet who fervently defended his church and was himself in minor orders.

How Spenser—and we—might compare how he and Ronsard pursued the life of a poet makes an interesting case not of intertextuality, exactly, but of what one could, in a pinch, call intercareerism. For the rest of this essay, as a tentative contribution to intercareerist studies, I will look at some recurrent if hardly unprecedented tensions in Ronsard's verse between his widely read love poetry and his abortive epic, the *Franciade.* Such tensions give further context to Spenser's own related if distinct sense of how to relate Eros to heroics. Noticing them (which it seems probable, if not provably certain, that he would have done) might have given him, being merely human, some now unquantifiable mixture of sympathy and satisfaction.

A few reminders: In 1550 Ronsard launched his career, aside from a few even earlier minor poems, with four books of odes, following these in 1552 with love sonnets to Cassandre and more odes. He was already planning an epic (toying for a while, he said later, with an Arthurian theme). A 1550 ode to Calliope tells the muse how he hopes to change the sound of Pindar to that of Homer, while another tells briefly of a projected poem tracing the adventures of Francus and the 20,000 Trojans he led to found Paris, the new Troy. (This is, even on Parnassus, known as staking a claim.)[4] As the years went by, new verses and revisions poured from his pen. In 1560 his collected *Oeuvres* had made an impressive edition for a still youngish man, and in 1584 when he was old and ailing—no longer in the forefront of fashion, grieved by the French civil wars and the court's corruption, but still very famous—his publisher talked him into preparing the great folio edition that shortly served, Gustave Cohen wryly remarks in the preface to his own edition of Ronsard, as both monument and tomb. Never in all those years, however, did he get Francus all the way from Troy to Paris, and late in life he was still writing love poetry. Ronsard had a talent for celebrity, but the contours of his career make a bad Virgilian wheel: generically speaking, he kept slipping backward.

In a recent book, Patrick Cheney suggests that we modify our sense of how Renaissance writers could conceive of poetic careers.[5] Traditionally, the Virgilian rota rolls from pastoral to georgic to epic, just as Spenser moves from the pastoral *Shepheardes Calender* to a hero named George at the start of a dynastic epic. But that, argues Cheney, is not the only way to invent a generic wheel, especially in a Christian culture, and he notes how in the Renaissance erotic lyric sometimes served the same function as the pastoral in implying an apprenticeship and in setting up both affiliations and tensions between epic and Eros, fierce wars and faithful loves. To the evidence he adduces I would add that Ronsard, although he himself had begun with odes, in a 1578 quatrain on the *Oeuvres* of J. de Boyssieres says that "[f]or practice, Virgil sang his pastoral, / And later sang Aeneas the Trojan: similarly, / Boyssières sang his amorous torment / And now sings Hercules in the long heroic line."[6] An odd apprenticeship, at first glance, for in most ways one can think of the love sonnet as the opposite of the epic: short, not long; private, not public; local, not national; fruitlessly erotic, not marital, genealogical, and dynastic. And yet not only do Renaissance love sequences often inscribe political commentary or desire, not only do some seem like short-winded parcels of a longer (not)Virgilian (not)epic impelled, like epic heroes and epic itself, by longing—some explicitly mention the epic that their authors have no intention of writing, have begun writing, should begin writing, will begin writing any moment now, will finish with just a little more time, reward, polish, or resting up. Meantime, of course, those long heroic poems frequently sing of love, whether the love that tempts the hero to linger like Aeneas in a cave with Dido or the one that will lead him to a marriage forming the basis of the dynasty celebrated by the epic's author.

As Cheney observes, Ovid himself had joked about the seeming conflict between epic and Eros. At the start of the *Amores,* it will be recalled, he tells how he was writing a poem in the high manner, dactylic hexameters and all, when Cupid laughingly stole a foot from the second line, converting brave heroics into soft elegiacs. When Ovid protests, Amor shoots him.[7] Not even the ensuing fifteen hundred years could teach the god better manners, for in the 1552 *Amours de Cassandre* Ronsard says that "Mars had already elected my trumpet, and in my verses Francus was speaking, already sharpening his lance on my (poetic) fury, goading my brave poetry; already Gaul had been seized with consternation, the Seine glittering with steel, and already Francus had led the Trojan name and Asian honor to Paris, when the little winged archer with a sure shot wounded me to the bone, appointing me minister of his secrets. Arms, farewell: Paphian myrtle yields not to Delphian laurel if Eros gives it with his own hand."[8] Spenser, though, blames the lady herself: *Amoretti* 80 tells Lodovic Bryskett that the poet cannot continue the "taedious toyle" of writing an epic so long as he has only one wit and that one beset by the "troublous fit, / of a proud love."

But the lover of Cassandre, even during this erotic interruption, keeps fingering those Delphian laurels, encouraged by the lady's name and its evocation of Troy. There really was a Cassandre Salviati, but falling in love with a young woman with a resonant name is not beyond the powers of a clever poet. And, yes, there are some allusions to Rome in Petrarch's *Rime,* serving what Thomas Greene calls the collection's lyricization of epic materials, as well as a gesture or two toward the author's epic *Africa* (115). Here in the *Amours de Cassandre,* however, the specifically Trojan connection, with its memories of grief, wandering, and unheard prophecy, gives Ronsard's love poetry more emotional energy and temporal depth while it also suggests some generic overlap with the promised *Franciade.*[9] Even a not unexpected *recusatio* (*Amours de Cassandre* 4) evokes the heroic world by negation when Ronsard tells his "guerriere Cassandre" that he is no Myrmidon, no Philoctetes (slayer of Paris), but rather mad Corœbus, lover of the Trojan Cassandra. And later he prays Cupid, skilled in herbal medicine, to cure his wound, the same wound the god had given Apollo near Ilion when the latter saw Cassandra (*Cassandre* 70). Had Homer, says sonnet 87, seen the lady who enslaves Ronsard he would not have sung the deeds of Mars (so far this loosely follows Petrarch's *Rime* 186), and if Paris had seen her he would have awarded her, not Venus, the apple. If, by the heavens' will,

Ronsard can sing *her* conquest, there will be no myrtle or laurel worthy of her or of his head. A bit arrogant, doubtless, but no more so than Spenser's quasi-epic boasting in *Amoretti* 69 of his "conquest" and his raising in verse an "immortal moniment" like the "Trophees" of "famous warriors of the anticke world." (In fact, Spenser of course outdoes Ronsard—and most other sonneteers—by actually performing a conquest of the lady, albeit one enabled by her own changed will; see *Amoretti* 67).

Two years later Ronsard published, in the 1554 *Bocage,* an elegy for Cassandre that he later moved to the *Amours,* where it could join the other poems to that lady. Only a detailed study would do full justice to the mixture of tones and motives in this farewell to love. Just as Ronsard had earlier told his readers that Cupid made him give up laurel for the myrtle, now he informs Cassandre that Henri II has made him exchange his lute for an epic trumpet. Ah, what serves it, he asks, to have read Tibullus, Propertius, Ovid, Catullus, and Petrarch now that the king has denied him power to follow them and made him hang up his now silent lyre? So much for his dream of showing the Tuscans that France can equal them in amorous plaint! He had already, he says, made many an elegy in the antique fashion, many a lovely ode, many a pastoral, believing that the French had not yet fulfilled their language's capacities in those genres. But do not weep, he tells his sweet friend Cassandre, because he could not finish his work in her praise. Henri is no savage beast, and if Ronsard is not mistaken he too has felt Cupid's arrow. He will forgive his poet if one day he returns from war to resume his lute and sing not of alarms but of Love, of the lady's beauties, and of his own tears. No bow can be always strung and even Achilles at times played on his golden lute (1: 98–100).

In terms of genre, career patterns, and the poetics of apology this is an interesting poem. In a striking revision of Ovid's witty explanation of why he does not write epic, here it is Cupid's work that is interrupted because of a mortal king. From an erotic point of view, Henri has blocked desire by making his poet give up a girl to celebrate a dynasty, to leave the apprentice genres and sing for his royal "maistre." But from a careerist point of view, the king's command is Ronsard's own wish (or so he thought, until he discovered Henri's perhaps understandable reluctance to pay for an unwritten epic). For nearly two decades, that combined royal and personal wish would be a source of Ronsard's frustration, hope, and at times anger. Nor, as he worked on the *Franciade* did he forget Amor, beauty, or tears. Much of the epic is taken up by the Ovidian (or Virgilian) passion of the king of Crete's two daughters (a "double Dido," Florence Weinberg astutely calls them [73–85]). It is passion that causes a degrading metamorphosis in one, Clymene, as she literally becomes a sea monster, and inspires self-abnegation and prophecy in the other, Hyante, as she foretells the fate of Francus and his founding of a dynasty by another woman. The *Franciade* has a splendid giant-fight strikingly like Arthur's battle with Orgoglio in book 1 of *The Faerie Queene*, but what sticks in the memory, aside from the endless roll-call of the Valois family's often violent and ignoble ancestors, is the *eros* that Ronsard transfers from his *Amours* and relocates in women who love the hero after being shot—like Ovid and Ronsard himself—by Cupid. (Indeed it might well require an arrow from Cupid to cause such depth of feeling, for Francus is not an appealing hero and would need the combined ministrations, Spenserians might suppose, of Guyon's Palmer, Britomart, and Calidore to fashion him into a prince any gentleman would want to serve or lady would want to marry.)[10]

In 1572, years after Henri II had died and only weeks after the horrifying St. Bartholomew massacre, Ronsard at last published what he had completed of his promised epic. The moment was hardly propitious: one authority has suggested that the poem, which was never to be popular, would have done better at a time when the French were not too anxious about their future to read about the glories of the past.[11] Nor, probably, was the poetry's effect helped by its meter. The *Franciade* is in decasyllables, Ronsard had already explained in his 1565 *Art poetique françois*, because even though it was he himself who had set the Alexandrine "en vogue et en honeur," those with "power to command"—he means young Charles IX—had demanded a shorter line (Ovid's Cupid had stolen only one foot per couplet; the French king took two). Ronsard never did finish the *Franciade*, although he certainly had the time, and later editions, when France had yet another king, add a quatrain: "Had King Charles lived, / I had finished this long work; / As soon as Death had conquered him, / His death conquered my courage."[12]

Then, in 1578 Ronsard published another major amatory sonnet sequence, impelled, it seems likely, by rivalry with the now fashionable Philippe Desportes—although the 1597 edition of Charles Binet's life of Ronsard reports that it was Catherine de' Medici herself who had asked the poet to sing again of love, and in a Petrarchan manner. Once more he chose a lady (or accepted Catherine's choice) with a Homeric first name: Hélène de Surgères, one of the queen mother's maids of honor. Even more than in his earlier *Amours*, Ronsard's two-part *Amours de Helene* uses a name to recall one of European civilization's originary stories of violence, treason, and consequent dispersion, indeed one with such ambiguity in its resonance that some critics have heard as much irony as love in the sequence.[13] Hélène's "nom si fatal," he says in *Helene* 1.3, her fatal/fateful name, recalls the "malheur des Troyens," the Trojan disaster. *Helene* 2.9 repeats the point: "ce beau nom fatal" once put all Asia and Europe "en pillage." Although it seems a curious piece of forensic cratylism, so to speak, to blame such terrible pillage on a mere name, not on a person, "Helen" had long been taken as cognate with words meaning "destroy" (so unlike the name "Elizabeth," Spenser may have thought, if he noted Ronsard's onomastic wordplay).[14]

To be sure, had the first Helen not lived, Francus—and Aeneas—would have stayed home, and the *Franciade*— let alone the *Aeneid* —would never have been made. In an important sense, then, Hélène is indeed Ronsard's sweet "haleine," as he punningly calls her near the start of the sequence (1.3). She is his "breath," his inspiration, the impetus for epic (recalling, if only coincidentally, that work of "longue haleine" on Francus he had promised in 1556) as well as for amatory questing.[15] As his "haleine" she is to him, if even more problematically, what "l'aura" was to Petrarch. Ronsard's choice of lady and name, then, makes for an ambiguous gesture in several regards. It performs a continuation of his epic by lyric means with an implicit flashback to the erotic origin of Francus's story, but it is also punitive in its evocation of Troy's fall, a fall that was, one could argue, in large part Helen's fault. The lover, like others before him, rewrites himself as a warrior, "du camp d'Amour pratique Chevalier" (*Helene* 1.13). And he is an epic writer after all, implies one sonnet that serves, without quite saying so, as a defense of his return to the love sonnet (*Helene* 2.68). Love animates him, he claims when defending his subjection to a new yoke, giving him better invention and a stronger muse. He must love, he argues, so as to have a better spirit with which to conceive the children (his verses, that is) who will make his name live on. Ronsard moves from ancestors to progeny, from the past to the future, from thrones to poems, and from the dynastic epic to the love sonnet. The last lines reinforce this: what more fertile subject could he have chosen, they ask, than the same one that was Homer's delight ("plaisir")—the divine and virtuous Hélène?[16]

Several other poems in the *Sonnets pour Helene* make a similar move. Urged on by his master Cupid, for example, Ronsard besieges Hélène as the Greeks camped before Troy, thus merging a medieval amatory topos with epic allusion (*Helene* 2.10). In the 1550s Henri II had told Ronsard to get on with his epic. Now, in the 1570s, the poet has a telling defense of his generic backsliding: had all his countrymen been in love, he says, there would have been no civil wars (a topic on which he had by now written some anguished polemics). May Venus, he prays, have pity on the French, descendants of her favored Trojans, and unbristle the mustaches of Mars.[17] Ronsard never quite says so, but as both goddess of love and mother of Aeneas, Venus has a complex and ambiguous relation to epic and love poetry; the sexual energies of which she is patroness can distract heroes from their tasks, but she is as necessary as Helen to the Trojan war, and her distractions make for event and narrative.

In his heart, I think, and doubtless with occasional nudges from his court milieu and its powerful female presences, Ronsard preferred desire's distractions, preferred (un)faithful loves to fierce wars. His career is a study in what happens when an urgently ambitious writer finds himself on a track laid down sooner by tradition than by his own "naturel," as Ronsard calls his inborn taste and talent. If the *Franciade* is a better poem than is sometimes supposed, one reason is that in it Ronsard so often allowed the Delphian laurel to cede once again to the Paphian myrtle; even his equivalent for Virgil's prophetic Anchises is a woman in love. Spenser had also thought about those same leaves with some ambivalence. Like Ronsard—and of course Petrarch—he works laurel into the leaves of his love poetry (both Ronsard's Astrée and Spenser's Elizabeth Boyle sport the victor's laurel leaf to the bemusement—and in Spenser's case pleasure—of their lovers).[18] But it was with a more unsettling irony that whereas Spenser puts Venus's myrtle, fittingly enough, in book 3's goodly and regenerative Garden of Adonis, he puts (Petrarchan?) laurel in book 2's more problematic and artificial, if engagingly beautiful, Bower of Bliss. That was in 1590. In 1596 he had produced more of *The Faerie Queene*, but he had also published love poetry with traces of concern that the lover might be, or might appear to be, neglecting his epic and his queen. *Amoretti* 33 blames his generic detour on his lady and, like Ronsard off and on throughout his career, *Amoretti* 80 promises that the lover will one day burst out into renewed effort. Spenser's maneuvers in *Amoretti* between lyric and epic are quieter than Ronsard's in *Helene* and later, yet they too suggest that whatever the course chalked out by tradition a poet can, in middle age (Spenser was in his forties, Ronsard in his fifties), find singing of love as much a fulfillment as an apprenticeship. Cupid does not always die young, whatever the intricacy of tones with which these two poets treat him.

My present venture in comparative careerism raises other issues as well. What if life goes on even after the generic rota, of whatever variety, has turned? Even without Cupid's (or a queen's) urgings, a poet may still want to work and to please. Thus Spenser's *Prothalamion* appears, for all its self-pity and for all the seeming discouragement at the very end of *The Faerie Queene*, like a bid for more notice from the increasingly powerful Earl of Essex.[19] Ronsard, despite his own age and occasional melancholy, had likewise looked forward near the end of his career. An unfinished late poem addresses Henri de Navarre, now clearly in line for the French throne. Here, it tells the Huguenot leader, he will find no frivolous thoughts and raging loves but rather Moses and his law (2: 666). Having responded in the 1570s to

Desportes's prominence as a love poet, Ronsard may now be taking on Du Bartas and the intensified fashion for biblical poetry. He is also, of course, prudently saluting the rising sun. So let me attempt an intercareerist fantasy. What if both poets had lived longer? Navarre's struggle to confirm his rights as king was to be a truly epic battle that ended only after he became a Catholic and that received wide, if eventually disappointed, attention in England. Spenser was disgruntled by the conversion, of course, and invented book 5's Sir Burbon to express his contempt mingled with grudging comprehension. Ronsard, though, would have rejoiced. After making a pious end to their careers with religious poetry, or perhaps joining a fashionable shift toward satire, but subsequently still living on, each poet might then have found fresh epic opportunity. With the support of Henri IV, aware that Ronsard had once written love poems to the mother of the new king's mistress, might a doddering Ronsard have begun a *Bourboniad*? And, with a nod from Essex or a forgiving James, would Spenser have worked on *The Faerie Duke* or, perhaps, a few years later, a *Jacobiad* on the founding of Jamestown by Brute's descendants? My more serious point is that the course of true careerism never did run smooth, and that one chief obstacle to its smoothness is, paradoxically, long life and professional success. Poets can die before they have a chance to burst forth into sudden blaze; they can also live to be sans matter, sans patron, sans everything.

In terms of Spenser's own intercareerist thoughts, there are other questions. For example, since major literary careers were by now represented in other countries largely through printed books, should we wonder which editions a writer like Spenser knew as he thought about Ronsard? In the absence of any close translations, it is perhaps impossible to determine which one(s) he saw, yet the physical presentation of Ronsard's career, the generic order, the typeface, prefatory poems, portraits, and commentaries—the public staging of France's "archipoete," in effect—varies with the date of publication. More important, for us, is the use, to our own thinking about Spenser, of observing how Ronsard's literary vocation played itself out. Remembering not just separate poems but the careers of other poets might modify the biographical narratives we construct by encouraging us to see as European phenomena those challenges or discourses that might otherwise seem peculiar to England or Spenser. England, for example, was not the only nation where poets had to deal with what Ronsard, addressing Elizabeth and Catherine de' Medici in 1565, called the two queens' wise "gyneococratie."[20]

It would also help to consider just how vocal Ronsard was in complaining, nearly from the start of his career, that France, together with its corrupt courtiers and tightfisted statesmen, lacked due gratitude to its poets in this mucky and dishonorable "siècle de boüe," one refusing to provide the wind without which Francus could not reach the Gallic shores; like Colin Clout, consequently, Ronsard can affect to prefer country life to the humiliations he finds at court.[21] In fact, whatever Spenser's and Ronsard's felt sincerity, their subjective experience of anger or frustration, we might ask whether poetic discouragement was not also to a large extent conventional, one of the posts marking the path of a poetic career. There is, I think, a poetics of artistic dejection that operates even when the dejected poet (an exiled Ovid, for example, or a Coleridge fearing the loss of inspiration) has objective reason to grieve. Laments, even sincere laments, invite imitation—a *translatio doloris,* Renaissance humanists might call it— even if each new lament is inflected by new conditions and by such specifics as gender, politics, religion, social and literary fashion, age, and geography. The fact that Ronsard, for all his productivity, fame, and hobnobbing with royalty, makes so many Cuddie-like complaints seems another good reason to treat skeptically any tidy chronology of Spenser's actual conception of his position. Yes, he could feel neglected or misread, and no, he never did gallop forth as promised like a refreshed horse to write six or eighteen more books of his epic. But he was not alone. In a poem attached to the *Franciade* in 1587, Ronsard explains in farmers' terms how exhausting it is to struggle with an uncultivated language in a still uncultivated nation. In a passage that modulates into a sad georgic on the author's failure to write epic, the verse bemoans the sheer toil involved in heroic enterprise, the drag of circumstance that slows the oxen and entangles the plow.[22]

Ronsard is franker than Spenser, much franker, about interfering monarchs and stingy magnates. Perhaps like Spenser in *Amoretti* 74, surrounded by the three Elizabeths whom he loves but who do seem a crowd, Ronsard wanted royal support but felt hemmed in by it. If Ovid had to shift meter because Cupid stole a foot and left the poet to limp in a lover's uneven elegiacs, Ronsard had to write his *Franciade,* in less-than-heroic decasyllables (or so he says) because Charles IX told him to and then, if his friend Binet is correct, to write again of love because Charles's mother told him to. Ovid's joke allegorizes his *own* desire; Ronsard's meter, like Hélène's chaste refusals, *counters* his own desire. Spenser shows traces of such concern: might Gloriana resent his praise of his other Elizabeth, the one who so fully favored him, and of the unnamed country lass on Mount Acidale in book 6? Does the moon peering in at him in *Epithalamion* recall England's Cynthia, and if so what does she want? If Cynthia can trash Arlo Hill, in the *Mutabilitie Cantos,* what might she do to poets? Spenser shared Ronsard's sense of the way power can swoop down, Argante-like, even on writers of epic.[23] Those who still find Spenser's praise of Elizabeth excessive or his politics servile might consider, for comparison, how Ronsard can both flatter nobles and rulers as gods and, in other lines, struggle painfully within the toils made by the power of others and by his own desires. Even a great Renaissance poet, not least one trying to write epic with a Trojan theme for a Renaissance dynasty, can look less like Virgil than like Laocoön.

Notes

1. On Ronsard's life, see Cohen, *Ronsard: Sa vie et son oeuvre.* In this essay I cite Cohen's convenient *Oeuvres complètes de Ronsard* by volume and page number (or sequences by book and sonnet number), but since Ronsard so often revised, adding and dropping poems, it is wise also to consult the twenty-volume chronological edition by Paul Laumonier, Raymond Lebègue, and Isidore Silver and the recent *Oeuvres complètes,* ed. Jean Céard, Daniel Ménager, and Michel Simonin (Paris: Galimard, 1993–1994). It is hard to believe that Spenser did not keep up with Ronsard's work, whatever the two poets' religious and temperamental differences. Satterthwaite may exaggerate these differences by overplaying Ronsard's "paganism." There are traces of Ronsard's "Adonis" in Spenser's *Astrophel,* echoes of two lyrics about Cupid in *The Shepheardes Calender* and the "Anacreontics," and quite a few parallels—although no clear "borrowings"—between Ronsard's various *Amours* and Spenser's *Amoretti.*

2. Smith says that lest Cecil should lack "newes" he is enclosing Ronsard's "Nues" (clouds), a satire of political gossip that includes a rumor that an Englishman (Leicester?) will marry his mistress. Good for a wry laugh back home, Smith must have thought. See my *French Poets and the English Renaissance* 83.

3. The Trojan aspect of Ronsard's *Franciade,* like that of Spenser's *The Faerie Queene,* is not merely a way of imitating Virgil or appropriating a share of antique glory. The Habsburgs' imperialist claim, their assumed right to muscle their way "plus ultra" through the gates of their ancestor Hercules, was often expressed in terms of a Trojan inheritance, implausible though those terms now seem. To celebrate French or British Trojans, if only as a shared literary fantasy, is to advance one's own monarchy and to deny the global pretensions of Charles V and, later, Philip II. On those pretensions, see Tanner. On Ronsard's complex relation to his own epic models see François Rigolot, "Homer's Virgilian Authority: Ronsard's Counterfeit Epic Theory."

4. 1: 433–34; 1: 361 (in a 1550 ode to Henri II on peace with England).

5. See P. Cheney's *Spenser's Famous Flight.*

6. "Virgile, pour essay, chanta sa Bucolique, / Puis le Troyen Ænée: ainsi premierement / Boyssieres a chanté son Amoureux tourment, / Et ores son Hercul' d'un long vers heroïque" (2: 944).

7. *Amores* 2.1: "Arma gravi numero violentaque bella parabam / edere, materia conveniente modis. / par erat inferior versus—risisse Cupido / dicitur atque unum surripuisse pedem." Cheney (157) notes the significance of these lines for Spenser. At the start of the third book Ovid meets Elegy, a sweet-scented and loving lady whose charms are only increased by her limp, but also mighty-paced Tragedy, with grim forehead ("fronte . . . torva") and scepter, who

scolds Ovid for writing love poetry. The frown and scepter might remind Spenserians of the proem to book 4 and its nervous allusion to the "rugged brow" of the statesman—some say William Cecil—who disapproves of Spenser's recently published *Amoretti and Epithalamion*. Other Roman poets played on the tension between Amor and Mars, elegy and epic. For examples, including *Amores* 1.1, see Hallowell 85–93.

    8. *Amours de Cassandre* 71 (1552):

> Ja desja Mars ma trompe avoit choisie,
> Et dans mes vers ja Francus devisoit;
> Sur ma fureur ja sa lance aguisoit,
> Empoinçonnant ma brave poësie;
> Ja d'une horreur la Gaule estoit saisie,
> Et sous le fer ja Sene tre-luisoit,
> Et ja Francus à Paris conduisoit
> Le nom Troyen et l'honneur de l'Asie,
>   Quand l'Archerot emplumé par le dos,
> D'un trait certain me playant jusqu'à l'os,
> De ses secrets le ministre m'ordonne.
>   Armes adieu. Le Myrtre Pafien
> Ne cede point au Laurier Delfien,
> Quand de sa main Amour mesme le donne.
> (1: 30–31)

(Ronsard was fond of laurel and myrtle leaves as generic signs, adopting them often to express tension—or ties, as in my epigraph—between epic and Eros.) Muret's 1553 edition of the *Amours de Cassandre* quotes the Ovid; see his *Commentaires au premier livre des "Amours" de Ronsard* D2v. Muret's was not the only commentary on Ronsard: see Marie-Madeleine Fontaine and François Lecercle's preface to Belleau's 1560 *Commentaire au Second Livre des "Amours" de Ronsard*. Such commentaries gave Spenser another precedent for his *Calender*, says Adams.

    9. His friend Joachim Du Bellay would later attempt the same generic sleight of hand in his *Antiquitez* (1558, translated by Spenser in his 1591 *Complaints* as *The Ruines of Rome*): these antiheroic sonnets, with their mingled echoes of Lucan, Ovid, Virgil, and Augustine, evoke and participate in the *Romanitas* they lament, criticize, and resurrect. Compare Quint's *Epic and Empire*, which shows how those frères-ennemis, epic and romance, relate to each other and how epic can incorporate romance as inner dissent.

    10. Ronsard's insertion of an erotic element may have surprised some readers, for his outline of the story in a 1555 ode to Henri II (1: 469–73), a sort of letter to Ralegh with even less application to the poem as we have it (for example, it says that Francus conquered Rome), has nothing on love. Although in theory the *Franciade* celebrates the Valois dynasty, Ronsard's treatment of Henri's ancestors, like Spenser's genealogical lists in book 2 of *The Faerie Queene*, is unexpectedly candid concerning their faults. Weinberg (85) calls Francus a "cad, though a divinely sanctioned one" and no worse than his models. Doubtless, she suggests, had the epic been finished we would have seen him improve.

11. Dassonville (103–22) argues that the *Franciade* was never popular but was never intended to be; perhaps, he says, it would have done better under François I.

12. "Si le Roy Charles eust vescu, / J'eusse achevé ce long ouvrage; / Si tost que la mort l'eut veincu, / Sa mort me veinquit le courage." The poet went on alluding to his epic, though. Even in 1584, bidding farewell (again!) to Venus's doves and landscape, he ends Ode 5.33 by noting that Francus had passed that way as he led his army to the Seine's bank.

13. In the early 1550s Ronsard could complain of being unheard, his voice unanswered with approbation and belief in high places. By the mid 1570s, although now much listened to, he was troubled by Huguenot scoffs (and the success of younger writers). It is intriguing, then, that he would now address a lady named not for an ignored prophetess but for a trouble-making Greek. On the name "Helen" and its complex meaning in Greek tragedy and rhetorical display, see Simonin. Cohen quotes Binet (257).

14. On "Helen" as pillage, see Simonin 132.

15. For the allusion to the *Franciade* see 2: 860, in a poem to the Cardinal de Lorraine dropped from the 1584 edition. Another pun may lurk in his self-mocking comment (*Helene* 2.65) that climbing up the stairs to her more than Olympian palace apartment makes him sweat and lose "haleine." It would be pleasant, if difficult, to find similar wordplay in *Amoretti*. Puns on "Boyle"— "boil"? "bile"?—could be only unfortunate, however. Some Elizabethans thought the name "Elizabeth" combines "Eli" and "Sabbath" to make a word in (bad, I am told) Hebrew meaning God's peace or rest, but evidence that Spenser plays with this in his love poetry, even when urging his "warrior" to make peace or hoping to find "rest" with her, seems tenuous. On the infusion of epic elements into Ronsard's late love poetry see also Jean M. Fallon, *Voice and Vision in Ronsard's "Les Sonnets pour Helene."* Bruce R. Leslie argues in *Ronsard's Successful Epic Venture: The Epyllion,* that whatever the *Franciade*'s aesthetic and conceptual failures, such poems as the *Hynne de l'Hyver* succeed as brief epics.

16. *Sonnets pour Helene* 2.68:

> Ah! belle liberté, qui me servois d'escorte,
> Quand le pied me portoit où libre je voulois!
> Ah! que je te regrette! helas, combien de fois
> Ay-je rompu le joug, que malgré moy je porte!
> Puis je l'ay rattaché, estant nay de la sorte,
> Que sans aimer je suis et du plomb et du bois,
> Quand je suis amoureux j'ay l'esprit et la vois,
> L'invention meilleure et la Muse plus forte.
> Il me faut donc aimer pour avoir bon esprit,
> A fin de concevoir des enfans par escrit,
> Pour allonger mon nom aux despens de ma peine.
> Quel sujet plus fertil sçauroy-je mieux choisir
> Que le sujet qui fut d'Homere le plaisir,
> Ceste toute divine et vertueuse Helene?
> (1: 270)

17. *Helene* 1.51. Ronsard's polemics had drawn the attention of the English diplomatic community in Paris. In 1568 a translation of Ronsard's *Discours des miseres de ce temps* was published there by Thomas Jeney, who gently nudged it away from a specifically Catholic stance (although Jeney himself later converted to Rome). With a dedication to the ambassador, Sir Henry Norris, and elegant Neo-Latin commendations by Daniel Rogers, the handsome little volume has the look of a quasi-diplomatic gesture. Evidently in this social and political circle, one with ties to the Sidneys (and so, later, with Spenser), Ronsard was associated with more than love poetry and humanist imitation; see my *French Poets* 84–88, 258; and J. van Dorsten ch. 7.

18. "Sonnets et Madrigals pour Astrée" (1578) 11 (1: 210), and *Amoretti* 28 and 29. Ronsard says, "Le Laurier est aux victoires duisant," and Spenser quotes Elizabeth: "The bay (quoth she) is of the victours borne." In neither case is the laurel's meaning left quite stable. Ronsard modeled Astrée, like Cassandre and Hélène, on a real woman, Françoise d'Estrées, mother of the Gabrielle who was to be the mistress of Henri de Navarre and, says Cohen's note, one of seven sisters nicknamed "the Seven Deadly Sins" (she was Lust).

19. Like Ronsard in a bitter 1563 poem to Catherine de' Medici, he walks out along a river feeling unappreciated. The poem, from *Le Bocage royal* (1: 865–72), is worth quoting to show how France's seemingly most successful poet could repine, first to himself and later to a sage he encounters near the Seine, concerning his bad fortune, the death of friends, and the failure of the great to support the arts. Oh, had the learned François I lived! But Ronsard has deceived himself in praising lords. As for an epic, he tells posterity:

> Toy qui viens apres moy, qui voirras en meints lieux
> De mes escrits espars le titre ambitieux,
> De Francus, Francion, et de la Franciade,
> Qu'égaler je devois à la Grecque Iliade,
> Ne m'appelle menteur, paresseux, ny peureux:
> J'avois l'esprit gaillard et le coeur genereux
> Pour faire un si grand oeuvre en toute hardiesse,
> Mais au besoin les Rois m'ont failly de promesse;
> Ils ont tranché mon cours au milieu de mes vers;
> Au milieu des rochers, des forests, des deserts,
> Ils ont fait arrester, par faute d'equipage,
> Francus qui leur donnoit Ilion en partage.
> Pource j'ay resolu de m'en-aller d'icy
> Pour trainer autre-part ma plume et mon soucy,
> En estrange pays, servant un autre Prince;
> Souvent le malheur change en changeant de province.
> Car que feray-je icy sans aide et sans support?
> L'espoir qui me tenoit, se perdit par la mort
> Du bon Prince Henry, lequel fut l'esperance
> De mes vers, et de moy, et de toute la France.

The sage performs some magic rites and says Ronsard is sick with poetry ("Ta teste en est malade"). Pray to the great gods of the court, he says: follow, serve, sit at their tables, tell them delightful tales, court them, see them, urge them often ("Les courtizer, les voir, et les presser souvent") or your work will be nothing but wind. Luckily, Catherine de' Medici governs France by "naturelle amour" so as to make ancient virtue flower once more. If *she* does not change your destiny, then leave ungrateful France and seek a better fate elsewhere.

20. See my *French Poets* 83–84. Spenser would have noted with pleasure or irony that the same flurry of poems directs some of its most abject flattery at William Cecil. Ronsard had lived in Scotland for a time when a boy, attending Mary Stuart's mother, and his poetry on Mary has real warmth (she in turn admired his poetry); he would not, I think, have enjoyed Spenser's recreation of her as Duessa.

21. In a poem to Villeroy, secretary of state (1: 279–83); on wandering near the brooks and the fields, singing to fauns and dryads, see Ronsard's long 1560 "Discours contre Fortune" (2: 399–409), which also has a prayer by the muses on Ronsard's behalf, a temple of Fortune, and a dismayed description of a trip to court. Similarly, but later in his career, Du Bellay, who had worked epic tonalities into his *Antiquitez,* returns home to write "Le poete courtizan," satirical advice to would-be court poets on seeking to please and winning treasure.

22. Ronsard cites Homer and Virgil, then laments his own fate:
Ces deux grands demy-Dieux, dignes chacun d'un temple,
L'un Romain, l'autre Grec, à qui les Cieux amis
Et les Muses avoient tout dit et tour permis,
Et non à moy François, dont la langue peu riche,
Couverte de halliers, tous les jours se desfriche,
Sans mots, sans ornemens, sans honneur et sans pris,
Comme un champ qui fait peur aux plus gentils esprits
Des laboureurs, actifs à nourrir leurs mesnages,
Qui tournent les guerets pleins de ronces sauvages
Et d'herbes aux longs pieds, retardement des boeufs,
A faute d'artisans qui n'ont point davant eux
Defriché ny viré la campaigne feruë,
Qui maintenant revesche arreste leur charruë,
Luttant contre le soc d'herbes enrivonné.
Mais quoy! prenons en gré ce qui nous est donné,
Achevons nostre tasche, et croyons d'asseurance
Que ces deux estrangers pourront loger en France,
Si la Parque me rit, reschaufant la froideur
Des hommes bien adroits à suyvre mon ardeur,
Sans craindre des causeurs les langues venimeuses,
Pourveu que nous rendions nos provinces fameuses,
Non d'armes, mais d'escrits; car nous ne sommes pas
De nature inclinez à suyvre les combas,
Mais le bal des neuf Sœurs, dont la verve nous baille
Plus d'ardeur qu'aux soldars de vaincre à la bataille.

Ils ne sont ulcerez sinon par le dehors,
Aux jambes et aux bras, et sur le peau du corps;
Nous, au fond de l'esprit et au profond de l'ame,
Tant l'eguillon d'honneur vivement nous entame. . . .
(2: 640–42)

The poem continues: poets are thus melancholy, fantastic, whimsical; conduits for the gods' instruction, badly dressed and with rural words, they express Nature's decrees or destiny.

23. Spenser did a better job than Ronsard of keeping his techniques under his own control. If only as coincidence, it seems symbolically fitting that the "Spenserian" stanza expands that of rhyme royal (used by James I of Scotland), whereas Ronsard's line was shortened by a royal critic with motives far different from Ovid's syllable-snatching Amor.

III. Spenser and the English Other

GLORIANA, ACRASIA, AND THE HOUSE OF BUSIRANE

Gendered Fictions in
The Faerie Queene as Fairy Tale

Mary Ellen Lamb

Spenser's use of such highly literary texts as Ariosto's *Orlando furioso,* Tasso's *Gerusalemme liberata,* and Virgil's *Aeneid* has been well documented. Scholarship has demonstrated the extent to which many episodes of *The Faerie Queene* represent rereadings of these formative texts in ways that make them absolutely central to its meanings. It is easy to forget that the visibility of their determinative presence within Spenser's work is also enabled by their survival as written texts. Editions of Ariosto, Tasso, and Virgil are easily accessible to twentieth-century readers. By contrast, Spenser's evident debt to an oral literature of fairy tales, announced in his title *The Faerie Queene,* has received comparatively little attention because it is more difficult to trace.[1] English fairy tales did not enter the written literature until the seventeenth century; even then the most popular early written collections, such as *Mother Bunches Tales,* came from France (Warner 166–67). While this oral tradition remains somewhat elusive in its very nature, some information still, however, remains available—in ballads, in references to contemporary practices, in early allusions to tales that later reached written form, and in a consistent pattern of contempt expressed for "old wives' tales."

To neglect the centrality of this vernacular tradition for *The Faerie Queene* is to remain blind to the breathtakingly bold narrative maneuver that Spenser's epic performed in making simultaneously visible two competing forms of texts. Bringing these oral tales, and the culture that transmitted them, into narrative awareness required a rethinking of the written texts as well. The cultural meanings—the symbolic capital—of written texts were formed in part as a response to their identity as written, rather than oral texts, as products of a culture that was educated, male, and literate rather than uneducated, female, and illiterate. While oral texts conferred little symbolic capital, they assumed significant cultural power of a different sort, as the first experience of fiction-making most early modern subjects encountered as children. The association of fairy tales with the feminine had less to do with the gender of their authors than with their transmission. Children often heard fairy tales from the women who raised them: their nurses and women servants as well as their mothers. These "old wives' tales" shaped early modern perceptions of fiction, finally to create them as dangerously (or pleasurably) effeminizing. Presenting itself as simultaneously an epic and a fairy tale, *The Faerie Queene* reveals the gendered conflicts at the core of its own narrative act. In particular, this paper explores the gendered conflicts produced by the presence of fairy tales in Spenser's representations of Gloriana, Acrasia, and the house of Busirane.

The title of *The Faerie Queene* identifies Spenser's epic with a tradition of fairy tales. Fairy queens appeared prominently in ballads discussed below such as "Thomas Rhymer" and "Tam Lin." Ballads of mortals pining for their fairy brides or lovers lie behind Arthur's unceasing desire to find the fairy queen, and his paleness as he describes his love (1.9.13–15). The claim that mortal children were stolen by fairies and that fairy or elf children were left in their place appears from the other side of the fairyland/mirror: instead of the changelings left by fairies, *The Faerie Queene* presents the mortals stolen as children and raised by fairies in the characters of Artegall and the Redcrosse Knight ("such men do Chaungelings call, so chaungd by Faeries theft" [65]).[2] Isabel Rathborne has pointed out the parallels between the familiar dancing fairies of folklore and Calidore's vision of the dancing graces on Mount Acidale, who vanish at Calidore's intrusion (205–15). In addition to the fairy queen, pining mortal lovers, changeling children, and dancing immortals, *The Faerie Queene* includes many other elements easily recognizable from fairy tales: elves, dwarves, evil witches, ogres, giants, loyal lions, and birds that carry mysterious jewels.

It was this fairy tale aspect of an early drafted portion of Spenser's epic that his friend Gabriel Harvey simply could not fathom. His often-quoted letter to Spenser records his shock at Spenser's decision to write an epic that included a fairy queen: "If so be the *Faerye Queene* be fairer in your eie than the *Nine Muses*, and *Hobgoblin* runne away with the Garland from *Apollo:* Marke what I saye, and yet I will not say that I thought, but there an End for this once, and fare you well, till God or some good Aungell putte you in a better minde" (Harvey 628). Often this passage is interpreted in terms of the conflict between a native and a classical tradition; but the extent of his disapproval suggests that something more is at stake. Beginning with "Marke what I say" to "fare you well," Harvey's incredulity verges on incoherence. The two forms of narratives were not merely mutually exclusive; Harvey's confidence in the absolute superiority of the classical tradition is exceeded only by his unapologetic contempt for a tradition including a fairy queen and hobgoblins. Praying that no less a force than God or an angel might put Spenser "in a better minde," Harvey washes his hands of the entire project. Rather than dismiss Harvey's response as the idiosyncratic blindness of an insensitive pedant, I would claim that his contempt for the fairy queens and hobgoblins of fairy tales was a widespread phenomenon. Accounting for the strength of Harvey's disapproval, as well as recognizing its deeper cultural sources, is crucial for understanding the gendered nature of Spenser's poetic project.

The social historian Peter Burke has described educated early modern males as "amphibious, bicultural and also bilingual" (*Popular Culture* 28). Like other literate males, Gabriel Harvey had intimate and personal experience of life both within the popular and the educated cultures. While Burke notes that for the elite, the "great" or high-status tradition was "serious" while the popular tradition was "play," Burke's model for these cultural "amphibians" does not acknowledge the conflicts between the popular and the elite cultures, or the extent to which early modern child-rearing practices gendered these conflicts, internalizing them within the subjectivities of early modern males. These social tensions became narrative tensions, as vernacular folk tales, and especially fairy tales, became identified with the degraded feminine culture known in childhood.

Fairy tales gained specific cultural meanings from the gendered circumstances of their transmission and reception. Not only were women the primary narrators of these tales to children, but boys also heard fairy tales before they themselves were considered wholly male. As described by Laqueur, the gender of boys was rendered indeterminate according to a one-sex system, in which masculinity was an achieved social characteristic more than a biological given. Dominated by women and wearing skirts until at least the age of three, boys younger than seven years of age were still considered effeminate (Aries 58–59; Rackin 74–76; Orgel 14). Some early moderns revived a classical discourse to go even further: before the age of seven when rationality set in, children were not even entirely human, and they were to be whipped and petted or "cockered" like small animals (Stone 117; Marcus, *Childhood and Cultural Despair* 10).

If a man's later memories of fairy tales aroused anxiety over an earlier effeminacy or even bestiality, that anxiety would have been only exacerbated by the memory of the pleasures they provided. As Greenblatt has noted, the early moderns approved pleasures that served a useful function; inordinate pleasure was characterized not by its intensity as much as by its absence of purpose (176). Contemporary descriptions portrayed women as telling stories for no more practical purpose beyond occupying long winter nights by the fire (Boccaccio 54; Shakespeare's *Macbeth* 3.4.59; Peele's *Old Wives' Tale*). Even worse, the pleasures provided by women's stories, and by their songs and lullabies, were profoundly sensual. Performed rather than read, any oral literature gains powerful meanings through the sounds of the teller's voice, in the expressions of her face, perhaps in the warmth of her body, and certainly in her personal interactions with her audience (Degh 112–19). Acknowledgment of the power of this pleasure remained largely unspeakable within a literate culture, but a modern analogue suggests the probable impact of this experience: Carolyn Cooper describes the effects of the oral culture of her Jamaican childhood as unceasing and visceral, as "noises in the blood" (2–3, 8).

These cultural meanings of fairy tales—their associations with effeminacy, with sensual pleasures, with domination by women—were not necessarily apparent to small boys or women. These meanings were produced within a highly masculinized culture of the schoolroom. Taught only by men and in the presence of other boys, youths learned Latin under highly ascetic and sometimes punitive circumstances. Walter Ong's representation of this experience as a puberty rite recognizes its cultural meaning, to inculcate older boys into a stage of masculinity distinguishing them not only from women, but from the self-indulgent and effeminate creatures they once were. They were to experience, according to William Kerrigan, a birth of a "linguistic ego" into the male culture of Latin (277, 285). This rebirth was not only linguistic; it also involved a denial of earlier sensual pleasures. Keith Thomas has described the grammar school project as a system of "instinctual renunciation" ("The Articulation of Ego" 8). The discipline internalized through long hours of translating, sometimes accompanied by canings, left little time for bodily pleasures or even for play. According to T.W. Baldwin, Elizabethan schools purposefully prevented boys from playing to transform them into men (1: 561). This rigorous physical as well as mental training was designed to create a disciplined student body whose mastery over their own sensual desires fitted them as leaders able to rule others.[3] Unlike fairy tales, the narratives of the masculinizing schoolroom—the myths, epics, the histories of the classical world—were designed for high purposes: to further the eloquence and instill the morals to train the leaders of the next generation (Crane 163; Helgerson, *Elizabethan Prodigals* 32). Through their familiarity with classical narratives, young men were to present themselves not only as learned, but as masculine.

Fairy stories and classical myths proceeded not only from two opposing cultures, but from two opposing forms of masculine self. Abruptly removed from the female culture at about the age of seven, early modern males had little opportunity to reconcile the inner contradictions proceeding from these two highly gendered cultures. In this context, Harvey's sense of the incompatibility of the creatures from two forms of narrative—a fairy queen and the nine muses, a hobgoblin and Apollo—becomes more than a merely aesthetic distaste. His contempt for fairy queens and hobgoblins participates in a general and perhaps inevitable hostility of the learned culture for the childhood culture of women. This hostility emerges forcefully from Erasmus's admonition to remove boys at an even earlier age from women's dominance. Most notably, Erasmus also expresses this aggression in terms of incompatible narratives: "A boy [may] learn a pretty story from the ancient poets, or a memorable tale from history, just as readily as the stupid and vulgar ballad, or the old wives' fairy rubbish such as most children are steeped in nowadays by nurses and serving women" (214). Erasmus's contempt for fairy tales, like Harvey's, reveals an unexpected vulnerability in the hegemony of patriarchal power. Fairy tales, and the culture that produced them, potentially competed with classical myths for the loyalty of boys. Thus, Erasmus dismissed ballads as "stupid and vulgar," appropriate only to the uneducated lower classes; knowledge of fairy tales demonstrated the regrettable influence of lower-class women over children and especially over young boys, who could better spend their time learning classical myths and histories in the schoolroom. One wonders if, in their sometimes inevitably painful interpellation into this elite version of early modern masculinity, boys necessarily agreed or if, in the course of long hours of Latin translation, boys occasionally felt nostalgic for the creature comforts of childhood. If so, then a desire to sit again at the knees of women, to hear yet more "fairy rubbish," was not easily integrated into their newfound sense of masculinity. Harvey's hostility to Spenser's "Faerye Queene" suggests that the tensions between schoolroom and childhood narratives did not necessarily diminish with age.

Erasmus's solution, like Harvey's, was simply to stamp out the narratives of childhood, and in the process to displace the "soft" effeminate boy with a "hard" disciplined youth. Other strategies were also possible. Arthur Golding's translation of Ovid's *Metamorphoses* blends the Latin and native cultures by translating the "di" of Medea's speech as "elves," and Shakespeare retains Golding's merging of cultures as he quotes Medea's lines, "Ye elves of hills, brooks, standing lakes, and groves," in the *Tempest*

(5.1.33; Kermode 142–45, 147–50). Later, King James's *Daemonologie* identified Diana's followers with fairies: "That fourth kinde of Spirits, which by the Gentiles was called Diana, and her wandering court, and amongst us was called the Phairie (as I told you) or our good neighbors" (132; Latham 52). Does this accommodation represent an attempt to integrate not only these competing cultures, but the competing selves of boys formed within them? Or does it represent an appropriation of an early female discourse by a more powerful male discourse? A similar question can be raised for Spenser's use of these two competing forms of narrative in *The Faerie Queene*. It could be said that the use of classical narratives in *The Faerie Queene* displaced or appropriated childhood fictions to redeem fiction itself for masculinity. But the process may have worked both ways. While boys were, in theory, to leave behind vernacular fairy tales for classical myths, *The Faerie Queene* may also have reversed the process, by placing classical works within a large "fairy tale."

To recreate early modern meanings of Spenser's representation of Elizabeth as a fairy queen, it is necessary to look at contemporary legends of fairy queens. They were not, on the whole, complimentary. In a masterful 1930 survey of Elizabethan English fairy literature, Minor Latham puzzled over the noncongruence between the evil reputation of fairies and Spenser's honorific use of the title *Faerie Queene* to refer to Elizabeth: "In all the pages of their record, with the exception of the fairies of Shakespeare's mythology, and the fairies of Spenser, the fairies as a race are never referred to as good spirits, except when this adjective is applied to them as a matter of propitiation or of fear, or to single out some particular member of the race who is pleased, for some reason or other, to show a favor to mortals. This conception of fairies seems almost incredible when it is remembered that *The Faerie Queene* was written in honor of Elizabeth" (143). Since 1930, scholarship by such scholars as Louis Montrose and Susan Frye has demonstrated the cultural complexities shaping representations of Queen Elizabeth whether by herself, her courtiers, or early modern writers. Within this theoretical context, Spenser's use of the fairy queen to refer to Queen Elizabeth ceases to be incredible. It has now become possible to interpret negative as well as positive aspects of fairy queens as playing a role in Spenser's characterizations of female sovereignty.

Within a context of competing learned and popular cultures, Spenser's figure of a fairy queen becomes an ideal vehicle for representing and managing a subject's ambivalence over domination by Queen Elizabeth. This fairy figure from childhood narratives accurately locates ambivalence about a woman's rule at its source, in the gendered significances attached to women's rule in childhood. In this respect, Spenser is doing what I believe he does best in *The Faerie Queene:* he embodies cultural issues—even cultural nightmares—in his text in ways that make them accessible but by no means simple. Within the context of childhood fairy tales, the identification of Elizabeth as Gloriana can easily be presented in opposing ways, performing the opposite functions of confirming or containing her power. The recapitulation of the female dominance of childhood through the identification of Elizabeth as a fairy queen, for example, allays gender anxieties of male subjects as needless. Far from effeminate, male knights in *The Faerie Queene* become even more manly under Gloriana's influence, as they engage in heroic quests and achieve courageous deeds to gain her favor. Alternatively, Spenser's topical allusions to Elizabeth as a fairy queen denigrate her power as a transitory phase, like the dominance of women in childhood, through which questing males should pass. In either case, by naming Gloriana as the queen of his own large fairy tale, Spenser has created issues of gender dominance as part of his own narrative act.

To understand the cultural implications of Spenser's identification of Queen Elizabeth as the fairy queen, it is necessary to explore the contemporary folklore of fairies. One significant characteristic shared by Queen Elizabeth and fairy queens was the capacity to bestow wealth; in this capacity they also both conformed to a small child's perception of any adult who produces goods and moneys by an unknown mysterious force. Various allusions to early modern fairies described their propensity for leaving coins or silver in the shoes of housemaids who performed their cleaning duties well (Aubrey 203; Latham 132–33); these domestic rewards were surely given by employers to encourage hard work. Fairies in ballads promise and sometimes deliver gifts of gold and jewels to favored mortals; these may well derive from an association of the barrows concealing the wealth of the ancient dead with the gorgeous underground caverns imagined as the habitats of fairies (Wimberly 180–86; Latham 138–39). The belief in fairy wealth was widespread enough by the early seventeenth century to enable con artists to convince trusting stooges that with their help, available for a substantial fee, a fairy queen would reveal to them the whereabouts of concealed treasure (*Brideling*). Generosity emerged as a prominent characteristic of the female "fairies" bestowing gifts on Elizabeth in her progresses: fairies gave her jewels at Apthorpe and Quarrendon, and the fairy queen gave her a rich gown at Woodstock (Latham 143; Baskerville). While fairy queens paid her homage, in none of these progesses was Elizabeth actually identified as herself a fairy queen; it was left to Spenser to make that association explicit. This association of fairy queens and generous gifts, especially in Elizabethan entertainments, perhaps expressed

Spenser's own hopes for ample rewards from his own personal fairy queen, Elizabeth.

Fairies, including fairy queens, did not only reward; they also punished. Housemaids who did not clean well were pinched at night. The pinching of Shakespeare's Falstaff by townspeople disguised as fairies and directed by a "fairy queen" in *Merry Wives of Windsor* enacts a belief that fairies pinched lechers as well. In "Childe Roland," a story mentioned in *King Lear,* the hapless Burd Ellen is taken to Elfland because she runs in the wrong direction ("windershins") around a church to catch a ball thrown by her brother; her brother is almost caught in the act of rescuing her when he nearly eats fairy food (Jacobs 137–45). While relatively few other fairy tales can be proven to derive from this period, collections of early tales often detail grave consequences for neglecting to follow rules set by fairies: seven-year lameness, blindness in one eye, pining to death for an absent fairy lover (Hartland 95–104, 116–19, 123–25). Numerous contemporary allusions represent fairy tales as frightening, although surely fright at scary stories implies rather than precludes delight. Reginald Scot describes the fear they inspired as lingering even into adulthood: "In our childhood our mothers maids have so terrified us with an ugly devil having hornes on his head . . . and they have so fraied us with bull-beggers, spirits, witches, urchens, elves, hags, fairies . . . and such other bugs, that we are afraid of our own shadows" (153).

Spenser's Gloriana does not punish her knights, although Belphoebe, another version of Elizabeth, punishes Timias with a vindictiveness that almost causes his death from unrequited love. The fear of fairy punishment represents the dark side of the hope for fairy rewards. A tradition of fairy malice perhaps accounts for the occasional nervousness in the narrator's tone as he addresses Gloriana as, for example, his "dearest dred" (1 proem 4). As a glittering figure of arbitrary and irrational power, capable of conferring immense treasure or wasting diseases, Gloriana the fairy queen becomes an apt vehicle for expressing the hopes and fears structuring a male subject's feelings for Queen Elizabeth. As a character from childhood tales, the figure of the fairy queen also associates the powers of queens with the terrible power of mothers and nurses to thwart or to indulge their young charges' desires or even their most essential bodily needs.

These powers were associated not only with the fictional character of fairy queens, but with the women who told the stories that created fairy queens. Just as the "mother's maids" of Reginald Scot were able to terrify children with fairy tales, the power imagined for the fairy queen Gloriana is also integrally tied up in acts of narration. Presiding over her court, the fairy queen assigns tasks to her knights; and it is to her court that they return to recount their adventures. The fairy queen does not appear as a character in her own person, but perhaps like the women of childhood, she remains an absent presence whose favor motivates knights—such as the Redcrosse Knight—to accomplish many of the adventures that compose *The Faerie Queene*.[4]

> Upon a great adventure he was bond,
> That greatest *Gloriana* to him gave,
> That greatest Glorious Queene of *Fairie* lond,
> To winne him worship, and her grace to have,
> Which of all earthly things he most did crave.
> (1.1.3)

In this respect, Spenser is not so different from the Redcrosse Knight; his writing of the epic *Faerie Queene* is itself an arduous and even a heroic adventure performed to gain the favor of Gloriana. Although her power resides in listening rather than telling, Gloriana's presence (perhaps like Elizabeth's) creates her court as the hidden scene of stories affecting faraway events. In this sense, Gloriana represents a principle of narration.

The centrality of Gloriana to the narrative act of *The Faerie Queene* is perhaps most apparent, however, in her effect on Arthur, who wishes to win not only her "worship" but her love. As Arthur tells the sympathetic Una, Gloriana appeared to him in a dream as a "royall Mayd" who made "most goodly glee and lovely blandishment" to identify herself as she left as "the Queene of Faeries hight"; on waking, he found only "pressed gras where she had lyen" (1.9.13–15). Arthur's desire for Gloriana assumes structural significance for Spenser's epic, for as the allegorical figure of Magnificence comprehending the other virtues (Spenser 407), Arthur represents its unifying principle. His desire for Gloriana sets in motion a narrative desire, by creating the expectation that Spenser will continue to write, and that readers continue to read, until Arthur's glorious marriage with Gloriana ends his quest, and with it, Spenser's epic itself. As Craig Berry has noted, "Spenser defers the completion of Arthur's quest in order to keep us reading" (165). As a triumphant conclusion to Spenser's epic, Arthur's anticipated marriage represents the narrative desire of readers as proper and wholesome. We expect, like Arthur, to be satisfied.

But the identity of Gloriana as the Queen of the Fairies releases a counter-expectation for those knowledgeable in fairy lore. In his desire for Gloriana, Arthur models a less healthy form of narrative desire. In fairy tales and especially fairy tale ballads, erotic desires for fairies seldom end well. Perpetually dissatisfied, mortal lovers pine and die. From this perspective,

Arthur's paleness (16), as well as his vow never to rest until he finds Gloriana, already identifies him as under the spell of a fairy lover. From this perspective, he is a doomed man. This ending is never realized in the unfinished *Faerie Queene*.[5] Rather than displacing or negating an expectation of a triumphant conclusion, I believe that this alternative ending released a lurking anxiety over Arthur's fate, which was at the same time a lurking anxiety over the nature of narrative desire in *The Faerie Queene* itself. For Harvey, as for other adult males of the early modern period, the revival of an old narrative desire for childhood fairy tales was fundamentally unhealthy. Like doomed lovers, grown men who yearned to return to these fairy pleasures could never be satisfied.

Or if adult male readers could be satisfied, if they could temporarily find fulfillment of the narrative desires of childhood, they perhaps found themselves in the position of the Redcrosse Knight, whose dream-experience so cruelly parodied Arthur's. Like Arthur, Redcrosse dreamed of physical pleasures with his beloved. Unlike Arthur, Redcrosse woke to find Una (or the simulacrum of Una) beside him and receptive to his desires (1.1.49–55). The response of the Redcrosse Knight was rage, contempt, and finally flight. To remain, to succumb to sexual/textual desires, was to risk a regression like Verdant's, supine in Acrasia's arms.

While Gloriana's influence is at least superficially beneficial and Acrasia's is sinister, both figures conflate the authority of fairy queens with the powerful effects of stories themselves. Through its allusions, its imagery, and its plot, the Bower of Bliss episode announces its topic as the dangers potential to early modern fiction-making itself. Critics have already noted the ways in which lyric poetry, including the lyric poetry of Spenser's *The Faerie Queene*, is implicated in the art of Acrasia's Bower of Bliss: the art of the bower imitates nature, yet its highest goal is to the conceal its effort (Greenblatt, *Renaissance Self-Fashioning* 189). I believe that nothing has yet been said about the association of women's tales with Acrasia's art through the figure of Phaedria.

In book 2, Phaedria clearly acts as a version of Acrasia. Her effect on men is described in terms identical to Acrasia's; in fact, Guyon and the Palmer themselves encounter her on Idle lake on their way to Acrasia's bower (2.12.17). In canto 5, Cymochles has already abandoned himself to "idle pleasures" in Acrasia's bower, where "his warlike weapons cast behind," he "pourd out his idle mind / In daintie delices, and lavish joyes" (2.5.27–28). Roused by Atin who found him "in Ladies lap entombed" (36), Cymochles rushes off to fight Guyon only to fall prey to Phaedria, who subdues him to the very same plight. Taking him on her shallow ship to cross Idle lake, she seduces him with "merry tales" told for "pleasant purpose," along with other forms of "light behaviour" (2.6.8):

> And all the way, the wanton Damzell found
>   New merth, her passenger to entertaine:
>   For she in pleasant purpose did abound,
>   And greatly joyed merry tales to faine,
>   Of which a store-house did with her remaine,
>   Yet seemed, nothing well they her became;
>   For all her words she drownd with laughter vaine,
>   And wanted grace in utt'ring of the same,
> That turned all her pleasance to a scoffing game.
>   (2.6.6)

Successfully distracting Cymochles from his warlike aim, she leads him into a "shadie dale" to lay "his head disarm'd / In her loose lap" while she lulls him to sleep (14). In the only extended lyric attributed to a woman character, the canto includes three stanzas of her haunting lullaby, which would persuade men to forsake their "toilesome paines" to choose "pleasant pleasures" (15–18).

Phaedria's narrative acts—her merry tales and lullaby—reduce Cymochles to the same state in which Guyon finds Verdant, his "warlike armes" hung on a tree, "slombering / in secret shade," his "sleepie head" laid in Acrasia's lap (2.12.72, 76, 80). While she herself does not sing, music surrounds them: "whence that Musick seemed heard to bee, / Was the faire Witch her selfe now solacing, / With a new Lover" (72). What would appear to be a condition of erotic and aesthetic fulfillment is portrayed, in the book of Temperance, as a terrible fate. Appalled by Verdant's shameful condition as "in lewd loves, and wastful luxuree, / His dayes, his goods, his bodie he did spend" (80), Guyon steps forward and captures them in a net. Leading Acrasia away in chains, he frees her lovers whom she, like Circe, had turned to beasts. Only Grill chose to retain his pig's shape and his "hoggish mind" (86–87).

Beyond a vague allusion to "witchcraft," Acrasia's techniques of seduction were never specified. The reduction of Cymochles and Verdant to the same shameful state of pleasure suggests that she, like Phaedria, may also have told merry tales and sung a lullaby. But Acrasia is identified in another way with the narrative arts of childhood: whatever her other literary allegiances, Acrasia is herself fairy queen. Not only does she possess the traditional fairy character flaws of cruelty and lust (Greenlaw 113), she also kidnaps mortal men to serve her selfish sexual purposes. In the ballad of

"Thomas Rhymer," for example, the queen of Elfland takes True Thomas up behind her on her horse, with practically no preliminaries, and keeps him as her paramour in Elfland for seven years. If he wishes ever to return to his own land, True Thomas, like Verdant, must remain speechless for the entire period:[6]

> "But Thomas, ye maun hold your tongue,
>   Whatever you may hear or see,
> For gin ae word you should chance to speak,
>   You will neer get back to your ain countrie."
> (Child 1: 37)

Tam Lin had even less power to refuse his role as his fairy queen's paramour. In version G of "Tam Lin," he was kidnapped at the age of three by the fairy queen (Child 1: 350). Raising him up in fairy land until he was old enough to serve her sexually, Tam Lin's fairy queen becomes an Acrasia-like combination of mother and lover. Tricked out of her lover by a mortal girl bearing his child, Tam Lin's fairy queen was not generous in defeat:

> Up then spake the Queen o Fairies,
>   Out o a bush o rye:
> "She's taen awa the bonniest knight
>   In a' my cumpanie.
> But had I kennd, Tamlane," she says,
>   "A lady wad borrowd thee
> I wad taen out thy two grey een,
>   Put in twa een o tree.
> 'Had I but kennd, Tamlane," she says,
>   "Before ye came frae hame,
> I wad taen out your heart of flesh,
>   Put in a heart of stane."
> (Child 1: 356)

As destructive lovers who retain their paramours against their will, the fairy queens of "Tam Lin" and "Thomas Rhymer" embody, like Spenser's Acrasia, a nightmare version of possessive sexuality. Unlike the Bower of Bliss, however, these ballads manage sexual anxiety without capturing the fairy queen or destroying her bower. Thomas Rhymer returns safely from her realm after seven years. This length of time, which corresponds to the period when mothers and nurses were to have the care of children, perhaps introduces a maternal subtext into Thomas Rhymer's confinement in fairy land. This subtext is more explicit for Tam Lin, who was stolen as a child before he became his fairy queen's lover. Tam Lin also successfully escapes, to assume his adult responsibilities as husband and father. The content of these ballads would seem, if anything, to reassure children of their eventual independence from female domination. But as mentioned above, the cultural meanings of fairy tales lay in their transmission by women to children, including effeminate boys. For early modern males, the cultural meaning of fairy tales lay in their associations with effeminacy, with sensual pleasures, with domination by women. It was only a small step from ballads sung by women to lullabies.

The perception of Acrasia as a fairy queen creates another level to the threat she poses in the Book of Temperance. Abandoning quests to lie in women's laps represented not only sexual indulgence, but a childish regression to an earlier effeminate self (Montrose, "The Elizabethan Subject" 329–30; Parker, "Suspended Instruments" 57). Atin even calls Cymochles "a womanish weake knight" (2.6.36) as he wakes him from Acrasia's bower. The competition between cultures, internalized within the subjectivities of early modern youths, invested this regression with a particular horror, or perhaps with a particular pleasure. Spenser's own narrative describes Acrasia's bower through the appalled eyes of Guyon. Even if they did not necessarily share it, Guyon's perspective would have been familiar to men who had attended early modern grammar schools. Guyon's formidable mastery of his passions, developed or revealed throughout the Book of Temperance, formed the basis for the disciplined masculine self it was the object of the grammar schools to produce. The temporary success of Acrasia in dominating Verdant embodied a cultural nightmare: that the childhood culture of women could finally win out, that nostalgia could prevail, that the masculine schoolroom could fail in its efforts to shape the subjectivity of early modern youths. In her role as a fairy queen, Acrasia posed the unthinkable possibility that fairy tales could emerge victorious in their competition with Latin texts, and with the masculine culture which produced them.

Acrasia was not only a fairy queen. She was also an adaptation from Tasso's Armida; and Spenser even quotes a song from the *Gerusalemme* to make this connection between his text and Tasso's explicit. The many echoes from Homer's *Odyssey* culminate in identifying Acrasia as Circe, who also turns men into swine. Perhaps no scene in *The Faerie Queene* is as intertextual as Acrasia's Bower of Bliss. Simultaneously a version of Circe, Armida, and a fairy queen, Acrasia blurs boundaries between learned and popular texts. Like all three of her sources, Acrasia seduces men in an attempt to prevent them from fulfilling heroic tasks. Taken together, these four characters suggest that the threat, real or imagined, posed by women's sexuality to active manhood was widespread throughout Western culture.

The emphatic intertextuality of the Bower of Bliss episode raises another even more menacing possibility. As she merges the figure of fairy queen with the figures of Armida and Circe, Acrasia steps across the boundary separating the degraded culture of childhood and the masculine schoolroom. Even written texts in foreign languages are no longer safe from her seductive charms. The actual source of a narrative—whether it is written or oral, classical or native—is no longer a dependable determinant of its influence on gender. Its effect on masculinity depends instead on the nature—the extent of purpose—of the pleasure it offers. Any fiction, no matter how high its cultural capital, which can elicit purposeless pleasure, can be as effeminizing as the fairy tales of childhood.[7] Real men had better turn to philosophy and history.

If this anxiety about the effeminizing influence of fictions seems extreme, it was not unique to Spenser's *The Faerie Queene*. The Acrasia episode created an extended fiction from a common metaphor occurring often in early modern works. The famous metaphor for the wrong sort of poetry in Sir Philip Sidney's *Apology for Poetry*, for example, almost forms a first draft of Spenser's Bower of Bliss episode: "[Poetry] is the nurse of abuse, infecting us with many pestilent desires; with a siren's sweetness drawing the mind to the serpent's tail of sinful fancies . . . both in other nations and ours, before poets did soften us, we were full of courage, given to martial exercises, the pillars of warlike liberty, and not lulled asleep in shady idleness with poet's pastimes." This passage sketches the outlines of both Acrasia and Verdant. Like the seductive Acrasia, poetry conflates a nurse's unhealthy nurturing with a siren's sexuality. Like the effeminized Verdant, "we" the readers neglect our duties as virile warriors to be lulled asleep idly in the shade. Poetry that elicits pleasure without any definite moral purpose is only a pastime, a form of child's play. Poets have rendered our once-hard pillars soft. In these metaphors, Sidney is drawing on specific social practice. The dichotomies between nurses and warriors, idleness and martial exercises, recapitulate the internalized conflicts, produced through the competition between female and male cultures, which tainted pleasures, including narrative pleasures, with gender anxiety.[8] As in the Bower of Bliss, amoral pleasure elicited by *any* poetry—not just fairy tales—can return adult readers to an effeminacy experienced in childhood.

In the Bower of Bliss episode, Spenser pushed contemporary anxieties about the gendered effects possible to poetry to their most extreme form. One might think that these anxieties, expressed in this way, would have brought

The Faerie Queene to a halt. It was perhaps the very direness of this scenario that led to its reformulation in book 3, literally from a different perspective. The horror of Verdant's lapse depended on Guyon's gaze, which judged Verdant through assumptions about masculinity codified as the virtue of Temperance, or the mastery of passions through reason. With book 3, a woman knight replaces a male knight as hero, to demonstrate a virtue especially pertinent to women. With this entry into a female domain, the entire situation looks different. This change of perspective is signaled in the proem, which re-views the gender dynamics of the Bower of Bliss in the narrator's praise of Ralegh's poem to Elizabeth:

> Then that sweet verse, with *Nectar* sprinckeled,
> In which a gracious servant pictured
> His *Cynthia*, his heavens fairest light?
> That with his melting sweetnesse ravished,
> And with the wonder of her beames bright,
> My senses lulled are in slomber of delight.
> (3 proem 4.4–9)

The proem has recast Ralegh as a ravishing Acrasia and Spenser's narrator as the sleeping Verdant. After the Bower of Bliss, the narrator's claims to be "ravished" with the "melting sweetness" of Ralegh's poem and, even worse, to feel his "senses lulled . . . in slomber of delight" are disturbingly familiar. But what was cause for blame in book 2 becomes grounds for praise in book 3. The paradigm has shifted entirely.

This change of perspective requires a change in the reader's gaze; and in its directions to its royal reader, the proem guides all readers to undergo just such a dramatic reversal:

> Which that she may the better deigne to heare,
> Do thou dred infant, *Venus* dearling dove,
> From her high spirit chase imperious feare,
> And use of awfull Maiestie remoue:
> In sted thereof with drops of melting loue,
> Deawd with ambrosiall kisses, by thee gotten
> From thy sweete smyling mother from above,
> Sprinckle her heart, and haughtie courage soften,
> That she may hearke to love, and read this lesson often.
> (4 proem 5)

Instead of a sovereign who would use her "awfull Majestie" to judge,

Elizabeth should read this book as a compassionate woman. As he prays the "dred infant" Cupid to move Elizabeth's heart to "melting love" by placing there "ambrosiall kisses" received from his mother Venus, the narrator sexualizes her act of reading in terms absolutely conventional for constructions of women readers of the time (Lamb, *Gender and Authorship* 7–8, 52–58,72–74; see also Quilligan, *Milton's Spenser* 179–208). These terms were antithetical to masculinity. A masculine reader whose reason has subdued his sensual passions would not willingly receive Cupid's kisses from Venus in his heart. No narrator would have advised Guyon to "soften" his "courage" and lived to tell the tale. To read book 3 according to these instructions, a male reader must mentally cross-dress. Verdant's effeminacy, which produced such horror in book 2, becomes a necessary precondition for the reading of book 3. The narrator's expectations continue to obtain throughout the book, receiving even more emphatic expression in the review of book 3 placed in the opening to book 4:

> Of lovers sad calamities of old,
> > Full many piteous stories do remaine,
> > But none more piteous ever was ytold,
> > Then that of *Amorets* hart-binding chaine,
> > And this of *Florimels* unworthie paine:
> > The deare compassion of whose bitter fit
> > My softened heart so sorely doth constraine,
> > That I with teares full oft doe pittie it,
> And sometimes doe wish it never had bene writ.
> (4.1.1)

In assuming that the readers of book 3 have responded with the compassion imagined for women readers, the narrator also portrays his own compassionate response. In the process, the opening presents Spenser as a woman writer. Exhibiting the compassion expected of women readers, he actually weeps in pity for the love-plights of his own female characters, Amoret and Florimell; and his effeminacy is further suggested in the image of his "softened" heart. His near-regret for writing can be taken in two ways. He may, like a stereotypically emotional woman, be subject to changes of heart because he does not really know his own mind. Or alternatively, his effeminacy, evident in his "softened heart" and abundant tears, causes him so much regret that he questions his act of writing book 3 at all. These readings are not mutually exclusive. Together they suggest that the response of an adult male writer (or reader) effeminized by writing (or reading) fiction may have ranged from judgmental shame to deviant pleasure.

An understanding of the gender change in the reader and writer of book 3 is essential to an appreciation of its new formulation of the problem posed by competition between narratives produced by male and female cultures. Susanne Wofford's brilliant explication of the gendered opposition of character and allegorical figure in the house of Busirane is absolutely germane to this issue. Wofford argues that book 3 represents allegorical characterization as a male mode of writing, as exemplified by Busirane's "penning" of Amoret. A looser construction of character typifies a female mode of writing, as exemplified by Britomart's "openness of character that leads her into unexpected adventures and makes her respond in unpredictable ways" (15). The interpretive looseness of book 3 dramatizes the "impossibility of expressing absolute meaning in a poem" as the gap between the "male meanings imposed by narrator or magician" and the "female understandings represented and acted upon within the story as story" (15). Only Britomart, a character written in the female mode, can be "bold" enough to free Amoret from the meanings imposed upon her by Busirane. With Britomart's rescue of Amoret, book 3 places its own narrative within "an alternative, female authority" opened up through this "dialectic between character and figure" (3).

A seldom-mentioned folklore source for the Busirane episode suggests that this gendered conflict in narrative is even more encompassing, and even more grounded in early modern narrative practice, than Wofford has imagined. In its notes to this episode, the *Variorum Spenser* mentions a small discovery in a 1921 dissertation by Earle Fowler, published as *Spenser and the Courts of Love.* In a passing footnote, Fowler notes that the often-quoted words written over the doors in Busirane's castle—"Be Bold," "Be Bold," "Be Not Too Bold"—derive from the folktale of Mr. Fox, where they were written over a doorway in Mr. Fox's hallway, (56). While not published until the early twentieth century, "Mr. Fox" was apparently already an "old tale" in the 1590s, according to another quotation noticed by Fowler appearing in Shakespeare's *Much Ado about Nothing* (1598–99). In 1.1.207–08, Benedick mocks Claudio's reticence in admitting his love for Hero: "Like the old tale, my lord: 'It is not so, nor 'twas not so, but indeed, God forbid it should be otherwise.'" The "Be Bold" quote identifies Busirane's castle as Mr. Fox's house, and Busirane's torture of Amoret with Mr. Fox's murder of various young ladies. Just as Acrasia merged the figures of Circe, Armida, and a fairy queen, the figure of Busirane merges the figure of a male writer, and especially a Petrarchan poet, with the figure of a fairy-tale villain. In this instance of intertextuality, however, the gendered narratives are not equal. The references to Mr. Fox invest the entire Busirane episode with the wonder and the terror of an old wives' tale.

Here is the story of Mr. Fox, as reported by Halliwell-Phillips (1: 291): "Once upon a time," Lady Mary went with her brothers to the country, where they befriended a neighbor bachelor Mr. Fox. One day Lady Mary visited Mr. Fox's house and, finding no one there, she entered alone. When she went through the door with the words written over it ("Be bold, be bold—but not too bold, lest that your heart's blood should run cold"), she found "skeletons and tubs full of blood." Just then, Mr. Fox came home with his sword drawn and dragging a young woman by her hair. As Lady Mary hid, she saw the girl grab the banister of the stairs. Mr. Fox cut off her hand, which wore a beautiful bracelet; and the hand and bracelet both fell into Lady Mary's lap. The next day, when Mr. Fox dined with other guests at Lady Mary's house, she related the crime she had witnessed, pretending that it was a dream. At several intervals in her story, she repeated the words, "It is not so, nor it was not so; and God forbid it should be so." Finally, as she ended her story, she cried: "But it is so, and it was so, and here's the hand I have to show." Halliwell-Phillips relates that at this point she displayed the bracelet she took from the murdered girl's detached hand, but the phrase "and here's the hand I have to show" surely indicates that she showed the hand, as well. The satisfyingly gruesome response of her guests to her story ends "Mr. Fox": "Whereupon the guests drew their swords, and cut Mr. Fox into a thousand pieces."

Perceiving the house of Busirane episode as a version of "Mr. Fox" foregrounds other fairy-tale features. Busirane's castle is surrounded by enchanted fire which cannot be quenched. Only the chosen person can pass through (11.21, 22, 25). Like the castles later appearing in "Beauty and the Beast" tales, it is at first mysteriously empty of people. When the magician recites his lines backwards, the castle disappears into air and (of course) the captive princess Amoret is restored to her own true love. This is a childhood story that elicits an irrational delight that has nothing to do with a recognition of Petrarchan tropes, and everything to do with becoming a child again. A sense of this ridiculous childish pleasure is necessary to understand the remarkable narrative effect of enclosing the densely "meaningful" episode of Busirane within the tale of "Mr. Fox." The unexpected encounter with the words "Be bold, be bold—but not too bold" may well have affected an early modern reader in the same way as the inclusion of the Disney song "Hi ho, Hi ho, / It's off to work we go" in a classical opera would affect an audience today.

The references to Petrarchan lyric, to courtly masques with allegorical figures, and especially to classical myths woven in tapestries only heighten what was already an intense cognitive dissonance. In the house of Busirane, these lyrics, masques, and myths all contribute to the patriarchal "spell" of a culture that holds Amoret captive. Britomart refuses to interpret the meanings of the tapestries, and it is this "typical lack of comprehension" (Cavanagh, *Wanton Eyes* 156) that creates her immunity to their power. Classical myths don't matter to her.[9] If we read this episode for the pleasure of suspense rather than for "meaning," perhaps they don't really matter to us either. In this episode, women's narratives have won, hands down. As Busirane is forced to read his spell backwards, Amoret is not the only figure freed from the chains of allegory. Just beyond the verge of sight, in the deep structure of Spenser's narrative act, Acrasia also shakes off her chains.

NOTES

1. Critics who have written on fairies in *The Faerie Queene* include Greenlaw; Rathborne; Latham; Duffy; Woodbridge; and the editors of *The Spenser Encyclopedia*. See also Briggs. Wooden notes that "doings of the fairies were an essential part of childhood during the English Renaissance" (104), but that Spenser's *The Faerie Queene* was essentially the first literary text to popularize fairies in this period (98).

2. Eberly has recently theorized changelings as an early modern way of explaining various forms of infant retardation or failure to thrive.

3. Henry Sidney states this rationalization in a letter to Philip Sidney at Shrewsbury: "Be humble and obedient to your masters, for, unless you frame yourself to obey others—yea, and feel in yourself what obedience is, you shall never be able to teach others how to obey you" (12). Crane (6) describes early modern schools as providing "common cultural capital enabling social mobility without threat to hierarchy." This instilling of discipline into youths as training to rule revived a powerful classical discourse of self-mastery as, ideally at least, a precondition for mastery of others; See Foucault, *The Use of Pleasure* 84–85. For a less harsh account of humanist education, see Bushnell.

4. For this insight, I am indebted to my graduate student Marlo Belschner.

5. The unfinished literary source for Arthur's vision, Chaucer's *Tale of Sir Thopas*, complicates even this ambiguity for, according to Lee Patterson, Chaucer swerved from classical and courtly forms of "makyng" to find a new paradigm for authorship in minstrel performances (123); the "elvyssh" narrator of a rhyme he "lerned longe agoon" further allies his form of authorship with a late medieval desire to return to childhood (166). On this issue, see also Berry, "Borrowed Armor." Bennett speculates on the centrality of Arthur's dream to the evolution of *The Faerie Queene*. Lehrer demonstrates a late medieval and early modern reception of Chaucer as domestic literature appropriate for children. My thanks to Craig Berry for alerting me to the literature on this issue.

6. According to Child (1: 37), "Thomas Rhymer" was written about a fourteenth-century figure; allusions to "Tam Lin" exist from 1549 and 1568 (1: 336, 340).

7. An amazing amount of brilliant work has been done in the past few

years on poetry and/or narratives as effeminizing: see Dolan, "Taking the Pencil"; Fleming; Herman; Levine. Acrasia's power is also generalized in Gosson's image of poetry as "Circe's cup," as noted by Levine 12. Hayes discusses a similar hybrid of aristocratic and popular intertextualities in Jonson's use of popular Maid Marian and Robin Hood materials for his play, *The Sad Shepherd.*

8. This issue is discussed more thoroughly in Lamb, "Apologizing." By the time James Cleland wrote his *Institution of a Young Nobleman* (1607), these metaphors were so widely circulated that they had become cliches: "I am so afraid of *Poesie,* that I dare not councell you to read much thereof privately, it is so alluring, that whoever is not aware, shal bee inchanted by this minister of voluptuousness, and so inticed, that he will have no other delight, then to lie sleeping in pleasure; use it therefore only as a recreation after your serious study" (5.3ʳ–5.3ᵛ).

9. For a brilliant analysis of the House of Busirane, see Silberman's description of Britomart's battle with Busirane as a "battle for interpretation" in which Busirane "covertly seeks to retain the power of interpretation exclusively for himself" (59–60).

WOMEN AT THE MARGINS IN SPENSER AND LANYER

Susanne Woods

> I permit not a woman to teache, nether to usurpe autoritie
> over the man, but to be in silence.
>
> (1 Tim. 2.12; Geneva Bible)

Edmund Spenser is generally acknowledged to be the most admired model
for poets of his own and the next generation. Even as writers moved to a
plainer style, they continued to look to the eloquent Elizabethan for
inspiration and strategy. Aemilia Lanyer, the Jacobean poet who may well
have been the first Englishwoman to think of herself as a professional writer,
was no exception. This essay relates one Spenserian device, his use of
marginal figures to center important ideas, to Lanyer's effort to center
women's voices and experience.

A woman publishing was a transgression that many enterprising
Renaissance women found ways to circumvent (Lewalski, *Writing Women*
1–11; Wall, 282–83; Woods, "Vocation and Authority"). Women were not
alone, however, in the need to develop techniques that allowed them to
speak publicly. Any admonitory address from lower to higher class in
Renaissance England was technically a transgression. Elizabethan and
Jacobean literature, which was in large part the product of a humanist-
educated trade class or minor gentry (Spenser, Daniel, Shakespeare,
Jonson), is nonetheless filled with injunctions directed to queens, king, and
various members of the nobility. No matter how humble the prefatory
address, how serviceable the vision to those in power, or how entertaining
the tale, the risk of offence was always at hand.

Renaissance poets were plainly aware of the traps and dangers of
addressing the great and developed numerous strategies to sidestep the

charges of sedition that Lord Burghley might see in Spenser's *Mother Hubberds Tale* or the Queen herself in a production of *Richard II*. High-born sponsors and examples (such as Sidney) were of course very useful. Among techniques of approach, metaphor and fiction were the poet's primary disguises, as Spenser makes clear in the letter to Ralegh. In this he follows a well-understood tradition of fictive eloquence that eschewed plain speech not only because it was considered inelegant, but because it was dangerous. As the ghost of "The Poet Collingbourne," executed for verse critical to Richard III, is feigned to tell William Baldwin, compiler of the popular *Mirror for Magistrates:* "Warne poetes therefore not to passe the bankes / Of Hellicon, but kepe them in the streames, / So shall their freedome save them from extreames" (Campbell 358, ll. 278–80). In the riddling language of metaphoric discourse, in the indeterminacy between signifier and signified, the poet may avoid the "extreames" (including death) exercised by those in power.

Yet a poet who wishes to influence as well as reflect culture must risk crossing the boundary between fiction and the experiential world of his (or her) time. So Spenser specifies some of his allegorical meanings in the letter to Ralegh, and brings the Blatant Beast to the contemporary world of the Elizabethan court at the end of book 6. Less obviously, Spenser sometimes blurs the focus of his narrative to effect solutions from the margins of a story's action, reminding the reader that an authorial consciousness is directing and manipulating the story. One effect of this technique is to decenter expectations, whether of plot line or power relationships.

So, for example, the marginal (in book 5) Britomart rescues Artegall, and the briefly seen Colin Clout explains the crucial doctrine of grace to the intruding courtier Calidore on Mt. Acidale in book 6. In the first instance, Artegall's adventures on behalf of justice come to an abrupt halt, overcome as he is by the Amazon queen Radigund and "trapt in womens snare" (5.6.1). Yet despite Radigund's passion for her captive, he remains true to Britomart, the woman who has captured his heart, allowing Britomart to effect a rescue from her marginal role of waiting for his return. Despite her ladylike worries and "jealous feare" (5.6.4), when Talus brings her word of Artegall's plight she casts off the woman's role she has assumed since her betrothal in book 4, gets an infusion of allegorical force in Isis Church (5.7), destroys Radigund, and frees Artegall. In one of Spenser's nicer ironies, Britomart then takes charge of the land of the Amazons in order to place herself and all women back in their subordinate (and therefore marginal) roles:

> . . . she there as Princess rained,
> And changing all that forme of common weale,

The libertie of women did repeale,
Which they had long usurpt: and them restoring
To mens subjection, did true Justice deale.
(5.7.42)

Calidore centers book 6 until his remarkable vision of the graces, who circle and center "that faire one / . . . to whom that shepheard pypt alone" (6.10.15). "That shepheard" is of course Colin Clout, a figure for the poet Spenser, and the courtier Calidore's intrusion on his inspired rhapsody dissipates the vision of the graces. The poet must teach the courtier what lies at the heart of true courtesy, unachieved grace, a fragile image on the edge of experience: "soone as [Calidore] appeared to their vew / They vanisht all away out of his sight" (6.10.18). The source of grace is the beautiful woman, who may be of modest birth (6.10.25–27). Spenser uses this episode to take class and gender from their marginal positions in society and in book 6 and put them at the heart of the poet's vision and the courtier's hope of grace.

Spenser's tendency to bring marginal figures into the center extends to a tendency to blur some boundaries altogether. The classic instance is book 3, so neatly bound together at the end of the 1590 *Faerie Queene*, in 1596 changed to defer all conclusion, and then to open suddenly into a book 4 that wanders across plots, structures, and themes as if friendship itself were amorphous, and solid connections always just eluding the human condition. These crucial narrative asides and anticlassical structures often involve women, with Una at the heart of those tendencies in the more classically structured book 1. While Una centers 1.3 and 1.6, for most of book 1's narrative she is literally and allegorically at the side of Redcrosse Knight, marginal to much of the story though central to the achievement and achievements of Holiness.

Spenser's decentering approach to narrative, particularly as embodied by the figure of Una in book 1, may have provided a model for Lanyer's unprecedented empowerment of women in her poem on Christ's passion, *Salve Deus Rex Judaeorum* (1611). Lanyer's dedicatory poems, all to women, tend to conflate gender and class, destablizing the ability of either one to hinder the authorial voice. Yet a key issue for Lanyer remained how women derive and exercise authority, how they may be seen as the authors and right interpreters of experience. In her principal poem (the title poem of the volume) she negotiates the male-centered narrative to make women central to the meaning of the story. In the biblical versions of Christ's passion, women appear only on the outskirts of the grand drama of Christian salvation. By contrast, Lanyer creates a community of female virtue and response that reorders and reinterprets the story, that teaches its true meaning, incidentally defying the Pauline injunction cited in this essay's epigraph. Spenser's technique of centering marginal figures at crucial moments may have provided a useful model for an aspiring transgressor.

The Faerie Queene displays an eclectic syncretism that does not serve a carefully articulated world view, but questions simple doctrines and assured categories, including power relationships, whether of love or rule. Spenser's famous *copia,* multiple metaphors and examples that refine and illustrate similar topics and issues, defy the neatness of one-to-one allegory, creating instead "a perpetually self-displacing mode of discourse" (David Lee Miller, *The Poem's Two Bodies* 12). In the unwinding of his narrative, all apparent boundaries, whether structural or thematic, blur as attention to them intensifies. Spenser's allegorical suggestions resonate like chords rather than sing like a single voice.

Una is a case in point. Her name is a common one in Ireland, but allegorists have long seen its many allusions in Spenser's use: to singularity, perfection, completeness, to the truth that is one, to the one True Church (*Variorum* 1: 178, 196; Hamilton, ed. 30, 41). Central as she must be to the concept of "Holinesse," the early tradition sentimentalized her even while acknowledging her importance as an agent in Redcrosse Knight's salvific journey (*Variorum* 1: 496–500—e.g., "for all her strength of endurance and of affection, she is a frail and tender being, exposed to the roughest buffetings of fortune" [499]). A key reason for the response of Una's early commentators is her similarity to the traditional heroines of medieval romance and to the praying lady in the background of illustrations from the legend of St. George. Una's power to represent the True Church is limited by the medieval Arthurian tradition from which she comes (Shaver). In Arthurian romance the lady is a passive inspiration at best, who does not direct her own rescue or save her rescuer from danger. Una is neither a woman warrior, like Bradamante, nor a sorceress, like Morgan Le Fay; neither her tradition nor her circumstances give her much ability to act on her own.

Nonetheless, like the grace she sometimes receives and sometimes represents, Una blurs the traditional equations of male=active, female=passive, and leans in from the margins to direct Redcrosse Knight at crucial moments. In the familiar approach to the battle with Errour in book 1, she cautions him against foolhardy action:

> Be well aware, quoth then that Ladie milde,
> Least suddaine mischiefe ye too rash provoke:
> The danger hid, the place unknowne and wilde,

Breedes dreadfull doubts: Oft fire is without smoke,
And perill without show: therefore your stroke
Sir knight with-hold, till further triall made.
(1.1.12)

He argues against the shame of retreat, but she continues her warning, though she acknowledges that his honor impels the battle to come:

Yea but (quoth she) the perill of this place
I better wot than you, though now too late
To wish you backe returne with foul disgrace
Yet wisedome warns, whilest foot is in the gate,
To stay the steppe, ere forced to retrate.
This is the wandering wood, this *Errours den,*
A monster vile, whom god and man does hate:
Therefore I read beware.
(1.1.13)

Una knows how to interpret the environment she sees, how to "read." A Sophia figure here, she advises and urges caution, but she does not intervene in the forward movement of her knight's adventure. Her intervention becomes more direct in the battle, however, when she shouts encouragement and instruction:

His Lady sad to see his sore constraint,
Cride out, Now now Sir knight, shew what ye bee
Add faith unto your force, and be not faint
Strangle her, else she will surely strangle thee. (1.1.19)

Much like a modern coach, Una directs the central action from the sidelines. Perhaps her aggressiveness in this encounter makes Redcrosse more willing to believe in her sexual aggressiveness when the false Una importunes him in canto 2.

The true Una, however, reverts to the more traditional passive lady in distress in the middle of the book: she subdues the Lion by her beauty, accepts his protection (1.3.5), and is subject to deception by Archimago (30) and abduction by Sansloy (43–44). I confess that when I first read, and later first taught, book 1, my tendency was to skip canto 6. Una's helplessness in the face of Sansloy, her rescue by the fauns and satyrs, and the appearance of Satyrane seemed tame stuff on the way to Redcrosse's dalliance with Duessa and fight with Orgoglio in canto 7. Yet Una has a more-than-passive role in canto 6. As she had guided Redcrosse, so she seeks to guide "the woodborne people" who "fall before her flat" (1.6.16):

> Glad of such lucke, the luckelesse lucky maid,
>   Did her content to please their feeble eyes,
>   And long time with that salvage people staid,
>   To gather breath in many miseries.
>   During which time her gentle wit she plyes,
>   To teach them truth, which worship her in vaine,
>   And made her th'Image of Idolatryes;
>   But when their bootlesse zeale she did restraine,
> From her own worship, they her Asse would worship fayn.
> (1.6.19)

As she could not keep Redcrosse from hasty battle with Errour, so she cannot keep the satyrs from idol worship. Nor could Sir Satyrane's human mother fully tame him by instruction (1.6.27–28), though Una's beauty and "her wisedome heavenly rare, / Whose like in womens wit he never knew" inspire him to rescue her (31, 33).

Una is to some degree an agent of her own rescue even in canto 6, in part because of her traditional inspirational beauty, but in part because of her less traditional, but allegorically necessary, "wisedome heavenly rare." In canto 7, though she manages to swoon a theologically correct three times when the dwarf tells her the news of Redcrosse's capture, she takes heart and takes charge, "resolving him to find / Alive or dead" (28). Her purposive wandering allows her to encounter Arthur, who rescues Redcrosse from Orgoglio's dungeon (1.7.29, 1.8). At first Una is the fawning lady, bemoaning the sad state (and lost innocence) of her beloved. Next she decides the fate of Duessa, choosing to let her live, but spoiled "of her scarlot robe" and therefore revealed as the disfigured creature she truly is.

Una's most notable intervention is in canto 9, when the tantalizing rhetoric of Despair tempts the fallen Redcrosse "to worke his finall smart." Up to that point the focus has been completely on Despair and Redcrosse, two figures locked in a duel of mental anguish. In canto 52 the focus shifts to Una who, after a ladylike short swoon, takes charge of the action and of Redcrosse:

> Out of his hand she snatcht the cursed knife,
>   And threw it to the ground, enraged rife,
>   And to him said, Fie, fie, faint harted knight.

What meanest thou by this reproachful strife?
Is this the battell, which thou vauntst to fight
With that fire-mouthed Dragon, horrible and bright?

Come, come away, fraile, feeble, fleshly wight,
. . .
Arise, Sir knight, arise, and leave this cursed place.
(1.9.52–53)

Una completes her authoritative intervention by leading the Redcrosse
Knight to the "house of Holinesse."

From this point forward allegorical pieties and a holy hermit take over
preparing Redcrosse for his final duel with "that fire-mouthed Dragon,
horrible and bright" that has Una's parents in thrall. Narrative moves into
denser allegory in canto 11 as comic and heroic merge in the concluding
betrothal. Una may wait for her man to complete his quests at the end of
book 1's frame, but she has been anything but passive within the book's
narrative adventures. Yet her active power is always balanced by traditional
romance passivity (first a quick swoon, then take charge), and her
interventions always seem to reach into the main scene from the sidelines.

In Aemilia Lanyer's remarkable poem on Christ's passion, *Salve Deus Rex
Judaeorum,* the story is presented entirely from women's points of view and
women have vital roles to play, yet Lanyer recognizes their traditional
political marginality. If a poet writing in the first decade of the seventeenth
century were searching for models of women in a narrative of salvation, Una
is an excellent one. Spenser's example is a powerful authority for exercising
the virtues of women in a narrative poem, and there is every reason to believe
that Lanyer was familiar with *The Faerie Queene.*

Lanyer undoubtedly read contemporary poets. She refers directly to
poems by Daniel and Drayton in the *Salve Deus* (225–40), and I have argued
elsewhere that she was acquainted with Ben Jonson (Woods, "Patronage").
It is more than likely that Lanyer had read Spenser. The 1590 *Faerie Queene*
appeared while she was still Aemilia Bassano, at Elizabeth's court as the
mistress of Henry Cary, Lord Hunsdon, who, as Lord Chamberlain, was
responsible for court entertainments. If we credit her report to Simon
Forman that "she hath bin favored moch of her mati [majesty, Queen
Elizabeth]," Aemilia may even have been among those who heard Spenser
read his poem "at timely hours" in the Elizabethan court (Woods, ed. xviii;
Spenser, *Colin Clouts,* l. 362). One of Spenser's patrons was Margaret,
Countess of Cumberland, who was to be Lanyer's principal patron and

dedicatee of the *Salve Deus*. By 1596 Aemilia was married to Alfonso Lanyer and living in Westminster, near St. James. Her parish was St. Margaret's, Westminster, in 1598 when her daughter was christened, and she is not likely to have missed the great funeral for the "prince of poets" at the Abbey next door in 1599. In 1619 the Countess of Cumberland's daughter and Lanyer's friend and patron, Anne Clifford, then Countess of Dorset, erected the monument to Spenser in Westminster Abbey. Although the only male poet Lanyer mentions by name is Sidney ("The Authors Dreame" 138), it is probable that Lanyer met Spenser during his first court visit (1589–91), and even more probable that she knew that most famous of Elizabethan poems, *The Faerie Queene.*

The *Salve Deus* is not at all like *The Faerie Queene* in genre or style. The similarity is in how Lanyer interjects the active authority of female figures, who come into the picture at key times to warn or affect the actions of men. Despite its apparent uniqueness, Lanyer's poem does not exist in a poetic vacuum, nor does she give her women power as if no poet had ever done so before. The example of Una is a logical one for Lanyer's effort to situate women in the Christian story. The poem's narrative action begins at line 333, as Christ goes to the Garden of Gethsemane, and ends at line 1320, after a short song of his resurrected beauty, based on the Canticles. Surrounding the story proper is a dedicatory frame to the Countess of Cumberland in which her virtues and sufferings are extolled and consoled.

The narrative loosely follows Matthew 26.30–28.10, and consists primarily of men who are at worst wicked, and at best misguided (Simon of Cyrene and Joseph of Arimethea are the exceptions), contrasted with women who are the prophets and revealers of truth. Peter, James and John fall asleep in the garden, and Peter denies Christ three times. These are the best. Judas and Caiaphas are wicked, Herod is a fool, and Pilate is the ultimate self-serving politician. In themselves, these are familiar characters who (along with the ever present figure of the suffering Christ) center the action. Less familiar are the women who appear from the margins, take center stage long enough to make important points about the perfidy of men, and then blend their voices into that of the narrator.

The narrative voice, which has so forcefully characterized itself as female (273–96), intrudes and comments at will. Here, for example, is her interjection on those who came to arrest Christ:

How blinde were they could not discerne the Light!
How dull! if not to understand the truth,
How weake! if meekenesse overcame their might;
How stony hearted, if not mov'd to ruth:

How void of Pitie, and how full of Spight,
Gainst him that was the Lord of Light and Truth:
  Here insolent Boldnesse checkt by Love and Grace,
  Retires, and falls before our Makers face.
(505–12)

A narrator has the right to comment as well as describe, and though she does more of the former than Spenser, she does enough of the latter to keep the familiar story moving in interesting new ways. The homiletic moments in themselves do not constitute centering a female voice.

The first and most radical intrusion of a woman's voice is that of Pilate's wife, whose single biblical verse (Matt. 27.19) Lanyer expands into a lengthy speech in defense of Eve and all women against the terrible masculine sin of the Crucifixion. Like Una commenting on knowledge, discretion, and experience before the encounter with the dragon Errour, Pilate's wife reaches in, unasked, from the margins of the action and, while acknowledging the power of men, makes herself the prophetic voice that should be heeded:

Let barb'rous crueltie farre depart from thee,
And in true Justice take afflictions part;
Open thine eies, that thou the truth mai'st see,
Doe not the thing that goes against thy heart,
Condemne not him that must thy Saviour be;
But view his holy life, his good desert.
  Let not us women glory in Mens fall,
  Who had power given to over-rule us all.
(753–60)

Like Una, Pilate's wife is able to "read" the situation, and she goes on to reread the story of the fall. In her version, Eve meant no harm, "But surely *Adam* cannot be excusde, / Her fault though great, yet hee was most too blame / What Weaknesse offerd, Strength might have refusde" (777–79). And just to blur the categories of ignorance and knowledge a bit more:

If *Eve* did erre, it was for knowledge sake,
The fruit beeing faire perswaded him to fall:
  No subtill Serpants falshood did betray him.
  If he would eate it, who had powre to stay him?

Not *Eve,* whose fault was onely too much love,
Which made her give this present to her Deare
. . .

    Yet Men will boast of Knowledge, which he tooke
    From *Eves* faire hand, as from a learned Booke.
(797–802, 807–08)

Eve herself becomes the Book of Knowledge in this rhetorical tour de force, and (like Una) though women are weak, they read aright.

So it is with the daughters of Jerusalem, who read correctly the procession of the cross:

First went the Crier with open mouth proclayming
The heavy sentence of Iniquitie,
The Hangman next, by his base office clayming
His right in Hell, where sinners never die,
Carrying the nayles, the people still blaspheming
Their maker, using all impiety;
  The thieves attending him on either side,
  The Serjeants watching, while the women cri'd.
(961–68)

Their weeping moves these women from the sidelines to the center, as Christ turns to them, comforting and speaking to them as he would not speak to his accusers (969–84). The women are blessed (985–87) and seek by their example to turn the hearts of the men:

They labor still these tyrants hearts to move:
  In pitie and compassion to forbeare
  Their whipping, spurning, tearing of his haire.

But all in vain, their malice hath no end,
Their hearts more hard than flint, or marble stone.
(998–1002)

Like saints and martyrs, like medieval heroines, they try to inspire by their examples and (in vain) to refocus the attention of the men.

The poem turns immediately to "The sorrow of the virgin Marie," whose grief and tears are most directly reminiscent of Una ("To see his bleeding body oft she swouned" [1012]). But if she swoons like Una, also like Una she acts, and she, too, reads the scene correctly:

> Her teares did wash away his pretious blood,
> That sinners might not tread it under feet
> To worship him, and that it did her good
> Upon her knees, although in open street,
> Knowing he was the Jessie floure and bud,
> That must be gath'red when it smell'd most sweet:
>   Her Sonne, her Husband, Father, Saviour, King,
>   Whose death killd Death, and tooke away his sting.
> (1017–24)

Lanyer turns full attention to Mary, with a hymn of praise that extends the story of the annunciation and Mary's own Magnificat (Luke 1.48–49), concluding with a return to Christ's sacrifice, and then back to Mary on the sidelines of the procession (1025–136). As Mary fades from view, the scene moves inexorably to the Crucifixion itself. The story has two more women, "The *Maries*" who come to anoint the body of Christ and find the tomb empty, but Lanyer gives them only two lines (1287–88). The mighty act of sacrifice has been done, the Resurrection and the risen Christ are next in order, and then a return to the frame of praise for the Countess of Cumberland.

The line between the narrative and the framing praise of the Countess has in fact been breached before the report of the Resurrection, as Lanyer addresses her patron directly at the moment of crucifixion. "To my Ladie of Cumberland," says the marginal note:

> This with the eie of Faith thou maist behold,
> Deere Spouse of Christ, and more than I can write;
> And here both Griefe and Joy thou maist unfold,
> To view thy Love in this most heavy plight.
> Bowing his head, his bloodlesse body cold;
> Those eies waxe dimme that gave us all our light.
>   His count'nance pale, yet still continues sweet,
>   His blessed blood watring his pierced feet.
> (1169–76)

Like Mary and the daughters of Jerusalem, the Countess enters the narrative to read the story aright ("and more than I can write"). More important, she enters the narrative as the "Deere Spouse of Christ," the Church born at the moment of the Crucifixion, and fulfills a symbolic importance suggested in the opening frame: "Thy constant faith like to the Turtle Dove / Continues combat" (157–58): "thou, the wonder of our wanton age, / Leav'st all delights to serve a heav'nly king" (169–70); "Thou faire example, live without compare" (177). In the concluding frame Lanyer completes the circle by filling out the portrait of the Countess as the perfect type of the church. The poem's structural margin—its frame—becomes its center.

Lanyer's principal device in the frame is to compare the piety and devotion of the Countess of Cumberland to the love and piety of a series of famous women, beginning, interestingly, with Cleopatra (1409–46), and concluding with an extended comparison with the Queen of Sheba, who (like the Countess) sought wisdom (1569–608). The comparisons themselves are subtle and sometimes unexpected. Their net effect is to underscore the Countess as the true spouse of Christ. The section that precedes these comparisons (1321–408), the point at which Lanyer moves from the passion narrative back to the frame, allows the poet to present her gift of the passion story to the Countess, who in turn becomes both the reader of the book of Christ and herself the model for all perfect piety.

First, Lanyer brings the countess in from the margin of her narrative, and recenters the entire passion story in her patron's heart:

> . . . (good Madame) in your heart I leave
> His perfect picture, where it still shall stand,
>   Deepely engraved in that holy shrine,
>   Environed with Love and Thoughts divine.
> (1325–28)

Her heart engraved with Christ, the Countess is able to recognize His presence in all its guises:

> Thou call'st, he comes, thou find'st tis he indeed,
> Thy Soule conceaves that he is truly wise:
>   Nay more, desires that he may be the Booke,
>   Whereon thy eyes continually may looke.
> (1349–52)

Seeing Christ in the sick and poor, she performs acts of mercy that confirm her own salvation and imprint her with the power "to heale the soules of those that doe transgresse" (1371). Rejecting wealth and honor if "it prooves a foe / To virtue, learning, and the powres divine" (1390–91), she brings others to Him:

> . . . in thy modest vaile do'st sweetly cover
> The staines of other['s] sinnes . . .

That by this means thou mai'st in time recover
Those weake lost sheepe that did so long transgresse,
Presenting them unto thy deerest Lover.
(1394–98)

Like Una, the Countess reads the book of holiness correctly and performs right actions, then becomes herself a text by her example. Her sufferings are never merely passive, as they move her to acts of charity and mercy. The veil that hides Una's face becomes the veil the Countess throws over the sins of others. The marginal figure embodies the triumph of the story's action, and both Una and the Countess end up properly betrothed.

Blurring traditional categories of active and passive, story and reader, both Spenser and Lanyer privilege the marginal. In Spenser's story Una becomes the agent for Redcrosse Knight's redemption. In Lanyer's passion the scorned Christ and the apparently helpless women share the triumph. An important question in Lanyer criticism is how a nonaristocratic woman can write with such authority. Spenser provided an excellent model for Lanyer's unapologetic stance. Figures like Una and Britomart, the imposing presence of Gloriana real and feigned, could easily have a major impact on a young woman who saw for herself the power of a Queen. Spenser's narrator, himself both observer and actor, provides additionally an ungendered model for the marginal figure—the author—who centers and directs the action. Colin Clout teaches Calidore the reciprocity of grace, and Edmund Spenser may have taught Aemilia Lanyer about the authority of the poet.

These observations suggest a number of broader questions about the relation between biblical injunctions and transgressive speech, and between men and women artists of the period. I want to conclude this essay with just one of them. How do Spenser and Lanyer's examples of female prophetic voices, delivering spiritual virtues from the margins of the narrative but from the center of the poem's thematics, define the paradoxes of gender, authority, and power confronted by women writers (especially) in the English Renaissance?

The Pauline epigraph with which I began this essay was used ubiquitously to silence women in this period, yet the Protestant doctrine of the unmediated conscience could not allow any authority to gainsay a woman's belief that she had "been appointed to performe this Worke" (Lanyer, "To the doubtfull Reader"). Further, women poets found examples of transgressive women among the male writers, who themselves struggled "not to pass the bankes / Of Helicon" so much as to be rendered voiceless. The device of allegory, with its long tradition of supporting the humble voice who would speak to the higher born, provides the opportunity for figuring prophecy in female garb. And all the Pauline injunctions in the world could not escape the model of a great Queen, in relation to whom Spenser must carefully calibrate his images, and whose overriding force Lanyer herself personally remembered. Whatever ambivalences and confusions Elizabeth may have created in the men who depended on her and then followed her, her presence as a person, a Queen, the head of the English church, and the dedicatee of Spenser's work, helps a poet such as Lanyer read a signifier such as Una as more than allegorical, her gender relevant to her consequences. Perhaps Lanyer's best answer to St. Paul is in her vision of Elizabeth in heaven, anticipating the women of her poem and the spousal role of the Countess of Cumberland. The woman poet transforms the Faerie Queene into the very Queen of Heaven: "crown'd with everlasting Sov'raigntie; / Where Saints and Angells do attend her Throne, / And she gives glorie unto God alone" (*Salve Deus* 6–8). Patronage and prophecy merge in such a vision. What more authority does a poet need?

Spenser's poetry is present in the work of many of his contemporaries and followers, whether or not the admiration is explicit in their verse, and even when they have abandoned allegorical technique and generous rhetorical *copia*. *The Faerie Queene,* with its dedication to a powerful queen and its complex use of female characters, has such clear appeal to women that Suzanne Hull has rightly included it in her bibliography of renaissance books for women. Spenser allows his female figures, including Una, Britomart, Colin's graces, and the Queen herself, to offer male experience a glimpse of true authority. In *The Faerie Queene* that authority is presented and explained by the male poet, whose voice and vision, given a signature in the episode of Colin Clout and the graces, ultimately centers the richly shifting episodes and allegories. Lanyer's transgression is to offer not only marginal female figures as glimpses of God's true hand in the world, but to be herself their author and explicator.

LADY MARY WROTH IN THE HOUSE OF BUSIRANE

Jacqueline T. Miller

The House of Busirane episode that concludes book 3 of *The Faerie Queene* has proved to be an enduring locus of interpretive intrigue, inviting a range of critical approaches and resistant to consensus. Spenser's own decision to revise the ending of the episode—in a way that leaves it ever more unfinished—serves as a mirror of the provisional nature of our attempts to understand it and of its own status in the text.

Particularly interesting in this regard is the way this episode is rewritten—again and again—in Wroth's *Urania*. As several readers have noted, Wroth rescripts the Amoret-Busirane episode in the fourth book of the *Urania;* for Quilligan, this is evidence of how in the *Urania*, moral values are "completely reversed" ("Female Authority" 263); for Lewalski, it shows how Wroth's romance explores "female rather than male heroism" (*Writing Women* 269). But the revision is significant for more than thematic reasons; Wroth's text reinscribes the provisional nature of the episode by rewriting it more than once.[1] First Pamphilia sees Amphilanthus, in "a place like a Hell of flames" (583) standing with his heart exposed and her name written on it; Musalina, the female enchantress who is one of Pamphilia's rivals, stands ready, with sword in hand, to raze the name out. Undaunted, Pamphilia (Britomart-like) attempts to run through the fire, but (Scudamore-like) is repulsed—she learns, because of her constancy. Later, near the end of book 4, we discover that Amphilanthus gets a view of the same place, and sees in it "Pamphilia dead . . . her breast open and in it his name made, in little flames burning like pretty lamps which made the letters"; he tries to save her, is "instantly throwne out of the Cave" which he learns is the "hell of deepe deceit," is lured away by Musalina and Lucenia and forgets Pamphilia for quite some time (655–56). Finally, as the book ends, Amphilanthus, "disinchanted" by Musalina, reunited with Pamphilia, returns to the Hell of Deceit, "now no more to be abused," "recovered his Sword, and brought home his Armour, resolving nothing should remaine as witnesses of his former ficklenes, or the property of that place, destroying the monument, the Charmes having conclusion with his recovering" (660–61).

The gendered nature of Wroth's revisions are of course significant: the female Musalina replaces the male Busirane; both male and female (Pamphilia and Amphilanthus) are susceptible to being figured as her victims *in* the visions, and both are also susceptible as witnesses *of* them.[2] This emphasis on the viewer of the represented scenes—and on how the view changes with the viewer—is especially provocative when we consider Wroth's text as a reading of Spenser's. Wroth exploits the instability of the precursor text—to which Spenser himself draws attention—by establishing its availability to be appropriated and reappropriated, not only by the seventeenth-century female author of the *Urania,* but also by the female enchantress Musalina, who orchestrates the visions within it. If, as Lauren Silberman has suggested, Spenser's House of Busirane stages a "battle for interpretation" in which we see "the interaction of reader and text as a vigorous and highly charged exchange" (60, 61), then Wroth has taken up the challenge with a vengeance. The impotence of the readers/viewers, Pamphilia and Amphilanthus, in the first two accounts is foil to Wroth's own active engagement with the Spenserian moment, and it also stands in sharp contrast to Wroth's third and final allusion, which provides a resounding (if temporary) sense of closure: Amphilanthus dismantles the Spenserian site in an action as much reminiscent of Guyon's ransacking of the feminine and effeminizing Bower of Bliss as of Britomart's act of recovery in the House of Busirane.

I am suggesting that when Wroth deliberately and explicitly rewrites this episode from *The Faerie Queene,* she chooses a focus that not only highlights the issues of gendered writing and interpretation so paramount in Spenser's original, but also uses them to show how she grapples with his legacy. Though the Sidney heritage has been most commented upon in Wroth criticism, many have noted Spenserian and other (including especially Shakespeare) sources as well.[3] For my purposes, however, it is less important to see that Wroth "unsettles" or "revises" certain generic traditions for what they can tell us about a Jacobean woman's position in her culture, than to see what those revisions can tell us about how Wroth read and perceived a major literary precursor: how, in short, *The Faerie Queene* figured for this most prolific early modern writer/reader. As Carrell has noted, in the *Urania* "Wroth offers as background a sort of greatest hits parade of the most memorable episodes from masterpieces of romance." But it may not be entirely true that "[f]or Wroth, reading and writing a romance is . . . a rebellion in the form of control," a control she exerts by "becoming the author of her own ideal romance" (90).[4] Wroth stages an inconclusive debate about her own autonomy as writer and reader; she does this, in response to Spenser, by establishing how open his text is to rewriting even while her rewriting discloses her reliance on his as she attempts to close down that work he himself claims is "endless." The openness of Spenser's text that invites Wroth in (that seems to beckon her to reconfigure the work in active appropriation) also seems to threaten a confinement reminiscent not only of Busirane's penning of Amoret but also of his inscriptions on the palace walls that Britomart so intently "oft and oft . . . over-red" (3.11.50) and yet cannot satisfactorily "construe" (54). Indeed, at what appears to be a parallel and deeply symbolic moment in the *Urania,* at the threshold of the Theatre of Love, Pamphilia and her entourage of women encounter pillars upon which letters are "ingraven," but "they understood not the meaning." Pamphilia, "more desirous of knowledge than the rest" (and more active in her desire to understand than her Spenserian counterpart who proceeds without comprehension), goes off to search for clues, discovers open spaces and plains deceptively inviting in their presumed promise of an unmarked space between the inscribed phallic pillars; here, "finding her imagination likely," she locates a keyhole and a key, but only to enter and then immediately be trapped within the enchanted theater (373).

The *Urania* is, of course, a book filled with storytellers, poets, readers, and writers; and it, like *The Faerie Queene,* is endless.[5] It is, also, like *The Faerie Queene,* obsessed with the idea of ending, and in its most Spenserian moments these concerns come to the forefront. In a curious way, the *Urania* seems to become most allusively Spenserian precisely at the moments when it becomes intent on resolution, and it is doubly curious because one of the things it seems intent on resolving is its own relation to (the influence of) the prior Spenserian romance. Yet resolution and conclusion become increasingly elusive goals in the *Urania.*

This becomes clear in the major scenes of enchantment in the *Urania,* which are, as Waller has noted, some of the most Spenserian moments in the text (249; see also Lewalski, *Writing Women* 267). They are also all, almost as soon as they begin, about how to find endings, how to release those who are confined, how to conclude the scene and the charms. The first enchantment, which imprisons Urania, Selarina, and Urania's servant in the Palace of Love, alludes, as Roberts suggests, to Spenser's Temple of Venus ("Labyrinths" 187). Amphilanthus and Pamphilia end this enchantment: we are told at the outset that when "the valiantest Knight, with the loyallest Lady come together," then "all these Charmes shall have conclusion" (48–49)—and Pamphilia correctly announces "wee will surely bring an end to it" (168) when she and Amphilanthus agree to approach together. As they easily pass through the three towers, the prisoners are freed and, reminiscent of the disappearance of Busirane's castle, "the Pallace and all vanished" (170).

The second enchantment poses a more difficult challenge. Coming to the Theatre of Love with Urania, who fears a new enchantment, Pamphilia is initially full of assurance: "Let it be what it will . . . I will see the end of it." Urania provides some cautionary words of wisdom: "You may . . . having had such success in the last, yet take heed, all adventures were not framed for you to finish" (372). Urania's words prove true: Pamphilia is caught within this enchantment and "conclusion" must come from without, and not easily. Others who try to end it also end up inside it. At one point, when Selarinus bemoans Philistella's captivity in the Theatre of Love, Rosindy belittles his concern: "Why waile you thus . . . since shee is but inchaunted?" Selarinus's passionate reply reveals the source of the enduring power of enchantments that Rosindy so exasperatingly underestimates: "But enchanted, why call you that nothing? . . . but enchaunted, and but for ever for any thing wee know; what old fables blind you, led by enchauntments?" (411). Selarinus's association of old fables with enchantments implies that they both are unreliable guides while insisting on the potential endlessness of their influence. Though Rosindy insists that "[n]ever was any such thing made . . . but to be ended" and specifically recalls how the first enchantment was "concluded by Amphilanthus and my Sister" (411), this second one will be harder to end (indeed, it has several false endings) and will conclude, at least for Pamphilia—who becomes victim and audience in this scene, rather than active agent as in the first—far less satisfactorily (since it pairs Amphilanthus with Musalina, the force behind the third enchantment(s) at the Hell of Deceit.)

The first confrontation with the Hell of Deceit occurs after a false sense of resolution has been achieved. Pamphilia and Amphilanthus have been reunited, "love expressing itselfe, not only lively but perfectly in their eyes" (568); even Pamphilia finds it hard to believe that she has lived to see this. But they are separated during a hunt (Amphilanthus disappears into the wood), and Pamphilia assumes a more final end: finding his hacked and bloody armor, his horse dead, and a huge, slain boar, she concludes that Amphilanthus too is dead. Making a shrine of the pieces of his armor where she finds them, Pamphilia, with the help of Polarchos, hangs them up, and then "under-writ some lines, Pamphilia both making them, and ingraving them." It is only then, after making her inscription, that Pamphilia sees the ring of iron, which she pulls, revealing the "hell of deceit." What she finds inside is another scene of writing featuring a woman: "at last she saw Musalina . . . and Lucenia holding a sword, which Musalina tooke in her hand, and before them Amphilanthus was standing, with his heart ripped open, and Pamphilia written in it, Musalina ready with the point of the sword to conclude all, by razing that name out, and so his heart as the wound to perish" (583).

In *The Faerie Queene* Busirane "cruelly pend" (3.11.11) Amoret; his palace contains inscriptions that the rescuer, Britomart, cannot understand; and he is discovered "figuring straunge characters of his art" (12.31) with the blood from Amoret's heart which he has opened her breast with a knife to excise. What is compelling about Wroth's revision of the scene is not just the gender reversal of victim and victimizer, and the failure of the virtuous to perform the rescue, but that the scene of writing has become a scene of erasure. Spenser's malignant male artist pens, figures and inscribes; Wroth's Musalina (or "little muse")[6] is intent on "razing" out a prior inscription, and her endeavor in doing so is "to conclude all." For this incarnation of Wroth's female artist/enchantress, conclusion is to be achieved by erasing a prior inscription; and while the malevolent Musalina is specifically intent here on erasing Pamphilia as both inscription and inscriber, the careful allusions to *The Faerie Queene* in this scene register another type of prior text with which female authors must contend. In any event, there is no conclusion in this scene: Pamphilia and Polarchos accept the futility of their efforts to end this enchantment, and Musalina remains frozen in this anticipatory moment of being "ready" to perform her final and villainous act of erasure/conclusion.

We may pause here to consider another less literal but telling moment of erasure that records Wroth's complicated sense of her relation to the Spenserian model of female agency: this occurs in the story of Nereana, who is seeking her beloved Steriamus. Pamphilia first hears of Nereana from Amphilanthus, immediately after we have been reminded of her own status as a poet—and one who adds to a formerly finished piece (after hearing prophesies from Melissea, she takes her customary walk in the woods, goes to the tree where she had earlier engraved "her sad sonnet" [191] and adds four new lines under it). Within a page, Pamphilia meets Nereana in person: certainly one of the most Spenserian of the *Urania*'s characters, Britomart-like in her pursuit of Steriamus. The king remarks upon the rarity of a woman undertaking such a journey, but it is Pamphilia through whom Wroth seems to erase the very existence of the heroine of Spenser's Book of Chastity, as she remarks, "before your coming hither, I heard the fame of you, which came swifter then your self, though brought by love: and in truth I am sorry, that such a Lady should take so great and painefull a voyage, to so fond an end, *being the first that ever I heard of, who took so Knight-like a search in hand*" (194).[7]

Of course, Nereana is no replica of Britomart: as Pamphilia professes ignorance of Spenser's female knight, Wroth substitutes a very ambivalent version of her.[8] Nereana is "ignorantly proud" (192) but both mocked and admired "since for a woman it was unusuall to love much" (195); thrown off course by a tempest, she finds a pleasant place where she decides, with a stunning independence of spirit, "to recreate her selfe after her owne liking." Yet like Redcrosse Knight and the Spenserian punning that accompanies him, she enters a Wood, and "as she wandered in amaze" she "at last quite lost her selfe" (196). Discovered and mistaken for Liana/Diana by the crazed Alanius who would worship her, she is tied to a tree, undressed, and recostumed so that when she sees her image in a clear stream, "the picture of her owne selfe did so amaze her, as she would not goe so neere unto her metamorphos'd figure" (198). In short, Wroth erases the Spenserian model in a way that conspiciously recalls her, and replaces her with a figure whose desire for autonomy and self-fashioning is (in her first appearance in the *Urania*) thwarted by a "madde man" (197) who turns her into an image of his own fantastical vision.

What do we make, then, of Wroth's final treatment of the very Spenserian Hell of Deceit? Amphilanthus's first encounter with this enchantment, as noted earlier, reverses the images of Pamphilia's first encounter: he sees his name written in her heart, first in "little flames," then (more Busirane-like) "ingraven at the Bottome in Characters of bloud" (655). There is more to his version of the story, however: first, after he kills the boar, he battles a group of armed men, and one "young man unarmed" in particular, whom Amphilanthus slays, and who then transforms into Pamphilia whose body is carried beneath the crown of stones. Unable to recover her, Amphilanthus takes the pieces of his hewed armor and arranges them on the stone as "his monument," resolves to die or release her, and then responds to a call for help from Musalina and Lucenia because "the force of charmes prevaile," though he is still so enchanted that he is blind to their continuing influence and can claim, in ludicrous error, "now . . . I am disinchanted." In this scene, in a sense, Musalina succeeds in razing Pamphilia's name from Amphilanthus's heart: the first vision in the Hell of Deceit is realized here as "Pamphilia is forgotten" (656). But when Amphilanthus returns to Germany, and hears stories of Pamphilia and her experience, a reinscription occurs: "These things wrought in him, like drops falling on soft stones, they weare in to them at last, though in the beginning touch and slide off; more and more this pierced, and so much strengthned with his owne affection, as hee resolves to see her" (659). Erasure can never be complete; the first inscription will be reinscribed as the stories are renewed and retold.

But it is precisely this—a state of affairs whose liabilities are matched by its benefits—that Wroth's characters resist acknowledging. As this reinscription occurs, and Amphilanthus recovers his memory and is happily reunited with Pamphilia in the last pages of the published *Urania,* he returns to the scene of enchantment for a presumably final act of razing/erasure. In the scene quoted earlier, Amphilanthus eliminates the original site of all those inscriptions and removes the signs of his own errancy, bringing, we are told, "conclusion" to those charms that parted him and Pamphilia. Yet Amphilanthus's actions, as noted above, recall the unsettling and unsatisfactory nature of Guyon's destruction of the Bower of Bliss at the end of book 2 of *The Faerie Queene.* They also reject and yet oddly fulfill the Spenserian image of the emasculated Verdant's discarded armor, "full of old moniments, / . . . fowly ra'st, that none the signes might see" (12.80): Amphilanthus reclaims his sword and armor but also resolves that "destroying the monument" will wipe out "the property of that place" and all evidence ("nothing should remain as witnesses") of his implication in it. Though a prior inscription haunts his every move here, it seems that "conclusion," as conceived and enacted by Amphilanthus, requires not just the collaborative transaction of rewriting but the more aggressive force of eradication. The wry narrator affirms his view—"now all is finished"—only, within the same (long) sentence, to reject it: "Amphilanthus must goe" (661). The lovers will part again, the story continues, and the text itself inscribes the provisionality of conclusion by ending in the middle of a sentence barely begun.

It is tempting to posit that Wroth scripts her own vexed relation to her precursor texts in the figure of the book that makes more than a single appearance in the *Urania.* In one scene, Pamphilia walking in a "delicate thicke wood," reads from "a booke shee had with her"; the story is of a Lady who loves "a brave Gentleman who equally loved" but is inconstant and "left her for a new."[9] Pamphilia at this moment feels safe in the happiness of her love, and railing at "all storyes" and "every writer" for so "apparrelling" love "according to their various fancies," wondering how love can "suffer thy selfe to be thus put in cloathes, nay raggs" (in imagery recalling Alanius's re-dressing of Nereana), "then threw she away the booke" (317). Though Wroth allows Pamphilia this forceful gesture of detaching herself from the previously written story, she also insures that we see (though Pamphilia doesn't) the many ways it informs her own, exposing the false illusion of assuming that her version can be so easily divorced from those precedents.[10]

Another striking and telling appearance of a book in the *Urania* occurs at the "end" of the second enchantment in the Theatre of Love. There are a series of partial endings forecast for this enchantment: first the "man most loving, and most beloved" (Amphilanthus) can release those captured from their charms, but he himself will be enclosed and unable to bring them or himself forth until "the fairest creature in disguise" comes (Veralinda) to release them all, and "then should all bee finished" (373, 400). But after Amphilanthus and Veralinda have fulfilled their roles (outlined on an "inscription" on the gate of the theatre), we all discover that there is more to do. The chairs upon which the enchanted sat vanish, but a "Pillar of Gold stood in their stead, on which hung a Booke" which only Urania can take down. Still the enchantment is only "partly ended": Urania must have Veralinda's help to open the book, whereupon "the house then vanished" (455). What the book contains is the "story of Urania" and next, the (very similar) story of Veralinda; we learn that the man who orchestrated this enchantment was he who had preserved Urania's life when she was abducted as an infant, and Veralinda discovers the identity of her true father and eventually reunites with him. So, this enchantment, framed by a man, the conclusion of which can be rendered by a woman, is actually not over until a book is discovered and read, a book that records the indebtedness of the titular heroine to the man and reveals the paternal origin of the woman who supposedly brings all to conclusion.[11] The place of enchantment is replaced by a book; the book reveals the men at the source of both enchantment and existence. But only the women whose stories are inscribed within the book may open it, read it, and thereby end the enchantment so that their and others' stories may be continued.

The gendering of romance, according to Patricia Parker, associates the digressiveness of the genre with female speech and female sexuality that thwarts the masculine quest for closure.[12] Wroth's concern with concluding texts (her own and others) and the association of that concern especially with enchantments (Parker identifies the female enchantress [Circe, Acrasia] as the figure that most endangers the possibility of closure) may provide a new perspective on that issue. Especially significant is the way Wroth associates female romantic/sexual desire with questions of narrative deferral and closure. As Pamphilia and Urania contemplate entering the Theatre of Love at the onset of the second enchantment, Urania expresses her fear: "if it be an inchantment, woe be to us, who may be bewitched to the misery of never seeing our desires fulfil'd" (372). Once inside, however, what the women "see" is indeed the fulfillment of desire: "all the comfort their owne hearts could imagine to them selves, they felt there, seeing before them (as they thought) their loves smiling, and joying in them" (373). Even Pamphilia, who had voiced her assurance that she would "see the end" of this enchantment, is held passive thrall by her own vision of happiness. The failure of the women to work on their own behalf to "end" this enchantment is due to their fictive visions of fulfilled desire, which render them unable to function to achieve true closure (either of their desire or their stories). Female agency is rendered useless by the pleasures of fictions of closure (of fulfilled female desire); agency, and the real possibility of closure (and the coming together of male and female),[13] is activated only when the fictions dissipate.

It is precisely this closure that never existed for Britomart in book 3 of *The Faerie Queene* and that was forever obliterated for Amoret in the 1596 revision and continuation. Before I conclude, I want to emphasize how frequently and thoroughly the *Urania* revisits Amoret's unfinished story, and not only in the reinscriptions from the *Urania*'s last published book that I have already discussed. The *Urania* opens with an echo of Britomart coming upon the haplessly lamenting Scudamore at the site of Amoret's torture, when Urania herself happens upon the similarly positioned Perissus, lamenting his lost and now presumed dead love Limena, who married her torturer Philargus but remained faithful in her love for Perissus.[14] Amoret's story, we may recall, cannot be concluded—desire cannot be fulfilled, she cannot be united with Scudamore—so long as she is enclosed by Busirane. Yet though she is released, and though we read of the origins of her story (her birth, her rearing in the Garden of Adonis) she resists conclusion, and her story remains unfinished. Through Limena's story Wroth provides a different anatomy of gendered desire and the possibility of closure. Limena is discovered, not dead but on the verge of being killed by her torturer/ husband, in an explicitly Spenserian scene (like Amoret, she is tied to a pillar, naked from the waist up, and like her even pleads for the life of her torturer when she is saved). Limena is not only rescued, however, but also reunited with and married to her beloved Perissus, for whom she has endured so much torture. The unfinished Spenserian text is concluded, we may be inclined to say: Wroth inscribes the closure that unites male and female and fulfills both sexual and textual desire for conclusion. Yet what is the true nature of that conclusion and how is it effected? The wounded and dying Philargus—the evil torturer/husband—has a deathbed conversion, repents, and makes everyone promise in advance to comply with one last dying request of his "which granted [he says] I shall dye with all content" (86)— and that is that Perissus and Limena will marry each other ("Limena, deny not this to your dying husband"). In the end, the fulfillment of female desire, the long-sought and long-deferred conclusion, becomes a story for which the man who thwarted and denied it claims responsibility. The question Wroth asks as she obsessively revisits the unended Spenserian story that seems to be such a powerfully founding moment for her own narrative may well be the one with which I will conclude: though she may desire it, and struggle mightily to achieve it, can conclusion ever truly bear the signature of a woman, or is she compelled to inscribe it always as compliance with masculine desire?

NOTES

1. Lewalski cites the three versions but does not comment on the significance of the repeated recastings of the scene. All quotations from Wroth are taken from *The First Part of The Countess of Montgomery's Urania,* ed. Roberts.

2. Also noted by Naomi Miller, *Changing the Subject* 57. Miller's book appeared after I had written this essay for the Yale Spenser conference; I have tried to acknowledge and address her argument in my footnotes.

3. In addition to those already cited, see Waller; Roberts, "Radigund Revisited" and "Labyrinths of Desire"; N. Miller, "Not much to be marked" and "Engendering Discourse"; among others.

4. At the end of her article, Carrell acknowledges that "Wroth's control remains in the end limited and temporary" (102).

5. For an analysis of some scenes of writing and reading in the *Urania,* see Lamb, *Gender and Authorship* and "Women Readers"; and Hackett, "'Yet Tell Me Some Such Fiction.'" For a recent analysis of the theme of ending and beginning in Wroth's work, see Alexander.

6. Roberts notes this meaning of her name in her edition of the *Urania,* 756n397.5. I am indebted to Roberts's notes and their suggestiveness concerning Spenserian subtexts.

7. Emphasis mine. Roberts, in the notes to her edition of the *Urania,* points out the Spenser connection here and elsewhere in this scene (741).

8. For a positive reading of Nereana, see Swift 344–45; for a negative reading, see Hackett, "'Yet Tell Me Some Such Fiction'" 53–55. Shaver views the portrayal as ambivalent. Nereana's story continues sporadically throughout the first three books of the *Urania;* I focus here only on her first appearance.

9. This scene is frequently commented upon; see, e.g., Lamb, *Gender and Authorship* 191, "Women Readers" 218–19; and Swift 336.

10. It is interesting to set this scene of Pamphilia's active displeasure with what she reads against the most explicit scene of reading in *The Faerie Queene*: Arthur's and Guyon's engrossed reading of books in Alma's castle, "ravisht" and "beguild" with "delight" (2.10.69, 77).

11. Compare N. Miller's more optimistic reading of this scene emphasizing female bonding and agency (*Changing the Subject* 221).

12. See Parker, *Literary Fat Ladies,* esp. ch. 2.

13. See Eggert's incisive analysis of romance form and female power in *The Faerie Queene,* and her identification of "marital union as the joining of man and woman" as an unsatisfactory "feminine ending" that the text resists (270–71).

14. The echo of this scene is noted by others, including N. Miller, "Not much to be marked" 128; and Quilligan, "Female Authority" 261.

"MIRROURS MORE THEN ONE"

Edmund Spenser and Female Authority in the Seventeenth Century

Shannon Miller

In *Feminist Milton,* Joseph Wittreich provides convincing and thorough support for the influence that John Milton—particularly in his representation of Eve—had on women thinkers and educators in the eighteenth century. Countering a contemporary critical resistance to Milton's portrait of Adam's "help meet," Wittreich argues instead for the authority that many women were able to derive from the gender dynamics within *Paradise Lost.* His evidence suggests that Milton powerfully influenced eighteenth-century women thinkers and educators, even enabling the development of their thought about gender relationships and women's rights. Milton, it appears, offered authority to these writers. So too did Edmund Spenser. For women writers in the century following the publication of *The Faerie Queene,* Spenser was a powerful literary influence as well as a figure who could provide legitimacy to women beginning to publish their work. As we will see, the use that women writers such as Aemilia Lanyer and Mary Wroth make of Spenser's epic poem argues against an isolated tradition of women's writing. Instead of viewing women's production of texts as a reaction against male-authored texts, the form of and significance of Spenser's influence upon seventeenth-century women writers suggests the productive interplay of literary influence and gender.

Spenser's influence on writers in the seventeenth century was obviously extensive. We would expect to see a growing number of women writers during the period drawing on his work and, consequently, his validating identity as an epic poet.[1] Within Aemilia Lanyer's 1611 *Salve Deus Rex Judaeorum* and Mary Wroth's 1621 *Countesse of Mountgomeries Urania,* both writers draw extensively upon portions of book 3 of Spenser's

The Faerie Queene. In their use of what Thomas Greene has called the "subtext" of Spenser's poem, Aemilia Lanyer and Mary Wroth employ Spenser "heuristically": in drawing upon, but then distancing themselves from, their subtext, they "force us to recognize the poetic distance traversed" (40). Greene's model helpfully distinguishes this form of *imitatio* from what he terms a "reproductive" or "sacramental" strategy that "celebrates an enshrined primary text by rehearsing it liturgically" (38). By stressing the conscious use of, instead of simply a rehearsal of, the previous text by the writer, Greene's paradigm allows the reader to view the "poetic distance traversed" by the work. That distance is observable because the "heuristic" text makes explicit where it comes from: "it acts out its own coming into being" (41). But it simultaneously "creates a bridge" from the original work to the new text. This bridge, this "poetic distance traversed," is the experience that the reader has of the new text.

Explicit in my reading of Lanyer and Wroth is their awareness of Spenser's text and their reworking of it. The distance that Lanyer and Wroth, as well as the reader, travel from Spenser's *The Faerie Queene* to their poetic and prose works is a function of the productive interplay between the "subtext" and their new texts. Ann Jones has suggested how gender influences, even redirects, such a process of imitation or transmission: when women choose philosophic traditions or literary models that had been traditionally employed by men, this choice offered legitimation to the women writer. Yet it simultaneously transgressed traditional gender boundaries of authorship; further, these concepts or ideas were now in the hands of a woman.[2] Like the distance traveled between the source text and the imitating text, we see meaning produced in the space between the traditional, legitimating text and the new text penned by a woman. I will also suggest how these new meanings produced along the way are not necessarily stable, nor in the control of the writer who employs a legitimating text such as Spenser's *The Faerie Queene.*

Both gender and class shape the use that Lanyer and Wroth are making of Spenser; these categories contribute to the making of new meanings that we observe in the distance from, the gap between, the subtext or influencing text and these seventeenth-century works. Book 3 of *The Faerie Queene* provides extensive material for Lanyer and Wroth to draw upon as readers and rewriters of Spenser's text. This portion of Spenser's epic highlights Queen Elizabeth and issues of female authority, yet it is Lanyer's and Wroth's respective class positions that determine which elements in Spenser's text will offer them legitimacy as writers. Wroth emphasizes her class position as a Sidney; her turn to the romance motifs within Spenser's Busirane sequence are in keeping with the class conventions she stresses on the frontispiece of the *Urania:* "Daughter to the right Noble Robert Earle of Leicester And Neece to the ever famous, and renowned Sr Phillips Sidney knight. And to the most excelent Lady Mary Countesse of Pembroke late deceased." Lanyer, as a middle-class woman, was working to provide legitimation for her presentation of self as a writer along both the axes of gender and class and draws repeatedly upon the patronage and other prefatory material in Spenser's epic and the book 3 proem. The literary authority that Spenser's text can provide is consequently employed by these writers as they, and their works, balance the demands that gender and class interject into the act of producing literary texts. The strategic use that each writer is making of Spenser relies upon a fracturing or dividing of one's source; as we will see, the interplay of gender and class "cuts up" Spenser in their respective texts in distinct ways. Lanyer will modify Spenser's presentation of the Queen within his prefatory material in order to restage patronage as an event occurring between a cadre of women. Wroth will turn to the romance conventions in Spenser's poem, renarrating central elements of Spenser's book 3 Busirane episode to offer a new vision of men and women's view of the world, as well as the new position of the female author.

When Aemilia Lanyer published her passion poem, *Salve Deus Rex Judaeorum,* in 1611, she was writing in one of the few traditions allowed to women writers—religious meditations and poetry. As Margaret Hannay summarizes, "women were permitted to break the rule of silence only to demonstrate their religious devotion . . . to encourage religious education and publication by men, by translating the religious works of other (usually male) writers, and, more rarely, by writing their own devotional meditations" (4). This cultural approval of women who involved themselves in the production of religious works provided Lanyer limited authority to publish as a woman. This form of authority is further sustained by the generic tradition of female mystic writing: during much of the Medieval period, women mystics had gained access to both God and speech through their writings, and this convention continues into the Renaissance.[3]

While these generic and subject-based choices offered her some authority in a culture that heavily restricted women's access to publication, Aemilia Lanyer also turns to another source in order to acquire authority— Edmund Spenser's *The Faerie Queene.* We can observe Spenser's extensive influence within a series of textual parallels between *The Faerie Queene* and *Salve Deus Rex Judaeorum.* The use of the phrase "cunning thiefe" at line 177 of the dedicatory poem to Mary Sidney recalls the use of this same phrase in Spenser's dedicatory sonnet to "All the Gratious and Beautifull Ladies in the Court." The motif of the "deep Characters, writ with blood" (1725), which peppers the text of *Salve Deus* and the dedications ("deepe Characters of due punishment" in the poem to Katherine, Countesse of Suffolke, 68), recalls the fate of Amoret's heart in the hands of the enchanter Busirane. The "woefull bands" of Christ (748) evoke the portrait of "that same woefull Ladie [Amoret], both whose hands / Were bounden fast, that did her ill become, / And her small wast girt round with yron bands" (3, 12, 30, 6–8).

These parallels initially establish Lanyer as a reader and refashioner of Spenser's text. As a literary figure, Spenser served Lanyer's purposes particularly well: her middle-class status could be elevated along the lines of Edmund Spenser, England's epic poet born the son of a cloth-maker. Spenser was to become a landowner in the colonial sphere of Ireland, thus leaping the class category of landownership to acquire the status of a gentleman. And his aspiration to a higher social class position is recorded both within his poetic production and his pursuit of a career within Elizabeth's extensive political bureaucracy, his active role in the "profession" of a secretary that secured him both employment and promotion under Lord Grey.[4] Lanyer's interest in Spenser focuses on his aspiration as a literary figure and the possible court promotion that such activities could provide to him. While a position as a secretary to Lord Grey may have been a coup, rather than an insult,[5] such options for court, or class-located, promotion were unavailable to women. Instead, it is Spenser's assertion of artistic promotion that become recorded into Lanyer's text: these echoes explicitly invoke a Spenser who desired to ascend the social ladder as a poet, a path of recognition more available to Lanyer than service within James's state bureaucracy. Spenser's use of the phrase "lowly Shepheards weeds" occurs in book 1's proem and establishes Spenser's inheritance of Virgil's assumption of the role of epic poet.[6] While it is Spenser's first and probably most significant assertion of poetic authority within his national epic, the reference also evokes his social position, and his desire to aspire, within Elizabeth's court. Lanyer's use of this exact phrase in her own poem, her repetition of "lowly shepheards weed" (1714) in her portrait of Christ, signals her own aspiration to the position of poet in Anne's court. While Lanyer reconfigures the context, she sustains a line of poetic and class authority through her repetition of Spenser's second line in his epic poem.

Spenser operates as a perfect model for Lanyer in her negotiation of the class-based patronage system within *Salve Deus Rex Judaeorum*. Spenser had successfully aligned himself with powerful patrons within Elizabeth's court, and these alliances are recorded within the various dedications to his works and the series of prefatory poems to *The Faerie Queene*. Spenser employs both his relationship with this circle of and series of patrons to establish a particular relationship with Queen Elizabeth, a connection highlighted by his dedicating of his epic to her. While Spenser serves as a model for working the patronage system, he also models for Lanyer a strategy for addressing one's female monarch. Lanyer actively employs the dedicatory apparatus of *The Faerie Queene* to justify her address to Queen Anne and to the circle of women patrons within her court, consequently acquiring protection for her text.

It is within the dedicatory apparatus of *Salve Deus Rex Judaeorum* that we see Spenser's greatest influence. As numerous critics, including Barbara Lewalski, have remarked, Lanyer constructs an ideal community of women readers through the ten dedicatory poems that preface her passion poem, "addressing these ladies as a contemporary community of good women" (220). Lewalski here gestures to an evocative link with Spenser: the multiple dedications in the poem are "a comparable strategy [to Spenser's], making the several ladies an ideal version of Queen Anne's own court and entourage" (220). Yet the strategies of patronage are repeatedly reshaped by the conditions of gender. Lanyer does not position her male monarch at the heart of her multiple dedications: instead, she constructs a portrait of Queen Anne patterned upon Spenser's representation of Elizabeth. Consequently, Lanyer's use of the multiple dedication form actively rewrites, and rethinks, the strategies that marked Spenser's dedicatory apparatus.

While Lanyer does gesture at poetic authority through the echo to Spenser's book 1 proem, her most striking use of Spenser derives from motifs within his book 3 proem; her dedicatory sonnets, in form, context, and imagery, draw extensively from this portion of Spenser's epic. In the book 2 proem, Spenser asked his queen and patron to see herself within his poem:

> . . . O fairest Princesse vnder sky,
>   In this faire mirrhour maist behold thy face,
>   And thine owne realmes in lond of Faery,
> And in this antique Image thy great auncestry.
> (2 proem 4.6–9)

Such acts of viewing and reading of the self within his text continues into the book 3 proem where he again directed the Queen to engage his poem by gazing at it via images of herself that she will find there:

> Ne let his fairest *Cynthia* refuse,
> In mirrours more then one her selfe to see,
> But either *Gloriana* let her chuse,
> Or in *Belphoebe* fashioned to bee.
> (3 proem 5.5–9)

Though Spenser sustains this mirror motif though the narrative of book 3,[7] Lanyer employs this image within the more focused space of the dedications to *Salve Deus Rex Judaeorum*. Lanyer's poem begins in much the same way as Spenser's: she too addresses herself to a great queen, one who—like Queen Elizabeth in Spenser's poem—is asked by her client to "view" and "read" this text:

> Renowned Empresse, and great Britaines Queene,
> Most gratious Mother of succeeding Kings;
> Vouchsafe to *view* that which is seldome seene,
> A Womans writing of divinest things:
> *Reade* it faire Queene. . . .
> (1–5)

In addressing Anne in these terms, Lanyer invokes Spenser's appeals to his queen to read his poem.

The initial emphasis on reading and viewing continues through each poem, and the list of parallels between the two works suggest how actively and purposefully Lanyer was turning to Spenser. While the openings of Spenser's and Lanyer's texts are rather conventional in directing the patron into the text, Spenser's motif of the mirror becomes the dominant strategy employed by Lanyer throughout her dedicatory poems, both in the dedication to Anne and to numerous other patronesses who appear within Lanyer's prefatory material.[8] The motif of the mirror dominates the opening poem to Anne as she instructs the queen to "Looke in this Mirrour of a worthy Mind, / Where some of your faire Virtues will appeare" (37–38). This phrase explicitly parallels Spenser's request to Elizabeth that she acquiesce "[i]n mirrours more then one her selfe to see" (3 proem 5.6). Both phrases enact the process by which the patron is to see elements of herself while gazing into the poem. Such parallels continue: at line 90, Lanyer asks Anne, "Let your faire Virtues in my Glasse be seene," a phrase invoking Spenser's request, "Ne let his fairest *Cynthia* refuse, / In mirrours more then one her selfe to see" (3 proem 5.6). Here, both the request and implied action are repeated, while the placement of the verbs "let" and "see" at, respectively, the beginning and the end of the lines, align the two phrases in terms of word choice and sound. The final two feet of this Spenserian line are also repeated within the poem "To all vertuous Ladies in generall." Queen Anne, now implicitly joined by these ladies, will turn again to the poem: "Let this faire Queene not unattended bee, / When in my Glasse she daines *her selfe to see*" (6–7; my emphasis). These mirror images recur throughout the dedicatory sonnets to *Salve Deus Rex Judaeorum*, appearing in the poems to Margaret,

Countess of Cumberland (35), her daughter Anne, Countess of Dorcet, and Susan, Countess of Kent.

Both poets, then, inscribe their relationship to their patrons through numerous acts of gazing. Lanyer's invocation of the relationship of poet and queen through this motif of viewing and of vision draws upon the "subtext" of *The Faerie Queene*'s prefatory material, but also reworks this characteristically Spenserian strategy of gazing to her own ends. Through her use of Spenser, Lanyer can reconfigure her needs as a female client to a female patron. Her gender transforms Spenser's motifs, allowing Lanyer new strategies for requesting patronage from her Queen. Most significantly, Lanyer's use of the mirror motif establishes a connection to an authorizing epic poet, but also to his patron, Queen Elizabeth. One of the first consequences of Lanyer's use of the mirror image is to produce a portrait of Queen Anne that reflects aspects of Queen Elizabeth: she is "her selfe to see," and yet that "selfe" is a double for or a reflection of Queen Elizabeth. Lanyer employs the resonant metaphor of the "mirror" in her poem to produce a reflection of the previous queen. This process allows Lanyer to construct a portrait of Queen Anne as a single, ruling monarch; as such, Anne reflects many of Elizabeth's traits. Yet this portrait of Anne is unique, diverging significantly from other contemporary representations of Queen Anne.

The traits conventionally associated with Anne in seventeenth-century dedications stress her role as the wife and mother of kings. Early references to Anne, such as Andrew Willet's 1603 dedication to her in *Joy of the English Church for the Coronation of a Prince,* actually define the title of "queen" back into the much more limited figure of regent: the figure of Anne is distanced from Elizabeth as it is linked explicitly to the biological reproduction that she offered to England. As Anne is positioned as an appendage to James, "the ladie increaseth with her lord," her fate and identity are made dependent upon her ruling husband. The phrase is simultaneously evocative of the acts of reproduction that define her role. Anne's position as a mother is further highlighted in the comparison of Anne of Denmark to Anne Bullen who brought the "happie issue of his ladie," Queen Elizabeth, into this world. Because Willit compares Anne to Elizabeth's mother, the title of queen is radically distanced from an association with Elizabeth: instead, the figure of queen regent is reconstructed.

An overview of other dedications to Queen Anne during James's reign consistently reveals the portrait of a queen who neither rules nor operates in her own right. In *The Fall of Man,* Godfrey Goodman refers to "our most gracious King" throughout his dedication to the queen and uses this opportunity to comment on the great happiness of James's deliverance from the Gunpowder Plot; the dedication to the queen, then, becomes a vehicle in which to address the real source of power. John Florio's *Queen Anna's New World of Words,* which identifies her as the "Crowned Queen of England," stresses her position as a queen in relation to others: the dedication identifies her as the daughter of a great king, the wife of a great king, and the mother of future great kings. She is most important as the producer of future generations, an identity Samuel Daniel makes much of in his *Collection of the Historie of England:* "Queens, the Mothers of Kings, by whome is continued the blessing of succession that preserves the Kingdom." Anne's identity is flattened out to the definition of "queen" provided here, explicitly separated from the act of reigning and assigned the sole role of reproduction. In Willet's tribute, Anne will give to the country "whole royal offspring [that] this land may long have fruition of like golden and happy dayies" (4).[9] Though Daniel will refer to Anne as "mighty," as "the Majesty of Anne of Denmark, Queene, of England, Scotland, France and Ireland," the titular—or traditional—role of the queen is that applied to and praised in Anne.

Anne's representation as wife and mother thus dominates the dedications of the period. Lodowick Lloyd's dedication to *The Choice of Jewels* (1607) positions Anne amongst a series of famous biblical wives, associating this mother of future kings and princes in Great Britain with the mothers of the tribes of Israel, such as Leah and Rachel. At one point in Goodman's *The Fall of Man,* Anne is referred to as our "Princess"—a title that Elizabeth left behind early in her career as monarch[10]—and is set again and again within the context of "his Maiesties most happie Marriage." The 1619 *Mirrour of Maiestie* by H.G. spatially illustrates the relational identity of this queen. He positions a tributary emblem and accompanying poem to Anne between a poem to James and one to Prince Charles, thus defining her through and positioning her between the roles of wife and mother. While the poem accompanying the emblem does establish a connection between Anne and Elizabeth, applying the phoenix image to both—"One phoenix borne, another phoenix burnes"—the "semper eadum" motto of the previous queen is reapplied to Anne: "Your rare worths (matchless Queene) in you alone / Live free, unparalleled, entirely one." The rebirth imagery of the phoenix, so central in Spenser's work, is now applied to the figure of a queen placed between her husband and her offspring. Consequently, the motif becomes physicalized rather than the metaphor used by Elizabethan writers. The poem also positions Anne as exceeding Elizabeth as she, "matchless," absorbs the title of "entirely one." This absorption or usurpation of Queen Elizabeth's image, flanked as it is by the traditional position of wife and mother, attempts to reconfigure the associations with Elizabeth, domesticating them within the figure of Anne.

While most contemporary encomiasts of Queen Anne emphasize her relational and dependent identity, Lanyer is rewriting the conventional imagery of Anne to grant greater authority to Lanyer's own queen and patroness. Lanyer can simultaneously create the expectation of Anne's reception of this poem. Spenser offers Lanyer especially powerful imagery of Elizabeth from *The Faerie Queene* that Lanyer can then rework. Through the invocation of Spenser's text, then, Lanyer constructs a patronage situation that allows her to negotiate the issues of authority facing a woman writer. Spenser's primary dedication to Elizabeth is actively echoed in Lanyer's tribute "To the Queens most Excellent Majestie." In addressing Anne as "Renowned Empresse, and great Britaines Queene" (1), Lanyer inverts the very title signifying monarchical authority that Spenser had used to address his queen: "Magnificent / Empresse Renow / med" (dedication, 4–6). Spenser's address to his "Empresse" granted great power, even colonial sites such as "Ireland" and "Virginia" to his queen. Lanyer draws explicitly upon this nexus of tribute, power, and control as she introduces Anne as "Renowned Empresse." Further, these gestures to Spenser generate a pattern throughout the dedication that highlights Queen Anne's identity as an independent ruler; in the "mirror" that is Lanyer's poem, Anne can read the title of "Empresse Renow / med" and observe such traits applied to her. Consequently, Lanyer's portrait stresses aspects of rule unlike those generally attributed to Anne, the first queen regent that England had experienced since the revolving door of Henry VIII's queens. As we have seen, the title of "Empresse" is an unusual one for King James's queen within dedications to her, a term of imperial power applied to her only once in Samuel Daniel's dedication to "The Queen's Arcadia."

Instead of superseding Elizabeth and her identity as queen, a strategy that many dedications to Anne employ, Lanyer's queen is positioned as an echo of, a memory of, and most important, a reflection of the former Queen Elizabeth. In order to make her dedication serve as a mirror within which Anne will see herself as an independent queen, Lanyer's dedicatory poem rejects many of the conventions employed within contemporary dedications to Anne. Instead of the figure of the mother, "Cult of Elizabeth" images circulate within the opening of "To the Queens most Excellent Majestie." At line 23, Anne is told that "shining Cynthia with her nymphs attend / To honour you" (23–24), and again at line 29, Lanyer instructs Anne, "Be like faire *Phoebe*, who doth love to grace / The darkest night with her most beauteous face" (29–30). "Cynthia" and "Phoebe" both associate Queen Anne with imagery of the virgin goddess of the hunt, and as such with

Elizabeth. The figure of Diana was so commonly employed by poets that it became shorthand for the queen; we see this within Spenser's Belphoebe, one of the "mirrours" in which Elizabeth was "her selfe to see" (3 proem 5.5). And while such examples offer general points of contact between Queen Anne and Elizabeth, Lanyer also establishes explicit linguistic parallels to Spenser's address to Elizabeth within the book 3 proem. Spenser had used the title of "Cynthia" for the queen extensively in addition to directing Queen Elizabeth to see herself within Belphoebe.

The centrality of Anne in her own dedicatory poem recalls the most significant part of Elizabeth's rule: as a virgin queen, she reigned alone. "To the Queenes most Excellent Majestie" works to produce such a portrait of Anne by eliding the king in whom power actually resided: the reflection that Anne is to observe is of an "Empresse Renow / med," not the queen regent of King James I. The opening line of the poem, which addresses her as "Empresse" and grants her the markedly independent identity of "great Britaines Queene," accords to Anne an authority sustained throughout this poem. While the second line, "Most gratious Mother of succeeding Kings," alludes to the more usual identity of Anne as the mother of the Princes Henry and Charles, the poem never mentions James. After having established a monarchical identity for Anne, the text at one moment does seem as if it is going to turn to the king, her husband: "Here may your sacred Majestie behold / That mightie Monarch both of heav'n and earth" (43–44). Yet this "mightie Monarch" is not James. The third line of this stanza of the poem describes this as yet unnamed figure as "He that all Nations of the world controld" (45); the text announces Christ to be the monarch who reigns with this "Renowned Empresse." By eliding James at the very moment the text seems to prepare us for his appearance, Lanyer positions Anne as analogous to Elizabeth; she alone will reign with Christ.

Even the poem's reference to Queen Anne as "Most gratious Mother of succeeding Kings" highlights the more independent, and distinctly more female-centered, portrait of Anne. The dominant position awarded to the Princes, first Henry and then Charles, in most dedications to Anne is absent here: after this limited reference to succession, maternal traits simply do not become a sustained motif. The one child referred to at any length in the dedicatory poem is the queen's daughter, Princess Elizabeth, and this reference linguistically reflects Queen Elizabeth through the repetition of the name. As the poem moves on, it will employ refractive imagery to link the two Elizabeths. Lanyer directs us to an image of the queen's daughter after beseeching Anne, "Let your faire Virtues in my Glasse be seene" (90):

> And she that is the patterne of all Beautie,
> The very modell of your Majestie,
> Whose rarest parts enforceth Love and Duty,
> The perfect patterne of all Pietie:
>> O let my Booke by her faire eies by blest,
>> In whose pure thoughts all Innocency rests.
> ("To the Queenes most Excellent Majestie," 91–96)

By presenting Princess Elizabeth at this moment in the text, Lanyer is allowing Anne to see "mirrours more then one" of herself, first in the reflection of Queen Elizabeth and then in an image of her own daughter Elizabeth. Spenser's use of multiple reflected images of the queen is here telescoped by Lanyer as Anne is offered a view of herself and her progeny.

While the mirroring motif in the dedication to Anne invokes Spenser's Elizabeth, the motif of reflection bestows an identity onto Princess Elizabeth; within the second of the dedicatory poems, the young Elizabeth—already described as a reflection of Queen Anne—becomes the reflected image of the dead queen, "great Eliza" (110).

> Most gratious Ladie, faire *Elizabeth,*
> Whose Name and Virtues puts us still in mind,
> Of her, of whom we are depriv'd by death;
> The *Phoenix* of her age, whose worth did bind
> All worthy minds so long as they have breath,
>> In linkes of Admiration, love and zeale,
>> To that deare Mother of our Common-weale.
> ("To the Lady *Elizabeths* Grace" 1–7)

The resurrection of the former queen's memory, and even her body, is achieved through seeing Queen Elizabeth via the portrait of the princess; when the mirror is placed in front of the young Elizabeth, the view one receives is of the former queen. The poem to Princess Elizabeth thus employs a complicated refractive process by which triangulated images of Queen Anne, Queen Elizabeth, and Princess Elizabeth are constantly referring to one another: Queen Anne is to "[l]ooke in this Mirrour of a worthy Mind" which will show back the traits of Queen Elizabeth (37); "The Lady Elizabeths Grace" is the "very modell of your Majestie," Queen Anne, in whom Anne can see "your faire Virtues in my Glasse" (90–92); and Princess Elizabeth "puts us still in mind" of the former Queen Elizabeth ("To the Lady *Elizabeths* Grace," 2). Anne is a reflection of Queen Elizabeth; Queen Anne reflects the image of her own daughter; and Princess

Elizabeth reflects the former queen: this sequence of mirrored images constantly moves us from the present royal family to the image of the previous monarch. Whatever reflection of Anne we see in the "mirrour" of Lanyer's dedicatory poems leads us back to Queen Elizabeth.

This form of visual substitution through the metaphor of the mirror, substitutions that continually direct us back to Queen Elizabeth, is repeated within analogous linguistic slides punctuating the poem. The elusive referent of the phoenix achieves the same effect as the mirroring technique within the first two dedicatory poems. While the mirror motif casts Princess Elizabeth as a stand-in for the dead queen, the eighth line in her dedicatory poem, "Even you faire Princess next our famous Queene," effects yet another set of possible substitutions. The line unmoors the referent of "our famous Queene," allowing for another mode of mirroring Elizabeth within portraits of Anne and her daughter: is "our famous Queene" Anne, the acknowledged subject of the first dedicatory poem, or Queen Elizabeth, who is the famous queen discussed by the poem's opening lines? The description of "that deare Mother of our Common-weale" at line 7 only sustains such slides from Anne or her daughter to the former queen. Since Elizabeth's maternal relationship to her country was used to offset her barren condition, the verbal iconography of the mother holds the reference in suspension. The association between Queen Anne and Queen Elizabeth is thus continued through this dedicatory poem to Princess Elizabeth

Lanyer's reformulation of Spenser's mirror imagery—through which he drew his own queen into reading and supporting his poem—sustains the echo of Elizabeth within the portrait of Queen Anne. And these extensive parallels between Anne and Elizabeth also serve to validate Lanyer's appeal for patronage: Elizabeth acknowledged and rewarded Spenser, thus Anne should recognize Lanyer. But the reflective process that Lanyer institutes within her poem also results in many other images of female patrons as her dedicatory poems sustain the process by which one figure can be transformed into another through the technique of mirroring.

We have seen the extensive influence of Spenser's mirror imagery on *Salve Deus Rex Judaeorum*. Consequently, we might expect parallels between Spenser's many dedicatory sonnets and Lanyer's multiply dedicated format. Lanyer's text begins with a series of ten dedicatory poems (one dedication, to the Countess of Cumberland, is actually in prose) followed by the prose address "To the Vertuous Reader." While Barbara Lewalski compares Lanyer's use of multiple dedications to the dedicatory apparatus of *The Faerie Queene,* Spenser's poem positions his dedicatory sonnets very differently than does Lanyer: you might even say that his poem begins much more abruptly. In every edition of *The Faerie Queene* up to 1611 (the year

Salve Deus Rex Judaeorum was published), the shaped dedication to the Queen was immediately followed by the text. The commendatory and multiple dedicatory verses, which Arthur Marotti has described as "signal[ing] the breakdown of the old system of artistic clientage" (45), were either placed at the back of the text or eliminated in every edition.[11] Instead of following Spenser's use of multiple dedications, then, Lanyer reconceives his strategy. Spenser had placed the multiple dedicatory poems literally in the margins. Lanyer chooses to place at the forefront of her text what, in Spenser's presentation of his poem, was so much more secondary. While Spenser marginalizes the other dedicatory poems, and perhaps their consequences, Lanyer transforms them into the organizing aspect of her text. Like Spenser, Lanyer dedicates her text to the current Queen, but reworks Spenser's final dedicatory sonnet, "To all the Gratious and Beautifull Ladies in the Court," into her collection of female dedicatees.

The potential subversiveness embedded within Spenser's ploy to address multiple patrons is thus highlighted by Lanyer's placement of her many dedicatory verses at the head of her poem. After the poem's extensive process of reflecting Queen Elizabeth within the portrait of Anne throughout "To the Queenes most Excellent Majestie," the poem casts Margaret, Countess of Cumberland, and her daughter Anne, Countess of Dorcet, as *Salve*'s primary patrons, ultimately awarding the crown of virtue to them.[12] We see this accomplished through Lanyer's use of mirrors; again, Lanyer builds upon Spenser's play of reflected images that dominated the book 3 proem. In parts of his poem, Spenser stresses Elizabeth's image as producing the "reflection" that is his poem, while in others he directs her to see herself produced within the poem. Thus Spenser presented Elizabeth as the "Mirrour of grace and Maiestie diuine" in the proem to book 1 (4, 2), offering her the status of producer of his work, while in the book 2 proem she is directed "[i]n this faire mirrhour . . . [to] behold thy face, / And thine owne realmes in lond of Faery / And in this antique Image thy great auncestry" (4.7–9): here, she is a reflected image within his poem. Within book 3, she occupies both positions. Initially presented as the model for chastity, and thus for this book of Spenser's epic "[f]or which what needs me fetch . . . / Forreine ensamples" (1.3–4), she is then directed "[i]n mirrours more then one her selfe to see" (5, 6); now Elizabeth both produces and is produced by Spenser's poem as he positions *The Faerie Queene* as a mirror into which she is to gaze.[13]

Spenser's strategy of illustrating Elizabeth's influence on the text, but also its influence on her, recurs in Lanyer's account of Margaret and Anne and their effect on her text. In *Salve Deus Rex Judaeorum*, however, Lanyer now can benefit from a multiplicity of patrons for her poem. She divides the form of influence that each woman has on the text. While Queen Anne is consistently allowed to see herself reflected in Lanyer's poem, the Countess of Cumberland becomes the source of that poem. Lanyer has told Anne that she can see herself within Lanyer's text: "Looke in this mirrour of a worthy Mind, / Where some of your faire Virtues will appeare" (37–38). Yet while Queen Anne is directed to "[l]ooke in this Mirrour of a worthy Mind" (37), Margaret becomes that worthy mind reflected in *Salve Deus:* within Margaret's dedication, the poem is described as "the mirrour of *your* most worthy minde" (30–31; my emphasis). Margaret is thus awarded the identity as producer of Lanyer's poem. The two identities awarded to Elizabeth—the one who is producing and the one who is produced by the poem—here become split between Queen Anne and Margaret, Countess of Cumberland.

Lanyer thus succeeds at exchanging, through the slight of hand of a mirror, one patron for another. After establishing Anne as her seemingly primary patron, and a patron who could provide the most for author and poem, she replaces her with the less powerful Countess of Cumberland. This slide between patrons becomes most explicit as the text of *Salve Deus Rex Judaeorum* begins. Lanyer invokes the dead queen, a figure who has been consistently linked to Queen Anne throughout Lanyer's imagery. "Sith *Cynthia* is ascended to that rest / Of endlesse joy and true Eternitie" (1–2), the poem suggests that a substitute for the former queen must be sought. But the figure offered is not Anne; just as her husband was elided in the poem at the moment we would expect to see him, now too is the current queen. Queen Elizabeth's image is no longer reflected by the present queen and her daughter. The poem turns in its second stanza to an invocation of Lanyer's ultimate patron, Margaret, the Countess of Cumberland: "To thee great Countesse now I will applie / My Pen, to write thy never dying fame" (9–10). Lanyer may be invoking here Spenser's reorientation of book 4's proem. Though he initially addresses Burleigh, "The rugged forhead that with graue foresight / Welds kingdomes causes, & affaires of state" (4 proem 1.1–2), Spenser then directs us to his better reader, and his better patron, Elizabeth: "To such [as Burleigh] therefore I do not sing at all, / But to that sacred Saint my soueraigne Queene" (4 proem 4.1–2). Lanyer fuses such a shift of addressee with the complex mechanism of the mirror in her treatment of the countess. And this same process occurs again with the daughters of her patronesses, Princess Elizabeth and Anne, Countess of Dorcet. Of these two daughters, it is Anne who becomes "the Heire apparant of this Crowne / of goodnesse, bountie, grace, love, pietie" (65–66). While Princess Elizabeth reflected the image of the previous crowned queen, Anne ultimately is crowned as the mirror of virtuous perfection. The Cumberland family now "crowned" by Lanyer's verse, her use of the mirror essentially leaves the poem. Having effectively employed this strategy to reflect and refract images of patrons in her search for patronage, Lanyer turns away from the motif.

The "distance" that Lanyer travels from her subtext both records and revises Spenser's own poetic strategies. She employs Spenser's mirroring techniques, creating new meaning in *Salve Deus Rex Judaeorum* through the images produced by the reflective process. She explores the implications of multiple dedications and multiple patrons, finding within a potentially subversive strategy a forum for creating an audience. Lanyer's use of Spenser as a "source" of authority was powerfully influenced by her class position; as a middle-class woman, she needed to seek out an elusive patronage situation that would have been more easily available to male and noble writers. Mary Wroth, in publishing her 1621 *The Countesse of Mountgomeries Urania,* had far less need for patronage because of her identity as a Sidney, but she turns to Spenser's *The Faerie Queene* in order to achieve literary authority from the generic tradition of romance.[14] Wroth did model portions of her romance on her uncle Philip Sidney's *Arcadia*. Yet Wroth's work has been overly characterized as a reworking of the romance conventions of her uncle's narrative. *The Faerie Queene,* particularly episodes from book 3, occupies an equally significant role within her work as Wroth turns to Spenser's Busirane episode to model aspects of her romance.

Wroth's interest in Spenser's Busirane episode matches that of contemporary Spenserian critics. A highly original episode in *The Faerie Queene* with fewer sources than most other sequences of the poem, the account of Amoret's entrapment by the magician/lover/poet Busirane highlights the romance convention of women encased within an enchantment for or because of love. While the episode details Amoret's physical restraint and the accompanying violence directed onto her, it gestures towards the limitations that literary genres could place upon female heroines: Amoret's imprisonment may be a magical manifestation produced by Busirane, but the details of the masque illustrate Amoret's containment by the conventions of courtly love.[15] Spenser's criticism of these conventions, and of aspects of love poetry itself, transforms the scene into commentary about the figure of the male poet. In her article "Gendering Allegory," Susanne Wofford elegantly illustrates how Britomart operates both as Amoret's rescuer and as a reader and interpreter in her own right: "Britomart and the reader interpret in parallel" in their travels through the House of Busirane, the house of a male poet. In addition to examining the interaction between Britomart and Busirane, Wofford illuminates the relationship between the emergent character of Britomart and Spenser as author: "The figurative struggle between a female character and an evil male artist, then, points to a struggle between modes of writing, modes which in this episode are associated with male and female perspectives" (15). Though she may not become a figure for the author herself, she does manage to reverse the charms that Busirane has created to entrap Amoret. Though Britomart does not assume the role of a writer in this episode, she does un-write the romance conventions that encase the victimized Amoret. Wofford's suggestive reading of this episode argues that the allegorical rendering of Britomart breaks down in this episode to reveal a modern, perhaps even feminist, subject.

Britomart, particularly her actions within this sequence, consequently provides Wroth intriguing models for Wroth's own engagement with the conventions of romance within the *Urania*. If, as Wofford argues, "Spenser looks at Busirane's art from the point of view of a woman and condemns it" (12), then Wroth's extensive use of the episode allows her to draw upon Spenser's criticisms of the male tradition of, and dangers within, romance. Like Britomart, Wroth attempts to rewrite, perhaps even to un-write, the Petrarchan conventions and expectations that Spenser embodies within Busirane. Through her own use of the Busirane episode, then, Wroth may begin to "posit . . . an alternative female authority that reverses the male plot and creates a different kind of female character" ("Gendering Allegory" 15): a female writer. The main figure within the *Urania* is Pamphilia, a writer who has numerous biographical parallels to Wroth herself. Through the figure of Pamphilia, Wroth attempts to reverse the generic conventions within her romance much as Britomart attempts to un-write the verses of, and the consequent power of, the male poet Busirane.

The extensive parallels between the *Urania* and book 3 of *The Faerie Queene* have been noted by critics such as Maureen Quilligan and Elaine Beilin. But while numerous critics have noted the parallels between, in particular, the book 4 Hell of Deceit sequence and Spenser's episode in cantos 11–12 of book 3, few have noted the manner in which Wroth revises one of her main sources and the consequences this will have for a woman writer. In reworking Spenser's scene, Wroth will construct a space for female creative power, yet—as we will see—it comes with an analogously dividing threat to the figure of the female writer. Wroth employs numerous motifs from the book 3 Busirane episode into her narrative. Busirane's enchanted space, where he binds and tortures Amoret, is variously described as a "Castle," a "house," a "secret den," and a "deepe dungeon." These distinct traits of Busirane's residence, along with the plot elements of the Busirane sequence, become divided between Wroth's Throne of Love and Hell of

Deceit episodes. She adapts the architectural layout of Busirane's house to the three towers that comprise the Throne of Love. Pamphilia moves through the towers—a space of enchantment where lovers are bound until freed by Pamphilia and Amphilanthus—much as Britomart passed through the House of Busirane: Britomart enters at the "Castle gate," moves into the "vtmost rowme," into "the next roome," and finally penetrates "the inner roome" where Amoret is bound.[16] Pamphilia also ends the enchantment of the Throne of Love, passing through three towers that are a match for the three rooms in Busirane's house. In the Hell of deceit episode, alternately, Wroth integrates the cave-like characteristics of Busirane's abode along with images evocative of the enchanter's possession of and violence toward Amoret. Certainly the words written at the entrance to the cave, "This no wonder's of much waight, / 'Tis the hell of deepe deceit" (656), echo the confusing instructions to Britomart, "Be bold, be bold," and then "Be not to bold." Further, the "letters ingraven at the bottome in Characters of bloud" (655) that scar Pamphilia's heart are a reimagining of Busirane's "[f]iguring straunge characters of his art," which he "wrate" with "liuing bloud . . . Dreadfully dropping from [Amoret's] dying hart" (3, 12, 31, 2–4).

Wroth thus establishes a conscious intertextuality between her two episodes and Spenser's poem. Yet just as Britomart wrests authority away from Busirane—and perhaps from Spenser—Wroth rewrites Spenser's episode through a motif of fragmentation. Wroth separates the "castle" aspect of Busirane's abode from its cave-like or dungeon traits as she divides Spenser's episode between books 1 and 4 of her own narrative. The resolution of the Throne of Love enchantment is also significantly dilated since she leaves it unresolved through much of book 1: the title character of Urania is trapped within the Throne of Love approximately fifty pages into the narrative and not freed until the final pages of the 174-page book. Wroth thus takes up the plot device of the separation of lovers that Spenser adds to the 1596 version of *The Faerie Queene:* instead of unifying Scudamore and Amoret at the close of the Busirane episode, he leaves them divided.

In the book 4 episode, Wroth significantly extends this pattern of separating lovers as she sustains the fragmentation of her Spenserian source. In the Hell of Deceit episode, Pamphilia and Amphilanthus individually come upon rock structures that open onto nightmarish images of the other encased within a cave structure. In each one's vision, the lover is bound, their hearts exposed to view. The enchanted space refuses entrance, and the viewing lover departs after each one's unsuccessful attempt to save the other. Pamphilia and Amphilanthus are consequently physically divided from each other, just as are Amoret and Scudamore in Spenser's 1596 revision to book 3. More significant, though, is Wroth's psychic separation of the lovers.

Each has a distinct vision, one that reveals a much more fundamental fragmentation of Spenser's original hermaphroditic union, which concludes the 1590 version of Amoret and Scudamore's adventure. As Pamphilia peers into the Hell of Deceit, "as last she saw Musalina sitting in a Chaire of Gold, a Crowne on her head, and Lucenia holding a sword, which Musalina tooke in her hand, and before them Amphilanthus was standing, with his heart ript open, and Pamphilia written in it, Musalina ready with the point of the sword to conclude all, by razing that name out" (583). When Amphilanthus gains entrance to the cave where Pamphilia's heart is exposed to view, his name is ultimately discernible within her heart as well, though here the parallels begin to diverge: "there did hee perceive perfectly within it Pamphilia dead, lying within an arch, her breast open and in it his name made, in little flames burning like pretty lamps which made the letters, as if set round with diamonds, and so cleare it was, as hee distinctly saw the letters ingraven at the bottome in Characters of bloud" (655).

While Pamphilia's name can be removed from Amphilanthus's heart, Pamphilia's heart will never lose the imprint of his name. An allegorical tableau for their identities in the romance—Pamphilia is the "loyalist of ladies" while Amphilanthus means "lover of two"—their alternate visions suggest that men and women cannot share a single vision of the pains of love. Spenser may revise the original ending of book 3, transforming the hermaphroditic union of Amoret and Scudamore into an unresolved story of separated lovers, but Wroth suggests that men and women are psychically, and permanently, distinct. She further stresses this division between the visions by her distancing of them within the text itself: their particular visions occur seventy pages apart. Wroth's explicit use of Spenser's episode—the encasing of the body, the image of the heart punished by a weapon-wielding enchanter, the writing on the heart or with its blood—is transformed into a commentary about gendered perspective. While all readers of the Spenser episode, male and female, see the same torturous experience of Amoret, Wroth implies that such visions, such interpretations, are different for men and for women.

While Wroth's rewriting of the Busirane episode points towards her increasingly fragmented representation of the relationship between the sexes, this fragmentation of her "source" allows her to make the material her own. Wroth's rewriting of this male tradition—her reconstruction of Spenser's narrative into her own—transforms the male-produced spaces of tradition into sites of female creativity. In both the *Urania* episodes for which Spenser is a source, the creative force behind these episodes becomes a woman. Venus, "thinking her self in these latter times, not so much, or much lesse honour'd then in ages past, hath built this, calling it the throne of

Love" (48). The vision of the Hell of Deceit is created by the enchantress, Musalina. In perhaps her most significant revision, then, Wroth replaces the male creative force behind Spenser's original episode (Spenser and Busirane) with figures of creating women.

Yet the authorizing narrative of Spenser's book 3 episode carries within it a powerful threat to Wroth's attempted construction of a space for female creativity. Wroth is the creative power behind Musalina. But this figure of a powerful, creating woman simultaneously threatens to dismember another image of Wroth in the narrative: Pamphilia. Commentators on the *Urania* have unanimously agreed that Pamphilia is a figure for Mary Wroth within the romance, an interpretation buttressed by numerous biographical parallels between author and character. Pamphilia's name and the self that is gestured at through one's name are faced with erasure within the Hell of Deceit scene: Musalina stands "ready with the point of the sword to conclude all, by razing that name out" (583). As the creative power behind Musalina, Wroth thus becomes both this enchantress and Pamphilia. Consequently, we see one figure for female creativity attempting to erase the other such figure in the text. Of course Spenser has modeled for Wroth some of the dangers of authorship: Busirane is only one of a series of poet figures who are either threatening or threatened within his epic. Yet Wroth infuses this Spenserian observation with a powerfully gendered element: in the *Urania,* the figure of one female creator attempts to destroy the other major female writer. While the threat of writing is clear in both texts, the consequences are much more extreme for this figure of Wroth in her own text. In constructing a space for female authorship, Wroth represents the potential division, even dismemberment, of the female artist. She is simultaneously representing the potential for that same division in herself. The act of writing, the act of expressing a female self, can cause that very self to splinter. Wroth's attempts to create and express her position as an autonomous, speaking subject threaten to erase that very self constituted by the act of writing.

The book 4 episode suggests the state of division Catherine Belsey identifies within the Renaissance female subject: while men of the period were gradually becoming defined as unified subjects, "single . . . stable" and "continuous," women, though "able to speak [and] to take up a subject-position in discourse . . . were nonetheless enjoined to silence" (149). Yet Wroth's strategies for incorporating, but also necessarily reworking, the demands of male tradition offer her a path, though treacherous, out of the silence that underlies Belsey's formulation. While women may have found a "place in discourse" within the domestic sphere (*The Subject of Tragedy* 193), Wroth published a full-length sonnet sequence and circulated in manuscript both a pastoral play and a continuation of the *Urania*.[17] Despite cultural limitations on women's writing, Wroth nonetheless moved beyond appropriate female spaces and chose to pass through, and actively reconfigure, the powerful literary structure of Edmund Spenser's *The Faerie Queene*.

Wroth enters into the romance tradition, reconfiguring it and its possibilities for granting authority to a woman writer. Lanyer, whose production of religious poetry was considered less culturally threatening, imitates both Spenser's language and his patronage techniques in order to acquire, and trade, literary protection. Acts of dividing and rewriting one's source thus mark Lanyer's and Wroth's respective uses of Spenser as both writers fragment their "subtext" to allow for innovations necessitated by their location within the matrixes of gender and class. Certainly, both writers were consciously turning to Spenser: the parallels between Lanyer and Spenser's poetry and the influence of the Busirane sequence on Wroth confirm this. But the texts that Lanyer and Wroth produce as they rewrite, redraw, and variously segment or divide the line of tradition from Spenser's *Faerie Queene* are most profoundly inflected by the cultural identities assigned these women during the Renaissance.

This fusion of intertextuality and ideology produces multiple, even contradictory, meanings within Wroth's and Lanyer's texts. Wroth runs the risk that fragmenting her source will affect her own literary production, even threaten the act of writing itself. For Lanyer, the division her text makes between a royal and a noble patroness highlights the instability of her class position as she is forced to modulate between distinct figures for cultural and political power. It also suggests conflict with, even competition between, the individuals of the "ideal community" that literary critics have projected onto Lanyer's circle of dedicatees. In asserting that Lanyer transforms "the relationships assumed in the male patronage system into *an ideal community*" (221; my emphasis), Barbara Lewalski implies that the dedications to and the text of *Salve Deus Rex Judaeorum* construct a nonconflicted space. Yet patronage is a highly charged cultural practice through which writers vie for literary and social power; in her claims for her own writing, Lanyer cannot afford to stand outside of these conventions. Spenser thus serves the purposes of these two writers in analogous, yet quite distinct ways: he provides Lanyer with a model for creating a patronage circle, and he offers to Wroth an opportunity—with all of its attendant dangers—to reverse the male plot of romance. The *Urania* and *Salve Deus Rex Judaeorum* thus provide us with an opportunity to observe some strategies open to, and the consequences for, women writers during the seventeenth century.

NOTES

1. For a concise discussion of Spenser's influences on other poets until 1660, see the entry on "Imitations and Adaptations, Renaissance (1579–1660)" in the *Spenser Encyclopedia*. This account of Spenser's influence includes no female writers, suggesting the need for work that details how this group of writers viewed and employed Spenser's poetry.

2. According to Jones, "a transgression of gender rules occurs when a woman adopts the authority encoded" into the philosophical discourse of Neoplatonism. "Strict adherence to Neoplatonic ideals on the part of a woman poet, then, cannot be read simply as adulatory imitation (even if this is the reading she aspires to). It is, rather, the strategic adoption of a prestigious discourse that legitimates her writing. When a member of the sex systematically excluded from literary performance takes a dominant/hegemonic position toward an approved discourse, she is, in fact, destabilizing the gender system that prohibits her claim to public language" (4). Jones terms this act "negotiation," where the marginal woman writer draws upon dominant texts or the dominant ideology in order to produce her text. Her theory fuses the models of influence in Greene's *The Light in Troy* with Stuart Hall's theory of negotiation (4).

3. Wall has discussed the use Lanyer makes of both the authority of Christ and the figure of Mary Sidney to comprise her passion poem (319–30).

4. For a detailed exploration of Spenser's career as a secretary, see Richard Rambuss's *Spenser's Secret Career*. Rambuss intriguingly suggests within this book that "Spenser's career as a secretary provided him with a discursive practice and professional model that had a shaping effect both on his poetry and on the role he envisioned for himself as a poet" (28).

5. Brink, following Rambuss's lead, argues in "'All his minde on honour fixed': The Preferment of Edmund Spenser" that Spenser would have embraced, rather than have considered as an insult, his appointment as Grey's secretary. After many years of examining Spenser's work in light of his frustration with his level of promotion within Elizabeth's court, both Rambuss and Brink have shifted the focus to suggest that Spenser could well have been satisfied with the level of promotion he received from the diffuse Elizabethan court system. I remain much more convinced by Helgerson's view of Spenser's career as dominated by his goal to be recognized as a poet, rather than as simply a bureaucratic functionary. Rambuss's emphasis on the two-edged character of Spenser's "career" goals, though, I find a helpful adjunct to the growing work on Spenser's biography and its influence on his literary corpus.

6. I am drawing upon Helgerson's argument about Spenser's Virgilian-shaped laureate career in *Self-Crowned Laureates*. Rambuss's *Spenser's Secret Career* counters that Spenser is pursuing two careers, both that of a secretary as well as that of a laureate poet. I find Helgerson's argument about Spenser's sense of career more convincing. More significant for this essay, though, it is Spenser's identity as an epic poet—and not as a state functionary—that would have appealed to Aemilia Lanyer.

7. Walker discusses the full range of Spenser's use of the mirror images throughout the book. She argues that Spenser finds ways of "mirroring" the Queen within the character of Britomart, while Wofford, in "Gendering Allegory," argues that Britomart's subjectivity within the narrative is produced through the use of the mirror.

8. Besides these extensive linguistic parallels, Lanyer also employs the motif of the mirror at points structurally analogous to their use in Spenser's text. Spenser employs the mirror image within every proem of *The Faerie Queene* except that to book 4, yet the prominence of the image dissipates within the text. (In the 1590 edition of the poem, three of the ten references to mirrors occur within the proems, while five of the ten references occur within book 3.) So too with Lanyer's use of the mirror: while it dominates the relationship between her imagined readers (who are simultaneously her patronesses or protectors) and the poem, which is described within the ten dedicatory poems to *Salve Deus Rex Judaeorum,* the motif largely falls out of the body of the poem, only briefly appearing within the first thirty lines of her passion poem.

9. The apparent threat of the figure of Elizabeth is strongest at the beginning of James's realm when many of the dedications distance Anne from images of Elizabeth. By 1619, James Maxwell's *Carolanna: A Poem in Honor of Our King* can record the death of Anne in a pastoral poem through numerous motifs employed by Queen Elizabeth. In this posthumous dedication, Anne is associated with Diana, Mary, and various virginal motifs clearly eschewed by earlier dedications and writings.

10. For a full discussion of the use that Elizabeth made of different titles throughout her reign, see Marcus's "Shakespeare's Comic Heroines."

11. For a full account of the publication history of the commendatory and dedicatory sonnets, see Johnson's *A Critical Bibliography of the Works of Edmund.*

12. As Lewalski states, the inheritance of mothers to daughters characterizes the genealogy established within these commendatory poems: "Here the patrons' virtue descends through the female line, from mothers to daughters—Queen Anne and Princess Elizabeth, Margaret and Anne Clifford, Catherine and Susan Bertie, Katherine Howard and her daughters" (221).

13. See Montrose, "The Elizabethan Subject and the Spenserian Text," for an extended reading of Spenser's form of instructing and compelling the Queen to certain actions. Like Montrose, I am highlighting the interactive nature of textual production, both Elizabeth's effect on the text and the text's influence upon her.

14. Ironically, when Lord Denny attacks her after the *Urania*'s publication in 1621, Wroth is in much more need of the political and social protection that was an implicit aspect of the patronage relationship.

15. See Rose on the literalization of Petrarchan conventions within the House of Busirane. Berger has also discussed the tortures to which women have been subjected in male literary and erotic imaginings in "Busirane and the War between the Sexes."

16. Quilligan and Beilin have both remarked on the resemblance between the two Wroth episodes and Spenser's Busirane sequence. Quilligan suggests

that Wroth's rewriting of the Busirane scene is a reversal of the aspects of the Spenser episode. While Pamphilia's half of this dream certainly is reversed in almost every way, the torture of the female continues in Amphilanthus's dream. My discussion of a "division" of Spenser's episode is thus an attempt to accommodate both halves of Wroth's Hell of Deceit.

17. For Belsey, women find this "place in discourse" in the late seventeenth century as the humanist construction of the self turns towards liberalism. See "Finding a Place" in *The Subject of Tragedy*.

MILTON'S CAVE OF ERROR

A Rewriting of Spenserian Satire

John N. King

Book 1 of *The Faerie Queene,* or "The Legend of Holiness," has received little, if any, attention as a model for ecclesiastical satire in *Paradise Lost.* Nevertheless, Satan's encounter with Sin and Death bears the imprint of Sin's Spenserian prototype, Error, as a polemical figure for the Church of Rome. Milton styles Sin retrospectively as the ultimate ancestress of Spenserian Error in one of many intertextual allusions that take the shape of proleptic anticipations of allegorical debasement in *The Faerie Queene.*[1] *Paradise Lost* therefore pays homage to a lurid tradition of religious controversy when the monstrous offspring of Sin, sired by Death and descended from Satan, creep in and out of the womb of the mother upon whom they feed (2.795–800). By satire I mean the employment of parody, inversion, burlesque, and travesty to ridicule an object of attack.

   Sin mirrors the sinister maternality of Error, a monster incapable of suckling her famished brood of a "thousand yong ones" (1.1.15), who eventually devour her in a grotesque parody of transubstantiation and the Mass offered by yet another *mother,*[2] the Roman church: "They flocked all about her bleeding wound, / And sucked up their dying mothers blood, / Making her death their life, and eke her hurt their good" (1.1.25.7–9). Milton appropriates the opening episode of "The Legend of Holiness" as an important subtext for Sin's construction as a grotesque parody of the Church of Rome as a demonic mother. The complicated interchange between early episodes in *The Faerie Queene* and *Paradise Lost* highlights the transformation of Protestant militancy between the time of Spenser's conformity to the Elizabethan settlement of religion and Milton's heterodox rejection of organized religion, notably the episcopal hierarchy, doctrine, and ritual of the churches of Rome and Canterbury.

   In Spenser's religious allegory, Error joins Duessa as a latter-day variant of the Whore of Babylon and personification of the Roman-rite Mass. John Bale's *Image of Both Churches* had popularized such views, but they are ubiquitous in the writings by Luther, Calvin, Perkins, and others. The polymorphous sexuality and grotesque physicality of those monstrous females align them with sixteenth- and seventeenth-century Protestant polemics against the Roman church and ceremonial of the Mass as poisonous maternal feeders.[3] A syncretist like Spenser, Milton joins his predecessor by invoking the classical models of Echidna, who gives birth to Cerberus, the canine guardian of Hades, and Scylla, a beautiful nymph whose loins became "barking dogs" when Circe transformed her into a biform monster.[4] Scylla had come by the late Middle Ages to symbolize the uncontrollable appetite of sin according to texts like Dante's *Inferno* and the *Ovide moralisé*.[5]

Although censorship restrictions imposed under the harshly punitive Clarendon Code (1661–65), a set of statutes directed against non-conformists, may have forced Milton to veil the controversial aspect of the "genealogy of evil" that Spenser employed openly to allegorize the ontology of sin, polemical genealogies were published openly during the heyday of the English Reformation. Among the many anti-Mass satires published under Edward VI, *Pathose* (ca. 1548) by Luke Shepherd incorporates a funeral elegy for Mistress Missa,[6] a scurrilous personification of the Mass that functions as a poetic ancestress of Error, Duessa, *and* Miltonic Sin. The demonic descent of Mistress Missa as granddaughter of Pluto, illegitimate daughter of the Pope, and niece of Mohammed parodies the genealogical praise of epideictic rhetoric. Like Miltonic Sin, she commits incest with her papal father. Duessa's similar status as the "sole daughter" of the Pope anchors "The Legend of Holiness" in Reformation controversy (1.2.22).

Genealogies of papal evil were conventional in allegories by seventeenth-century Spenserian poets who afford a bridge between Spenserian Error and Miltonic Sin and Death. They coexist with an appropriation of the Gunpowder Plot as a focal point for religio-political satire in texts like Phineas Fletcher's *The Locusts, or Apollyonists* (1627)[7] and *The Purple Island* (1633). The former appeared at the same time as Milton's own Gunpowder Plot satire, *In Quintum Novembris* (c. 1626). Antipathy to both the papacy and the Jesuit Mission pervades the works of Spenser, Fletcher, and other Spenserian poets. *Apollyonists*, in particular, features a personification of Sin that functions as a composite model both for her namesake, Milton's Sin, who replicates her poetic forebear's role as porter of hell gate, and for Death, who shares the "shapeless shape" of Fletcherian Sin (1.10). In a work in which Fletcher's Satan laments that "Error's lost and fled" (1.25) as a consequence of the English Reformation, Sin shares the monstrous femininity and biform aspect of both Spenserian Error and Miltonic Sin:

> For she with art and paint could fine dissemble
> Her loathsome face: her back parts (blacke as night)
> Like to her horride Sire would force to tremble
> The boldest heart; to th'eye that meetes her right.
> (1.12)

Of course, she recalls Error's appearance as an "ugly monster plaine, / Halfe like a serpent horribly displaide, / But th'other halfe did womans shape retaine, / Most lothsome, filthie, foule and full of vile disdaine" (*FQ* 1.1.14). David Quint astutely notes that the leering response of Milton's Death to his delegation by Satan to feed upon mortal life (*PL* 2.846–48) "recalls none other than Fletcher's Guy Fawkes . . . contemplating the ruin of the House of Parliament" (*Epic and Empire* 273, citing *Apoll.* 5.10). Milton's Sin also inherits the biform femininity of Hamartia, the personification of sin born of Eve and "the firie Dragon" who, at the apocalyptic conclusion of *The Purple Island,* recalls the emetic response of Spenserian Error when he vomits his daughter and her hideous siblings (12.27–28). Based upon the Book of Revelation (16.3), Error's spewing of religious propaganda affords the model: "Her vomit full of bookes and papers was, / With loathly frogs and toades, which eyes did lacke" (*FQ* 1.1.20). The Geneva Bible gloss associates those apocalyptic beasts with Rome as Babylon, but the monster's spewing forth of controversial tracts is a witty invention. Attachment of the epithet "blacke as ink" to Error's brood has been taken as a stab against the black-habited Jesuits.

Milton's profound emphasis upon organic function, notably alimentary and sexual aggression, constitutes a legacy from generations of Protestant polemics and the Spenserian tradition of anti-Catholic satire. It pervades Satan's encounter, at the gates of hell, with the daughter whom he fails to recognize after her metamorphosis into one who

> seemed woman to the waist, and fair,
> But ended foul in many a scaly fold
> Voluminous and vast, a serpent armed
> With mortal sting; about her middle round
> A cry of hell hounds never ceasing barked
> With wide Cerberian mouths full loud, and rung
> A hideous peal: yet, when they list, would creep,

If aught disturbed their noise, into her *womb,*
And *kennel* there, yet there still barked and howled,
Within unseen.
(2.650–59; emphasis supplied)

Sin's hideous fecundity recalls not only Spenserian Error, but Milton's own attack in *Of Reformation* against Rome as the "*womb* and center of apostasy." That antiprelatical tract anticipates the canine aspect of the offspring of Sin and Death in its attack against English bishops, whose failures mean "we shall see Antichrist shortly wallow here, though his chief *kennel* be at Rome" (*CPW* 1: 547, 590). Milton uses the word *kennel* nowhere else in his entire oeuvre.

In Spenserian satire, the central trope of false feeding involves not mother's milk, but the body and blood upon which the hell-dogs feast in a travesty of transubstantiation and the Mass akin to the fate of Spenserian Error and Phineas Fletcher's affiliated attack against "Masse-Priests, Priests-Cannibal, / Who make their Maker, chew, grinde, feede, grow fat / With flesh divine" (*Apoll.* 1.1). Equating transubstantiation with cannibalistic gorging upon flesh and blood, Spenser's anti-Mass parody is a pre-text for Milton's representation of Sin. The retreat of her brood of hell-hounds within the womb where they "gnaw" upon their mother's "bowels" (2.798–800) recalls the feeding of Error's younglings upon their "dying mother's blood" (1.1.25). First Corinthians 15 underlies Death's unrestrained feeding as the archetypal predator delegated by his unholy grandfather to gorge upon living beings in the created world: "there ye shall be fed and filled / Immeasurably, all things shall be your prey" (2.843–44).

The monstrous femininity of Spenserian Error and Miltonic Sin may stem from a gynophobic aspect of patriarchal Protestantism,[8] in both its orthodox and heterodox manifestations, but it also slanders the Church of Rome as an unholy mother and Catholic devotion to the Blessed Virgin as an intercessor between the human and divine orders. As such, the episode recalls the fulsome sexuality of Duessa as a latter-day Whore of Babylon. In addition to the much-observed parody of the Trinity when Satan reunites with his offspring, the conception of Sin and her rape by both Satan and Death travesty both the Immaculate Conception of the Blessed Virgin Mary and the Virgin Birth of Christ Jesus. Sin's status as a perverse Mary, who receives praise in Roman Catholic tradition both as Christ's virgin mother and his queenly wife in heaven, inverts the Mariological formula of *Regina Coeli.* According to a variation of that scheme, Sin's *maculate* conception and Minerva-like birth through the sole agency of a male parodies the advent of Eve through the withdrawal of Adam's rib. Those parodic twists are disrespectful neither to the Father, Son, Eve, nor Mary per se. Indeed, the Protestant belief that Christ's mother deserves honor not as a miracle-working mediator, but because of the role that she plays in scriptural history, pervades Milton's construction of her role in *Paradise Regained.*

Puns and iconographical details associated with Sin and Death ridicule the papal claim to primacy over the church. Sin's bearing of the "fatal key" as "portress of hell gate" (2.725, 746) mocks the papal claim to apostolic succession from St. Peter as the first Bishop of Rome. Hers is the "key of the bottomless pit" conferred upon a fallen angel, most likely Satan, in Revelation 9.1. The Geneva gloss notes: "This authority chiefly is committed to the Pope in sign whereof he beareth the keys in his arms." The scene recalls the antipapal overtones of Spenser's attribution of rusted keys to Ignaro as a personification of spiritual ignorance (*FQ* 1.8.30). The rocky nature of Sin's "adamantine gates" hints further at an inversion of Jesus's charge to Peter—"Upon this rock I will build my church: and the gates of hell shall not overcome it" (Matt. 16.18)—not as the basis for apostolic succession, but rather as wordplay upon the literal meaning of Peter's name in both Koine Greek and Latin. The Geneva gloss interprets the "true" rock as faith. Milton's sardonic parody therefore directs blame not against Peter per se, but against the alleged episcopal perversion of his role in the primitive church.

"False wit," indeed, Joseph Addison would say, but Milton conforms not to neoclassical decorum, but to older paradigms for satirical wit (*The Spectator*). Similarly raffish humor suffuses the antipapal innuendoes attached to Death's employment of his "mace petrific" to solidify the inchoate matter of Chaos into a rocky bridge "by wondrous art / Pontifical" (*PL* 10.312–13). The spanning of Chaos with that "bridge / Of length prodigious" (2.301–02) provides a further overlay upon the punning attack against the claim of Roman pontiffs to *Petrine* supremacy.[9] The scene punningly inverts the Spenserian identification of petrification with divine grace as it is manifestated in the form of Arthur's wondrous shield: "Men into stones therewith he could transmew" (*FQ* 1.7.35).[10]

Reminding the reader of the fecundity of both Error and Sin, the womblike construction of Chaos further suggests that demonic insemination parodies inspiration by the androgynous Holy Spirit that bridges it, according to the opening invocation of *Paradise Lost,* "with mighty wings outspread / Dove-like sat'st brooding on the vast abyss / And madest it pregnant" (1.20–22). The "rock" upon which Jesus ordered Peter to erect the church is the spiritual antithesis of both the "massy iron or solid rock" of hell gate (2.878) and the "ridge of pendent rock" out of which Sin and Death build their bridge (10.313). Its "pontifical" aspect entails a ludicrous parody of the papal epithet of *Pontifex Maximus* ("supreme bridge-maker," a title once held by the chief priest of pre-Christian Rome). Reference to Death's "new wondrous pontifice" sustains the wordplay as the punning ramifies into a quibble upon Death's phallic dart. Sin's account of the birth of a well-armed son who immediately rapes his mother outrageously fuses an allusion to 1 Corinthians 15.55 with the seventeenth-century poetic sense of "death" as orgasm: "but he my inbred enemy / Forth issued, brandishing his fatal dart / Made to destroy: I fled and cried out Death" (2.785–87). I suggest, yet again, that the tableau recalls the disorderly behavior of Error's spawn.[11]

According to Archangel Michael's prophetic account of future history, the proliferation of Sin's offspring, human inheritors of the original sin of Adam and Eve, will be stamped with the disorderly sexuality of their ancestors. Indeed, the first consequence of the Fall is the discovery of crude sex by Adam and Eve, for the first time inflamed with "carnal desire" (9.1013). The spontaneity of lust recalls the coupling of Satan, Sin, and Death, and the proclivities of Error and Duessa. Discord, the "first / Daughter of Sin" (10.707–08), personifies the conflicted nature of the postlapsarian relationship of Eve and Adam, the latter of whom believes that their sexuality is infected with the consequences of original sin and with death:

> All that I eat or drink, or shall beget,
> Is propagated curse. O voice once heard
> Delightfully, *Increase and multiply,*
> Now death to hear!
> (10.728–31)

The satirical point is palpable. At the level of religio-political topicality, Sin and Death are the progenitors of generations of Roman pontiffs, English prelates, and other churchmen, whose sinister construction of the "false" church commits a metaphorical rape upon humanity that results in death, not birth, as reprobate souls hasten toward hell during history past, present, and future. The rape conceit had been conventional in antiprelatical tracts that attacked Archbishop Laud and the Caroline Church of England for ravishing England. In *Canterbury's Pilgrimage: Or the Testimony of an Accused Conscience for the Blood of Mr. Burton, Mr. Prynne, and Doctor Bastwick, and the Just Deserved Sufferings He Lies Under: Showing the Glory of Reformation, above Prelatical Tyranny* (1641), for example, Laud is "the Ork of Canterbury, that great monster, [who kept away] the Church of England from Christ her spouse, and . . . polluted her with popery" (A3ᵛ). According to *The Times Dissected, Or a Learned Discourse of Several Occurences Very Worthy of Special Observation, to Deter Evil Men, and Encourage Good* (1641), Laud introduced "innovations into the Church, making her of a pure virgin a very strumpet."[12]

The episode involving Sin and Death in *Paradise Lost* alludes to Spenser's construction of Error and Duessa as travesties of the Church of Rome. The grotesque sexuality of those monstrous females aligns them with Protestant satire against transubstantiation and the Mass as poisonous maternal feeders. Milton's engagement with Spenserian subtexts infuses religio-political satire into his allegorization of a text from the Epistle of James: "Then when lust hath conceived, it bringeth forth sin, and sin when it is finished, bringeth forth death"(1:15). At its most topical level, the Miltonic episode may represent the crypto-Catholicism of Charles II and the advent of the Restoration as a "pontifical" bridge that enables the importation into England of alleged ecclesiastical corruption. The promiscuous incest of the Satanic family may afford a sardonic parody of the king's notoriously profligate generation of bastard offspring. Satan's conception of Sin and their joint conception of Death is a fit complement to mockery of the Restoration as a new Gunpowder Plot aimed not *against* a Stuart monarch, but *by* a Stuart monarch against low- and high-church Protestants in England.[13] As such, the episode recalls genealogies of papal and Jesuit evil that infiltrate "The Legend of Holiness" and a variety of Spenserian satires that it gave rise to, notably Phineas Fletcher's *The Locusts, or Apollyonists.*

NOTES

I am grateful to Stephen R. Honeygosky, John G. Norman, and John T. Shawcross for comments on an earlier version of this essay. Grants from the Department of English, Center for Medieval and Renaissance Studies, and College of Humanities at Ohio State University supported the research upon which it is based.

1. See Bloom 125–43. Quotations from *The Faerie Queene* and *Paradise Lost* (hereafter cited as *FQ* and *PL*) are from Spenser, *The Faerie Queene*, ed. Hamilton; and Milton, *The Poems of John Milton*, ed. Carey and Fowler. Texts are modernized with the exception of quotations from Spenser and Phineas Fletcher.

2. In *Of True Religion*, Milton attacks "the Romish Church [as] Mother of Error." See *Complete Prose Works of John Milton* 8: 419–21; hereafter cited as *CPW.*

3. See Waters 1–20, passim; King, *English Reformation Literature* 61–64, and *Spenser's Poetry* 82–97.

4. Quotation taken from *Ovid's Metamorphoses Englished, Mythologized, and Represented in Figures,* trans. Sandys 14.50–74 [456–57]. On Echidna, see Hesiod, *Theogony* 295–305.

5. *Inferno* 6.13–33; n. on *PL* 2.659–61, in *Poems,* ed. Carey and Fowler.

6. The name derives from the priestly salutation at the end of the Mass, "ite, missa est" 'go, you are released.' See King, *English Reformation Literature* 265–66, 289; and Cable 43–44.

7. Quoted from Hunter; hereafter cited as *Apoll.*

8. On Sin's wombless birth, see Kerrigan, *The Sacred Complex* 184–87.

9. On Milton's bawdy wit, see Le Comte and Shawcross; and Rumrich.

10. See Gless 132.

11. For a comparable linkage between phallic quibbling and ecclesiastical allegory during the encounter among the Redcrosse Knight, Duessa, and Orgoglio (*FQ* 1.7.6–12), see Shroeder.

12. I am indebted to Deborah G. Burks for these examples.

13. See Quint, *Epic and Empire* 271, 278.

"AND YET THE END WAS NOT"

Apocalyptic Deferral and Spenser's Literary Afterlife

John Watkins

Throughout his career, Spenser fashioned himself as the Elizabethan laureate par excellence, a second Virgil destined to immortalize his queen as a latter-day Augustus. But as Spenserians have long acknowledged, he approached his laureate task with considerable ambivalence.[1] Whereas other scholars have attributed an anti-Elizabethan undercurrent in his verse to his disagreement with royal policies, I want to explore it as a manifestation of a conflict between his classicism and the apocalypticism he espouses as a writer in the Protestant, Foxean tradition.[2] Unlike Virgil, Spenser did not claim that the Tudor regime or any other human political order could endure forever. As an Elizabethan writing in the Virgilian tradition, he might uphold the *Pax Elizabetha* as the culmination of history, but as a Christian, he could honor it only as a shadow of a millennial kingdom. Historically, millenarianism had worked most effectively as an oppositional political discourse with which to threaten a dominant regime with its ultimate dissolution (McGinn; Firth). Like the apologists for Constantine, Frederick II, and other Christian rulers, Spenser only partially transformed it into a discourse that legitimated rather than subverted imperial authority.

Torn between the conflicting roles of laureate and millenarian prophet, Spenser changed the character of poetic influence within the English tradition. By incorporating multiple models of poetic and political authority in a single vision, he escaped an exclusive identification with one particular regime and became available as an influence on later writers espousing divergent ideological agendas. Within the first century after his death, for instance, his poetry inspired both royalists and parliamentarians, Whigs and Tories, who heard in it voices supporting their opposing causes.

David Norbrook (*Poetry and Politics* 195–214) and Richard Helgerson (*Forms of Nationhood* 21–62) have hailed Spenser as the model that later poets like Drayton, Wither, and Milton followed in their varying degrees of resistance to Elizabeth's Stuart successors. But Spenser also inspired the Stuarts' most ardent admirers. In 1648, a royalist publisher reprinted Artegall's encounter with the Giant (*The Faerie Queene* 5.2) under the title *The Faerie Leveller*. According to the preface, the episode represents under allegorical cover "the dangerous doings of these pernitious Sectaries, the confounders of orders, the movers of Sedition, the disturbers of Peace, the subverters of well-settled States . . . lately risen up and now raigneing amongst us, by the name of Levellers; and they were discryed long agoe in Queene Elizabeths dayes, and then graphically described by the Prince of English Poets whose verses then propheticall are now become historicall in our days" (*Faerie Leveller* A2ʳ). Honoring Spenser as the "*Prince* of English Poets," the preface links his allegorical vision inseparably to royalism. His "propheticall" verses provide a key to understanding the civil wars, with King Charles cast as "Arthegall the Prince of justice," the kings' forces as Talus, and "Col. Oliver Cromwell" as the "Gyant Leveller" (*Faerie Leveller* A2ᵛ). For the royalist pamphleteer, Spenserian prophecy provided a powerful antidote to a competing prophetic vision offered by the sectaries themselves, one that transferred sovereignty from the crown to God's Englishmen in anticipation of the millennial kingdom.

I want to examine an aspect of *The Faerie Queene*'s poetic structure that allowed its moral, political, and aesthetic conflicts to be projected onto future English writing: its cultivation of a forestalled apocalypse.[3] Like other apocalyptic writers, Spenser both envisions and defers an imminent exaltation of time into eternity. The moment Redcrosse's victory over the Dragon seems to usher in the church's apocalyptic marriage to the Lamb, the marriage rites turn out to be just a betrothal. Duessa's reappearance indicts a yet unreformed ecclesiastical order, and Redcrosse leaves Una "to mourne" his further service in Gloriana's wars (*FQ* 1.12.41). Just when Spenser approaches a language of temporal and spatial transcendence in describing the Gardens of Adonis, Time appears to forestall apocalypse. Sir Calidore interrupts the circling dance of the graces with its iconographic gestures toward eternity. Nature checks Mutabilitie's ambitions but leaves her sublunary authority intact until an apocalyptic sabbath. Spenser repeatedly brings his characters and readers to the threshold of eternity only to reassert their continued existence in time. Like Redcrosse on the Mount of Contemplation, readers of Spenser's apocalyptic fantasy glimpse the New Jerusalem only to be reminded that they cannot enter it.

Spenser's retreat from a final consummation exemplifies what Stephen

O'Leary sees as "the temporal paradox at the heart of apocalyptic discourse," the fact that "the declaration of the End of time is itself constitutive of a community which must then reconceive and redefine its place in universal history in the face of the apparently endless extensions of its earthly existence" (50). Although anticipations of imminent doom can create a community of believers, that community faces an overwhelming practical challenge in trying to preserve its collective identity when the End is not. *The Faerie Queene*'s historical allegory heightens this general paradox by treating the apocalypse as if it has already occurred in the establishment of a Protestant national church. Earlier in the century, writers and preachers like John Bale, the annotators of the Geneva Bible, and John Foxe employed apocalyptic rhetoric to consolidate their sense of themselves as a persecuted elect struggling against the papal Antichrist (Firth 32–110). But by the 1590s, over three decades of established Protestantism had transformed the significance of the apocalyptic equation of the Pope with Antichrist and the Roman church with the Whore of Babylon. The Reformation had taken place without ushering in the Second Coming, and an entire generation had grown up under a Protestant sovereign. Steeped in Foxe's *Book of Martyrs* and their parents' firsthand accounts of the Marian persecutions, these second-generation Protestants may have been as hostile to Catholicism as their parents. But for the most part, they did not share the earlier Protestants' longing for liberation from a tyrannical regime associated with Rome. Bernard Capp has noted, for example, that "the eschatological preoccupations of Jewel, the first major champion of Anglicanism, are conspicuously absent from the works of the second, Richard Hooker, a generation later" ("Millennium and Eschatology" 159). Apocalypticism, with its legacy of opposition to earthly authority, retained its original antiestablishment fervor principally among some sectarians. They argued that the English church still suffered under a Babylonian yoke because it was governed by bishops and retained dozens of popish liturgical practices (Capp, "Political Dimension" 95–101).

As a Protestant sovereign, Elizabeth posed for her Protestant apologists a problem like the one that Constantine posed for his Christian subjects after his conversion: once the *imperium* could no longer be identified with Antichrist, what role did it play in the eschatological narrative that had given a formerly oppressed population a communal identity? The moment Elizabeth ascended the throne, poets, preachers, dramatists, and artists transformed apocalypticism into a discourse that validated rather than opposed existing political structures (Helgerson, *Forms of Nationhood* 254–68). Byzantine Christians like Pseudo-Methodius had made a place for the good monarch in the apocalyptic tradition by introducing the figure of the

Last Emperor, a Christian king of the Greeks and Romans destined to defeat the Moslems and to inaugurate a reign of peace heralding Christ's imminent return (Cohn 31–32). As Bernard McGinn has argued, other European nations adopted the topos of the Last Emperor to give their ruling houses a sacred, eschatological aura (70–93). John Foxe used it when he concluded his *Book of Martyrs* with a description of Elizabeth's godly magistracy modeled in part on his earlier tributes to Constantine. According to Foxe, God appointed Elizabeth not only as the "amends and recompense, now to be made to England for the cruel days that were before" but also as a divine agent who "helpeth neighbours, reformeth religion, quencheth persecution, redresseth the dross, frameth things out of joint" (8: 600–01).

Whereas Foxe attributed an apocalyptic agency to Elizabeth during her reign's opening decades, Spenser attempted to do so at its close.[4] The Armada year marked the high point of her identification as a champion of the True Church against Antichrist (Bauckham 173–80; Capp, "Political Dimension" 97). But that validation of her apocalyptic role took place thirty years after her accession. By 1590, her advancing years resisted the most ingenious efforts to describe her reign as the culmination of British history. In *The Faerie Queene*, Spenser tried to reframe the apocalyptic scenario in the face of an inevitable forward movement in time. Britomart's visit to Merlin's cave exemplifies the difficulties Spenser and other writers found in reconciling their apocalyptic portrayal of Elizabeth with the embarrassment of temporal continuity. When Merlin reveals his prophecy of triumphs and disasters awaiting Britomart's descendants, his catalogue threatens to degenerate into a directionless chronology. But when he hails the Tudor dynasty as a restoration of the crown to its rightful British owners, he transforms the record of apparently random power struggles into a coherent narrative of fall and regeneration:

> Thenceforth eternall union shall be made
>   Betweene the nations different afore,
>   And sacred Peace shall louingly perswade
>   The warlike minds, to learne her goodly lore,
>   And ciuile armes to exercise no more:
>   Then shall a royall virgin raine, which shall
>   Stretch her white rod ouer the *Belgicke* shore,
>   And the Castle smite so sore with all,
> That it shall make him shake, and shortly learne to fall.
> (3.3.49)

Just as Christian eschatologies use the Parousia to shape the randomness of history, the unions between England and Wales, York and Lancaster, establish the significance for the Britons' previous sufferings as a prelude to a final triumph. Spenser depicts Elizabeth in unmistakably millenarian terms. "Sacred Peace" heralds her long-awaited appearance, and she transforms the Last Emperor's victory over the enemies of Christendom into a specifically Protestant triumph over Habsburg Catholicism.

But the moment Spenser reaches this millenarian culmination, he readmits the history that apocalypticism strives to resist. In medieval eschatologies, the Last Emperor's victory signals Christ's return and the end of time itself. In modifying this scenario, Spenser differentiates his figurative apocalypse from its earlier Christian prototype:

> "But yet the end is not." Then *Merlin* stayd,
>   As ouercomen of the spirites powre,
>   Or other ghastly spectacle dismayd,
>   That secretly he saw, yet not discoure.
> (3.3.50)

Although Merlin's fit conceals what will happen after Elizabeth's reign, his insistence that "yet the end is not" suggests that history has not reached its culmination.[5] Elizabeth is not the Last Emperor, and the Sacred Peace that she establishes merely prefigures rather than initiates the millennium. The final "end," marking the end of time itself, belongs to the future. Spenser's refusal to specify whether Merlin's "suddein fit, and halfe extatick stoure" (3.3.51) manifest prophetic exhaustion or dismay before some "ghastly spectacle" about to befall Britain readmits the possibility of national tragedy.

Several political considerations overdetermine this retreat from millenarian confidence. Specific questions about the royal succession exacerbated Spenser's more general predicament as an apocalyptic poet confronting the apparent endlessness of time. By 1590, Elizabeth was clearly going to die without a biological heir. Her crown was likely to pass into the hands of James VI of Scotland, the son of the same Catholic queen whose plots against Elizabeth contributed to Spenser's characterization of Duessa. No one could guarantee if a Stuart king would preserve the Tudor status quo in religion, diplomacy, or constitutional principle. By suggesting that Elizabeth, unlike the Last Emperor, will not be privileged to rule until the Parousia, Spenser may also vent some dissatisfaction with her policies. His earlier poetry had already situated him left of the ecclesiastical center, and he may have shared with other millenarian Protestants misgivings about the pace of the English Reformation. Laureate aspiration conflicted with prophetic vocation. As a self-proclaimed laureate, Spenser idealized

Elizabeth's achievements, but as a prophet, he examined them more critically from the transcendent perspectives of scripture and eternity.[6]

Anxieties about poetic authority intersect with these political and religious reservations. Here and throughout the poem, Spenser's apocalypticism rests uneasily beside his avowed ambition to write an English epic that would rival its classical and continental precursors. Poets in the Virgilian tradition fetishize their own artistry in ways that are incompatible with millenarian prophecy. The imminent collapse of time into eternity, which would confirm the prophet's visions, would render meaningless the laureate's celebration of a particular temporal order. Spenser needs to convince his patrons and readers that future generations will admire his work and the culture that produced it. He is committed far less to preparing his audience for the end of the world than to producing what they will honor as an enduring literary monument. He draws back from apocalypse in part because his poetic achievement depends on the projected judgment of future readers.

But if apocalypse threatened Spenser's future fame, so did time itself. As the laureate who helped create Elizabeth's mythic identity, he risked binding his poetry's future canonization to her posthumous reputation. If her successor discredited her policies by adopting a more conciliatory stance toward Spain and the Catholic continent, *The Faerie Queene* could lose its bid to become the consummate British epic and appear instead as a monument to a defeated religious and diplomatic vision. What finally saved it from becoming a mere period piece was its unstable juxtaposition of laureate and prophetic discourses. The critiques of the queen that provided a countertext to the poem's most extravagant compliments distanced it from Elizabeth just enough to secure its place in a post-Elizabethan future. Spenser's poetry could survive even if its laureate politics became dated. As its later reception proved, it could even inspire writers like Milton who believed that prophecy, like sovereignty itself, was invested in the English people.

Written at the close of the Tudor century, Spenser's poetry looks back to an earlier Protestant vision in which the monarch redeemed the English people from their Babylonian captivity and brought them closer to the New Jerusalem. But precisely because its faith in the godliness of monarchy is not complete, the poetry looks forward to an alternative political vision in which the English people themselves rather than their monarch become the agents of apocalypse. The constitutional, social, and religious conflicts that ultimately led to civil war provided divergent contexts for reading, interpreting, echoing, and imitating works like *The Shepheardes Calender* and *The Faerie Queene*. In the remainder of this essay, I want to explore how three competing responses to the Spenserian conflict between laureate and prophetic vocations shaped early-seventeenth-century literary history. In their responses to Spenser, the memorialists who first commemorated Elizabeth's death, the citizen-dramatist Thomas Dekker, and John Milton, the laureate of an imaginary free commonwealth, all grappled with the Spenserian predicament of the forestalled apocalypse.

James's accession immediately challenged one of the hallmarks of Elizabethan apocalyptic argument: the representation of sectarian conflict as an irreconcilable struggle between good and evil (Capp, "Political Dimension" 102–04). Some Englishmen questioned his right to the English throne solely because his mother was the woman popularly demonized as the Whore of Babylon (Willson 138–39; *Calendar* 9: 540). Rumors about his overtures to Catholics like Northampton and Northumberland alarmed an even larger section of the population into thinking that he might harbor secret sympathies for Mary's religion. James aggravated these anxieties further by making peace with Spain and by refusing to support Protestants in the Thirty Years' War. So much Elizabethan propaganda had characterized the Habsburgs as agents of Antichrist that his conciliatory gestures struck many as a violation of England's divine mission to lead a universal reformation of the church (Willson 148–49, 408–16).

Although Elizabeth herself tried everything in her power to prevent a war with Spain, Spenser and numerous other apocalyptic writers celebrated her so effectively as a champion of true religion against the servants of Babylon that their successors used this bellicose image of Elizabeth to challenge James's determination to keep England out of war. Apocalypticism, with its vision of a triumphant future, yielded to nostalgia for an imagined past in which time seemed once to have hovered on the brink of eternity.[7] From the moment James ascended the English throne, commemorations of Elizabeth veiled suspicions that he might be less disposed to carry on the war against Antichrist. In 1603, Spenser's septuagenerian schoolteacher Richard Mulcaster published a parallel Latin and English tribute to Elizabeth that celebrated her reformation of the church, her intervention in the United Provinces, her defense of England itself "with armed hand," and her escapes from Catholic assassins (A3). Mulcaster's conclusion honors James as her rightful successor, but uncertainty about the future hovers just below the celebratory surface:

> Now my liege Lord, successour to my Queene . . .
> Thou seest a mightie patterne in thine eie
> As to match her tis much, to passe her more.

Wherefore thy charge is doubled in our eyes,
Which are in hope that thou wilt follow her steps
And rule as she did raigne with equall praise . . .
And as she did auoid the Iesuites treacherous traines,
Whereby she gat her graue in drie and quiet death,
So good King *Iames* goe late to God and slip their snares,
For if thou stick'st to God, they'l not sticke to sticke thee.
(B2)

Mulcaster hedges everything he says about James with contingency. Since surpassing Elizabeth's example would be a virtual impossibility, Mulcaster *hopes* that James might at least follow it. God has given him a "triple British Crown" as king of England, Ireland, and Scotland with which to oppose "the Romish bane," but Mulcaster is conspicuously uncertain whether he will carry out his apocalyptic vocation. Almost paradoxically, Mulcaster will take comfort in future Jesuit plots as a sign that Elizabeth lives again in her successor's opposition to Rome. If James remains faithful to the Protestant God, the Jesuits will conspire against him. But God will allow him to "slip their snares" as effectively as Elizabeth had.

For poets with Mulcaster's political and religious convictions, writing in a flagrantly Spenserian style offered one way of perpetuating the Elizabethan struggle against Antichrist. When Elizabeth died, writers heightened the occasion's pathos by noting that the only poet who could ever successfully eulogize her was already dead himself: political nostalgia for Elizabeth became inseparable from an aesthetic nostalgia for Spenser.[8] His legacy as Elizabeth's laureate was so fundamental to William Browne, Christopher Lever, John Lane, and Richard Niccols's conception of the past that they treated his death as a prefiguration of the Queen's. For them, mourning Elizabeth was impossible without simultaneously mourning the poet who had immortalized her as the Faerie Queene.

Richard Niccols, a veteran of the Spanish conflict who served under the Earl of Nottingham at Cadiz, typifies the writers whose nostalgia for Elizabeth's seeming commitment to international Protestantism joined with nostalgia for Spenser's reign as the Prince of Protestant poets (*DNB*, "Niccols"). When Niccols added an account of *England's Eliza, or The Victorious and Triumphant Reigne of Elizabeth* to the 1610 edition of *The Mirrour for Magistrates,* he deferred to Spenser as the one poet who would have been equal to the task of commemorating her career:

O did that Fairie Queenes sweet singer liue,
That to the dead eternitie could giue,

Or if, that heauen by influence would infuse
His heauenlie spirit on mine earth-borne Muse,
Her name ere this a mirror should haue been
Lim'd out in golden verse to th'eyes of men:
But my sad Muse, though willing; yet too weak
In her rude rymes *Elizaes* worth to speak,
Must yeeld to those, whose Muse can mount on high,
And with braue plumes can clime the loftie skie.
(824–33)

Haunted by the proems to books 1 and 3 of *The Faerie Queene*, Niccols recalls Spenser's opening use of the modesty topos only to reverse its progression from diffidence to confidence. Like Spenser, Niccols foregrounds the discrepancy between his humble powers and the epic enterprise he undertakes. But after acknowledging the unfitness of his "enforst" task, Spenser yields to an unrivalled "Sacred Muse" who authorizes him to "blazon forth" his song (*FQ* 1 proem 1). Niccols, in contrast, finds his labors supported only by his own "sad Muse," a pathetically private and self-effacing entity who yields to other, better Muses. Whereas Spenser's opening stanzas challenge poetic precedent in their conspicuous departures from Virgil and Ariosto, Niccols aspires to resurrect his precursor or to be so infused with "his heauenlie spirit" that he would become nothing less, but also nothing more, than a second Spenser.

Niccols's advertised fidelity to Spenser should not be read as a failure to cultivate originality. Aesthetic originality was not his goal. By "resurrecting" Spenser in poetry conspicuously modelled on *The Shepheardes Calender* and *The Faerie Queene*, Niccols tried to preserve an imagined Elizabethan consensus against both political and aesthetic innovation. His idealization ignored Spenser's conflicted representation of Elizabeth and upheld him as an unwavering proponent of her policies. As Niccols recalled her reign, there was no room for conflict: all England united behind its queen against the papal Antichrist. By denying the debates over diplomacy and ecclesiastical polity that often complicated Spenser's own representations of the queen, Niccols excluded the dissatisfactions with the temporal order that motivated Spenser's longing for eternity. He differs most from Spenser in abandoning apocalypticism. Niccols's dissatisfaction with the present manifests itself in his nostalgia for the past rather than in expectations of future transcendence.

Poets like Niccols often work with *The Shepheardes Calender* rather than with *The Faerie Queene*, as if they were more comfortable relating themselves to the novice than to the mature poet. Unlike *The Faerie Queene*, which often glances toward a future apocalypse, the *Calender* anticipates the seventeenth-century Spenserians' own nostalgia for a lost golden age. Nothing could be more appropriate to their predicament than the *October* eclogue, with its anxieties about inadequacy before the great poetry of the past. When Spenser's Cuddie broached the possibility that the Virgilian moment was past and that great poetry could no longer be written, other voices refuted him. But when the seventeenth-century Spenserians revive the question by substituting Elizabeth for Augustus and Spenser for Virgil, nothing challenges their pessimism. Their own incapacity to rival him is a memorial to him and to his age.

No poet more exemplifies the Spenserians' fixation on the Elizabethan past than John Lane, a close friend of Milton's father. Although he lived into the middle of the century, Edward Phillips described him in his 1675 *Theatrum Poetarum* as "a fine old Elizabeth gentleman." By insisting that if more of Lane's works had been published, they "might possibly have gained him a name not much inferior if not equal to Drayton and others of the next rank to Spenser," Phillips confirms Lane's cultivated second- or third-ratedness (*DNB*, "Lane"). Lane's work repeatedly advertises its derivation from a Spenserian original. He devoted much of his career to an eight-canto completion of *The Squire's Tale* that was indebted to *The Faerie Queene*, book 4, in concept and execution. Similarly, his poem "Tritons Trumpet to the sweet monthes" imitates the procession of the Seven Deadly Sins from book 1 of *The Faerie Queene*." His 1603 "Elegie vpon the death of the high renowned Princesse our late Soueraigne Elizabeth" typifies the Spenserians' obsession with *The Shepheardes Calender*. Like Niccols, Lane echoes *The Faerie Queene*'s modesty topos to admit that he cannot follow Spenser into the higher regions of epic:

> I graunt at first I should but lowly maske,
> And not begin with such a loftie taske,
> But warble softly on a Shepheardes reede,
> The while my bleating flockes securely feede.

Lane's elegy turns out to be a recasting of the *Aprill* eclogue with "Beta" in place of the original "Elisa." Whereas Spenser had taken the first half of Elizabeth's name for his shepherd-queen Elisa, Lane chooses the second half in a gesture of conspicuous derivation and belatedness. Following Spenser, he calls on the "Shepheards daughters" and "Virgins chast" to join his song. Whereas Spenser asked his auditors to bind up their hair and crown Elisa with floral wreathes, Lane asks his to "rend [their] yellow heares" and to "embraue" Beta's "corse with flowres." Early in the elegy, he reveals the extent of his poetic ambition by urging his audience to mourn Elizabeth by rehearsing "the songs of *Colin Clout.*" Instead of inventing an original language suited to a new regime, he aspires to preserve the Elizabethan age by repeating Spenser's words.

For a time, the 1605 Gunpowder Plot stirred hopes that James might finally resume the Elizabethan war against Antichrist. Thomas Dekker voiced these hopes in his 1607 apocalyptic fantasy, *The Whore of Babylon,* a tribute to Elizabeth's triumph over the Armada that draws implicit parallels with James's more recent triumph over the Gunpowder conspirators. Although Dekker's nostalgia for Elizabeth links him to poets like Mulcaster, Niccols, and Lane, his belief that her example might spur her successors on to even greater accomplishments allowed him to write more in the heroic mode of *The Faerie Queene* than in the elegiac mode of *The Shepheardes Calender.* Dekker evokes the past primarily as an inspiration for the future. Opening with the funeral of Mary I and the accession of Elizabeth, his play recounts the major plots against Elizabeth's life and concludes with reenactments of the Armada and Elizabeth's Tilbury speech. Like Spenser in "The Legend of Holinesse," Dekker weaves the details of Elizabeth's struggles into an overarching confrontation between the fairy queen—here named Titania—and the Empress of Babylon.

Dekker advertises his Spenserian inheritance by naming several of Titania's courtiers after characters from *The Faerie Queene.*[9] The treacherous Paridell provides a mask for Dr. William Parry, who plotted against Elizabeth despite her earlier kindness toward him. Truth, who appears as a personified abstraction with her father Time and her close associate Plain Dealing, resembles Una as the victim of the Empress's calumnies. One of the Spenserian names has always struck critics as mis-assigned: the Earl of Leicester appears as Florimell. But the apparent gender confusion points to a crucial aspect of Dekker's Spenserian inheritance: the concern with false appearance that figures in the confusions caused by the False Florimell. In Dekker's play, Florimell is a loyal subject who makes the mistake of trusting the recusant Campanus and introducing him to Titania's court. He may not seem much like Spenser's Florimell, but he has much in common with her suitors who repeatedly fail to discern the difference between authentic virtue and mere appearance.

As the play unfolds, Dekker follows Spenser in incorporating the theme of double, antithetical identity into an apocalyptic vision of England's destiny. As in *The Faerie Queene,* England stands both as a Protestant champion against the Antichrist and as a corrupt society awaiting a more complete Reformation. Just when Titania rallies the troops to fight the

Armada, for instance, Plain Dealing complains at length about corruptions of the brokers, victuallers, and other professionals who attend the army. Like Spenser, Dekker never lets us forget that a gap exists between actual historical circumstances and his idealized representations of them. The Elizabethan past that he nostalgizes is just as imaginary as the Elizabethan present that Spenser projected, and both poets idealize Elizabeth's apocalyptic agency along the same lines. Dekker follows Spenser, for instance, in exaggerating Elizabeth's support for English intervention in the Netherlands. As an implicit celebration of the foiled Gunpowder Plot, his play similarly exaggerates the extent to which James was prepared to take on Elizabeth's mantle of opposition to the Catholic world.

For both writers, the monarch's failure to obliterate his or her enemies entirely indicates that the ultimate apocalyptic labor lies in the future. Spenser draws closest to Dekker in a perpetually deferred representation of apocalypse that attempts to bridge the gulf between England as it currently exists and England idealized as Faeryland. After the Tilbury festivities, Time reminds the company that the minutes of the Whore's "majestic madness with her sons / . . . are not yet run through Time's hand" (5.6.85, 87). A baby born at Tilbury and cradled in "the hollow back-piece of a rusty armor" is destined to service in a future, post-Elizabethan struggle against the assembled forces of Babylon (5.6.42). In a classic gesture of apocalyptic deferral, Dekker transfers Elizabeth's antagonism against the Whore of Babylon to her successor James I. A Babylonian cardinal prophesies that even Titania's death will not ensure a final Catholic victory, since her heir may prove to be an even more powerful antagonist:

> . . . out of her ashes may
> A second Phoenix rise, of larger wing,
> Of stronger talon, of more dreadful beak
> . . . and perhaps his talon
> May be so bony and so large of grip
> That it may shake all Babylon.
> (3.1.251–52, 260–62)

Dekker's manipulation of the apocalyptic timetable is even more complex than this passage might first suggest. Since *The Whore of Babylon* establishes a running parallel between the plots against Elizabeth and the Gunpowder Plot against James, the Second Phoenix's anticipated triumph commemorates James's victory over the 1605 conspirators. But if the play, entered in the Stationers' Register in 1607, recalls an event that had already happened in the past, it anticipates an even more complete destruction of

England's enemies in the indefinite future. While honoring James as the hero who triumphed over the Gunpowder conspirators, Dekker suggests that further challenges await him or his successor.[10] In exaggerating the militancy of James's anti-Catholicism, Dekker, like Spenser before him, vents his desire for a more aggressive, interventionalist foreign policy. In the future that he would like to see, James—or possibly his son Prince Henry— will emerge as the leader of a pan-European Protestant union against the Habsburgs and other Catholic powers.

Whatever doubts Dekker had about the likelihood of James's emerging as Last Emperor, he still worked within a monarchical eschatology. Yet as the years passed, writers inspired by Spenser returned to a pre-Constantinian vision of the future in which God opposes human kingship. Multiple political, social, and religious developments contributed to this eschatological shift. Prince Henry died before he could become the liberator of Protestant Europe, and Charles I outraged left-leaning Protestants and centrists alike by marrying a Catholic queen and by encouraging Arminian beliefs and Laudian ritual (Norbrook, "Milton's Early Poetry"). No Stuart king seemed likely to carry the gospel to all nations and then deliver his crown to Christ at the Second Coming. When Milton initiated his career as a poet in the Spenserian tradition, his greatest temptation was an even deeper retreat into nostalgia for the Elizabethan past. He overcame that temptation through a dramatic reconfiguration of the apocalypse as Spenser and other Elizabethan writers imagined it. Denying apocalyptic agency to any monarch, Milton invested it in the members of his own religious party and social class imagined collectively as God's Englishmen. Beginning with the 1629 "Ode on the Morning of Christ's Nativity," Milton transformed eschatological rhetoric into an argument for revolution and popular sovereignty.[11]

Although scholars often read the "Nativity Ode" as a criticism of classical myth that anticipates what they consider *Paradise Regained*'s more comprehensive repudiation of antiquity, the poem enacts an even more ambivalent critique of Spenser, the Protestant idealization of Elizabeth, and previous projections of apocalypse. The routing of the pagan gods masks Milton's simultaneous routing of mortal rulers endowed by earlier poets with a godlike aura. This departure from Spenserian precedent underlies several peculiarities that distinguish the ode from other treatments of Jesus's birth. Rosamund Tuve, for instance, remarks that Milton focuses more on the paradoxes of the Incarnation than the human drama of the Nativity (37–72). As an intertextual strategy, this incarnational emphasis challenges the hybris of the ruler elevated to deity with the humility of the Christian deity who "[f]orsook the Courts of everlasting Day, / And chose with us a darksome House of mortal Clay" (14–15). Milton's conspicuous inattention to Mary as the vessel of the Incarnation distances him not only from the Catholic cult of the Virgin but more obliquely from the Protestant cult of Elizabeth, the woman to whom Spenser and his heirs attributed Marian honors in endowing her with apocalyptic agency.

Milton mediates his critique of Elizabeth through a revision of the *Aprill* eclogue. John Carey has noted how archaisms like "ykindled" (155) and specific textual echoes of *The Shepheardes Calender* and *The Faerie Queene* give the "Nativity Ode" a Spenserian character.[12] Each stanza's hexameter conclusion reinforces this effect, and the Hymn section derives its canzonic form from *Aprill, Prothalamion,* and *Epithalamion* via Phineas Fletcher's *Elisa.* Like Spenser in *Aprill,* Milton prefaces his canzonic hymn with a pentameter exordium identifying its occasion. Thematic parallels complement these prosodic connections. Both poets celebrate a central, numinous figure who chastens the exuberance of nature and promises a millenarian cessation of warfare. Elisa, attired "like a mayden Queene" in "Ermines white," hails from a "heavenly race" guaranteeing that "no mortall blemish may her blot" (57, 58, 53, 54). In Milton, Jesus's transcendent purity encourages nature

> To hide her guilty front with innocent snow,
> And on her naked shame,
> Pollute with sinful blame
> The saintly veil of maiden white to throw.
> (39–42)

Chloris brings an olive branch to Elisa that symbolizes "peace, when wars doe surcease" (124–25), and the infant Jesus sends "down the meek-eyed Peace, / She crowned with olive green" (45–46) while the sounds of human war fall silent.

But if Milton joins such Spenserian writers as Lane and Niccols in a close textual engagement with *The Shepheardes Calender,* he shares neither their nostalgia for Elizabeth nor their withdrawal from apocalyptic vision. Here as in *Paradise Lost,* he looks forward to a final consummation, one in which "God will be all in all." In a passage that explicitly thematizes rivalry with prior authority, he challenges the *Calender*'s attributions of immortal characteristics to a mortal queen. He bases his personification of the sun's embarrassment before the Son of God on Spenser's description of Phoebus's embarrassment before Elisa:

I sawe *Phoebus* thrust out his golden hedde,
  upon her to gaze:
But when he sawe, how broad her beames did spredde,
  it did him amaze.
He blusht to see another Sunne belowe,
Ne durst again his fyrye face out showe:
  Let him, if he dare,
  His brightnesse compare
With hers, to have the overthrow.
(*Aprill* 73–81)

And though the shady gloom
Had given day her room
  The Sun himself withheld his wonted speed,
And hid his head for shame
As his inferior flame,
  The new-enlight'n'd world no more should need;
He saw a greater Sun appear
Than his bright Throne, or burning Axletree could bear.
("Nativity Ode" 77–84)

The topos of the Sun yielding to a new and higher authority provides Milton an image of the older royalist poetic order, epitomized by Spenser, yielding to a truly reformed poetic that invests apocalyptic agency in Christ alone. With the traditional pun on "sun" and "son," Milton discredits Spenser's precedent as a violation of natural hierarchies ordering relationships between the sexes and among the different levels of creation. In *Aprill*, a female human being triumphs over the sun's masculinized authority. In the "Nativity Ode," however, a masculinized sun yields neither to a woman nor any other mortal but only to the Son of God. Already in 1629, Milton harbored enough reservations about monarchy to present the Son's messiahship as a correction of kingly pretensions: neither the sun's "bright Throne, or burning Axletree could bear" the presence of the Son now manifest as the "sovran Lord" of all creation (60).

Poets like Lane and Niccols all but abandoned Spenser's apocalypticism by reorienting their poetry from his perpetually deferred "sabbath's sight" toward a golden age already past. As I have argued, this shift from millenarian expectation to nostalgia condemns them to repetitions of *The Shepheardes Calender* in an effort to revive the imagined optimism of Elizabeth's reign. Milton overcame this fixation on England's cultural and political past by reinvesting apocalyptic agency completely in the divine Son who will finally establish his reign on earth. But if Milton restores a millenarian vision to poetry in the Spenserian tradition, he does not free apocalypticism from deferral. Like Spenser in *The Faerie Queene*, he retreats into linear history after a brief glimpse of transcendence: "But wisest fate says no, / This must not yet be so" (149–50). The child whose birth almost overcame the limits of temporality must grow up and suffer crucifixion. Even then, "our bliss" will not be "full and perfect" until "the world's last session," a moment that Milton joins Spenser in deferring to an indefinite future (165, 166, 164).[13]

When Milton published the "Nativity Ode" in 1645, the collapse of Charles I's government made the "world's last session" seem imminent to thousands of English men and women (Hill 87–98, 190–92; Capp, "Political Dimension" 109–18). Within a context of heightened millenarianism, Milton revised his understanding of humanity's role in the final days. If God remained the ultimate agent of apocalypse, He manifested His power not through kings but through the collective actions of those whom Milton upheld as the godly men of England. The end of the world offered Milton and other midcentury Puritans a powerful instrument for wresting political authority from the monarch and investing it instead in their own class. If they dismissed any ascription of apocalyptic agency to the monarchy as blasphemous, the Second Coming's perpetual deferral allowed them to hail their own revolutionary actions as its harbinger.

By the time Milton defended the nation's execution of Charles I in *Eikonoklastes*, he so inverted the myth of the Last Emperor that he upheld the abrogation of monarchy as the ultimate apocalyptic accomplishment:[14]

> But what patrons [kings] be, God in the scripture oft enough hath expressed; and the earth itself hath too long groaned under the burden of their injustice, disorder, and irreligion. Therefore, "to bind their kings in chains, and their nobles with links of iron," is an honor belonging to his saints; not to build Babel (which was Nimrod's work, the first king, "and the beginning of his kingdom was Babel") but to destroy it, especially that spiritual babel: and first to overcome those European kings, which receive their power, not from God, but from the beast; and are counted no better than his ten horns. . . . Thus shall [kings] be to and fro, doubtful and ambiguous in all their doings, until at last, "joining their armies with the beast," whose power first raised them, they shall perish with him by the "King of Kings," against who they have rebelled; and the "fowls shall eat their flesh." (Milton 814)

Quoting Revelation 19—the same passage that inspired Foxe, Spenser,

Dekker, and dozens of other Elizabethan writers—Milton rejects their attempts to reconcile royalist and apocalyptic discourses. Like the writer of Revelation itself, he uses apocalyptic rhetoric to discredit rather than to support imperial authority. From his republican perspective, kingship appears as the ultimate evil, the source of the "injustice, disorder, irreligion" that have blighted human history. Scripture from Genesis to Revelation supports his revisionary association of Babylon less with Catholicism than with monarchy. In contrast to other early modern commentators, he treats the Tower of Babel episode as an indictment of kingship rather than idolatry. He finds in Revelation a prophecy of temporal monarchy's final defeat by its one true claimant, the King of Kings who routs all human pretenders.

Time itself limits the effectiveness of apocalyptic rhetoric. The most powerful prognostications are those that are specific enough to convince people that they are living in the Last Days but not so specific that they can be refuted when the End does not occur. Spenser published *The Faerie Queene* during the resurgence of millenarianism that accompanied the Armada (Bauckman 173–80). But as Elizabeth aged and the war with Spain dragged on, the apocalyptic fervor receded. The nostalgia expressed by seventeenth-century Spenserians for Elizabeth and her prophet-laureate marked a low point of millenarian belief. Focused on a glorious past rather than an even more glorious future, the Spenserians all but abandoned confidence in the reigning monarch as a champion of apocalyptic struggle against the Beast. Dekker's *Whore of Babylon* stands out as an anomalous and qualified resurgence of that confidence in the wake of the Gunpowder Plot. The more successful resurgence of millenarianism in the 1640s depended on Milton and his radical contemporaries' revision of the apocalyptic scenario itself. Prognostications attributing apocalyptic agency to the people are less easily refuted than those attributing agency to monarchs. Queens die, dynasties rise and fall, but the people endure in their collective identity. By imagining a godly nation preparing the way for Christ's Second Coming by driving out kings and prelates, Milton and his contemporaries planted the seeds for the postmillennialism that would dominate British eschatological thought for the next century.

NOTES

1. On Spenser's transformation of the Virgilian laureate career, see Helgerson, *Laureates*; D. Miller, "Spenser's Vocation"; Krier; Suzuki; Wofford, *Choice of Achilles;* and Watkins.
2. Among the many accounts of Spenser's place in the Protestant, Foxean tradition, I am particularly indebted to King, *Spenser's Poetry*; Norbrook, *Poetry and Politics*; and Hume.

3. Angus Fletcher cites Spenser's retreats from apocalyptic representations as evidence of a fundamentally nonapocalyptic imagination (3–10). Distinguishing the prophet from the apocalyptic visionary, Fletcher argues that Spenserian prophecy is nonpredictive: "He belongs to the broader tradition, which is only partially predictive, a tradition that balances anticipation of the future with a concern for the past and, even more important, for the present" (4). Fletcher's model of a unified prophetic imagination at work throughout *The Faerie Queene* minimizes the significance of its apocalyptic gestures. These gestures had a powerful impact on later writers like Dekker, Milton, Blake, and Wordsworth. I see Spenser's retreat from apocalypse as symptomatic of a crisis in late Tudor apocalyptic rhetoric, a broader cultural crisis that transcends the peculiarities of the individual poetic. Much early modern writing, moreover, resists Fletcher's rigid distinction between the prophetic and apocalyptic modes.

4. Numerous scholars have discussed Spenser's relationship to Protestant treatments of the Revelation. See especially Hankins; Sadler; O'Connell (38–68); King, *Spenser's Poetry* 71–109. Kermode anticipates my particular concern with the medieval figure of the Last Emperor (*Shakespeare, Spenser, Donne* 19–24).

5. See Fried's discussion of the prophetic uncertainties that underlie the interruption of Merlin's vision (268–69).

6. Critics have often commented on Spenser's ambivalence toward Elizabeth, particularly in *The Faerie Queene*'s middle books. See J. Anderson, "In liuing colours"; and Norbrook, *Poetry and Politics* 109–56.

7. See Norbrook's discussion of nostalgia as a reaction to Jacobean politics (205–08).

8. For further discussion of Elizabeth's posthumous reputation, see Spikes; Barton; Perry; Woolf; and King, "Queen Elizabeth I;" Walker, "Posthumous Images;" and Walker, "Reading the Tombs of Elizabeth I."

9. Marianne Gateson Riely catalogues Dekker's debts to Spenser in the introduction to her edition of the play (Dekker 46–51).

10. For detailed discussion of Dekker's place in Jacobean political debates, see Gasper 62–108.

11. For alternative discussions of Milton's relationship to Spenser, see Guillory; and Quilligan, *Milton's Spenser*. See also Labriola, "Milton's Eve and the Cult of Elizabeth I."

12. See Carey's discussion of the poem's sources, style, and versification (98–99). As Halpern notes, the *Aprill* eclogue and the "Nativity Ode" share a common origin in Virgil's Fourth Eclogue (9–10).

13. See Belsey's discussion of the poem's temporal slippages (*Milton* 1–2, 19–23). Patrides links the poem's temporal uncertainties to a peculiarity of Milton's apocalyptic thinking: a commitment to the revolutionary present that precludes extensive speculation about the future (217–18).

14. As Lewalski notes, Milton's understanding of the apocalypse developed throughout his career in response to changing political circumstances ("*Samson Agonistes*" 1053–54). For more general discussion of Milton's apocalypticism, see Fixler.

IV. POLICING SELF AND OTHER: SPENSER, THE COLONIAL, AND THE CRIMINAL

SPENSER'S FAERYLAND AND "THE CURIOUS GENEALOGY OF INDIA"

Elizabeth Jane Bellamy

I would like to begin with a question: can interpretations of *The Faerie Queene* benefit from postcolonial perspectives? I am not especially concerned that such a line of inquiry might be judged, by definition, as anachronistic. Although an important recent trend in Spenser studies has, of course, been the ongoing investigation of Spenser's *proto*-colonialist role in England's oppression of Ireland, I would also stress the timeliness and appropriateness of placing *The Faerie Queene* in a postcolonial context. If by the term "postcolonial" we mean, in its broadest scope, a critique of Empire, then of course *The Faerie Queene* as a key document of Eurocentrism, self-consciously written in the idiom of an "elect nation," and a literary work profoundly implicated in the social formations of western Europe (such as the rise of the concept of nationhood and the rise of territorial imperialism in England's transition from "saluage wildernesse" to empire), readily lends itself to postcolonial perspectives. But what is of even more concern to me is the possibility that the question of how postcolonial critique can most productively be brought to bear on *The Faerie Queene* runs the risk of overlooking the many confusions that have begun to accrue around the very term "postcolonial." All too often, recently, the term "postcolonial" has become an undifferentiated and unproblematized amalgam of such concepts as "Third World studies," "migrancies," "diasporas," "borders," "marginalities," "ethnicities," etc. In such an unnuanced framework, the term "postcolonial" (as a number of recent critics have pointed out) may be losing its descriptive force, such that the very posing of the question, Can *The Faerie Queene* be postcolonial?, could already be naively overlooking the controversies inherent in this relatively new discursive field.[1]

Maybe a more precise question to pose in this context might be, Even when we think we are bringing postcolonial perspectives to bear on *The Faerie Queene*, how can we be assured that we are being genuinely postcolonial? Presently, in the wake of the quincentenary that served as the occasion for so many long overdue rewritings of Europe's cultural encounters with the New World, a question that current readers of Spenser might wish to answer with greater specificity is how future readings of *The Faerie Queene* can be enriched by the still newly emergent discourse of postcolonialism.[2] As a major representative of the English literary canon, can *The Faerie Queene* ever really be part of what Gayatri Spivak, for example, envisions as a decolonized curriculum? Or will any attempt to forge a relationship between *The Faerie Queene* and postcolonial theory be merely catachrestic?[3] I will state from the outset my hope that *The Faerie Queene* will persist as an object of inquiry and knowledge in a curriculum seeking to participate in the compelling politics of much recent postcolonial critique; and I also believe that any historicizing approach to representations of empire in *The Faerie Queene* can benefit from an attentiveness to current concerns about the nature of "postcoloniality" itself. The challenge, then, is to fashion a meaningful critique of imperialism in *The Faerie Queene* that can both preserve the epic's historical embeddedness in Elizabethan culture and demonstrate its relevance for postcolonial concerns. And thus in this essay I will trace, among other things, the contours of a postcolonial rereading of *The Faerie Queene* through the lens of some recent controversies about what constitutes postcolonial studies—a rereading that can, I hope, considerably enrich our understanding of *The Faerie Queene*'s highly ambiguous and inconclusive hovering between "Old World" and "New World."

As I noted at the outset, the very invoking of the term "postcolonial" is beginning to elicit anxiety within postcolonial discourse itself. Quite predictably, perhaps, the more the term "postcolonial" has enjoyed a wide and influential circulation within academe, the more confusing it has become. Sara Suleri has observed that "the concept of the postcolonial itself is too frequently robbed of historical specificity in order to function as a preapproved allegory for any mode of discursive contestation" ("Woman Skin Deep" 756). And Ella Shohat has also thoughtfully addressed the problem of what she calls "the theoretical and political ambiguities of the 'post-colonial'" (99). In light of her warnings about the proliferating "ahistorical and universalizing" deployments of postcoloniality—and the potentially depoliticizing effects of such broad-based deployments—we should be concerned about the possibility that any attempt to forge a relationship between *The Faerie Queene* and postcolonial theory will only be catachrestic, or, worse, politically inconsequential. But I would argue that if we listen carefully to some of the anxieties that postcolonialism is experiencing as it seeks to configure itself as an emergent discipline, *The Faerie Queene* can begin to take on a new relevance for a decolonized curriculum of the kind that Spivak envisions. In particular, I will demonstrate how anxieties about the very definition of the term "postcolonial" can serve as a useful backdrop for a consideration of how India is embedded as a kind of political unconscious in Spenser's epic—an embeddedness that suggests ways in which we can rescue *The Faerie Queene* from the restrictive *imperium* of English studies and insert it into a broader global and, indeed, postcolonial framework. A return to *The Faerie Queene*, that most canonical of Western epics, can enable us to test, interrogate, and, in some cases, confirm some of the governing assumptions behind the discursive field known as "postcolonialism."

Before turning to Spenser's representation of India in *The Faerie Queene*, let us first look more closely at the problem of postcolonialism and its discontents by turning to Ella Shohat's essay, where the author discusses the problem of who can justifiably lay claim to a postcolonial status. She prefaces her discussion with the difficult question of origins: "When exactly, then, does the 'post-colonial' begin? The vague starting point of the 'post-colonial' makes certain differentiations difficult. It equates early independence won by settler-colonial states, in which Europeans formed their new nation-states in non-European territories at the expense of indigenous populations, with that of nation-states whose indigenous populations struggled for independence against Europe, but won it, for the most part, with the twentieth century collapse of European Empires" (103–04). Shohat expresses concern that the term "postcolonial" should not be so labile as to encompass both the histories of settler-colonial states founded in non-European contexts and nation-states that emerged after the collapse of European empires. In her concern for the open-endedness of the term "postcolonial," Shohat suggests, then, that the ambiguity of the term has at least one of its origins in a catachrestic and ill-conceived conflating of, say, India and America as sites of colonialist aggression that have nevertheless traced radically different trajectories vis-à-vis indigenous populations.

Using Shohat's essay as a cautionary backdrop, I would suggest that the ill-conceived conflating of Indian and American colonial experience that has increasingly characterized recent postcolonial studies may, in turn, have at least one of *its* origins in *The Faerie Queene*, which, in its broadest scope, undertakes the challenge of imagining a geopolitical space in the aftermath of Columbus's paradoxical sailing west to go east, his discovery that America was, in effect, the *not*-India. In the final analysis, we should be re(the ways in which *The Faerie Queene* may have almost as much to

India as it does with England (and the turning of its imperial gaze to America)—or, more specifically, with the cultural contradictions that accrue when imperialist epic tries to conceive of India and America as inhabiting the same, for lack of a better term, "*not*-Indian" and "*not*-English" space.[4] Phrased another way, *The Faerie Queene* may have everything to do with, in Shohat's words, "the vague starting point of the 'post-colonial'"—not just because its gaze is beginning to turn to the New World in the West, but also because its imperial scope struggles to accommodate India in the East.

To further contextualize the importance of Spenser's India as "the vague starting point of the 'post-colonial,'" we can also turn to Sara Suleri's *The Rhetoric of English India* and her emphasis on what she provocatively calls "the curious genealogy of India." For Suleri, the concept of "English India" (not unlike the peculiar temporality of *The Faerie Queene* itself) expresses "a disinterest in the continuity of tense" and chronology, and is not necessarily synonymous with British rule in India (3). In such a temporal scheme, Suleri suggests that the origins of "English India" can productively be considered prior to the actual moment of colonial encounter: "In historiographical terms, colonial trauma can be read only in the context of an apocalyptic 'end' or 'beginning' of empire, even though a merely cursory knowledge of the trials of English India makes evident the obsession of that idiom's . . . engagement with the transfer of power" (5–6). Here Suleri, among other things, is taking issue with Benedict Anderson's *Imagined Communities* and its "quest for national origins" in order to achieve a definitive account of how nationality becomes constituted.[5] By means of her emphasis on "the curious genealogy of India," Suleri is more concerned with "how the encounter of colonialism and the emergence of nationalism are secret sharers in an act of cultural transcription so overdetermined as to dissipate the logic of origins, or the rational framework of chronologies" (9). Suleri seeks something new in the narrative of empire, something that can move us beyond the oversimplified alterity of "colonizer" and "colonized," a different perspective on what she has called the complex "situatedness of nationalism in the colonial encounter" (3).

With what I take to be great significance for *The Faerie Queene*, Suleri objects that studies of English India usually begin no earlier than the eighteenth century; and thus I would like to answer her challenge of finding new ways to configure the origins of "English India" by examining how *The Faerie Queene*'s ongoing crisis of "name and nation" can enable us to tease out the inconsistencies between the idioms of British "empire" and British "nation" that in Suleri's view overdetermine the concept of "English India"—i.e., the ways in which the "curious genealogy of English India" can begin prior to the colonial encounter itself.

Let us glance briefly at how India is represented in three dynastic epics preceding *The Faerie Queene*. We could say that "the curious genealogy of English India" has its literary origins in the so-called "India topos," or the topos of "the extent of fame," conventionally stretching from India to Thule (presumably the northernmost region of the ancient world). As E.R. Curtius defines the topos, "To be known in India is obviously the greatest of fame" (160). To illustrate how this topos is invoked, Curtius turns to epic, reminding us of book 6 of the *Aeneid,* where Anchises prophesies to Aeneas that Augustus will extend his rule over all the Indians (160). Centuries later, the "India topos" informs Camões's 1572 epic, the *Lusíadas,* perhaps the first narrative of European dynastic epic's imperial zeal to seize the wealth of the East Indies. It is in Camões's famous canto 5 and its narrative of Vasco da Gama's rounding of the Cape of Good Hope and discovering a seafaring "passage to India" that we can detect perhaps the first traces in epic literary history of an ambiguous threshold between the eminently literary "India topos" and the mapping of real, historical trade routes: no longer simply a literary topos for a Western cultural imaginary, India is represented by Camões as distinctly conquerable.

In the *Orlando furioso,* canto 15 (19–35), Ariosto celebrates the Habsburg empire of Charles V and the "voyages of discovery" as extensions of his power. The paladin Astolfo travels past the shores of East India (*l'odorifera India*), past the Ganges, Ceylon, and Cochin. Not without significance for the transmutations of the "India topos" within the literary history of epic, it is not until India is out of sight that Astolfo asks the prophetess Andronica about the intriguing mysteries of sailing west. Andronica predicts that under Charles V, future mariners (the *nuovi Argonauti*) will sail far beyond the Pillars of Hercules and eventually discover seafaring passages to the Orient by sailing due west, implying that this *nuovo mundo* will render all the old maps of India obsolete.[6]

In canto 15 of Tasso's *Gerusalemme liberata,* the Christian knights Carlo and Ubaldo sail west, beyond Ascalon, Gaza, Syria, Rhodes, Crete, Tunis, and Cadiz, in a *barca aventurosa* piloted by a guide (an avatar of Fortune, if not Fortune herself) whose task is to take the knights to Armida's island to rescue Rinaldo. Armida's island is located somewhere in the "Fortunate Isles," both a vague location in the ocean far west of the Pillars of Hercules, and a real place on the map (the Canary Islands). The passage culminates in Tasso's encomium to Columbus (who, as David Quint notes, provisioned in the Canaries in 1492 before sailing west)—an encomium that signals, unlike the eastward impulse of the *Lusíadas,* a distinctly westward urge for imperial expansion (*Epic and Empire* 262).[7] As Carlo and Ubaldo's pilot predicts, "the time will come that the pillars of Hercules will be mere fable" ("Tempo verrà che fian d'Ercole i segni favola vile"[15.30]).[8]

Ariosto's and Tasso's celebrations of these Renaissance voyages of discovery are, of course, intended to predict an eventual founding of Catholic empire in the New World. And I would now like to turn to the extent to which their cartographic celebrations of these Catholic ventures become a kind of political unconscious for Spenser's Protestant epic of empire, originating, if not in India, then certainly in an (un)consciousness of a not fully obsolete India. Although *The Faerie Queene*, as Spenser's fashioning of a British version of the *imperium sine fine*, inherits epic literary history's westward pull of empire, for the author, as we shall see, the "India" topos presents much more of a narrative problem than in prior dynastic epics.

And thus, in offering specific suggestions for how *The Faerie Queene* can participate in some of the current debates about what constitutes the "postcolonial," I propose that we focus on his perpetually enigmatic "Faerie land"—a strangely contradictory locus (neither fully "East" nor fully "West"), a highly ambivalent and disjunctive moment in the westering of empire known as the *translatio imperii*, and a locus that, as we shall see, may have rendered *The Faerie Queene* "postcolonial" *avant la lettre*. Despite its dreamy existence as what Coleridge once referred to as a kind of "mental space" (36) and despite the poet's own odd baiting of the reader that no one "does know, / Where is that happy land of Faery" (2 proem 1.6–7)[9]—a claim, by the way, reinforcing readers' traditional impressions that much of *The Faerie Queene* does not take place in real geographic spaces—Spenser's "Faerie land" is conceived as a locus that can presumably, albeit with some difficulty, be *found;* and certainly no less than the central protagonist Arthur himself experiences a very real pressure to locate the faery city Cleopolis. (We will return to these pressures later in more detail.) As Spenser himself admits to the reader, "Of Faerie lond yet if he more inquire, / By certain signes here set in sundry place / He may it find" (2 proem 4.1–2).

Moreover, with no small significance for Suleri's probing "the curious genealogy of English India," it can be argued that where much of Faeryland can most likely be "found" is in India, as evidenced in Guyon's reading of the *Antiquitie of Faerie lond* in Alma's castle, where the knight learns of the vast dominion of his faery ancestor Elfin, whom "all India obayd, / And all that now America men call" (2.10.72.5–6), with Elfin himself serving as a version of the mythic Hercules conquering both East and West.[10] Over a decade ago, in a knowledgeable and valuable essay that has been often overlooked by Spenser criticism, Michael Murrin suggested a kind of "genealogy" of Spenser's Faeryland that could be traced through the literary history of epic romance, specifically through the matter of Charlemagne, whose various fairy lands were often located in the near and Middle East and what is now Southeast Asia ("Spenser's Fairyland," *The Allegorical Epic*). Murrin refers, for example, to the *Melusine* of Jean of Arras (1394), a romance chronicle whose fairy land is located in the Near East—not modern India, by any means, but a region that the *chansons de geste* virtually equated with India (most likely the homeland of, for example, Boiardo's Fata Morgana and of Ariosto's "Indian" princess Angelica). The fairy land of the thirteenth-century *Huon of Bordeaux* (translated into English in 1534) drifts even further eastward, featuring the fairy king Oberon—presumably the same Oberon whom Spenser will later identify as king of Faeryland and father of Gloriana (2.10.75–6). Murrin reasons that because, in the matter of Charlemagne and in the Italian epics, fairy land is depicted as drifting ever eastward, readers of *The Faerie Queene* may conclude (even without benefit of the Elfin chronicles housed in Eumnestes's archive) that much of Spenser's Faeryland can be located "in" India. (As Murrin claims, Faeryland is "a dream of empire" [130].) Thus, even though "India" as such is mentioned no more than a half dozen times in *The Faerie Queene*, it could be argued that the "curious genealogy of English India" is fully implicated in Spenser's faery locus.

As Murrin further argues, the eastward drift of the matter of Charlemagne's various fairy lands was one result of the imperialist wish fulfillments of the old Crusader myths, a geographic "symptom," as it were, of the dream of a final Christian military victory over Islam of the kind predicted in Ariosto's *Orlando furioso*. In other words, these romance fairy lands that stretched all the way to India are epic literary history's premature anticipations of the final outcome of the Crusades. In the particular case of *The Faerie Queene*, then, we could argue that the traditional, literary historical location of fairy land in the East calls for a reconsideration (particularly in light of Murrin's essay) of Spenser's "Faerie" realm as little more than an archaic, nostalgic, and outmoded vestige of much of the poet's source material, the older romance chronicles. The persistent yearning and nostalgia for "antique times" that pervade so much of Spenser's tone throughout *The Faerie Queene* (a tone that particularly characterizes much of his troubled book 5) also serve to introduce the reader to the faery knight Guyon early in book 2, where the poet reminisces: "Well could he tourney and in lists debate, / And knighthood tooke of good Sir Huons hand, / When with King Oberon he came to Faerie land" (2.1.6.7–9). When viewed in this literary historical context, Guyon, past hero of the *Melusine* and victor over Huon of Bordeaux, assumes a new complexity as the hero of Spenser's book 2. The point I wish to emphasize is this: Guyon, as Spenser's heir to literary history's many fairy lands, is perhaps *The Faerie Queene*'s most comprehensively "European" or "Old World" figure, embodying Western romance chronicle's last consolidating hope for the fulfillment of the Crusader myth—but also serving as the epic's most potentially outmoded hero.

But although Guyon may be Spenser's quintessentially "European" hero, we have also to consider his anticipations of English ventures in the West Indies and the Americas (i.e., the westernmost territory of Guyon's faery ancestor Elfin). Almost twenty years ago (but with renewed significance for the recent turn in early modern literary studies to Europe's colonial encounters in America), Thomas Cain argued cogently for "a recurrent New World motif" in book 2, with the proem to the second book presenting an imperial realization of Troynovant in "fruitfullest Virginia" (85). Whereas Murrin tends to emphasize the eastward drift of Spenser's Faeryland, Cain asserts that the geographical spaces of Faeryland (the Faeryland of book 2, at least) push ever westward such that Acrasia's Bower of Bliss, for example (and its obvious literary antecedent in Armida's island in the Fortunate Isles), should be viewed as a parody of "fruitfullest Virginia"; and the episode of the greedy Mammon of canto 7, surrounded by his "Great heapes of gold," should be interpreted as a warning to Ralegh and other English explorers of the ruinous temptations of the fantasy of El Dorado (93–94). Moreover, the very name "Guyon," echoing both Eden's River Gihon and Ralegh's New World project of Guiana, anticipates a vast realm where the traditional boundaries of India and Asia will also begin to overlap with the Americas.[11]

Neither fully "west" (as Guyon/Guiana) nor fully "east" (as Guyon/Huon), Guyon's story in *The Faerie Queene,* for all practical purposes, comes to an end following his destruction of the Bower of Bliss. That is to say, his narrative concludes somewhere in the Fortunate Isles, beyond the Pillars of Hercules. Thus the prospect of an "outmoded" Guyon (i.e., a Guyon who both anticipates New World ventures and continues to bear the burden of completion of the old Crusader myths from the matter of Charlemagne, or, phrased another way, "Guyon" as the narrative slot in *The Faerie Queene* where European literary history is stretched by the novelty of an Atlantic world) can perhaps give us a new perspective on why Spenser chose the figure of Arthur as the central protagonist of his epic—and, eventually, to a further consideration of Spenser's representation of "the curious genealogy" of India. Perhaps it is because of his outmodedness that Guyon's foes, the "paynim" brothers Pyrochles and Cymochles, swearing almost parodically by "Termagant" or "Mahoune," lack the heroic, adversarial urgency of, say, Orlando's battles with the formidable Agramante in the *Orlando furioso*—

and at this point we should pause to consider why it is not Guyon but Arthur who is the overarching hero of *The Faerie Queene* (aside from the immediately obvious reason that, as "England's Virgil," Spenser required an authentically "British" hero for his epic).

First, let us return to the significance of the poet's ambitious claim (Spenser's own version of the "India topos") that the expanse of Faeryland encompasses both India *and* America, i.e., the (once-and-future) territory of Elfin, whom "all India obayd, / And all that now America men call." As we have seen earlier, the "India" of the matter of Charlemagne is less the real India than an ambiguously mapped by-product of the dreamy, exotic "Orientalism" of the romance chronicles. But the faery "India" of *The Faerie Queene* must assume more real, geographic burdens because Spenser's Faeryland has committed itself to a territorial expanse that includes not just the "India" of the Near and Middle East, but also America—an ambitious representation of world empire that places unusual pressures on Spenser's appropriation of the faery topos. If we also keep in mind that since 1580 (the same year, we should note, as Sir Francis Drake's circumnavigation of the globe), both India and America had been ruled by Philip of Habsburg (following Philip's defeat of the Ottomans at Lepanto),[12] then according to Spenser's prophetic projections for *The Faerie Queene*, his epic narrative must not only logically anticipate England's final military triumph over Spain (and, by extension, India), but it must also ambitiously commit itself to epic history's ultimate *literary* triumph: *The Faerie Queene* (unlike Camões's *Lusíadas*, which was content with a story of the founding of real, mappable trade routes to India) must imagine a kind of meta-India, i.e., India as both the First World site of Christian victory over the "infidel," *and* a "New World" India, whose fictive representation can triumph—literarily, at least, if not historically—over Spanish gains in the Americas. Unlike the fairy lands of earlier romance chronicles, Spenser's Faeryland must, in other words, first go *west* in order to expand east: west, that is, to America, which may be one reason why Guyon, fully implicated in "European" literary history, must be rescued in book 2 and eventually replaced as hero by Arthur. Moreover, although Guyon eventually achieves his quest of destroying Acrasia's bower, the very act of imagining exactly where Acrasia's isle is located raises a kind of cartographical anxiety for the reader: Guyon is one of the few characters in *The Faerie Queene* who knows the precise location of Cleopolis, but one wonders if he could pinpoint the precise location of Acrasia's isle, situated, as it is, somewhere in the Fortunate Isles in a geographical space neither fully "European" nor fully "American." The narrative is even more overdetermined by the fact that in *The Faerie Queene*, any further realization of "faerie" destiny becomes, paradoxically, the "Briton prince" Arthur's task, such that the matter of Charlemagne must cede generic place to the matter of Arthur and its more westward drift, west of Europe to an implied, hidden isle of Avalon as Arthur's final destination— a geographic (or merely literary?) space (beyond the Pillars of Hercules?) that is, like Acrasia's isle, also neither fully European nor fully American.

Despite *The Faerie Queene*'s fragmented incompletion, the ultimate "prophetic moment" of Spenser's epic, as many Spenser scholars have noted, anticipates the Faerie Queene Gloriana and the "Briton prince" Arthur's eventually joining forces to triumph over the "Paynim King" and nothing less than Islam itself. But one result of the ambitious geographic (and literary) scope of Faeryland is that the "Saracens" of this latest version of imperialist epic are now (theoretically, at least) no longer the Saracens of the old Crusader myths (nor are they even Spanish Catholics-as-Saracens—a new kind of "Saracen" for, as it were, a distinctly Protestant reviling), but rather, increasingly, New World Spaniards rapidly gaining territorial advantage over the English in the Americas. The point I wish to emphasize here is that Spenser's ambiguous and unmapped literary threshold between "Old World" Saracen and "New World" Spaniard (i.e., the generic seam between the matter of Charlemagne and Spenser's newly conceived goals for the matter of Arthur) becomes a precarious space that cannot "speak" its own narrative contradictions within the bounds of epic.

Spenser's attempt to represent a fictive triumph over Spanish gains in the Americas may be one of the significant reasons why the narrative of *The Faerie Queene* cannot impel itself forward to Gloriana and Arthur's defeat of the "Paynim King." With Arthur as its hero, we could say that *The Faerie Queene* remains cartographically adrift in the Fortunate Isles because, unlike Ariosto and Tasso, Spenser is not prepared to record the culmination of the "voyages of discovery" in Catholic empire in the New World. In particular, the uncertain allegory of at least two of Arthur's adversaries in *The Faerie Queene* is one symptom of the narrative inconsistencies that accrue when a "Faerie" India must attempt to meet America on a common literary ground. One of Arthur's principal foes is the "Souldan," whom he resoundingly defeats in book 5—a violent encounter (during which the "Souldan" rides a chariot with hooked blades jutting from its wheels) that is sufficiently "heroic" and decisive to satisfy the generic requirements of the old Charlemagne romances. But in Spenser's restless and overdetermined allegory, this defeat is soon to be superseded by Arthur's encounter with the giant Geryoneo, who, in an "old" historical reading of the political allegory of book 5, embodies Philip II of Spain in particular and the institution of Roman Catholicism in general. Arthur's (anticipated) defeat of Geryoneo is a distinctly "Old World" vision in which the hero of (Protestant) Britain (or, more specifically, Arthur as the Earl of Leicester in the Protestant Netherlands) is foreseen as overcoming the Spanish Philip and Catholic idolatry. But Arthur's defeat of Geryoneo, though designed to supersede the significance of Arthur's earlier defeat of the ("European") Souldan, is allegorically inconsequential in light of Philip's territorial gains in the New World. The defeat of the newest Spanish enemy in the New World (Arthur's realm) cannot yet be portrayed with any allegorical stability.

We should also pause to consider the ambiguity inherent in the fact that in his battle against the Souldan, Arthur fights on behalf of the beleaguered queen Mercilla, a figure traditionally interpreted as evoking both the historical Elizabeth and the meta-historical Gloriana. That Mercilla (like Britomart, Belphoebe, Florimell, etc.) is another one of *The Faerie Queene*'s many surrogates for Gloriana, and not Gloriana herself, may not seem all that significant—but as the *not*-Gloriana, on whose behalf Arthur battles the Souldan so ferociously, Mercilla (who herself presides over an ambiguously mapped territory "[f]rom th'vtmost brinke of the Armericke shore, / Vnto the margent of the Molucas" [5.10.3]) does serve as a reminder that Arthur never succeeds in locating the *real* faery queen. And, as was mentioned earlier, the hero's chronically diasporic experience in Faeryland results in an inability to find even Cleopolis, the "kingdomes seat" where Gloriana resides. We can speculate that Cleopolis is precariously "located" on the generic seam between the matter of Charlemagne (India) and the matter of Arthur (somewhere west of Europe itself). But Arthur has been displaced from Cleopolis—much as he has been "displaced" from the matter of Charlemagne; and it is as if the city of "fame," perhaps epic literary history's ultimate First World metropolis, is locatable only by those, such as Guyon, who always already reside in it. We are reminded of this fact when, in one of *The Faerie Queene*'s more curious moments, Arthur, having confessed to Guyon that he has "sought the sight, / Yet no where can her [Gloriana] find" (2.9.7), is told by the faery knight, "were it not, that I am delaid / With hard aduenture, which I haue in hand, / I labour would to guide you through all Faery land" (2.9.8). On the basis of this brief, but inconclusive exchange between Arthur and Guyon, one suspects that knowing where Cleopolis can be found (being able to interpret the "certaine signes" of its whereabouts) is tantamount to knowing the location of the (geographic and literary) seam between India and the "westering" of epic toward America.

We could argue that Spenser's new generic emphasis on the matter of Arthur can be interpreted as the poet's refusal to be "colonized" by the Habsburgs—his literary strategy for superseding Spain by placing India in a new narrative realm. But we should also note that the chief narrative casualty of this impossible project is Arthur himself. Spenser intends Arthur as, in effect, the agent by which First World imperialism seeks to become the historical realization of Elfin's Indian-American meta-realm (a dominion whose existence is only theoretical in the *Antiquitie of Faerie lond*). But Arthur's strangely persistent inability to find Faeryland because of, among many other factors, the nonconvergence of the matter of Charlemagne and the matter of Arthur results in a narrative impasse. In *The Faerie Queene,* the literary history of epic attempts a coherent narrative of empire from India to America, but in the process, Faeryland becomes instead the site of cultural displacement, essentially unlocatable because of its premature attempts to smooth out the rough edges of an uneven, incommensurate process in British history—and, for that matter, in the "curious genealogy of English India."

Even as Spenser's Faeryland seeks to perpetuate the "bookish" fairy lands of the literary history of epic, then, the ambition of such a project virtually guarantees *The Faerie Queene*'s failure to incorporate within its literary scope the historical Real of England's colonial ventures in the Americas. Although the happy procession of rivers during the marriage of the Thames and the Medway in book 4 can conjure a global imagination capable of incorporating the "Great Ganges," "Deepe Indus," and the New World's "Rich Oranochy" (4.11.21) into the same imperial vision, a similar "marriage" of Old World fairy lands and New World expansion cannot be imagined within the larger narrative of *The Faerie Queene.*

The absent presence of the historical Real of England's colonial ventures in the Americas in *The Faerie Queene* prompts a return to Ella Shohat's provocative question, posed earlier in my essay, "When exactly, then, does the 'post-colonial' begin?" As mentioned earlier, Shohat's concern is that one "origin" of the growing vagueness of the term "postcolonial" is a careless conflating of India and America as sites of colonial aggression that trace entirely different trajectories with respect to their indigenous populations. To observe that this conflating may itself have at least one of its "origins" in *The Faerie Queene* is one way we can better anticipate some of the confusions of current attempts to define the "postcolonial," mentioned at the beginning of my essay. If we remember that implicit in much of the narrative of *The Faerie Queene* (particularly in the allegory of Timias and Belphoebe) are Ralegh's "voyages of discovery" (read mercantile ventures), first in "fruitfullest Virginia" and later in Guiana (as documented in his 1590 *Discoverie of Guiana*), then Spenser's epic seeks to encompass, among other things, the story of British merchants, competing with Spain and struggling to establish settlement colonies in the Americas. But we should also note that Elizabeth's support of Ralegh's mercantile ventures in the New World was at best inconsistent;[13] and at this point it is appropriate to ponder the role not of the New World, but of the real India as a possible origin of the "postcolonial" in Spenser's epic. To do so, we must first reconsider the vexed question, raised earlier, of exactly who Elizabeth is meant to be in *The Faerie Queene*. In other words, is Elizabeth the meta-historical "faerie queene" who, at some unspecified future point, will join forces with Arthur to supplant the Spanish Habsburgs in the New World? Or is she a historical Elizabeth—the same Elizabeth who near the end of her reign, on 30 December 1600 (four years after the final installment of *The Faerie Queene*), granted a charter of incorporation to the East India Company and, in the process, helped to inaugurate a new British imperialist era in India? What if Spenser's "faerie queene" is really an Elizabeth who was less preoccupied with England's mercantile ventures in the New World (in a kind of pseudo-mythic "fruitfullest Virginia") than in colonial expansion in India—not, however, the "faerie" India of the old Crusader myths (whose expansion to the West could only be a fictive representation), but a real India as the (once-and-future) site of British imperial ambitions in the East? For that matter, we could argue that it is perhaps the East India Company itself, as the ambiguous threshold between the "Orientalist" India of the outmoded Crusader myths and an early modern India as a nascent site of British venture capital, that may be the most unrepresentable moment of all within the narrative of *The Faerie Queene*.

Perhaps now we are in a position to understand more fully Spenser's enigmatic organization of space in *The Faerie Queene* and, in particular, the poet's urging the reader that "Of Faerie lond yet if he more inquire, / By certain signes here set in sundry place / He may it find." In *The Faerie Queene,* the shifting borders of the "India topos" of prior dynastic epics are presented as both an artifact of Troynovant's "antiquitie" and a mappable, geographical referent in the present. Faeryland can be "found," in other words, both in the bookish *Antiquitie of Faerie lond* and in the India of a nascent British imperialism. Thus in any effort to articulate the "place" of India in Spenser's epic, one must be attentive to a kind of cartographic play on words implicit in the "India topos" itself. All of which is to say that in *The Faerie Queene* India is both "topos" as literary citation (i.e., the topos of "the extent of fame," with Cleopolis, the city of "fame," as its capital, and a topos that has previously constituted the "India" of the literary history of dynastic epic), and India is also the more literal embodiment of "topos" as physical place.[14] When Spenser claims that India can be found by following "certain signes," he is challenging his readers to trace the enigmatic vectors whereby the "India topos" of the past becomes the mappable India of the present. In *The Faerie Queene,* the "India topos" (India as a vast cultural inheritance from past epics) is activated in such a way that India becomes both a real, geographical referent and also the place around which the "idea" of England as empire (the idea of England as national space) begins to organize itself.

In conclusion, I wish to return to the central question posed at the beginning of my essay: Can interpretations of *The Faerie Queene* benefit from postcolonial perspectives? Having for so long served as one of the more hoary representatives of the British literary canon, can *The Faerie Queene* now legitimately participate in a decolonized curriculum of the kind envisioned by postcolonial pedagogy? As we have seen, it is possible to argue that the narrative failures of *The Faerie Queene* are the beginnings of the "narrative" of English India; and I hope my essay has demonstrated that Spenser's epic and its overdetermined perspectives on the beginnings of a colonial encounter between Anglo and Indian would constitute a very compelling starting point for any course on the historical development of what Sara Suleri has called "the curious genealogy" of English India, the shaping of English India as what she calls a "discursive field" that is inclusive of both colonial and postcolonial narratives (*Rhetoric of English India* 3). In trying to conceive of new ways to read the inception of empire, Suleri offers a return to English India as a "family tree that is less chronological than it is perpetually at odds with the geographic location of cultures" (15). If, as she has argued, "the term 'English India' demands an explication that would render it both literal and figurative at the same time" (2), then the neither fully historical nor fully fictive locus of Spenser's "faerie" India can serve as just such an explication ("both literal and figurative") that Suleri calls for. Given *The Faerie Queene*'s notoriously ambivalent relationship to the "logic of origins" and its temporally fragmented narrative that fractures any "rational framework of chronologies," I contend that Spenser's Faeryland, perhaps the most overdetermined "cultural transcription" in all of epic literary history, is precisely the kind of obscure threshold between nation and empire, and between colonizer and colonized, that can enrich our ongoing investigation into the "curious genealogy" of English India and can be a major participant in postcolonialism's project to recapture its earlier energies as "the critical frame of Empire."

NOTES

For their willingness to read and provide valuable suggestions for this essay, I wish to thank my colleagues Elizabeth Hageman, Douglas Lanier, and Sandhya Shetty.

1. For a brief sampling of concerns about the growing amorphousness of the field of postcolonialism from within the discipline itself, see McClintock; Shohat; Suleri, "Woman Skin Deep"; Dirlik; Sharpe; and Seshadri-Crooks.

2. A question to pose in this context is, Are Spenser critics being "genuinely postcolonial" when the focus, for example, remains on such figures as the "faithlesse Sarasin" Sansfoy or the "paynim" brothers Pyrochles and Cymochles, demonstrating their status as marginalized, Saracen "others," as demonized caricatures of Spenser's (mis)representations of a militant Islam? Such is the project of Heberle's essay. His study of Spenser's embedded Orientalism is well perceived and enlightening. But one suspects that even here we are not yet "doing" a postcolonial study of *The Faerie Queene*. In focusing on how Spenser's Protestant epic of "national origin validation" must constitute itself at the expense of his marginalized, Saracen "others," otherwise well-intentioned critics are vulnerable to Spivak's claim that a mere focus on marginalization is not "doing" postcolonial critique at all, but rather inadvertently reinforcing a kind of "new Orientalism" that runs the risk of fetishizing an exotic Otherness—an endeavor potentially all the more fetishizing because its critique of imperialism is still contained within the *imperium* of canonical method as usual (277). To Spenserians seeking a "genuinely" postcolonial approach to *The Faerie Queene*, postcolonial critics might counter that the postcolonial project must seek to negotiate far more complex overdeterminations than simple issues of "marginalization" and "Otherness." (For an excellent reading of Spenser's treatment of national origins that, in my estimation, lays an effective groundwork for more genuinely postcolonial perspectives, see Mazzola. See also Archer's forthcoming book.)

3. Phrased broadly, "catachresis" is Spivak's privileged term for the attempt to combine discourses that are incommensurate with one another. In classical rhetoric, catachresis was a kind of concept-metaphor without an adequate referent. Spivak's use of catachresis points to the lack of an adequate referent within, specifically, postcolonial experience. For Spivak's strategy for the "dethroning" of the imperialist gestures of English canonical method itself, see her chapter "Scattered Speculations on the Question of Cultural Studies" in *Outside in the Teaching Machine*.

4. These cultural contradictions could be viewed as a "symptom" of what Mignolo has summarized more generally as the psychic crisis brought about by the "need to integrate a fourth part of the world into a European consciousness" (256). For a compelling "psychogenetic" reading of the idea of national space (and what he calls "cartographic writing") as embodied in methods of early modern mapping, see Conley.

5. B. Anderson's *Imagined Communities* is a definitive study of nationality as a "cultural artifact."

6. For a useful account of how Renaissance "voyages of discovery" were gradually rendering the old Ptolemaic map obsolete within the specific context of the *Orlando furioso*, see Biow's chapter "Ariosto, Power, and the Desire for Totality" in his *Mirabile Dictu*.

7. For more on Tasso's "boat of romance" and its prophecies of future "voyages of discovery," see Quint's chapter "Tasso, Milton, and the Boat of Romance" in *Epic and Empire*.

8. All references to *Gerusalemme liberata* are taken from *Torquato Tasso: Gerusalemme liberata*, ed. Caretti.

9. All references to *The Faerie Queene* are taken from *The Faerie Queene,* ed. Hamilton.

10. We might also note that in book 3, Glauce speculates that Britomart's future dynastic spouse, the elusive Artegall, might have to be sought as far away as "th'Indian Peru" (3.3.6), one of Spenser's conventional, trans-hemispheric terms throughout *The Faerie Queene* for India itself. In her valuable essay, Hendricks uses Spenser's link between India and Faeryland as the backdrop for an examination of what she calls "the figurative evocation of India" in Shakespeare's *A Midsummer Night's Dream* (see especially 43–48).

11. Nohrnberg suggests that Guyon's name derives from Gihon, the Edenic river of Temperance (*The Analogy of "The Faerie Queene"* 303). See also Fowler, "The River Guyon."

12. Murrin reminds us of the broad domain of Philip's rule in *The Allegorical Epic* (139).

13. For the definitive study of Elizabeth's ambivalent and less than enthusiastic support of Ralegh's ventures in the Americas, see Knapp. As Knapp argues provocatively, "The repeated failures of England and the continuing success of Spain in America . . . suggest that whether by necessity or choice, England's relation to the New World was essentially a frivolous one" (4). As a result, writes Knapp, Spenser developed "a diffident attitude toward empire in America" (106). See also Quint, *Epic and Empire* and Helgerson, *Forms of Nationhood* for the generic tensions between an "aristocratic" epic and "bourgeois" or "mercantile" romance adventure.

14. For a consideration of this dual meaning of topos, I am indebted to Artemis Leontis's chapter "The Topological Approach" in her *Topographies of Hellenism.*

SPENSER AND THE USES
OF BRITISH HISTORY

David J. Baker

To think of Britain as a whole, says J.G.A. Pocock, or to "desire such a synthesis would mean that one had become a 'British' nationalist, which I think no one ever has, ever will, or ever should." Britain is not a unified nation. Its history of disparities and conflict is precisely that of a "synthesis" that never took place, and an identity framed in its terms would be fragmented indeed. In this essay, I mean to consider how an awareness of the ruptured history of Britain and a concomitant impulse towards an overarching nationalism come together in the thought of one early modern "Briton," an Englishman by birth, a resident in Ireland—Edmund Spenser. It is true, I will say, that the "'British' nationalist" is a chimera. It is also true that the ironies of this disjunct phrase have their uses. In Spenser, we see a particularly apposite instance of the "different demands" that "Britain" and the "nation," as tropes, impose on "the subject's sense of identity" ("British History" 616).

In recent years, the problems of Britishness, past and present, have been addressed with particular rigor in the developing field of "British history." This tag has been attached to the work of a varied coterie of historians,[1] but many of them share an aim: to show that the histories of the geopolitical entities now called England, Ireland, Northern Ireland, Scotland, and Wales are and long have been mutually imbricated and mutually influencing. Pocock, himself an early and influential proponent of the approach, has said that to treat the affairs of the English apart from the doings of the other peoples on the so-called "British Isles" is to confirm, by exclusion, a long tradition of complacently Anglocentric history. On the contrary, "[t]he premises must be that the various peoples and nations, ethnic cultures, social structures, and locally defined communities, which have from time to time existed in the area known as 'Great Britain and Ireland,' have not only acted so as to create the conditions of their several existences but have also interacted so as to modify the conditions of one another's existence and that there are processes here whose history can and should be studied" ("Limits and Divisions" 317). Each British "nation" came into being within a dense interweave of intra- and interisland encounters among the various British peoples. Thus, British history (at least as it was initially defined) tries to decenter England so as to resituate it within the multicentric domain that has come to be known as "Britain."

To my mind, the most valuable contribution that this historiography can make to Spenser studies is an expanded sense of what "British" can mean. The term is usefully capacious; it can house disparate identifications and do so without necessarily obliterating them. In one usage, at least, "British" holds in equivocal tension "national" loyalties that, often, are more distinctly opposed to each other in political and/or historical fact. I should say from the start, though, that "British" sometimes has quite another connotation. It implies instead the *denial* of politico-cultural difference on the two islands off the coast of continental Europe. (The phrase "British Isles" itself is regularly denounced. As Pocock notes, the name is "one which Irishmen reject and Englishmen decline to take seriously" ["British History" 606].) The British history has its critics, and many of them are themselves historians of the early modern period. From these, we hear that the term is at once too imprecise and too unitary. Some of the deepest reservations arise from the suspicion that, as Keith Brown puts it, "the emergence of British History looks like a reincarnation of the history of the English state" (117). So much of what counts as the history of this period has been done and is still being done by English practitioners who ask English questions about English concerns that British history, whatever its pretensions, is just more of the same, albeit under a new, more ecumenical name. The great crises of England's past are "discovered" to have some of their causes and effects elsewhere on the British Isles, and the "over-production in the historiography of the English Civil War," for example, "is dealt with by letting the overspill be soaked up by Scotland, Wales and Ireland." A regnant establishment opens new areas of inquiry, but only, perhaps, as a "repetition of the original colonial project" (Maley, rev. 53). Nicholas Canny, a self-described "Brito-sceptic," declares that "much of what appears as 'new British history' is nothing but 'old English history' in 'Three-Kingdoms' clothing" ("Irish, Scottish, and Welsh" 147–48). Practically, he doubts whether most historians can truly master the "newly defined subject in all its aspects" since it requires "a good reading knowledge of three Celtic languages as well as English and Latin" (148). More programmatically, he charges that the British history attempts to "treat of developments within the three kingdoms of England, Scotland and Ireland as but parts of a single process" ("Anglicization" 49), "imply[ing] an integrity for 'These Islands' probably in excess of any that ever existed, and distract[ing] our minds from the lively but varied contacts that were maintained by the several different communities on the two islands with the European Continent" ("Irish, Scottish and Welsh" 147). It is a "holistic approach" that "emphasise[s] similarity at the expense of difference, and ignores the fundamental diversities that made it so difficult for the several peoples on the two islands to live within a single polity" (148). Derek Hirst too has wondered whether this approach attributes an ahistorical "supranationalism" to the various British peoples of this time. These were "nations," he says, that were usually more parochial in their sense of themselves: "[O]ur Olympian vantage, offering all the consolations of hindsight and a perspective that is at least potentially pan-British, risks obscuring the sense of their world held by [early modern 'Britons']. We may think we know what the term 'Britain' means; but we should pause a little—as successive rulers were forced to do— before requiring our forebears to think supranationally" (452).

Arguably, this is a misreading of the British historiography. Pocock notes that while critics such as Canny have a point that is "wholly valid," it is "most powerfully so when directed against a contention which I do not think anyone is currently putting forward: namely, that 'British history' is the name of a paradigm which offers to include every aspect of every people formed within the territory of the second United Kingdom (1801–1922) . . . and reduce it to a common history, the history of a single formed identity" ("Conclusion" 295). But, for the literary reader, perhaps the strongest argument against taking "British" in this sense, as a rhetorical device for either ignoring or transcending the many conflicts of a shared past, is how little use it is when it comes to making sense of early modern figures and of their writings. This sceptical understanding of "British" puts the emphasis in a single place, on imposed uniformity, whereas in the period itself, it seems to me, we often see the accent falling (though not always equally) on both uniformity *and* on "fundamental diversities." It may be that "British" was less susceptible of a single definition in an era before anything like a trans-island hegemony—a truly "British" empire—had been effectively installed in the early eighteenth century. Indeed, it is arguable that in this "pre-imperial" period, what "Britain" often implied, more than unity, were the dislocations of the islands' past. Here, therefore, I will take a specific work, Edmund Spenser's *A View of the Present State of Ireland*, and ask whether and in what sense the historiography he practices there can be thought of as prototypically British. Spenser, we know, was well versed in the British history of his own day. (In the *View* he draws heavily on William Camden's *Britannia*, among other works.) But more consequential, I suspect, were his observations of the British history shaping his adopted country of Ireland, which left him sceptical that "nations" on the two islands could be derived from anything but flux and accident. Though Spenser might share premises with today's British history, however, the conclusions he drew from those premises were strikingly different, and characteristically radical and severe. According to this poet's hard logic, what the historical predicament of Britishness necessitated was not a decentering of the "nation" that he called his own on the British Isles—England—but rather an ever greater imposition of its national order on its neighboring polities. For Spenser, to be British in late-sixteenth-century Ireland was to be conscious of an inevitable, though often deplorable, condition that could be escaped only by the forceful assertion of an authoritative and ultimately transcendent "nationalism" that exalted a single nation-state, England, over its British neighbors. Not a "supra-nationalism," that is to say, but a rigorous "super-nationalism." Ultimately, I argue, this idealization of England represents a triumph over its own history, since, as Spenser means to demonstrate, such a polity can be achieved only by eradicating the British contingencies that mark (and mar) its chronicle. And I will suggest further, and more speculatively, that by about 1596, when Spenser wrote the *View*, he himself was more British than he was English, and perhaps more so than he was New English. In saying this, I am not concerned so much with assigning Spenser a discrete identity as in learning what kind of work the designation "British" can do in opening up the complexity of that identity. By "British," then, I mean that for Spenser in Ireland, the ramifications of the British politics of his era were a lived reality, that he meditated deeply on those ramifications in both his prose and poetry, and that for him one such ramification may have been that the condition of Britishness superseded the more narrow "national" identity—Englishness—that we usually assign him. But, again, Spenser's Britishness would be misunderstood as a "supra-nationalism." Britishness will not do much work for us if we think that it implies the erasure of all distinguishing national marks—a pan-Britishness—so that we have Spenser as a cipher, a Renaissance man without qualities. Britishness, for Spenser, was not so much a coherent identity as an ongoing predicament, one that had been brought about by a long history of diaspora and intermingling among the diverse peoples on the British Isles—a history, thus, of the sort that is now being called to our attention by the emerging British historiography.

These are large claims, and here brief examples from the *View* will have to do the work of a longer demonstration. From these instances we can at least take away a sense of the argumentative links between British history and English nationalism in Spenser's thought. One of England's principal problems in Ireland, he claims through Irenius, is its permeability to "outside" agitators and the tendency of such agitators to link up with, and even become, "inside" agitators. This has long made it difficult to delimit Ireland and keep it under control. And even more disruptively, he implies, it makes it hard to know exactly what Ireland is and from where on the British Isles a threat is emanating. For instance, when Edward II reigned in England, the Scottish king, Robert Le Bruce, "bore [him] a most malicious and spiteful mind." This rival "annoy[ed Edward's] territories of England," but he also sent a "power of Scots and Redshanks into Ireland." These combined with indigenous clans, "got footing," and marched against the English Pale (17). Finally, these invaders were driven home to Scotland. But where is "home" for these Scots? From whence did this threat come? It might seem that the answer is simply "Scotland," but in the *View* coordinates will often shift. And, as Willy Maley has pointed out, Irenius's declarations are "hardly designed to clear the confusion" ("Spenser and Scotland" 9). How Scotland is to be distinguished from Ireland, or Ireland from Scotland, becomes more and more perplexing as Irenius's argument continues. Indeed, he goes to great lengths to prove that the Irish and the Scots both are derived "originally" from nomadic Scythians. Thus, he declares, "Scotland and Ireland are all one and the same" (38). Have we arrived at the end point here, at the ethnic, if not geographic, origins of the invaders? Andrew Hadfield has argued that in the *View* Spenser means to identify the Scythians as the true progenitors of the Gaels. "Irish culture, whatever additions have been made to it and whatever transformations it has undergone, is, at heart, still that of the ancient Scythians" (104). Irenius is disinclined to elaborate on other derivations; "[i]n contrast, he runs out of space attempting to list all the Scythian traits" (105). And, indeed, the weight of the *View*'s contention is distributed towards the Scythians. What keeps it unbalanced, though, are constant—and, surely, intentional— reminders that the Gaels trace an irredeemably multiple lineage. "At heart," they are a hybrid people. In this treatise, genealogy is as inconstant as geography; as another critic puts it, "the whole discussion rests on the assumption that there is no such thing as the Irish as such" (Maley, "Spenser and Scotland" 11). "[N]ot of one nation," says Irenius pointedly, "was [Ireland] peopled as it is" (37). The Irish are descended from the Scythians, but they are also descended from the Scots and the ancient Britons (and, some say, the "Spaniards or . . . Africans or Goths" [39]) and the ancient Gauls, whose speech, in turn, "is the very British, the which was generally used here in all Britain before the coming in of the Saxons, and yet is retained of the Welshmen, the Cornishmen, and the Britons of France." If locating the stock from which the Irish are derived is difficult here, it is because at every point of origin Spenser falls back to another, and in the *View* no origin is pure. None of the British peoples, as Spenser says, have remained unmixed with others. Even the "dialect" of the aboriginal British has been "greatly altered" through "time working alteration of all things and the trading and interdeal with other nations round." Though some "original words appear to be the same" (45), still, just who the "very British" were originally is left an open question, as is the derivation of the Irish from them. "The Irish," opines Irenius in an assertion that unravels as it goes, "are very Scots or Scyths originally, though since intermingled with many other nations repairing and joining unto them" (57). And for all this, Spenser takes as his warrant the British historiography of his own day. For those who "list to read in Camden or Buchanan," the etymologies that lead back to a variegated British past may be seen "at large" (45).

When Robert Le Bruce's troops marched out of Scotland, then, they did not present the English crown with a unified, readily identifiable foe. Instead, they came trailing behind them a long and complicated history that rendered the very term "Scottish" ambiguous. Stressing such historical "indeterminacies" in Spenser's *View* is worthwhile, if only because they help to undo the distinction between Spenserian "prose" and Spenserian "poetry" that has sometimes straitjacketed the argument of the treatise into a set of formulaic claims. But if we stop there, we mistake how pervasively ambiguous *and* how powerfully self-correcting his prose can often be. To this problem of "national" "interdeal," therefore, Spenser has a solution. Immediately following upon his description of the depredations of Edward Le Bruce, Spenser inserts praise for Lord Grey of Wilton, the former Lord Deputy whom Spenser had previously defended allegorically in book 5 of *The Faerie Queene*. Later in the *View*, Spenser will claim that Grey's policy failures were the result of unfounded accusations lodged against him and of a misplaced royal benevolence towards the Irish. Enemies alleged that Grey was "a bloody man, and regarded not the life of [Elizabeth I's] subjects, no more than dogs. . . . Ear was soon lent thereunto," a general pardon issued, and Grey's commendably rigorous "purposes were blanked" (106). The "sharp execution of the Spaniards" (107) at Smerwick was, contrary to reports, fully justified, and so on. Here, though, Spenser offers a less direct but more historiographically involved defense. Eudoxus, harking back to the incursions of Robert Le Bruce, laments the "desolation . . . made by those ragtails in Scotland," and draws an explicit comparison between it and the present "calamities," the "many evils, as every day I see more and more thrown upon" Ireland, "miserably tossed and turmoiled with these variable storms of afflictions." But Irenius reminds him that, although before Ireland's "principal parts have been rent and torn asunder," and "rebellion" has often "stretch[ed] itself into all parts" (19) of the kingdom, Grey, "like a most wise pilot," was able to keep it on course and safe, and "held her most strongly even against those roaring billows . . . by the space of twelve or thirteen years" (20). To the threat posed by the border-crossing Scots, that is, the hard policy of Lord Grey is the best response. The very predictability of Irenius's "ship of state" metaphor signals a shift in rhetoric that one often sees in the *View:* from a nuanced and open-ended statement of a difficulty— here, the political and even ontological uncertainties that arise from many centuries of imbrication among the British peoples—to a resolute and deliberately reductive statement of the remedy. It might be true that in the past the Scots and Irish have drifted across one another's nebulous borders, conspiring, fighting, and intermarrying. (Who "knoweth not," asks Spenser, that "the O'Neals [of Ireland] are nearly allied unto the MacNeals of Scotland, and to the Earl of Argyll, from whom they use to have all their succours of those Scots and redshanks"? [114].) And, of course, they did so still. But borders will be firmer, Spenser implies, when an effective war machine, guided by consistent strategies, can make them so. As he charts the political space of the British Isles in his *View,* Spenser relies only intermittently on a modern sense of "nationhood"—distinct boundaries, rigid control over ingress and egress, centralized authority, and so on. No one of the polities he treats—Ireland, Scotland, and even England—is autonomous enough in present actuality to be rendered historically distinct or politically independent. Spenser's sense of the space these "nations" define among them owes far more, in fact, to his knowledge of the complexity of the dealings among the British peoples. He was, and not at all despite himself, a British historiographer. But what Spenser wants out of this melange of histories is not a polyglot polity that reflects the diversity of its origins. Rather, Spenser militates for a single "nation" that will dominate, if not entirely subsume, the rest. As the *View* makes very clear, he is willing to contemplate what amounts to a campaign of official terror to establish it. Lord Grey is his exemplar because, when many among the Irish (or are they Scots? or Scythians? or Britons?) "conspired in one to cast off their subjection to the Crown of England" (19), he was able to forestall them and to consolidate Elizabeth's disparate realm under her single authority.

Or take, very briefly, another example from the *View* in which this same drift from British *exemplum* to English *apologia* can be seen. Spenser is, once again, tracing the derivation of the present day Irish to their disparate origins, this time to their Gaulish ancestors. They had bards among them, for instance, as do the Gaels, and "the profession . . . is not yet altogether left off by the Welsh which are their posterity." The Gauls also "used swords a handful broad, and so do the Irish now," and they "used to drink their enemies' blood and to paint themselves therewith." As evidence of the survival of this custom among the Irish, Spenser adduces "the execution of a notable traitor at Limerick called Murrogh O'Brien, [where] I saw an old woman which was his foster mother took up his head whilst he was quartered and sucked up all the blood running there out, saying that the earth was not worthy to drink it, and therewith also steeped her face and breast, and tore her hair, crying and shrieking out most terribly" (62). This passage is often quoted for effect. Sheila Cavanagh describes it as "sensationalism," a tale of the sort that "provided entertainment for a curious English audience as well as political ammunition" (129). And, admittedly, it is vivid and it does help to locate Spenser as an observer and agent of England's sharp policies in the Irish kingdom. Spenser accepts the brutality he witnesses as necessary and proper and appears to offer neither explanation nor justification. But we should note that the scene emerges as the conclusion of a distinct historiographical argument, and that its politics follows from that argument. This shrieking mother implies a widespread disruption; what she demonstrates for Spenser is the "Britishness" of her protest. Her howls resonate with other voices that can be heard across the Irish Sea, in Wales, in Gaul, in Scotland, all linked by a history of crisscrossing traditions that disperse challenges to English authority around the British Isles and beyond. It is not inadvertent, I think, that this tableau of official English violence is placed at this juncture in Spenser's *View.* Its powerful effect is called for by the overdetermined history that Spenser has been evoking, and it is the rhetorical antithesis to it. England, he seems to suggest, will be founded in such places and by such acts as these. And the Britain that Murrogh O'Brien's mother represents is what England must supplant.

In both of these examples from the *View,* two projects are juxtaposed. One is historiographical and retrospective, the recovery of a British past, and one is political and prospective, the establishment of an English nation. On the one hand, Spenser is committed to tracing the "origins" of the peoples he treats back through the tangled weave of many centuries of interisland history. However, when he arrives at those "origins," what he finds, typically, is mingling and dispersal. We might be tempted to say now that the first project cancels—or at least complicates—the second, that an awareness of the heterogeneity of national origins works against any assertion of a unitary national sovereignty. This assumption, of course, is tacit in Canny's belief that a British history must perforce be "holistic" and will inevitably "ignore . . . the fundamental diversities that made it so difficult for the several peoples on the two islands to live within a single polity." It also inheres in Hirst's suspicion that Britishness amounts to a "supranationalism," that is to say, to a transcendence of loyalty to an English (or Irish or Scottish or Welsh) nation. But for Spenser these projects are not in tension, but mutually linked. On the other hand, then, it is *because* no one of the British peoples—and this explicitly includes the English—can call upon a seamless, unadulterated history reaching back to pristine origins that one of those peoples—the English—must emerge as a nation-state capable of subordinating all of the British peoples to it. In the *View,* the English "nation" is established as an after-the-fact construct whose imperatives are all the more compelling because they attach to nothing but "alteration," "trading," and "interdeal" at their historical root. This British history is a history of chronic instability, and it puts "national" identity on the islands profoundly in question—so profoundly that it must be answered with a fervent and compensatory Englishness. But though a British history posed severe problems for the Tudor state, and though these were problems that Spenser wanted rectified, that it *was* a British history he did not deny. For Spenser, Britishness named a lived condition that was both impossible to ignore and, ultimately, imperative to escape.

Now, to return to Pocock's dismissal of the phantasmic "'British' nationalist." If Spenser did indeed have an acute sense of a British past distinguished by constant traffic and exchange, and if, consequently, he thought of himself as in some way a "Briton," as the (often reluctant) inheritor of this variegated past, then, what can we say of his "identity"? How did "Britishness" and "nationalism" intersect in this poet? It is, I think, the very impossibility of this term, "'British' nationalist," the contradictions this phrase houses, that make it useful in getting at the difficulties of Spenser's multifarious belonging. What term, if it comes to that, would best describe the author of the *View*? Was he "English"? "New English"? Of course, it is the first of these designations that is now under the greatest critical pressure. A long tradition in Renaissance literary criticism has taken Spenser as unproblematically "English" and has canonized him as such. Now that the implications of Spenser's sojourn in Ireland are being debated more and more, however, this is becoming harder and harder to do credibly. Spenser and his texts had "ceased to be 'mere English,'" Hadfield said recently, "when both left England in the late 1570s or 1580 and were 'corrupted' by their relationship with Ireland" (202). "Spenser cannot be read—and never should have been read—as a straightforwardly English writer" (11). Hadfield shares with many others the sense that Spenser's location—geographic and cultural—has too often been discounted. That Spenser lived for sixteen years (or more) in the Irish kingdom must surely have had ramifying consequences, both for his "nationality" and his writing. Inevitably, Englishness, both as a lived condition and as a literary trope, would have been quite different when England itself was elsewhere and Spenser's "here" was a place on the ragged edge of the Queen's empire. Among historians, it has been Nicholas Canny who has been most forward in urging us to think of Spenser as New English, as one among the cadre of English officials dispatched to early modern Ireland to reduce that seemingly intractable kingdom to civility. He holds that Spenser's *View* was clearly a New English polemic "designed to serve the interests of those engaged upon the conquest and colonization of Ireland at the end of the sixteenth century, . . . the advanced opinion to be found there can be explained by the peculiar, not to say precarious, circumstances in which these individuals found themselves" ("Edmund Spenser" 2). The New English, alienated from the Gaels they were sent to administer, distrustful of the Old English they were gradually supplanting, suspected by (and, often, ignored by) the royal administration they were mandated to serve, elaborated a distinct ideology out of the exigencies Ireland imposed on them. Not only was Spenser not simply an Englishman, insists Canny; he was a displaced Englishman who assertively took upon himself a very particular—indeed, site specific—sort of Englishness. His "nationality" was that of a governing elite so far removed from England that it had come to acquire an identity of its own and its own imperatives.

But, if it now seems implausible to argue that Spenser was "straightforwardly English," is it any more plausible to argue that he was "straightforwardly" New English? Hadfield, for example, agrees with Canny that Spenser was New English, that this is "the colonial class to which [he] belonged." But, as he also shows, it was by virtue of that very ascription that Spenser was "caught between a host of competing and intersecting identities." Indeed, he and his cohort were "worried that unless they defined their identity in an aggressive way it would disappear before their very eyes" (4). It is just this quandary, the result of a life lived on two islands and split across them, that is hardest to capture in any one term. Hadfield's way of putting it is appropriately imprecise. If Spenser was once English, perhaps there was a sense in which he remained so during his years in Ireland, but not "straightforwardly." But if he did transmogrify into another condition, New Englishness, when (and just how) did this happen? And, if it did, could that condition always be distinguished from his originary Englishness? From the debased Irishness he castigated? Or, for that matter, from the Britishness he sometimes promoted, sometimes condemned? My point is not that these distinctions could not be made. They were, and by Spenser himself. But for *us* to make them involves us, as it involved this author, in a labor of discrimination among simultaneously like and unlike identities that cannot, in the very nature of such work, reach an end.

We may need to think again about Spenser's long stay in the British kingdom of Ireland. Richard Rambuss has suggested that we have been too quick to assume that Spenser suffered from being consigned to the "margins" of England's domain. On the contrary, by seeing the "distance of exile as opening up a space for saying what cannot be said elsewhere, nearer the centers of power," Spenser "empowered" himself (107). We might take this further, though, and consider whether the space that Spenser found himself in was not only less marginal than has been thought, but less centered (and more British) altogether. Spenser's belonging in any one "nation," that of his birth, that of his "exile," was chronically uncertain, and it is well known that the "degeneration" of identity in the Irish kingdom is a preoccupying topic in the *View*. Englishness is always in jeopardy; Irishness is always threatening to subsume its ostensibly civil counterpart. But I have wanted to suggest that his texts imply further metamorphoses, and what these open up in Spenser studies is the problem of Britain. Perhaps, Spenser's "exile" actually propelled him into an unstable, transmogrifying political domain within which he achieved not only the view from the edge, but a perspective that was not reducible to the nationally centered outlook of any one of the coeval polities on the British Isles. It may be that Spenser's identity arose from a condition of displacement (*not* English, *not* New English, *not* Irish) whose complexities only "British" can begin to figure. In the early modern period, as Hadfield points out, Britain was still a "nebulously conceived ideal." Spenser's work, he says, "is defined by the Tudors' attempt to expand their boundaries and unify [this ideal in practice], as well as exploit and subdue other nations and cultures" (12). Caught between colliding "nations and cultures" and transfixed by a nebulous ideal, how hard must it have been for Spenser to arrive at *any* final identity. And how unlikely it is that he did so. After all, "no one ever has, ever will, or ever should" become a "'British' nationalist."

NOTE

1. For a brief overview, see Ellis, "'Not Mere English.'" Pocock first issued a call for a transisland history in "A British History," and then later in "The Limits and Divisions of British History." The range of recent work in this field is well represented in four recent anthologies: *Three Nations—A Common History? England, Scotland, Ireland and British History c. 1600–1920*, ed. Asch; *Conquest & Union: Fashioning a British State 1485–1725*, ed. Ellis and Barber; *Uniting the Kingdom? The Making of British History*, ed. Grant and Stringer; and *The British Problem, c. 1534 -1707: State Formation in the Atlantic Archipelago*, ed. Bradshaw and Morrill. For a discussion of this historiography as it relates to early modern English literature, see my *Between Nations*.

"A DOUBTFULL SENSE OF THINGS"

Thievery in *The Faerie Queene* 6.10 and 6.11

Heather Dubrow

"So clomb this first grand Thief into God's Fold" (4.192), Milton writes, thus troping Satan's transgression as neither deception, seduction, nor disobedience, though he presents it in those terms elsewhere, but rather as robbery. Though the subject of thievery in early modern texts has been neglected by most critics, it frequently recurs at charged moments: Hamlet, for example, calls Claudius "[a] cutpurse of the empire and the rule" (3.4.99), and the embittered Fifth Song of Sidney's *Astrophil and Stella* includes the accusation, "Yet worst then worst, I say thou art a theefe" (43). Why, then, does Spenser too focus on thievery in a climactic passage in his own epic, the invasion of the pastoral world in book 6? And what does his representation of that transgression suggest about its roles in his culture, his genres, and his own subjectivity? Answers to those questions about this episode, a narrative of boundaries and borders, can be found on the often tense and guarded boundaries between critical methods and approaches.

A close reading of the final seven lines of canto 10, stanza 39, suggests some answers—and in so doing poses further questions about the interplay between Spenser's language and cultural history:

> A lawlesse people, *Brigants* hight of yore,
> That neuer vsde to liue by plough nor spade,
> But fed on spoile and booty, which they made
> Vpon their neighbours, which did nigh them border,

The dwelling of these shepheards did inuade,
And spoyld their houses, and them selues did murder;
And droue away their flocks, with other much disorder.[1]

This passage, I suggest, indicates the crucial coordinates for mapping the position of thievery in Spenser's poem and his culture: the feared action often involves the home and hence threats of invasion, the feared agent is a neighbor reconstructed as an outsider, and the feared results include corruption and contamination, notably the blurring of epistemological categories.

Notice, first of all, that the invaders are termed "*Brigants.*" Delighting as he did in etymology, Spenser may well have realized that, as Cotgrave's early modern dictionary testifies, the word was associated both with foot soldiers and with a type of armor (Cotgrave s.v. "brigand"). Thus the term evokes contemporary fears of demobilized military men and arguably also suggests a contrast between the impermeable barriers of armor and the tragic permeability of this, though perhaps not all, pastoral worlds.

Determining the geographical and ethnic implications of Spenser's allusion to brigands is, however, more complicated. Some readers have constructed a defensible though not definitive case that the word evoked Continental bandits; but by and large it was associated with a people of Celtic origins living in the north of England (Dillon and Chadwick 19, 22), though some early modern sources cite only that geographical area without referring to ethnicity. Thus, for example, Stephanus's *Dictionarium historicum geographicum poeticarum* specifies the northern regions of England in which the brigands live but notes as well that Ptolemy describes them as Irish (Stephanus s.v. "brigantes"). Similarly, in his *Rerum scoticarum historia* George Buchanan, an author with whom Spenser was certainly familiar, associates brigands with the York area and stresses that they controlled the whole breadth of the island. Questioning claims that they hailed from Gaul, he suggests instead that they migrated from Spain to Ireland and from there to England and hence, like all the Irish, were of what he terms the Scottish race (bk. 2, fol. 26, sig. Eiiii). Another dictionary, Cooper's 1565 volume, simply glosses the term in question as, "an ancient people in the north part of England" (s.v. "brigantes").

In addition to contributing to the georgic allusions harvested in Anthony Low's study of that literary type (53–54), the succeeding lines link the brigands to another lawless tribe, the people who thought that Serena was good enough to eat. We learn that the brigands "fed on spoile and booty." "Fed" connects them to the description of Calidore's "hungry eye" (6.9.26) as he listens to Meliboeus, thus anticipating later connections between the heroic and the demonic intruders into pastoral. The notion of eating spoil may also have an undertow of taboo. More to my purposes now, however, "spoil" and its cognates, which occur no fewer than four times in stanzas 39 and 40 alone, serve to interrelate the results of war, the act of stealing, and the process of contaminating. Thus Spenser dovetails fears of a foreign invasion and of burglary, associating both with corruption.

By characteristically and insistently drawing attention to the etymology of "neighbor" in the sixth line of the stanza ("nigh them border"), the poet emphasizes that the brigands, though the opposite of the pastoral world in so many ways, live at its margins. They are, however, outsiders, as the word "inuade" in the following line reminds us—a crucial concept in this canto, and here highlighted by its crucial position as a rhyme word.

Notice, too, how the succeeding line describes what they invade: "the dwelling of these shepheards." While "dwelling" may be glossed as "locale" or "site," it also carries with it connotations of "home," which would have been absent had Spenser written, say, "the meadows of these shepherds." And, indeed, the next line explicitly lists "and spoyled their houses" among the three principal results of this invasion. Its perpetrators are, in other words, burglars, a point to which I will return. In another sense "dwelling" functions as a gerund; that is, the brigands destroy not only edifices but also the ability to dwell in the sense emphasized at the conclusion of "To Penshurst": remaining spatially and morally constant. This is, of course, a value as often invoked as it is threatened in pastoral, where the chasing that represents narrativity often challenges the dwelling that represents the lyric. It is no coincidence in this light that Spenser's Meliboeus evokes his classical namesake, who famously loses his home in Virgil's first eclogue, nor is it coincidental that pastoral itself often represents a lost home.

Spenser proceeds to describe the consequences of this invasion in telling terms:

> Amongst the rest, the which they then did pray,
> They spoyled old *Melibee* of all he had,
> And all his people captiue led away,
> Mongst which this lucklesse mayd away was lad,
> Faire *Pastorella,* sorrowfull and sad,
> Most sorrowfull, most sad, that euer sight,
> Now made the spoile of theeues and *Brigants* bad,
> Which was the conquest of the gentlest Knight,
> That euer liu'd, and th'onely glory of his might.
> . . .

For vnderneath the ground their way was made,
  Through hollow caues, that no man mote discouer
  For the thicke shrubs, which did them alwaies shade
  From view of liuing wight, and couered ouer:
  But darkenesse dred and daily night did houer
  Through all the inner parts, wherein they dwelt,
  Ne lightned was with window, nor with louer,
  But with continuall candlelight, which delt
A doubtfull sense of things, not so well seene, as felt.
(6.10.40, 42)

While linking this kidnapping with the story of Persephone (Blitch), the lines also intensify the focus on thievery in the passage quoted above. When we are told in the fortieth stanza that Pastorella is "made the spoile of theeues and *Brigants* bad, / Which was the conquest of the gentlest Knight," the apparent contrast between "spoile" and "conquest" ostensibly distinguishes but also links the two invaders in question, thus reactivating an earlier simile associating Calidore with that other marauder Paris, an image explicated well by Donald Cheney among others (Cheney 223–25). Moreover, no poet delights in the repetition of words more than Spenser (or fears the repetition of errors and sins more), and the recurrence of terms here is particularly telling. For these lines not only allude to "spoil[s]" yet again but also flag the brigands' alternative title as thief, a term Spenser insistently repeats throughout these cantos. He harps on the word, I suggest, to call up the nexus of fears it called up in his audience, a nexus that, as I will demonstrate, tied together cultural concerns about the three principal issues we are tracing: invasion of the home, insiders and outsiders, and contamination. And the connection of "spoil" with a beautiful virgin functions proleptically as well, hinting of the danger that she will be despoiled by the brigand who attempts to invade into that other private territory, Pastorella's body.

    Indeed, the syntactical parallel between Pastorella as the brigand's "spoile" and as Calidore's "conquest" at once invites us to consider the obvious moral parallel between the two invaders and warns us against the tempting assumption that they are being equated rather than just compared. To be sure, invasions are endemic in this and other pastoral interludes, as Spenserians have often noted (Parker, *Inescapable Romance* 103–04; Tonkin 289); here the long series of them includes the threats from the tiger, the arrival of the merchants, and of course Calidore's own disruption of the vision on Mount Acidale—so to speak, a disgraceful event. Yet Spenser, as he so often does, invites us to note the imbrications of similarities and differences; yes, Calidore is like the brigands in that he invades the pastoral world and targets Pastorella as his booty, yet on the other hand they enjoy a "close felicity" (6.10.38) that hardly characterizes her relationship with the maven of the brigands.

Similarly, the brigands are not the first robbers in this particular Eden. When Meliboeus describes the pleasures of his pastoral retreat, virtually all of his activities involve some sort of predation—he tells Calidore not about watching his flock but about hunting the foxes that threaten it, he takes the kid from its mother, and he traps birds and fishes. One of the presents Coridon, grandfather to Marvell's Damon in this regard, gives Pastorella is "litle sparrowes, stolen from their nest" (6.9.40). Such references remind us that this is indeed a postlapsarian paradise, and they too demand to be compared to—but again not equated with—the thievery of the brigands. Rather, borrowing from Paul Alpers the argument that pastoral typically suspends threats (*What is Pastoral?* 68–69, 173), I want to suggest that the negative resonances of Meliboeus's and Coridon's activities, like those of Calidore's conquest, are indeed suspended in the sense of neither cancelled nor activated—another point to which I will return.

Stanzas 41, 42, and 43 represent the brigands in terms of night, secrecy, and darkness, descriptions cogently analyzed by James Nohrnberg from biblical and other perspectives (*Analogy* 665, 731–72). More to my purposes, Spenser thus links robbery with indeterminacy. In particular, the Alexandrine of stanza 42 describes the thieves' underground lair as creating "A doubtfull sense of things, not so well seene, as felt," a hexameter whose slowness, intensified by the monosyllables and abstractions that weight it, aptly mimes the hesitancies of doubt. During the subsequent fight in the thieves' den, "the candlelight / Out quenched, leaues no skill nor difference of wight" (6.11.16). The crime that has confounded villains and the hero is associated with both literal and epistemological darkness and with the blurring of lines that results. Commenting on the mercantile references here, Clare Regan Kinney plausibly suggests the episode enacts the intrusion of material reality into the allegorical world (113–15); even more significant, however, is the way the thieves threaten material and other versions of reality.

Canto 10 concludes on references to selling the prisoners; the next one details the business negotiations between the brigands and the merchants. Thus, as Kinney and others note, Spenser links the brigands with another type of predation, the commercial. In these events, like Calidore's initial conversation with Meliboeus, money intrudes into pastoral, and arguably the whole episode allegorizes a nostalgia for a countryside before commerce. In any event, commerce almost by definition involves a crossing of borders that permits the outside to enter within and the inside to move without.

In short, then, thievery in this passage involves two principal types of spoiling, corresponding to the brigands' roles as those who live on the border between inside and outside. First, the felony in question effects the realization of predilections suspended in less extreme and less threatening form within that world until the entrance of the thieves, notably a propensity to trap and to take. And second, it introduces dangers that had been absent from pastoral, notably the depredations of the mercantile. In so doing, it apparently draws attention to distinctions between the pastoral and the commercial, the virtuous and the villainous, the inside and the outside, but in fact darkens and blurs such contrasts.

The status of thievery in sixteenth-century England provides many though not all answers to why it assumes these roles in Spenser's text.[2] Recent studies of crime in early modern England, manifesting a Foucauldian preoccupation with the outré and extreme, have focused mainly on such deeds as murder, witchcraft and treason (Dolan, *Dangerous Familiars*; Maus); but the more quotidian felony of stealing was not only more commonly practiced but also, I maintain, more deeply feared. The assize records indicate that thievery, a category including offenses like burglary, robbery, purse snatching, horse stealing, and so on, was the principal felony throughout the Tudor and Stuart periods in the many counties covered by these documents. In Essex 90 percent of all reported felonies were crimes against property (Samaha 22). Moreover, thievery apparently became particularly prevalent during the decade *The Faerie Queene* appeared; although studies of crime rates are complicated by a series of methodological problems, the historian J.A. Sharpe is persuasive in his assertion that crimes against property rose to a peak in the 1590s (190).

Thievery, I would suggest, was not only the most typical felony when *The Faerie Queene* was written but also a prototypical one in the sense defined by cognitive scientists and recently discussed from a different, more literary angle in a forthcoming essay by Alan Richardson and Mary Thomas Crane. Prototypes are specific instances of a set or category that a culture uses to define it, so that, for example, a robin not a gull might be the prototype of a bird. The thief, I maintain, became the prototype of all criminals in early modern England; this helps to explain the intensity of the fears manifest in Spenser's text and other cultural records such as the assize transcripts, as well as the tendency to trope other transgressions as thievery.

Those records of crime and prosecution also suggest particularly intense anxieties about burglary, the felony that generally involves entry into a house and hence invasion. For example, its alleged perpetrators, unlike most other types of thief, were not allowed to invoke the method for receiving a more lenient publishment known as benefit of clergy. As I noted earlier, the brigands invaded the "dwelling" of the shepherds and "spoyld their houses" (6.10.39), thus committing a particularly egregious form of thievery.

Assize transcripts also testify that by and large members of the same or adjoining communities were responsible for crimes in their own locales; typically, too, they worked alone or in small groups. Nonetheless, the highly popular literature of roguery, such as Greene's cony-catching pamphlets and Dekker's *Belman of London,* evokes well organized gangs of marauders; these predators, we are often informed, come from Ireland or from what is called "the North." They are presented as instances of categories of transgressors repeatedly cited in contemporary documents, the so-called "rogues and vagabonds." The local, individual thief metamorphoses, in other words, into an alien group, much as Spenser constructs his invaders as a gang of brigands. Thus the texts in question exaggerate, though perhaps do not wholly invent, the threat from roving gangs of outsiders. There is no better example of how and why crime is constructed—and reconstructed.

But why does a culture whose crimes were typically petty thefts committed by a neighbor instead read and write tracts about organized crime committed by rogues and vagabonds? The answers should not be surprising in our own culture, which has on occasion virtually suggested that the Mafia is the root of all evil. Crime was particularly threatening in Tudor and Stuart England partly because it was so often committed by members of one's own community. That situation might variously produce guilt about neglecting the needs of poor families (similarly, studies of witchcraft have suggested that such guilt lies behind accusations [Macfarlane 173–74]), concerns about the possible implication of one's own family, and anxiety about the category crises that result when the boy next door might be a thief. As in the case of the Mafia, constructions of the felony that literally displaces material goods effect their own version of displacement: they posit a criminal subculture reassuringly distinct and readily distinguishable from one's own community.

The Faerie Queene, then, variously adduces, intensifies, and rein-terprets fears of thieves prevalent in early modern England; thus, for example, the poem reflects the sense that burglars, those thieves who invade a home, are especially pernicious, and it rephrases the transformation of local thieves into outsiders by evoking the borderline state, as it were, of the neighbor who dwells just outside one's boundaries. Hence we should gloss the brigands in terms of anxieties about crime within England, not simply with fears of Ireland, pace the *Variorum* and strong essays recently published on the episode in question (Lupton; Stillman). Of course, those genealogies are by no means mutually exclusive. As I have indicated, sometimes—but by no means always—local thieves were perceived as, so to speak, illegal immigrants from Ireland in particular. Indeed, given that the brigands were often seen as Celts currently living in England, they provide a telling analogue to the construction of the category of rogues and vagabonds, and Spenser's passage arguably demonstrates and even models the imbrication of that cultural construction with myths and legends about brigands. Yet, while Spenser and his culture associated crime in England with the Irish, they did not simply equate the two. Indeed, these stanzas also direct our attention to a distinct though related strategy of Othering, the construction of the North as a category; this mode of classification deserves more attention than it has yet received.

But anxieties are often multiply determined, and the invasive thief, I suggest, tropes many other concerns. On the national level, critics have recently drawn attention to the pervasiveness of fears of invasion (Woodbridge, *Scythe of Saturn* 45–85). One sign of the current privileging of cultural over social history is that these anxieties have received the attention that is their due, while another element in the preoccupation with invasive thieves, a highly significant change in land law, has been neglected by students of Tudor and Stuart texts. Central to English common law is the concept of a so-called real action—that is, an action concerning land, which is defined as "real" in the sense of perpetual and hence always able to be recovered, as goods might not be. Such actions were notoriously cumbersome to litigate; for example, small technical mistakes in wording could determine the outcome.

The Tudor period saw the development of an alternative method of disputing title, the use of the so-called action of ejectment (Holdsworth 7: 4–23). This was a version of the laws concerning trespass, a large and amorphous category that included the situation of someone stepping onto the property of someone else but also encompassed a range of other imputed actions such as the less serious crimes against the person. This legal strategy was originally developed for the use of lessees, who could not pursue real actions because they were merely leasing the property in question. In the sixteenth century, however, freeholders began to use them in lieu of real actions, attracted by their less rigid and less technical rules and their provision of a jury trial. Doing so initially involved a maneuver that would entitle the would-be owner of the property to deploy procedures designed for lessees: he would lease the land to someone, who would then assume the role of plaintiff when the adversary trespassed on the land. Thus if A and B disputed each other's rights to land, A would lease it to C, who would then take out an action of ejectment against B, the current occupant of the land, who would then eject C from the property. As the early modern period progressed, however, the law recognized that such leases were pro forma and worked out a fictional formula involving an imaginary lessee. In short, both the actual practice and the later refinement of it involved fictions that echoed the incursions of literal thievery.

Other analogues to thievery were, as I have argued elsewhere, even closer to home. Because of the high mortality rates for both mothers and fathers, a number of Spenser's contemporaries were raised by stepparents or other guardians (Dubrow, "Message from Marcade"). Since many areas of England suffered a major mortality crisis in 1557–59, Spenser's immediate contemporaries were particularly likely to have come from what today would be called blended families. Analyzing the consequences of that situation is tricky: the stereotype of the evil stepmother probably shows more about the gendering of resentments than the machinations of second wives, and in fact some memoirs celebrate the behavior of stepparents (Baxter 12), though of course such statements are not without their own evidentiary problems. It remains clear, however, that stepparents and stepsiblings might not only introduce tension into a household but also have a material effect, in more than one sense of that adjective, on the inheritance a child by the first marriage had hoped to receive. Wardship was another potential consequence of losing a parent. Its consequences, thoroughly documented by historians (Bell; Hurstfield), also included threats to the money and property of the many children unfortunate enough to have unscrupulous guardians. Or, to put it another way, stepparents and guardians assigned to wards might well thievishly intrude into the putative pastoral serenity of a childhood, seizing an inheritance as their spoil.

If, as I have been indicating, some answers to the preoccupation with thievery that characterizes the episode of Pastorella lie on the borders of social, cultural, and legal history, others occupy the permeable boundaries between those fields and literary history and practices. To begin with, the anxiety of influence can on occasion criminalize literary imitation; Spenser and his readers were surely aware of the charge that literary imitation was, or could readily descend to, a type of thievery.[3] Sidney, always aware of his debts to other writers, famously insists that he is "no pick-purse of another's wit" (*Astrophil and Stella* 74.8). Even more to the point, the celebration in Ralegh's "Vision vpon this conceipt of the *Faery Queene*" culminates on a reference to the author of the epic as "that celestiall theife" (14), and Ralegh, it has recently been argued, saw all writing as a type of thievery (Bednarz 280–81, 298–99). Early in his career Spenser stages his own preoccupation with poets' debts to their predecessors by deploying the pastoral convention of one shepherd singing a song composed by another; thus the author of *The Faerie Queene* plays against each other multiple versions of giving and taking and of presence and absence. If the legends of rogues and vagabonds serve to Other thievery occurring close to home, writers may adapt the same strategy in relation to their own imputed pilferings. Marlowe, who frequently borrows from the work of others, repeatedly describes Tamburlaine as a thief (P. Cheney, *Marlowe's Counterfeit Profession* 301–02n30). And might not Spenser's portrayal of the tribe of brigands similarly distance an accusation to which the tribe of poets was liable?

The crime in question also figures in two of the most popular genres of the early modern period. Thieves feature as supporting actors in many dramas starring shepherds—witness the pirates in the Greek pastoral romance *Daphnis and Chloe* or Autolycus in *The Winter's Tale*. And witness too the haunting line that began this essay and sparked my own interest in thievery in the texts of early modern England, Milton's "So clomb this first grand Thief into God's Fold." More surprising and more revealing are inverted renditions of the relationship between pastoral and thievery in both canonical and popular literature. Thus in the cony-catching pamphlets, rather than antipastoral representatives of crime intruding on the countryside to wreck their evil, the denizens of a pastoral world enter the city. Similarly, the original audience of *1 Henry IV* would surely have heard distorted echoes of brigands intruding on pastoral serenity when the Law of the Father knocks on the tavern door. Yet from another perspective, the tavern is always already the Edenic world violated by thieves.

The tonalities of thievery in such episodes differ significantly, but all these instances draw attention to two reasons it is so significant in pastoral. Most obviously, pastoral repeatedly engages with the dynamics of loss and recovery (witness its predilection for the trope adynaton, which both erases and inscribes the impossible events to which it refers); thievery renders material and literal many other types of loss within pastoral. And connection is at once the ideology, the methodology, and the physiology of pastoral, the genre that variously links previous singers of a song to the current one, Eden to its fallen analogue, and one appearance of a refrain to the next one.[4] Thievery, in contrast, literally separates owner and object and on occasion literally ruptures locks.

Romance also enjoys a complex relationship with the practice of thievery, and studying these links provides a broader context for my reading of the episode of the brigands. Critics often cite *finding what was lost* as the praxis of that genre. A more precise and fruitful encapsulation, however, is that romance is the genre of *returning what was lost;* it resembles pastoral in this respect, though they differ in so many others. In romance the imperative to return what was lost is variously realized on the level of plot by the action of restoring lost children to their parents and on the level of narrative structure by the circularity so characteristic of this literary form. And romance is as well the genre of *protecting what is threatened,* which is why the ideologies of the Cold War generated its latter day incarnation in James Bond. Hence the thief is the archetypal enemy not only of the romance hero but of the genre itself: rather than returning he devotes himself to removing, and rather than protect, he threatens. Moreover, while romance attempts to purify, thievery, as we have seen, not only plunders but also contaminates and corrupts.

Pastoral and romance are, of course, two of the genres most attractive to Spenser; their representations of thievery are no doubt among the reasons for their appeal to him, and, conversely, his work in them may well have intensified his interest in the crime in question. But this is only one of several explanations for that interest. When the generally salutary emphasis on culturally constructed discourses hardens into a refusal to recognize the idiolects of specific writers, it replicates the rigidities of an approach with which it otherwise has little sympathy, the type of Freudianism that posits universal childhood experiences. Spenser's engagement with the significance of thievery is for many reasons particularly acute in both senses of that adjective. Unlike many other writers, he was a native Londoner, and that city is likely to have exposed him to more incidents of thievery than someone growing up in, say, Stratford would have witnessed. Lord Roche, Viscount Fermoy, whose confiscated Irish estate was given to Spenser, accused the poet of stealing his cattle (Bednarz 298). Moreover, many of the issues that concern him most throughout his career may be troped in terms of the felony in question. Some evidence, suggestive though not definitive, links thievery with one of Spenser's principal preoccupations, the threat of Catholicism: the literature of roguery is preoccupied with stealth, one of the mannerisms typically attributed to adherents of the Roman faith, and rogues and vagabonds, like Catholics, are typically portrayed as outsiders insidiously entering England to corrupt it. Though these connections necessarily remain speculative if based only on the literature of roguery, the episode of Abessa suggests that Spenser himself forged a link between these two types of transgression:

> He was to weete a stout and sturdie thiefe,
>   Wont to robbe Churches of their ornaments,
>   And poore mens boxes of their due reliefe,
>   . . .

> And all that he by right or wrong could find,
> Vnto this house he brought, and did bestow
> Vpon the daughter of this woman blind,
> *Abessa* daughter of *Corceca* slow.
> (1.3.17, 18)

Moreover, Abessa herself is associated with the crime in question.

As I just noted, in many of the tracts I mentioned thievery is described in terms of secrecy, surprise, and the unexpected, all preoccupations of Spenser; indeed, surprise and the unexpected are traced in an important article by Harry Berger as among the motifs of books 5 and 6 in particular (*Revisionary Play* 215–42), and their connection with thievery is yet another reason for the preoccupation with this crime in the Pastorella episode. Above all, throughout his career the unstable relationship between inside and outside intrigues Spenser—other genres intrude into his texts, Saint George's name resembles Orgoglio's, and so on. Burglary is of course the crime of the outside coming in and the inside being taken out, and hence, as my previous comments on the mercantile suggest, it is commerce rendered as transgression—which suggests yet another reason it interested Spenser and his contemporaries.

For the author of *The Faerie Queene* and his culture, in short, thievery, that crime of darkness, often involves the invasion of a home and the resulting spoiling of boundaries, contaminating inside with outside, the agrarian with the commercial, and the generous giving and returning variously represented by the Graces and by the genres of pastoral and romance with rapacious seizing. And studying how the episode of Pastorella orchestrates these issues may invite us to hear their notes, rendered in a different scale but recognizable nonetheless, in many arenas of our own culture. Might, for example, the murder mystery set in an English village or a country house replay the narrative of the pastoral intruder? And for certain late-twentieth-century inhabitants of the United States, might fears of illegal immigrants intensify and justify concerns about intrusive thieves, and vice versa?

NOTES

I would like to thank Paul Alpers, Thomas Herron, Anne Lake Prescott, A.W. Brian Simpson, and Susanne Lindgren Wofford for valuable assistance with this essay; I am also indebted to my audience at the Yale Spenser conference for fruitful suggestions and to my research assistant, Sarah Smith, both for helping practically and for supplementing my analyses of the intrusion of outsiders with a thoughtful observation about the parallel process of the inside moving without.

1. I retain Spenser's original spelling throughout, but in the case of other Renaissance texts I have regularized *i/j* and *u/v*, as well as the capitalization of titles.

2. A more detailed discussion of thievery, the loss of parents, and the loss of dwelling place appears in my forthcoming book *Shakespeare and Domestic Loss.* My discussion here is also based on the more extended analysis of thievery in my article "'In thievish ways.'"

3. I am indebted to Patrick Cheney for useful suggestions about this point.

4. Compare the related but distinct concept of convening in Alpers, *What Is Pastoral?* esp. chap. 3.

V. CONSTRUING THE SELF: LANGUAGE AND DIGESTION

"Better a Mischief than an Inconvenience"

"The saiyng self" in Spenser's *View*; or, How Many Meanings Can Stand on the Head of a Proverb?

Judith H. Anderson

The phrase "saiyng self" in my title comes from Nicholas Udall's introduction to Erasmus's *Apophthegmes* and refers to the individual apophthegm, or, as we would say, to "the saying itself."[1] To a modern ear Udall's phrasing also suggests both the self or subject who speaks an apophthegm and the one who is culturally spoken by it. The particular "saiyng self" of Spenser that I intend, "Better a mischiefe then an Inconvenience," occurs strikingly twice in the first half of *A View of the Present State of Ireland*.[2]

This saying, whose glossing I deliberately postpone, stands out in a modern setting because it is unfamiliar, but it also merits attention in formal and historical contexts. It may be the only proverb repeated in the *View*—at least it's the only repetition of one to catch my eye in numerous rereadings. First spoken by Spenser's character Irenius, it is curiously reiterated by Eudoxus, his other character, some fourteen pages later, soon enough for notice even by the mnemonically challenged modern reader. But this saying also stands out as a prefabricated syntactical unit—an instance of that oddity the frozen syntagm—and it is further notable as an instance of the popular rhetorical figure "paroemia," the sort of figure that Renaissance editions often flagged for emphasis and mnemonic reference with an indexical finger.[3] Of course as a proverb it is even more importantly a cultural nugget—a "gem" in Erasmus's phrasing—in the cultural code of a society that valued and collected the treasures of prudence and traditional wisdom.[4]

When Irenius initially invokes the saying, he is arguing that English common law is "inconvenient"—that is, unfitting—for Ireland, insofar as it was not framed for Irish circumstances.[5] Rejecting a conception of human law in accord with abstract justice, he maintains pragmatically that laws are only just if they can prevent current evils and provide for "the safetye of the Comon weale." He then offers an example of how this safety ought to be balanced against an abstract right, explaining, "It is a flatt wronge to punishe the thoughte or purpose of anye before it be acted, ffor trewe Iustice punisheth nothinge but the evill acte or wicked worde, yeat by the lawes of all kingedomes it is a capitall Cryme to devize or purpose the deathe of the kinge" because regicide would more harm the commonweal than subsequent "punishment of the Malefactours coulde remedye." It is to encapsulate this explanation that he concludes, "better is a mischief then an inconvenience" (65–66).

Before dealing fully with the interpretive possibilities that Irenius's concluding proverb embodies, I will need to describe its reiteration by Eudoxus, yet a couple of preliminary observations are possible here. First, the proverb's context suggests that a mischief is a wrong or harm done—in words cited by the *OED*—"to one or some particular persons" as distinct from a greater harm "to the whole Common-wealth in generall."[6] Second, if we take the word "capital" in Irenius's phrase "capitall cryme" at face value to indicate an offense deserving the death penalty, then his principle of preventive homicide agrees with the published views of Jean Bodin but goes beyond the penalty for such a crime of intention specified in the statutes of Ireland during the reign of Elizabeth.[7] In Ireland the statutory penalty was forfeiture of all the offender's possessions and "perpetuall imprisonment," although a repeat offense, which could even include *imagining* regicide, brought death (*Statutes of Ireland* 286–87). At the beginning of Elizabeth's reign, the statutes of England imposed the same penalty, but this was later toughened: in the thirteenth year of her reign, the English Parliament made the penalty capital on the first express offense and then, under the ever increasing apprehension of a Romish threat in the twenty-seventh year (1584–85), on the first imagined offense.[8] In passing it might be noted again, however, that the larger context of Irenius's explanation is the unsuitability of English law for Irish circumstances.[9] The heightened emphasis on an expedient safety in his explanation, in which this statutory contradiction participates, is further accentuated by the gratuitous, intensifying adjective in the phrase "*flatt* wronge" and by the macabre etymological connection between the words *capital* and *mischief*, both ultimately derived from Latin *caput*, "head," or in this case headlessness (*Oxford Dictionary of English Etymology*, s.v. "mischief").

The second time the proverbial saying in question occurs, it comes with a casualness, even a nonchalance, that is suspect. This time, Eudoxus is replying to Irenius's argument that the statutory designation of the Irish practices of "coigny" and "livery" as treason is "inconvenient," that is, "inconsistent with reason" (78–79).[10] (Roughly, these practices refer to the tenant's providing lodging, victuals, and fodder for his lord.) Eudoxus begins by agreeing that Irish lords are wronged by the punitive statute "since it was an antiente Custome and nothinge Contraye to lawe, for to the willinge theare is no wronge done." Verbally echoing More's *Utopia,* he opines, moreover, that there are "*even heare in Englande . . .* in manye places as lardge Customes." Then he supposes that the purpose of the statute was to forbid the violent taking of victuals from "other mens tennantes againste theire wills" (79; my emphasis). Such taking, he labels "a greate outrage and yeat not so greate . . . as that it shoulde be made Treasone, ffor Consideringe that the nature of Treasone is Concerninge . . . the Prince . . . it is hardelye wrested to make this Treasone, But as you erste saide, *Better a mischiefe then an Inconvenience*" (79–80).

This time, the saying self is even italicized for emphasis, as if to accentuate the discrepancy between Eudoxus's own argument and the nugget of proverbial wisdom that concludes it. "Oh, well," Eudoxus seems to be saying, "The statute is totally unjust, but what the hell, bring out the traditional slogans and let's get on with it." Something that exceeds a merely literal reading is clearly happening. Not merely echoing but explicitly asking us to remember Irenius's earlier use of the proverb—"But as you erste saide"—Eudoxus's statement puts a spotlight on it and opens both its use and its meaning to scrutiny.[11]

This may be the point at which we find out how many meanings can stand on the head of a proverb, in this case the contextualized one in question. Since both occurrences of the saying "Better a mischief then an inconvenience" in the *View* involve statutory contexts, legal employment of it in Spenser's historical context is the place to begin. Interestingly, this employment is at odds with that of Irenius and therefore at least on the surface with that of Eudoxus, who invokes Irenius's use of it. In late medieval and sixteenth-century English law, according to J.H. Baker, *Better a mischief than an inconvenience* has "a life of its own"; it is a legal maxim, a codified saying. In it, *inconvenience* means roughly "inconsistency," the idea being that it is preferable "to suffer a mischief in an individual case than the inconvenience which might follow from admitting exceptions to general rules."[12] Norman Doe labels the saying a "late medieval common lawyer's slogan" and similarly interprets *inconvenience* as "inconsistency, [or] not upsetting established practice, [albeit] at the expense of allowing injustice:

[thus] 'a mischief will be suffered sooner than an inconvenience'" (155, 173).[13] Here *mischief* again pertains focally to the individual, and *inconvenience* to the law and established practice. Doe is more expansive, however, noting that while "*mischief* related to abstract right and wrong," rather than to inconsistent results or "inconvenience," it nonetheless involved a "narrower and less moral idea than that of reason or conscience" and "specifically meant being without redress or procedural vexation" (155). In other words, the narrow application of the saying "Better a mischief than an inconvenience" does not align easily with the capital crimes of Spenser's offenders. Despite the more obvious discrepancy between Eudoxus's sense of justice and his ironic use of this saying to terminate discussion, the saying itself fits least well Irenius's endorsement of preventive homicide in the *View*, an injustice that would appear to extend well beyond procedural inequity. Indeed, Irenius's citation of a legal maxim *against exceptions* to justify an *exceptional* law in which an immaterial intention, as distinguished from a material word or deed, brings death is itself noticeably self-contradictory.

Christopher Saint German's *Doctor and Student*, a Henrician exposition of common law that was popular with practitioners and lay persons throughout the sixteenth century and beyond, attests to the same narrow legal use of the saying, invoking it conclusively in a question that weighs the face value of a legal document against the "conscience"—the knowledge and awareness—pertaining to its execution. The student's response to this question establishes that the law need only ascertain whether the document at issue is the party's "dede or not / and not whether the dede were made with conseyence or agaynst conseyence / and thoughe the partye maye be at a myschyefe thereby / yet the lawe wyll rather suffre that myschyefe then the sayd inconuenyence."[14] Here again the integrity of (merely) legal principles and procedures—law for law's sake, as it were—is what matters rather than equity or morality; in fact these hardly seem to count. Even the student of law later observes, however, that in the case under consideration the dictates of reason and conscience should on a private basis redress the legal decision, thus underlining the tension between the maxim legally understood and conscience or equity.

In the early 1620s the same legal principles prevail where this maxim occurs. For example, Sir Edward Coke refers a mischief to a "private loss" and an inconvenience to a "public evil" and declares that the former is preferable to the latter. It is an inconvenience, he explains, "that any of the maxims of the law should be broken, though a private man suffer loss" (White 80n199). With respect to Spenser's *View*, the interpretive stakes are therefore these: if a specifically legal meaning limited to procedure and consistency does not restrict the maxim at issue and if the maxim also applies self-contradictorily, as I've suggested, then the invitation in the text to scrutinize this maxim enables the moral and equitable considerations that the accepted legal meaning would exclude.

Outside contemporary legal sources, the proverb "Better a mischief than an inconvenience" turns out to have led another rich life, a condition that further colors and complicates its meaning as a prefabricated unit—an imported whole—in a political tract such as Spenser's *View*. Two relevant instances occur in a commercial document that bears on a legal context—Gerard de Malynes's *Consuetudo, vel Lex Mercatoria: or, The Ancient Law-Merchant*.[15] In the first of these, Malynes, describing an early modern form of insurance against maritime losses, explains that if the insured has "caused himselfe to bee assured" for more than his cargo is worth, then in the event of loss "the last assurors which haue subscribed to the Policie" will be exempt from payment, for "It is better to suffer a mischiefe than an inconuenience" (161, cf. 156).[16] Curiously, the inconvenience this time is to the principle that money is received only for risk taken, and in direct contrast to the instance I cited from *Doctor and Student,* the mischief is against the actual document of insurance in question, which does not correspond to the actual loss. As a consequence "a Law not observed is inferiour to a Custom well observed" (156).[17]

In a second use of the same proverb Malynes, himself a merchant, contends that the disallowing of interest on money in all circumstances, such as the support of orphans or the mechanisms of monetary exchange, is "to remedie a mischiefe [interest, or, "usury"] with a greater inconvenience" (329). His meaning here is moral or commercial and commonsensical rather than legal and procedural. While he continues to mean an inconvenience to the greater entity or whole and a mischief to the lesser entity or part and to intend the greater good over the lesser, he is no longer within the compass of statutory law.

In connection with usury or the interest on money, the proverb "Better a mischief than an inconvenience" also occurs twice in the learned Thomas Wilson's *Discourse Uppon Usurye* (1572). In the first occurrence, the proverb is implicated in an unprincipled action born of necessity: for princes must do what "they would not of themselves doe yf it were not for very necessity, to avoide a greater inconvenience" (186). Wilson, a member of Parliament, a master in the Court of Requests, ambassador to the Netherlands, secretary of state, dean of Durham, and author of a logic and a rhetoric, obviously knew something of Machiavellian politics as well as of law and religion. One of his personae in the *Discourse,* a temporal or common law lawyer, observes that a number of statutes have permitted usury, "which I woulde they had contynued, to avoide further evell, for (as we say) bettre it is to suffer a mischiefe then an inconvenience" (237). Although attributed to a lawyer, Wilson's use of the proverb is clearly nontechnical, simply privileging the greater good over the lesser. Perhaps more striking is the fact that it is used *against* the current law on the books regarding usury and thus contradicts its proper legal usage in support of statutory integrity.

In a more explicitly political tract, *The Supremacie of Christian Princes* (1573), Bishop John Bridges invokes the same proverb to conclude an argument opposing rebellion against "an heretical, a scismatical, or a symoniacal King." "The lawiers woulde briefly say to this," writes Bridges, "better suffer a mischiefe, than an inconuenience." He adds that even if such an unjust king were considered an inconuenience, "we may not take away one inconuenience with an other greater inconuenience," and recommends instead "conuenient remedies of pacience & constancie" (1058).[18] Although Bridges too identifies his saying with lawyers, his use of it does not accord with theirs in the narrow senses of procedure and consistency. The inconvenience he envisions is a radical social disruption, rebellion, and his convenient remedies are "fitting" or "appropriate" ones. Of course the lawyers also envisioned radical disruption from a violation of legal formalism and opposed it in the maxim at issue. If Bridges's saying actually originates in the law, it might be seen as an instance of the violence of analogical extension—homologism—that is not unlike one possible reading of Irenius's use of it. To repeat: *one* possible reading.

Better a mischief than an inconvenience also occurs in contemporary literary contexts, where its use gravitates toward a moral rather than strictly legal meaning and further contributes to its instability. For example, in *The Resurrection of Our Lord,* a miracle play dating from the decades 1530 to 1560, the high priests Annas and Caiaphas twice urge the soldiers guarding Christ's tomb to lie about the circumstances in which his body has disappeared, thus suffering the mischief of a falsehood rather than the greater inconvenience of discrediting "Moyses lawe" (15–16).[19] Here, in distinction to the saying's force in a legal context, the mischief to be countenanced is clearly immoral and against conscience. In two of John Lyly's plays, the saying appears again, both times with moral coloring. In *Mother Bombie* (1594) it registers the difference between "a little shame" or "mischiefe" and "an infinite griefe" or "continual inconuenience." In *Gallathea,* where the saying refers to the sacrifice of a virgin to appease Neptune, Gallathea's father is accused of "preferring a common inconuenience, before a priuate mischiefe" because he wants to shield his daughter.[20] In *The Roaring Girl* (1611), an oblique, reversed version of the saying occurs when Master Gallipot suggests that he report his wife adulterous in order to discourage her supposed former suitor, and she retorts, "You embrace a mischiefe [a worse harm], to preuent an ill [a lesser harm]."[21] From Mistress Gallipot's viewpoint, the "ill" or rival's claim is lesser because she would actually like to be bedded by the supposed suitor. Since she has already told her gullible husband that she was formerly contracted to this supposed rival, the threatened "ill" appears to Gallipot a rightful claim rather than a legally inconsistent one. In this context the saying hardly carries the force of the legal maxim for either Gallipot.

In four other contemporary texts, Lyly's *Euphues and His England* (1580), Brian Melbancke's *Philotimus* (1583), Shakespeare's *Merry Wives of Windsor* (1597–1602), and Gabriel Harvey's "New Letter of Notable Contents, 1593," *Better a mischief than an inconvenience* occurs with a similarly radical modification or even reversal of the legal meaning. Lyly's Camilla, offended by Philautus's letter of love, debates with herself whether she can honorably answer it and then decides that she should "commit an inconuenience," that she "might preuent a mischiefe, chusing rather to cut . . . [him] off short by rigour then to giue . . . [him] any iot of hope by silence" (2.127). This time the mischief, "harm," "distress," or "evil consequence" is decidedly greater than the inconvenience, which amounts to an "impropriety."[22] Such is also the case in *Philotimus,* when the unfortunate Philotimus, hoping for money to appease his creditors, tells his presumptive benefactor that although he realizes "how litle thou owest me . . . yet must I commit an inconuenience, to preuent a mischiefe, and for auncient benevolence, craue your benificence." Here again "inconvenience" means "an unseemly act" or, perhaps, even a mere "discomfort" (173).[23] Another variation on the saying, in which the word "extremity" replaces "inconvenience," bears a similar but stronger sense of distress in Shakespeare's *Merry Wives of Windsor,* when Falstaff, offered the option of an indecorous escape in woman's clothing, gasps, "any extremity rather than a mischief" (4.2.73–74). However demeaning his disguise, it is clearly less of a threat than the mischief he anticipates at the hands of an irate husband.[24]

Spenser's friend Gabriel Harvey actually reverses the proverb in a letter that treats Nashe's attacks on him, for which Nashe at least temporarily appears contrite. Harvey, although highly skeptical and often derisive, presents himself as willing to suppress a counterattack (by the mysterious gentlewoman) long enough to await further signs of Nashe's penitence rather than quash his suspect overtures. For this purpose Harvey cites both the proverb and its inverse, introducing a distinction between its public and private applications: "Howbeit as in some publique causes, better a mischief, then an inconuenience: so in many priuate cases *better an inconuenience, then a mischief.* Though an Orient Gemme be precious, and worthy to be gazed vpon with the eye of Admiration, yet better an Orient Gemme sleepe, then the Penitent man perish."[25] While Harvey's concessive clause ("Howbeit . . . inconuenience") affirms the usual form of the proverb, his reversal of this form in the apodosis of his sentence further destabilizes the proverb's potential as a cultural signifier. It also enscapsulates what has appeared to this point in nonlegal sources of the later sixteenth century to be a translation of the legal maxim to a usage that is personal and equitable and thus opposite to it. The uncertain ground this "saiyng self" now traverses includes not only the relation of statute to equity and of law to morality but also that of a public domain to a private one.

If the saying thus participates in a tension within the law and another between the law and popular usage, its potential for instability is further intensified both by other legal uses of the terms *mischief* and *inconvenience* and by other nonlegal ones.[26] In law, these terms often appear as a seemingly synonymous pair, their doubling a means of emphasis, as in the phrase "tresgrand mischief & inconuenience."[27] In legislation, *mischief* had sometimes a thoroughly moral and not only a legal connotation, referring, for example, to a harm "'contrary to the pleasure of God'" or to "wilful premeditated murder . . . 'by the laws of God and of natural reason forbidden'" (Doe 156–57). Specifically within common law, *inconvenience* appears to have had a more stable meaning, but once outside the *practice* of common lawyers, it could appear in legislation describing riot, robbery, and murder (Doe 167).

Outside legal sources, both words had broader ranges of meaning, as we have already seen reflected to an extent in the saying itself. In the Tudor period, *mischief* could additionally mean anything from "misfortune," "trouble," and "distress" to "disadvantage" and "injury," to "wickedness," "troublemaker," or even "morbidity," while earlier usage, still present in extant documents, further extended the meaning to "need, want, [and] poverty."[28] Besides an inconsistency in law, *inconvenience* applied to any "want of agreement," "incongruity," or "absurdity" with respect to reason or rule; to "moral or ethical unsuitableness" or "unseemly behavior," "impropriety." Like *mischief,* it could also mean "harm," "injury," "misfortune," and "trouble," or "problem" in the sense of an unforeseen obstacle.[29]

In *A View of the Present State of Ireland* occurrences of the word *mischief* and particularly of the word *inconvenience* outside the proverbial saying further bear on a translation of the "saiyng self." On the few occasions that *mischief* occurs nonproverbially, it indicates "harm" or a synonym for "troublous practize" (74, 144) and therefore does not indicate a more technical legal usage. In contrast to the relative infrequency of *mischief,* *inconvenience* and its cognates weave threadlike through the pages on either side of the two proverbial instances of it, appearing elsewhere in the tract with some regularity as well. Usually they signify an inconsistency with reason, as in the instance of Irish folkmotes or tenancy (131, 134). When the inconsistency relates specifically to the laws, as it often does, it exists between the law and reason or circumstances rather than between legal cases or discordant results in a single case. Thus nowhere does the inconsistency appear to amount to a technically legal meaning.[30] While *inconvenience* sometimes merely indicates "harm," "trouble," or "injury," in adjectival form its other major signification besides "inconsistent" is "unsuitable," or "unfitting," as the native Irish garb and the speaking of Irish by the Old English are said to be.[31] In short, other occurrences of both words in the *View*, a number of them referring to law, offer no evidence for a strictly legal and thereby safely contained interpretation of the proverb, as Irenius invokes it. In no way do they restrict a reading of it open to the moral and ethical ambivalence that Eudoxus's use of it invites. In other words, whether through simple incompetence, moral discomfort, or cultural critique, Spenser's deployment of the proverb "Better a mischief than an inconvenience" in a way that is discrepant with both its legal contexts in the *View* and thus with its use both by Irenius and by Eudoxus questions the meaning of the proverb itself, the circumstances or instances to which it is applied, and the kind of justice they embody. Here the "saiyng self" carries a heavy and equivocal cultural burden.

What else this ambivalence implies, of course, is another issue. More than half a century ago, Raymond Jenkins, later followed by Spenser's biographer Alexander Judson, concluded that Spenser was "very familiar with the operation of the law-courts of Munster," basing his assertion on the discovery that Spenser was deputy clerk of the Council of Munster.[32] The implications of Jenkins's large claim are themselves unclear, however, since they could imply the superficiality of Spenser's legal expertise as easily as the depth of it: not unlike Chaucer's summoner, the far more educated Spenser might well have learned a number of law terms "out of som decree— / No wonder is, he herde it al the day."[33] In other words, it is possible that Irenius's misuse within a legal context of the saying "Better a mischief than an inconvenience" results from incompetence, his own or Spenser's, although Eudoxus's clearly ironic repetition of the saying inclines against the merely authorial alternative. Moral discomfort, cultural critique, or perhaps some combination of these remain the other interpretive possibilities, and they are the ones supported both by the genuinely dialogic form of the *View*'s review of law and by the more fully contextualized voice of Spenser's epic romance *The Faerie Queene*.[34]

If we think that the poet of faery wrote the *View* (and there is considerable verbal evidence that he did), we really shouldn't be surprised that his twin—his duplicitous—personae Irenius and Eudoxus should manage between them to utter a "saiyng self" that lands us in cultural quicksand, even though this possibly bottomless miring directly implicates the special nature of sovereignty, the danger of regicide, and more exactly the threats, including that of the imagination, to Spenser's queen. The potential for instability and for appropriation in any prefabricated unit of meaning, perhaps any "saiyng self," is a subject of which the poet of *The Faerie Queene* is demonstrably aware. Witness the sophistical use the character Despair makes of the resources of proverbial knowledge drawn from scripture, the classics, and other traditions or the stichomythic exchange of conflicting, relatively valued sayings between Prince Arthur and Una when they first meet in book 1. Even more to the point is the proverbially expressed conflict in Spenser's Book of Justice between Artegall and Burbon regarding the unity or expedient duplicity of truth itself—a conflict between the saying "To temporize is not from truth to swerue" and the opposite saying "Knights ought be true, and truth is one in all" (5.11.56).[35] The fundamental *duplicity* or equivocity of sayings in *The Faerie Queene*, another perception that Spenser could have found both in Chaucer, his poetic father, and in such a schoolboy-text as Erasmus's *De copia*, may well be one of the features defining its specific voice.[36]

Still more relevant than the instances in books 1 and 5 that I've cited to the force of the saying at issue in the *View* is the vexed treatment of the execution of Mary Stuart in Spenser's fifth book—the Book of Justice. Here, recalling multiple proverbs, the narrator endeavors to balance the claims of justice and mercy, referring first to justice, which "from iust verdict will for nothing start, / But to preserue inuiolated right, / Oft spilles the principall, to saue the part" (5.10.2). Whether justice spills the principal or the principle, a distinction often honored more in the orthographic and orthoepic breach than in the observance, it would seem to align readily both with the consistency that honors the integrity of the legal system over that of the individual life and with the numerically greater part over the numerically lesser "principall." In contrast with these possibilities, the narrator tells us that the principle of mercy, which is of "[s]o much more . . . powre and art" than justice,

> . . . seekes to saue the subiect of her skill,
> Yet neuer doth from doome of right depart:
> As it is greater prayse to saue, then spill,
> And better to reforme, then to cut off the ill.
> (5.10.2)

How mercy saves rather than spills and reforms rather than cuts off without departing from "doome of right," the poem does not tell us, and the oft-remarked discrepancy between mercy and Mary-Duessa's fate suggests its inability adequately to do so. The point I would make is that this discrepancy finds an echo in the odd ambiguity regarding the numerically "greater good" detectable in the exchange first between Irenius's and Eudoxus's deployments of the "saiyng self" and then between their ambivalent saying and its use in the circumambient culture. It finds another echo in the image of Malfont, the poet who has been silenced, his tongue nailed to a post for a trespass "adiudged so by law" in the court of Mercilla (5.9.25). And it finds still another in the uneasy oscillation Debora Shuger has seen emerging in the Renaissance between the "right to life" and the "solidarity of the patriarchal family and tribal community," between the "autonomous subject" and "his archaic subjection to the *mystica conjunctio*," and thus between what I have identified as the individual, private right and the greater, public good in Spenser's deployment of the maxim.[37] Far from being a modern invention, this is an oscillation—indeed, a tension—that traces back at least to the thirteenth century.[38]

On the basis of one saying in a tract of 188 *Variorum* pages, I can contribute to discussion of the writer's engagement in the views of his personae, whether direct, ironized, or otherwise mediated by his culture, but hardly resolve this issue. What I can conclude is that the immediate or seeming sense of Irenius's conclusive proverb is questioned first by its seeming affirmation but actual derision in Eudoxus's mouth and then by its interplay with the tensions of usage, including voice, in the broader culture. On the basis of what I discovered when I began seriously to wonder about the meaning and function of the saying in question, I would also conclude that we could profitably pay a good deal more attention to the rhetorical and historical details of the *View* before deciding who is saying what in it.

In an essay like this, I am also struck by the possibility of still another kind of conclusion, a final meaning to stand on the head of my proverb. There was a time when I might have reviewed the historical-cultural materials in this essay and then proposed a reading of the passages from the *View* in question without displaying extensive documentation except, radically abbreviated, in the notes. In this way I would have kept my eye firmly on what I determined the text to be. Now I exhibit these materials within the body of the essay, for they have become a more significant part of its subject, participating in a multiplicity or qualified indeterminacy of self and voice. But this remains an indeterminacy qualified for me, as it has been in this essay, by a relation to *The Faerie Queene*—by what I shall term the "volume" of this epic romance, not merely its mass but also its specific audibility, the recurrent, demonstrable effect of a rhetoric that is at once communal and distinctive. Moreover, this relative indeterminacy, which first appears so selfless and impersonal a reading practice, is ultimately dependent on some conception, if only a questioning, of self and voice: conceptually, a self must underlie an indeterminate self, a concept of person underpin one of impersonality. A characteristic feature of modernity, Anthony Giddens tells us, is self-reflexivity, self-evaluation that is institutionalized and culturally ingrained as never before (*Modernity and Self-Identity*, e.g., 1–9, 32–36, 52–55). In the deliberate exchange between Irenius and Eudoxus and the open-ended exchange with a larger cultural textuality that it extends, I cannot help wondering whether we might be seeing the beginning of something remotely similar.[39]

Notes

1. "To the Reader," in Udall, ed., *iii*[r]. I wish to thank Vincent Blasi for reading and commenting helpfully on the legal nuances of this essay.

2. Spenser, *Works* 10: 80. Unless otherwise specified, subsequent reference is to this edition, cited as *Var. A View of the Present State of Ireland*, 10, ed. Gottfried, is cited as *View*.

3. See J. Anderson, *Words That Matter* 21–23, 25–26, 33–42; Barthes, *Elements of Semiology* 19, 62; and Hoskyns 153–54. I borrow the analogy between a saying and a "prefabricated unit" from Barley 740.

4. Erasmus, cited in Phillips edition (3); see also Barthes, *S/Z* 100; Barley 740–41; Crane chap. 1; and J. Anderson, "Prudence."

5. J.H. Baker, *Manual of Law French* s.v. "enconvenient": "absurd, unfitting, logically inconsistent, unnecessary, undesirable."

6. *OED* s.v. "Inconvenience," 3.c (Malynes) ; "Mischief" n., 3.b (Spenser's *View*).

7. For the relevant quotation from Bodin, see *Var.* 10: 297, lines 648–62; and for incisive remarks about Bodin's treatment of natural law, see Shuger 78.

8. See *Statutes of the Realm* 4.365 (1 Eliza., chapter 5); 526 (13 Eliza., chap. 1), cf. 657 (23 Eliza., chap. 1); 705 (27 Eliza., chap. 1). See also Bellamy, chap. 2.

9. The Irish parliament that met in the second year of Elizabeth's reign (1560) passed the treason legislation making a second offense capital. Although Irish parliaments also met in 1569–71 and in 1585–86, they failed to enact specific legislation pertaining to capital treason against the crown. During the sixteenth century the relation of English to Irish parliamentary law is unsettled and evolving both theoretically and practically. For a sampling of diverse views of the legal situation, see Brady 22–30, 40–41; Ellis, *Tudor Ireland* 178–79, 192–95, and "Henry VIII" 516, 520, 531; Canny, *Elizabethan Conquest* 61, 102–03, 117–20, *From Reformation to Restoration* 22, 75, and "Edmund Spenser" 3–4; Bradshaw 263–67, 282, 287–88; and MacNeill, 1–8. See also, Crawford 41;

Beckett 18–19, 22–23; and Falls 18–23, 64–65. A sampling of relevant documents can be found in *Elizabethan Ireland* 112–23.

10. See *OED* s.v. "Inconvenience," 1.

11. A. Patterson offers a review of the place of Spenser's tract in the valuable historical work on sixteenth-century Ireland done in the last two decades by Nicholas Canny, Brendan Bradshaw, and Ciaran Brady (*Reading between the Lines* 82–86). None of these writers, including Patterson, directly address the proverbial saying in question, although the passage in which it occurs at times proves of interest to them.

12. I am grateful to Professor Baker for personal correspondence and the introduction to his edition of *The Reports of Sir John Spelman* 2.38; cf. Baker, *Manual of Law French* s.v. "enconvenient," "enconvenientise." In correspondence, Baker makes the additional point that the legal maxim in question is the equivalent of the modern saying "Hard cases make bad law." It countenances a principle that is "in a sense, the antithesis of equity."

13. By "late medieval" Doe mainly means the fifteenth century, but he includes Christopher St. German's *Doctor and Student* (1529–31) and corroborating Renaissance citations to the writings of such figures as Thomas Smith and Richard Hooker.

14. See chap. xlvi (mislabeled xlv). The rest of this paragraph derives from the same chapter of *Doctor and Student,* its customary title.

15. Although *Lex Mercatoria* was published in 1622, I consider the thinking of Malynes (fl. 1586–1641) roughly contemporary with that at the turn of the century; he treats a subject steeped in custom and precedent, as the full title of his treatise indicates. See, for example, the sixteenth-century petitions to the Privy Council regarding marine insurance in Raynes, *History of British Insurance:* "'the order of assurance is not grounded upon the laws of the realm but [is] rather a civil and maritime cause to be determined and decided by civilians,' . . . 'forasmuch as the matter . . . consisteth and standeth much upon the order and usages of merchants by whom rather than the course of law it may be forwarded and determined'" (29).

16. The context of the proverb is somewhat ambiguous: more exactly the statement that "the last assurors which haue subscribed to the Policie, shall enioy the benefit thereof, as hath beene declared" (161). The problem is the referent of "thereof." The only explanation I have found for this benefit comes on page 156: "those Assurors that have last subscribed to the Policy of Assurance, bear not any adventure at all." Instead, Malynes continues, they refund the premium to the holder of the policy, but they also take a cut of it because they are ipso facto subscribers to it. I thus take the Assurors' being bound "*ipso facto* to the said Assurance" (161) to indicate not merely the fact of having signed a document but the fact of the declared value of the cargo in question. See also note 15, above.

17. Cf. a bill regarding marine insurance introduced into Parliament in 1601: "our Courts have not the knowledge of their [merchants'] terms, neither can they tell what to say upon their causes, which be secret in their science proceeding out of their experience" (Raynes 56).

18. For this reference and those that follow, I have consulted *The Oxford*

Dictionary of English Proverbs; Tilley; Dent, *Proverbial Language in English Drama;* and *Var.* 10: 297.

19. I have assumed some corruption in the text, which initially seems to make the discrediting of Mosaic law a mischief rather than an inconvenience (462–64). But the surrounding context clearly indicates that this discrediting is the larger concern or "inconvenience."

20. *Works,* 3: 216: *Bombie* 5.2.26–27; and 2: 457: *Gallathea* 4.1.38–39.

21. Middleton and Dekker, *The Roaring Girl,* ed. Farmer F4. Gomme, ed., *The Roaring Girl,* follows the earlier dating of R.C. Bald, 1608, for the play; he offers no annotation for the inverted proverb in question (3.2.135–36); Mulholland, ed., *The Roaring Girl,* dates the play 1611 (12–13); he cites Tilley's listing of the proverb "Better once a mischief than always an inconvenience" without further comment (3.2.139–40).

22. *OED* s.v. "Inconvenience" n., 2; "Mischief" n., 1.a, 2.a-b: with the phrase "evil consequences" I borrow a later refinement in the *OED*'s equivalence because it accounts for the "evil arising out of or existing in certain conditions" (2.b).

23. *OED* s.v. "Inconvenience" n., 2, 4. Although the meaning "discomfort" is not recognized by the *OED* until 1653, a case can be made for it in this earlier citation.

24. Dent, *Shakespeare's Proverbial Language* (143), notes the relevance of *Better a mischief than an inconvenience* to *Merry Wives.*

25. "A New Letter," in *Works,* 1. 284. On relevant details of the Harvey-Nashe feud, see Nashe, "To the Reader," *Christs Teares over Jerusalem,* 1593, 1595, in *Works,* 2. 12–13, 179–81; and discussion of the Harvey-Nashe feud in Nashe, *Works,* 5. 66–67, 90–105. See also Stern 106–08, 110–13.

26. Cf. Doe : "[legal] usages of mischief and inconvenience reflect two fundamentally opposing concerns" (169).

27. *A Discourse upon the Exposicion & Understanding of Statutes* 79n165.

28. *OED* s.v. "Mischief" n., 1.a-c, 2.a-b, 4.b, 6, 7.

29. *OED* s.v. "Inconvenience" n., 1–3, 4.b.

30. See Doe 163; *View,* e.g., 52, 60, 74–75, 198–200.

31. *View* 100, 118; cf. 75, 225–26; for the meaning "harm," "trouble," "injury[ous]," see, e.g., 176, 214, 226, 229.

32. Jenkins, "Spenser: The Uncertain Years" 350; cf. his "Spenser and the Clerkship"; for Judson, see *Var.* 9: 113–16.

33. Chaucer, *The Canterbury Tales* (General Prologue 639–41).

34. On discomfort, see A. Patterson, *Reading between the Lines* 110. For a provocative exchange regarding dialogue in the *View,* see Breen, esp. 123–24; and Hadfield, "Who Is Speaking," esp. 236–37. While the tenor of my essay and the possibilities considered here are at odds with those of Fogarty's provocative essay "The Colonization of Language," there is much in her essay that I admire and find generally relevant to my concerns. Cf. also D. Baker.

35. The quotations are taken from Spenser, *The Faerie Queene,* ed. Hamilton.

36. See *Copia,* 24. 646–48; I thank Kathy Eden for reminding me of the

relevance of Erasmus's text. Kahn's discussion of training in the Renaissance to argue *in utramque partem*, "on both sides," of a question is pertinent. See 11, 38–39, and chap. 4 passim. On Chaucer's use of proverbs in *Troilus and Criseyde*, see Taylor 286–87.

37. See Shuger, *Renaissance Bible* 81, 87, and chap. 2 passim.

38. See Tierney, "Origins of Natural Rights Language," and his "Aristotle and the American Indians." My qualification "at least" is based on F. Miller 87–139, 373–78. Shuger declines to call the "oscillation" or "differentiation" (her preferred word) between "autonomous subject" and common weal a tension, which she describes as an "achieved polarization" (53). Tensions are arguably more subtle. This one has a persistent, not to say an abiding, shape. Additional definition of it can be found in Herrup's investigation of law enforcement in England during the late sixteenth and seventeenth centuries, which attempted to balance absolute considerations of justice with individuating history and circumstances and public order with personal error.

39. Recently, Willy Maley (*Salvaging Spenser* 115) and Andrew Hadfield ("Spenser and Republicanism") have suggested that Spenser had republican sympathies, possibly derived from the writings of Bodin, Buchanan, and Machiavelli. My findings regarding Spenser's deployment of the maxim "Better a mischief than an inconvenience" could be used to support their suggestion. To it, I would add the consideration, however, that the questioning of monarchical absolutism and the revaluation of individual right are historically and causally related.

THE CONSTRUCTION OF INWARDNESS IN *THE FAERIE QUEENE*, BOOK 2

Michael Schoenfeldt

> Intestines stretch out all the way to the curvatures of the brain.
> The two don't look much different, and they aren't and they
> are.
>
> Norman Maclean

> The human body is the very best picture of the soul.
>
> Ludwig Wittgenstein

Very popular (and frequently imitated) in its own day, the Castle of Alma has seemed to most subsequent readers a counterproductive grotesquerie. Critical opinion of this episode has altered little since John Hughes wrote in 1715 that the allegory of the House of Temperance is "debas'd by a Mixture of too many low Images, as *Diet, Concoction, Digestion,* and the like; which are presented as persons" (267–68). Underpinning Hughes's criticism of Spenser's allegory is a deeply anachronistic notion not only of literary decorum, but also, and more tellingly, of the relationship of body to self. Hughes assumes a realm of low and therefore irrelevant corporeal processes from which Spenser misguidedly draws the material for his allegory of the self. In *The Anatomy of Melancholy,* by contrast, Robert Burton asks a question that demonstrates great sympathy for the possible motives for including an account of the body's sundry details in a depiction of the construction of an ethical self: "And what can be more ignominious and filthie . . . then for a man not to knowe the structure and composition of his owne body, especially since the knowledge of it, tends so much to the preservation of his health, & information of his manners" (1: 139–40). For Burton, unlike Hughes, true filthiness inheres not in attending to the sordid details of corporeal processes but in ignoring them. Underpinning both Burton's and Spenser's somatic explorations of the interior self is the assumption that knowledge of physiology is knowledge of psychology, that knowing the body is not just gaining information about the corporeal machine the self inhabits but actually learning something about the self. Both assume, moreover, that the discrimination of noxious from nutritious matter in digestion is a physiological version of the discrimination between good and evil. If the alimentary path traversed by Spenser's knights seems to us a particularly grotesque and inappropriate route to knowledge of self, as I think it still does, perhaps the fault lies not so much in Spenser's aesthetic as in our own historically contingent and severely attenuated conceptions of what areas of knowledge pertain to the comprehension of self. Our own inability to apprehend and appreciate the controlled corporeality that is at the core of Spenserian temperance measures our distance from Spenser and from the early modern regime of the self he helped to shape.

Unlike the Gulf of Greediness, an orifice of indiscriminate consumption whose "griesly mouth . . . / Suck[s] the seas into his entralles deepe" (2.12.6), and unlike the various gates in the Bower of Bliss, which are "wrought of substaunce light, / Rather for pleasure, then for battery or fight" (2.12.43), and seem to be erected simply for the erotic pleasure of transgressing them, the gates of the Castle of Alma are "fast barred, . . . / And every loup fast lockt," even to the two virtuous knights who request entry (2.9.10). Spenser here emphasizes the tense blend of porousness and fortification that marks the physiological self the castle represents—without passages for nutrition and (as we will see) excrement, the self would experience the corporeal mortality that Guyon glimpses in his faint at the end of his time in the Cave of Mammon. Spenser, moreover, underscores the urgency of monitoring closely these passages. Indeed, Arthur and Guyon are allowed in only after they have skirmished with Maleger's troops.

On the first leg of what A.C. Hamilton wittily refers to as "their Cook's tour" of the Castle of Alma, Arthur and Guyon pass through the well-guarded mouth (the teeth are "warders . . . all armed bright / In glistring steele, and strongly fortifide" [2.9.26]), and proceed down the gullet in order to explore the stomach, the place where the substance of a dead other is made into something familiar and alive, where nutritive material begins the remarkable transformation that will allow it to nourish mortal flesh.[1] Giving the well-worn metaphor of the self as a castle a particular emphasis, Spenser likens the stomach to a "stately Hall, / Wherein were many tables faire dispred, / And ready dight with drapets festivall, / Against the viaundes should be ministred." The hall is presided over by a steward named "Diet," a figure "rype of age, / And in demeanure sober, and in counsell sage." His marshal is "Appetite," whose job is to "bestow / Both guestes and meate, when ever in they came, / And knew them how to order without blame" (2.9.27). These figures of dietary and social order lead Alma, Guyon, and Arthur into the stomach proper,

> a vaut ybuilt for great dispence,
> With many raunges reard along the wall;
> And one great chimney, whose long tonnell thence
> The smoke forth threw. And in the midst of all
> There placed was a caudron wide and tall,
> Upon a mighty furnace, burning whot.
> (2.9.29)

The lungs function as a "huge great paire of bellowes, which did styre / Continually, and cooling breath inspyre." A dynamic balance between the heat necessary for cooking and the cooling breath of respiration—a balance central to definitions of temperance as a form of moderation between extremes—is thus attained organically. The stomach is not a passive receptacle but an area of immense bustle: "about the Caudron many Cookes accoyld, / With hookes and ladles, as need did require." The immense complexity of the digestive process is indicated by the number of figures Spenser finds it necessary to include; apparently for Spenser, too many cooks do not spoil this vivid broth, but are required to accomplish the nearly magical transformation of dead matter into the nutritive fluid which sustains life.

Spenser's portrait of the stomach as a kind of kitchen draws on a vast literature that uses culinary metaphors to explain digestive processes. "Our stomake is our bodies kitchin," remarks William Vaughan in his popular *Directions for Health* (168). "Concoction," the technical term for digestion, derives from the Latin *concoctus*, "boiled together." A very literal kind of cooking occurs within the stomach of the individual consumer, carefully preparing the food for delivery to various parts of the body as a cook prepares meals. The stomach receives such extensive attention in Spenser's account of the well-tempered individual because it is a central site of physiological and psychological inwardness. Indeed, the name of the figure who presides over this castle, "Alma," may be short-hand for "anima," "soul," as many commentators urge, but it also means "nourishing," and this without having to buy any vowels or consonants. The point is that for the pre-Cartesian regime of the self Spenser inhabits, soul does not reside in a realm separate from the body but is in large part constituted by it.[2] As the process by which dead matter is assimilated to the substance of the self, digestion is a central process of psychological and physiological self-fashioning. The stomach, moreover, is the primary organ through which one can actually alter the temperature—a concept that is at once physiological and psychological—of the body. In *A View of the Present State of Ireland,* Spenser endorses Galen's principle that the psychological proclivities of the soul are in large part derived from the humoral temperature of the body. Irish wet nurses have a pernicious influence on the English infants to whom they give suck, Spenser admonishes, because the infants "draw into themselves together with their suck, even the nature and disposition of their nurses, for the mind followeth much the temperature of the body" (68). Juxtaposed with Spenser's frequent recourse to neoplatonic spirituality, then, is an aggressively materialist notion of self, a notion that puts particular ethical and psychological pressure on all acts of consumption. In the most literal way, you are what you eat. Under this regime, temperance assumes a double urgency: it is a virtue that not only exhibits proper ethical conduct, but also actively alters the moral condition of the self that practices it.

Just as a central part of food preparation is the separation of edible from inedible matter—we are told that the bustle of concoction includes "[s]ome to remove the scum as it did rise; / Others to beare the same away did mind" (2.9.31)—a critical issue in the assimilation of nutritive material is the successful and thorough elimination of what cannot be digested. Spenser thus calls appropriate attention to the technology of waste disposal:

> But all the liquour, which was fowle and wast,
>   Not good nor serviceable else for ought,
>   They in another great round vessell plast,
>   Till by a conduit pipe it thence were brought:
>   And all the rest, that noyous was, and nought,
>   By secret wayes, that none might it espy,
>   Was close convaid, and to the back-gate brought,
>   That cleped was Port Esquiline, whereby
> It was avoided quite, and throwne out privily.
> (2.9. 32)

This notorious passage is perhaps less indecorous when we remember that the unsuccessful elimination of waste is the primary cause of illness in the Galenic regime. That is why the urine flask came to represent the medical profession, and why almost all medical therapies in the period involve ridding the body of the excess fluids that cause disease. The multitude of therapies for accomplishing the necessary elimination of pernicious excess include phlebotomy, purgation, and clysters. "Physicke," notes Robert

Burton in *The Anatomy of Melancholy*, "is naught else but *addition and subtraction*" (2: 18). A temperate, well-regulated body is not a classical immured structure but a dynamic and porous edifice continually producing "superfluous excrements" from the very matter that nourishes it, excrements that must be purged. As William Vaughan writes: "Natures providence hath devised and framed sundry passages needfull for the purging, conveiance and evacuation of all such superfluous humours: to wit, the Kidneyes and the Urine-pipes, the empty or fasting Guts, . . .the Bladder, Eares, and Pores, appointed for the avoydance expulsion of sweat. And in the most part of these, if obstructions should happen, all the whole filthy masse of noysome humours is thereby kept within the body, and then gives violent assault to some of the principall parts" (168).

Disease is a product not of flow but of obstruction. The "violent assault" that Vaughan asserts will be made by "noysome humours" is simply another version of the irruptive forces that Maleger and his troops represent. The intricate processes of digestion, assimilation, and elimination portrayed within the Castle of Alma are thus intimately related to the heroic labor that Arthur accomplishes outside Alma's walls, and to Guyon's ultimate destruction of the Bower of Bliss. Rather than being an indecorous interruption of Spenser's ethical pattern, Port Esquiline supplies an absolutely essential component of it. The ejection of noxious material it accomplishes is psychologically, physiologically, and ethically necessary to Spenser's portrait of the temperate individual.

In one of the most sustained and compelling recent accounts of the Castle of Alma, David Miller argues in a chapter entitled "Alma's Nought" that Freudian psychoanalysis can usefully "summon into representation what Spenser's poetic intentions necessarily exclude from view. What Spenser's intentions exclude are the genitals" (*The Poem's Two Bodies* 190). It is true that Spenser does not give a genitally based sexual identity to the Castle of Alma (although most readers have interpreted the "wandering vine" over the portcullis as a male-specific moustache[3]). It is also true that Spenser seems to give the castle a deliberately hermaphroditic cast, even though the terms of that hermaphroditism involve conventional expressions of masculine superiority:

> The frame therof seemd partly circulare,
>   And part triangulare, o worke divine;
>   Those two the first and last proportions are,
>   The one imperfect, mortall, foeminine;
>   Th'other immortall, perfect, masculine.
> (2.9.22)

I would argue that here psychoanalysis, rather than providing us with a key to an earlier site of repression, encourages us to impose our own sense of the primacy of the genitals onto a culture where other forms of somatic activity—including, as we have seen, the alimentary tract—assumed equal if not greater importance.[4] Indeed, as Michel Foucault has argued of the Galenic system that Spenser portrays, "it is a trait manifested by all Greek and Roman medicine to accord much more space to the dietetics of alimentation than to that of sex. For this medicine, the thing that matters is eating and drinking" (*History of Sexuality* 3: 141). The seemingly unexpected turn that Arthur and Guyon make from the stomach to the brain (with a brief stop in the parlor of the heart), moreover, involves not the act of repressing genital sexuality that Miller posits—certainly the poet who conceived Ollyphant, that ambulatory phallus, could deal with the genitals when he chose—but rather a logical anatomical progression, since, as John Huarte and others assert, "albeit the stomacke abides so far distant from the braine, yet . . . the brain and the stomacke are united and chained together with certaine sinewes, by way of which they interchangeable communicate their dammages" (26). These mysterious sinews, canals that connect the stomach to the brain, explain an itinerary that seems so curious by modern physiological standards.[5]

The prominence of digestive and defecatory technology in Spenser's portrait of the well-tempered individual thus underscores the fact that the regime of the self Spenser depicts is very different from our own. The very title of Sir Thomas Elyot's popular *Castel of Helth* (1541) demonstrates the pervasiveness of the metaphor that underpins Spenser's Castle of Alma. Psychological, ethical, and physiological health is an edifice perpetually being constructed and in need of continual maintenance. In *Passions of the Minde*, Thomas Wright tellingly compares the control of one's insurgent emotions to the defense of a military fortification: "For these rebellious Passions are like craftie Pyoners, who, while Souldiers live carelessly within their Castle, or at least not much suspect, they undermine it, and breake in so upon them, that they can hardly escape" (69–70). The self that Spenser endorses is a profoundly constructed being, one that discovers individuation in regulating a repertoire of desires possessed in some degree by all. The notorious Grill, who prefers to remain a hog, represents essential, unregulated, and unreconstructed humanity, "the mind of beastly man." Where Jonathan Sawday argues that "Acrasia's sexuality is all mastering, able to transform the rational masculine intellect into a world of beast-like appetite associated with the feminine" (219), I would suggest that Grill is not so much the victim of Acrasia's powerful magic as the beast that all are capable of becoming in a moment of moral relaxation. Laurentius describes

the ethical processes by which the essential beastliness of humans can be
unleashed through faulty ethical conduct: "when a man by his malicious will
becomming an apostate and revolt, defaceth the ingraven forme of the
Deitie, and commeth by the filth of sinne to defile the holy temple of God,
when through an unruly appetite, he suffereth himselfe to be carried in such
headlong wise after his passions, either of choler, envie, or gluttonie, as then
he becommeth more outragious then a lyon, more fierce then a tyger, and
more filthie and contemptible then a swine" (bk. 2, chap. 2). Grill is just this
swine, transformed by his failure to control his own passions. When Spenser
inaugurates canto 12's trajectory of destruction by announcing, "Now gins
this goodly frame of Temperance / Fairely to rise," he reminds his readers
that temperance is a "frame," a structure, at once aesthetic and ethical,
imposed on the inherently unruly desires and beastly passions that inhabit
all.

The fetish of order and discipline that is the essence of this regime
immediately arouses our suspicions of authoritarianism. The fact that book
2 concludes with the violent destruction of a sensuous and beautiful
landscape has done little to allay those suspicions. These suspicions have
encouraged a kind of ideological enjambment between the self-control that
Spenser articulates and the colonial domination in which the poem also
participates. Spenser himself even provides the terms for the enjambment
when he compares the forces of Maleger to "a swarme of Gnats at eventide"
rising "out of the fennes of Allan" (2.9.16), a bog in Ireland. Spenser,
moreover, describes Maleger's troops in terms that are, Thomas Healy
suggests, "remarkably similar to Irenius's descriptions of Irish dress and
manners recounted in *A View*" (99–100):

> A Thousand villeins round about them swarmd
> Out of the rockes and caves adioyning nye,
> Vile caytive wretches, ragged, rude, deformd,
> All threatning death, all in straunge manner armd,
> Some with unweldy clubs, some with long speares,
> Some rusty knives some staves in fire warmd,
> Sterne was their looke like wild amazed steares,
> Staring with hollow eyes, and stiffe upstanding heares.
> (2.9.13)[7]

In *Renaissance Self-Fashioning*, Stephen Greenblatt has extended the links
between Spenser's experience as a colonial administrator and the portrait of
temperance in book 2 into a cogent interpretation of the Bower of Bliss and
its destruction as representing the vehement unease of western Christian

culture towards sexual pleasure. Citing a passage in Freud's *Civilization and Its Discontents*—"Civilization behaves toward sexuality as a people or a stratum of its population does which has subjected another one to its exploitation"—Greenblatt sees the book's violent conclusion as revealing the covert violence on which western civilization depends: "The Bower of Bliss must be destroyed not because its gratifications are unreal but because they threaten 'civility'—civilization—which for Spenser is achieved only through renunciation and the constant exercise of power" (173). It is I think significant that Greenblatt's account barely mentions the Castle of Alma, since that baroque presentation of regulated pleasure would complicate his compelling account of the apparently gratuitous destruction of the Bower of Bliss. Where Greenblatt frames his analysis of the Bower of Bliss in terms of an opposition between pleasure and control, Spenser frames his narrative in terms of an opposition between two kinds of pleasure: illicit, immoderate pleasure, which is to be resisted, even eradicated, and the salutary pleasure made possible by control, which is to be enjoyed, even relished. We need to remember that Alma's castle is not the site of ascetic self-denial; Alma's "bounteous banket" is rather "Attempred goodly well for health and *for delight*" (2.11.2; my italics). Gustatory pleasure, as well as the more ineffable pleasures of good health, are the goal of its bustling but carefully regulated activity. We need also to remember that it is the forces of Maleger, not the Castle of Alma, that inhabit a strangely disembodied state: "though they bodies seeme, yet substance from them fades" (2.9.15). Temperance involves not a turn from the body but rather the direction of rigorous attention toward it.

I would argue, furthermore, that despite these obvious links between Spenser's own experience as a colonial administrator in Ireland and the assault on Alma, the sense of order that emerges from book 2 is not a discipline necessarily complicit with colonial suppression, as Greenblatt and others have maintained, but something very different, potentially even opposite: a discipline intended to inculcate the internal stability that makes possible the subject's liberation from the passions that rage within all. It is not temperance but rather intemperance that Spenser portrays in terms of political violence and unjust subjugation: intemperance involves the physiological equivalent of the political violations of tyranny and usurpation. It is "[w]hen raging passion with fierce tyrannie / Robs reason of her due regalities, / And makes it servant to her basest part" (2.1.57). The Castle of Alma, by contrast, represents an ideal of self-government, whereby the body

> which doth freely yeeld
> His partes to reasons rule obedient,

And letteth her that ought the scepter weeld,
All happy peace and goodly government
Is setled there in sure establishment.
(2.11.2)

Self-governance here is articulated in the language of obedience to sovereign power. But as Milton and others demonstrate, there are no guarantees that the demands of these two authorities will always be synchronized. In his sonnet to Gabriel Harvey, Spenser describes his friend as one who "freely does, of what thee list, entreat / Like a great lord of peerless liberty."[8] This internal freedom from external and internal pressure is exactly what Spenser intends the precise and demanding disciplines of temperance to achieve. Greenblatt, then, leaves little room for the positive aspects of the self-regulation Spenser here endorses. One cannot respond properly to the compelling blandishments of the Bower without remembering that Guyon's overarching mission is to avenge the deaths of Mordant and Amavia, who together present "the ymage of mortalitee, / And feeble nature cloth'd in fleshly tyre, / When raging passion with fierce tyranny / Robs reason of her due regalitee / And makes it servant to her basest part" (2.1.57). The "due regality" of reason is opposed to the "fierce tyranny" of "raging passion." As Foucault argues in *The Use of Pleasure*, discipline is not necessarily complicit with political domination: "in classical Greek thought, the 'ascetics' that enabled one to make oneself into an ethical subject was an integral part—down to its very form—of the practice of a virtuous life, which was also the life of a 'free' man in the full, positive and political sense of the word" (*History of Sexuality* 2: 77). Freedom emerges from discipline rather than being opposed to it.

Spenser imagines the self as a fragile and unstable edifice, eternally under construction, and assailed on all sides (including the inside) by insurgent passions. As the Palmer tells Phedon, affections are to be controlled, or they will "cruell battry bend / Gainst fort of Reason" (2.4.34). We should remember that Spenser's declared purpose for the entire epic in the letter to Ralegh is "to fashion a gentleman or noble person in virtuous and gentle discipline." Identity is achieved not, as we might imagine, in the discovery of a hidden self buried deep beneath the encrustations and inauthenticities of civility; rather, it is achieved through discipline, through the forceful imposition of rational order on energies that tend naturally to the twin poles of tyranny and anarchy. The temperance Spenser portrays is not "The dull shore of lazy temperance" mocked by Lord Rochester ("The Disabled Debauchee") but an active, even heroic maintenance of order in the face of perpetual insurrection. If Spenser's portrait of the temperate subject has more traffic with the conduct of the colon than with the suppressions of colonialism, and finds the entrails to be a more significant locus of identity than the genitals, confronting such a seemingly alien formation of the human subject can perhaps remind us of the implicit strangeness of our own models of self.

NOTES

1. *The Faerie Queene,* ed. Hamilton 252; the note is to stanza 29. References to *The Faerie Queene* are to the 1978 edition of Roche.

2. For a cogent critique of Descartes from the viewpoint of modern neurophysiology, see Damasio.

3. See, though, Sawday's assertion that the House of Alma "is undoubtedly feminine," a claim that is less convincing than his brief but cogent observation on "the sexually undifferentiated body-interior" (162–63, 160).

4. On the difference between "the modern definition of the body as the sexual body" and the early modern definition, in which "sexual desire is an inflection of erotic longing, not its origin or essence," see Shuger 176–81. For a fuller discussion of the stomach as a locus of identity, see my "Fables of the Belly in Early Modern England."

5. Huarte (11) also develops a parallel between the processes of intellection and digestion that suggests a parallel between the activity observed in the stomach and that observed in the brain. "Knowledge," he says, must "have his due digestion . . . for as the bodie is not maintained by the much which we eat and drinke in one day, but by that which the stomacke digesteth and turneth: so our understanding is not filled by the much which we read in little time, but by that which by little and little it proceeds to conceive and chew upon." Carruthers observes that "[m]etaphors which use digestive activities are so powerful and tenacious that 'digestion' should be considered another basic functional model for the complementary activities of reading and composition, collection and recollection" (165–66).

6. See also the *Variorum* 282, quoting M.M. Gray *RES* 6, 414–15

7. "To the right worshipfull, my singular good friend, M. Gabriell Harvey," cited from *The Shorter Poems of Edmund Spenser,* ed. Oram et al. 773.

AFTERWORD

The Otherness of Spenser's Language

David Lee Miller

We cannot speak of "Spenser and the Other" without invoking Spenser *as* the other, for our interest in how literary texts of the Renaissance represent their others is precisely what marks the distance between their early and our late modernity. In writing *The Faerie Queene,* though, Spenser from the start took up a position marked as "other": England's arch-poet, as the title page of the 1611 Folio calls him, was also England's dark poet, a master of obscurity and hard things. What evidence there is suggests that *The Faerie Queene,* for all its canonical status, was more often admired than read and more often read than understood. What makes this text so difficult, even more than its allegorical method, is its style, that dense and peculiar matrix of linguistic invention and deformation, neologism and archaism, punning, typographical play, etymological imbrication, and portmanteau-coinage. I wonder how resistance to this style, or its resistance to readerly expectations, has limited the poem's social and cultural orbit—how it has affected the places *The Faerie Queene* occupies in English literary history, in popular culture, and in the American college curriculum today.

Consider the historical fortunes of Spenser's style. Everyone knows that Shakespeare is the genius of a latter-day idiom, whose power of phrase not only informs the history of literature but resonates throughout the popular and elite cultures of England and America from the mid-eighteenth century on, whereas Spenser, as a contemporary purist of English diction remarked, "writ no language." By the middle of the seventeenth century D'Avenant could note in passing that this had "grown the most vulgar accusation that is lay'd to his charge."[1]

There is, however, a time lag preceding Shakespeare's ascendancy. Bentley shows that for most of the seventeenth century Ben Jonson was more widely cited and admired, though "Shakespeare leads in quotations used in context for their aptness. . . . Evidently," Bentley concludes, "at least by the end of the century, Shakespeare's unsurpassed ability to phrase effectively the popular truth was recognized" (134–35). And yet, even though with each new reading of Shakespeare I seem to experience his unsurpassed gift of phrase all over again, I cannot help wondering to what extent his ability to render "the popular truth" really *was* unsurpassed, or to what extent it even existed, before the end of the century. Between the publication of the First Folio in 1623 and Shakespeare's emergence seventy years later as the word-hoard of the empire, forces of social, political, and cultural change produced the interregnum and the royal society, transforming the popular conception of truth and, in the process, making the conception of "popular truth" intelligible in a historically new way. Could such changes have lent Shakespeare's habits of phrase a kind of exemplarity they did not originally possess, appropriating them for social and cultural purposes they did not initially serve? A body of avowedly "materialist" work on the editing of the plays, for example, shows what a significant role textual selection and emendation have played in shaping Shakespeare's language as the prized idiom of individualism. What might we learn if the approaches of critics like De Grazia and Randall McLeod were incorporated into a cultural history of Spenser's reception that focussed on the *un*popularity of his style?[2]

Spenser's popularity never matched Shakespeare's, but his prestige was much greater. It wanes, though, like Ben Jonson's, as Shakespeare's status grows. Unlike Jonson, however, Spenser from the very beginning loses prestige largely for linguistic reasons, which may in an extended sense be political ones. Shakespeare's cultural ascendancy follows the rising curve of modernity; he is celebrated as the supreme artist of "human nature" in terms loaded with the values of Englightenment individualism. The same historical forces render Spenser progressively less intelligible.[3] Jonson's phrase—Spenser "writ no language"—has stuck because it catches something important about Spenser's style, which resists memorization and may resist in a fundamental way the linguistic production of Enlightenment culture and cultural politics. Spenser is not, as he said of Chaucer, a well of English undefiled. That was reserved to Shakespeare. Spenser's language is instead a semantic field that will not generate normative idioms for an increasingly modernist and progressivist political culture. What if the most profound alternative to authoring the language of the dominant political culture were precisely to have *writ no language*?

Modern Spenser criticism boasts some splendid achievements, but I do not think these include an adequate response to the act of linguistic invention by which Spenser fabricated an artificial discourse for his work.[4] We create the appearance of an attention to Spenser's language by making extensive use of it for our own critical purposes. There's plenty of work around, including mine, that exploits the signifying capacity of Spenser's text without theoretically and historically accounting for it. Harry Berger, Jr., in "Narrative as Rhetoric in *The Faerie Queene*," makes an impressive effort to historicize the textuality of the poem. Berger may in part have been responding to the charge by Louis Montrose, in the introduction to *Revisionary Play*, that "Berger's [recent] essays strongly imply that . . . linguistic slippages are not so much a general condition of discourse as manifestations of the author's ironic mastery of the imaginative world of his text—a mastery that the critic expounds and thereby shares" (16). The essay develops an impressive response to this objection, and yet it still seems strange, in the end, that for Berger the poem's sexual politics are so close to those of American English professors in the late-twentieth century. One still has the impression that Berger is exploiting a general, if now more persuasively historicized, condition of textual slipperiness in order to give us a politically amenable Spenser.

Montrose's objection, on the other hand, begs the question it raises: we all, to the extent that we engage the text, exploit the slippages of its language, and no one can locate the difference Montrose invokes, between stylistic effects that testify to authorial mastery and those that simply reflect a general condition of discourse. What are the implications for our critical practice of such a distinction? How might we try to respect it? If we are going to invoke the author, shall we assume that he, too, was aware of this problem? Did he respond to linguistic slippage as his seventeenth-century follower Digby would, by resisting it, idealizing an archaic and unchanging English that would triumph as the true idiom of the kingdom?[5] If so, then we must conclude that Spenser was indeed both naive and inept, for the consequences of the text he actually created were not to install a new idiom but to render his writing obscure; not to limit and resist the general slipperiness of language but to intensify and multiply its effects.

We might assume that Spenser deliberately cultivated such ambiguity. Elizabethan definitions of allegory stress the need for readers to exercise their powers of invention, and Spenser's style extends this demand to the details of semantics, syntax, even orthography. Seventeenth-century readers resist this aspect of the text and pretend that it can be overlooked; they recommend reading "past" Spenser's style for the sake of his "matter"—an approach that has its modern advocates as well. But the poet of *The Shepheardes Calender* loved secrets; he delighted in making reading a mysterious game. Why should we not believe that he deliberately, rather than ineptly, created a text that would survive not because it carries a set of determinate original meanings forward into imperial perpetuity, but because it retains an endless capacity to signify in historical circumstances no one could anticipate?

The Spenser I am invoking is close to the one Jonathan Goldberg describes as the author of an "endlesse worke" of reading. We need to know more about this work as it has proceeded over the last four hundred years. If Spenser's style is both resistant and accommodating, hard to make sense of (as the history of its reception shows) and yet (as the history of modern criticism shows) able to repay varied and often opposed ways of reading, how has this amphibious style affected Spenser's place as the most marginalized major author in the canon? In the poetic tradition he has been at once central and largely invisible, a "poet's poet" whose influence moves through later writing like an underground river, less easily mapped than Shakespeare's or Milton's. In the classrooms of American colleges and universities today Spenser plays a similarly double role: the standard undergraduate major in English lists three authors—Chaucer, Shakespeare, and Milton—as "major figures" in the early period, yet even as Spenser fades from the undergraduate curriculum he holds a prominent place in graduate seminars as an occasion for some of the most interesting and challenging criticism being produced. How long, I wonder, will this continue to be true? As postcolonialism and cultural studies provide increasingly dominant paradigms for literary study, will *A View of the Present State of Ireland* dislodge *The Faerie Queene* as Spenser's best known and most frequently studied text? I hope not. Before we exchange Spenser's verbal otherness for Spenser as our political other, I would like to know more about the politics of his strange and excessive style. Is Spenser really our fool? Or is he not rather, as Feste would have it, our corrupter of words?

NOTES

1. *Spenser: The Critical Heritage,* ed. Cummings 187. The introduction provides a useful account of Spenser's early reputation; Cummings suggests that the poem "may have overwhelmed and confused its earliest readers" (9). One in particular who neither admired nor understood the poem left a record of what Stephen Orgel calls his "angry dialogue" with it in the margins of a copy of the 1611 Folio. I am grateful to Professor Orgel for sharing with me his transcription of the marginalia and for letting me see his discussion of them in "Margins of Truth."

2. See De Grazia's *Shakespeare Verbatim.* McLeod's work has mostly circulated in manuscript, but see Random Cloud [Randall McLeod], "'The very names of the Persons': Editing and the Invention of Dramatick Character." See also Marcus, *Unediting the Renaissance.*

3. The earliest Jacobean editions of Spenser's work already show in their

patterns of emendation and proofreading a "failure to recognize archaisms" such as the syllabic -*es* that makes two-syllable words out of plural forms (Wurtsbaugh 5–6). By midcentury the first glossary of Spenser's language appears, appended to a Latin translation of the *Calender*. By century's end *The Faerie Queene*, like *The Canterbury Tales*, has been recast in heroic couplets, unfortunately not by Dryden.

4. Blank offers the most recent cultural history of "uncommon" language in Renaissance literary texts, including valuable insight into the language of *The Shepheardes Calender*, but beyond quoting one of those chimerical eight-line stanzas that bedevil proofreaders (27; Spenser's poem resists more than just memorization), Blank has almost nothing to say about *The Faerie Queene*.

5. Sir Kenelm Digby hopes that the poet's work "will be a meanes that the english tongue will receive no more alteration and changes, but will remaine & continue settled in that forme it now hath." He goes so far as to express confidence "that noe fate nor length of time will bury Spencers workes and memory, nor indeed alter that language that out of his schoole we now use untill some general innovation happen that may shake as well the foundations of our nation as of our speech" (Cummings, ed. 148–49). General innovation was already shaking the foundations of the nation and its speech as Digby wrote these words. But while his desire for linguistic and political stasis now appears both reactionary and unrealistic, he does grasp clearly the link between language and politics.

WORKS CITED

Adams, Marjorie. "Ronsard and Spenser: The Commentary." *Renaissance Papers* (1954): 25–29.

Addison, Joseph, and Richard Steele. *The Spectator.* Ed. Donald F. Bond. 5 vols. Oxford: Clarendon, 1965.

Alexander, Gavin. "Constant Works: A Framework for Reading Mary Wroth." *Sidney Newsletter* 14 (1996–97): 5–32.

Allen, Don Cameron. *Mysteriously Meant: The Rediscovery of Pagan Symbolism and Allegorical Interpretation in the Renaissance.* Baltimore: Johns Hopkins UP, 1970.

Alpers, Paul. "Narration in *The Faerie Queene.*" *ELH* 44 (1977): 19–39.

———. *The Poetry of "The Faerie Queene."* Princeton: Princeton UP, 1967.

———. *What Is Pastoral?* Chicago: U of Chicago P, 1996.

Anderson, Judith. "Arthur, Argante, and the Ideal Vision." *The Passing of Arthur.* Ed. Christopher Baswell and William Sharpe. New York: Garland, 1988. 193–203.

———. "The 'Couert Vele': Chaucer, Spenser, and Venus." *English Literary Renaissance* 24 (1994): 638–59.

———. "'In liuing colours and right hew': The Queen of Spenser's Central Books." *Poetic Traditions of the English Renaissance.* Ed. Maynard Mack and George deForest Lord. New Haven: Yale UP, 1982. 47–66.

———. "Prudence and Her Silence: Spenser's Use of Chaucer's Melibee." *ELH* 62 (1995): 29–46.

———. *Words That Matter: Linguistic Perception in Renaissance English.* Stanford: Stanford UP, 1996.

Anderson, Benedict. *Imagined Communities: Reflections on the Origin and Spread of Nationalism.* London: Verso, 1983.

Archer, John Michael. *Old Worlds: Egypt, Southwest Asia, and India in Early Modern English Writing.* Forthcoming.

Aries, Philippe. *Centuries of Childhood.* New York: Knopf, 1962.

Ariosto, Lodovico. *Bellezze del Furioso di M. Lodovico Ariosto. Scielte da Oratio Toscanella.* Venice, 1574.

———. *Orlando Furioso.* Ed. Cesare Segre. 2 vols. Milan: Arnoldo Mondadori, 1976. Trans. Guido Waldman. Oxford: Oxford UP, 1974.

————. *Orlando Furioso di M. Lodovico Ariosto alquale di nuovo sono aggiunte le Annotationi e gli Auuertimenti e le Dichiarationi di Girolamo Ruscelli.* Venice, 1556.

————. *Orlando Furioso di M. Lodovico Ariosto con Allegoria di Gioseffo Bononome.* Venice, 1584.

————. *Orlando Furioso di Messer Lodovico Ariosto, con Allegorie a ciascun Canto di Thomaso Porcacchi.* Venice, 1577.

————. *"Orlando Furioso."* Translated into English Heroical Verse by Sir John Harington. Ed. Robert McNulty. Oxford: Clarendon, 1972.

Asch, Ronald G., ed. *Three Nations—A Common History? England, Scotland, Ireland and British History c. 1600–1920.* Bochum: Universitätsverlag Dr. N. Brockmeyer, 1993.

Aubrey, John. "Fairies and Robin Goodfellow." *Remaines of Gentilisme and Judaisme.* In *Three Prose Works.* Ed. John Buchanan-Brown. Carbondale: Southern Illinois UP, 1972.

Baker, David J. *Between Nations: Shakespeare, Spenser, Marvell, and the Question of Britain.* Stanford: Stanford UP, 1997.

————. "'Some Quirk, Some Subtle Evasion': Legal Subversion in Spenser's *A View of the Present State of Ireland.*" *Spenser Studies* 6 (1985): 147–63.

Baker, J.H. *Manual of Law French.* 2nd ed. Aldershot, Hants, England: Scolar P, 1990.

Bakhtin, M.M. "Epic and Novel." *The Dialogic Imagination: Four Essays.* Ed. Michael Holquist. Trans. Caryl Emerson and Michael Holquist. Slavic Series 1. Austin: U of Texas P, 1981. 3–40.

Baldwin, T.W. *William Shakspere's Small Latine and Lesse Greeke.* Urbana: U of Illinois P, 1944.

Barkan, Leonard. *The Gods Made Flesh: Metamorphosis and the Pursuit of Paganism.* New Haven: Yale UP, 1986.

Barley, Nigel. "A Structural Approach to the Proverb and Maxim with Special Reference to the Anglo-Saxon Corpus." *Proverbium* 20 (1972): 737–50.

Barthes, Roland. *Elements of Semiology.* Trans. Annette Laves and Colin Smith. New York: Hill and Wang, 1968.

————. *S/Z.* Trans. Richard Miller. New York: Hill and Wang, 1974.

Barton, Anne. "Harking Back to Elizabeth: Ben Jonson and Caroline Nostalgia." *ELH* 48 (1981): 706–31.

Baskervill, Charles Read. "The Genesis of Spenser's Queen of Faerie." *Modern Philology* 18 (1920): 49–54.

Baswell, Christopher. *Virgil in Medieval England.* Cambridge: Cambridge UP, 1995.

Bauckham, Richard. *Tudor Apocalypse.* Courtenay Library of Reformation Classics 8. Oxford: Sutton Courtenay P, 1978.

Baxter, Richard. *Reliquiae Baxterianae.* London, 1696.

Bec, Christian. *Les livres des florentins: 1413–1608.* Florence: Olschki, 1984.

Beckett, J.C. *The Making of Modern Ireland, 1603–1923.* London: Faber and Faber, 1966.

Bednarz, James P. "The Collaborator as Thief: Ralegh's (Re)Vision of *The Faerie Queene.*" *ELH* 63 (1996): 279–307.

Beilin, Elaine. *Redeeming Eve: Women Writers of the English Renaissance.* Princeton: Princeton UP, 1987.

Bell, H.E. *An Introduction to the History and Records of the Court of Wards and Liveries.* Cambridge: Cambridge UP, 1953.

Bellamy, John. *The Tudor Law of Treason.* London: Routledge and Kegan Paul, 1979.

Belsey, Catherine. *John Milton: Language, Gender, Power.* Oxford: Basil Blackwell, 1988.

————. *The Subject of Tragedy: Identity and Difference in Renaissance Drama.* London: Methuen, 1985.

Bennett, Josephine Waters. *The Evolution of "The Faerie Queene."* Chicago: U of Chicago P, 1942.

Benson, Pamela. *The Invention of the Renaissance Woman.* University Park: Pennsylvania State UP, 1992.

Bentley, Gerald Eades. *Shakespeare and Jonson: Their Reputations in the Seventeenth Century Compared.* Chicago: U of Chicago P, 1945.

Berger, Harry, Jr. *The Allegorical Temper: Vision and Reality in Book II of Spenser's "Faerie Queene."* New Haven: Yale UP, 1957.

————. "Busirane and the War between the Sexes: An Interpretation of *The Faerie Queene* III, xi–xii." *English Literary Renaissance* 1 (1971): 99–121.

————. "The F-Fragment of *The Canterbury Tales.*" *Chaucer Review* 1 (1966–67): 87–102, 135–56.

————. "Narrative as Rhetoric in *The Faerie Queene.*" *English Literary Renaissance* 21 (1991): 3–48.

————. *Revisionary Play: Studies in the Spenserian Dynamics.* Berkeley: U of California P, 1988.

Berry, Craig. "Borrowed Armor/Free Grace: The Quest for Authority in *The Faerie Queene* I and Chaucer's *Tale of Sir Thopas.*" *Studies in Philology* 91 (1994): 136–66.

————. "'Sundrie Doubts': Vulnerable Understanding and Dubious Origins in Spenser's Continuation of *The Squire's Tale.*" *Refiguring Chaucer in the Renaissance* . Ed. Theresa M. Krier. Gainesville: U of Florida P, 1998. 106–27.

Bhabha, Homi. *The Location of Culture.* London: Routledge, 1994.

Biow, Douglas. *Mirabile Dictu: Representations of the Marvelous in Renaissance Epic.* Ann Arbor: U of Michigan P, 1996.

Blank, Paula. *Broken English: Dialects and the Politics of Language in Renaissance Writings.* New York: Methuen, 1996.

Blitch, Alice Fox. "Proserpina Preserved: Book VI of the *Faerie Queene*." *Studies in English Literature* 13 (1973): 15–30.

Bloom, Harold. *A Map of Misreading*. New York: Oxford UP, 1975.

Blumenberg, Hans. *The Genesis of the Copernican World*. Trans. Robert M. Wallace. Cambridge, MA: MIT, 1987.

Boccaccio, Giovanni. *Boccaccio on Poetry: Being the Preface in the Fourteenth and Fifteenth Books of Boccaccio's "Genealogia Deorum Gentilium."* Trans. Charles S. Osgood. 1930. New York: Liberal Arts, 1956.

Boehrer, Bruce Thomas. *Monarchy and Incest in Renaissance England: Literature, Culture, Kinship, and Kingship*. Philadelphia: U of Pennsylvania P, 1992.

Bradshaw, Brendan. *The Irish Constitutional Revolution of the Sixteenth Century*. Cambridge: Cambridge UP, 1979.

Bradshaw, Brendan, and John Morrill. *The British Problem, c. 1534–1707: State Formation in the Atlantic Archipelago*. London: Macmillan, 1996.

Brady, Ciaran. "Court, Castle and Country: The Framework of Government in Tudor Ireland." *Natives and Newcomers: Essays on the Making of Irish Colonial Society, 1534–1641*. Ed. Ciaran Brady and Raymond Gillespie. Dublin: Irish Academic P, 1986. 22–49.

Breen, John M. "Imagining Voices in *A View of the Present State of Ireland*: A Discussion of Recent Studies Concerning Edmund Spenser's Dialogue." *Connotations* 4 (1994–95): 119–32.

The Brideling, Sadling and Ryding, of a Rich Churle in Hampshire, by the Subtill Practise of one Judeth Philips. London, 1595.

Bridges, John. *The Supremacie of Christian Princes*. London, 1573.

Briggs, Katherine. *Anatomy of Puck*. London: Routledge and Kegan Paul, 1959.

Brink, Jean R. "'All his minde on honor fixed': The Preferment of Edmund Spenser." *Spenser's Life and the Subject of Biography*. Ed. Judith H. Anderson, Donald Cheney, and David A. Richardson. Amherst: U of Massachusetts P, 1996.

Brown, Keith M. "British History: A Sceptical Comment." Asch 117–27.

Buchanan, George. *Rerum scoticarum historia*. Edinburgh, 1582.

Burke, Peter. *Popular Culture in Early Modern Europe*. New York: New York UP, 1978.

Burton, Robert. *The Anatomy of Melancholy*. Ed. Floyd Dell and Paul Jordan-Smith. New York: Tudor, 1941.

———. *The Anatomy of Melancholy*. Ed. Thomas C. Faulkner, Nicholas Kiessling, and Rhonda Blair. 2 vols. Oxford: Clarendon, 1989.

Bushnell, Rebecca. *A Culture of Teaching: Early Modern Humanism in Theory and Practice*. Ithaca, NY: Cornell UP, 1996.

Cable, Lana. *Carnal Rhetoric: Milton's Iconoclasm and the Poetics of Desire*. Durham, NC: Duke UP, 1995.

Cain, Thomas. *Praise in "The Faerie Queene."* Lincoln: U of Nebraska P, 1978.

Calendar of State Papers and Manuscripts Relating to English Affairs, Existing in the Archives and Collections of Venice, and in Other Libraries of Northern Italy. Ed. Rawden Brown. 7 vols. London, 1864.

Campbell, Lily Bess, ed. *The Mirror for Magistrates.* Cambridge: Cambridge UP, 1938.

Campbell, Mary B. *The Witness and the Other World: Exotic European Travel Writing, 400–1600.* Ithaca, NY: Cornell UP, 1988.

Canny, Nicholas. "The Attempted Anglicization of Ireland in the Seventeenth Century: An Exemplar of 'British History.'" Asch 49–82.

———. "Edmund Spenser and the Development of an Anglo-Irish Identity." *Yearbook of English Studies* 13 (1983): 1–19.

———. *From Reformation to Restoration: Ireland, 1534–1660.* Dublin: Helicon, 1987.

———. "Irish, Scottish and Welsh Responses to Centralization, c. 1530–c. 1640: A Comparative Perspective." Grant and Stringer 147–69.

———. *The Elizabethan Conquest of Ireland: A Pattern Established, 1565–76.* New York: Barnes and Noble, 1976.

Capp, Bernard. "The Millennium and Eschatology in England." *Past and Present* 57 (1972): 156–62.

———. "The Political Dimension of Apocalyptic Thought." Patrides and Wittreich 93–124.

Carey, John, ed. *Milton: Complete Shorter Poems.* London: Longman, 1968.

Carrell, Jennifer Lee. "A Pack of Lies in a Looking Glass: Lady Mary Wroth's *Urania* and the *Magic Mirror of Romance.*" *Studies in English Literature* 34 (1994): 79–107.

Carruthers, Mary. *The Book of Memory: A Study of Memory in Medieval Culture.* Cambridge: Cambridge UP, 1990.

Cavanagh, Sheila T. "'The fatal destiny of that land': Elizabethan Views of Ireland." *Representing Ireland: Literature and the Origins of Conflict, 1534–1660.* Ed. Brendan Bradshaw, Andrew Hadfield, and Willy Maley. Cambridge: Cambridge UP, 1993.

———. *Wanton Eyes and Chaste Desires: Female Sexuality in "The Faerie Queene."* Bloomington: Indiana UP, 1994.

Cervantes, Miguel de. *Don Quijote de la Mancha.* Ed. Martin de Riquer. 2 vols. Barcelona: Juventud, 1971.

———. *Don Quixote.* Trans. J.M. Cohen. Harmondsworth: Penguin, 1950.

Chaucer, Geoffrey. *The Riverside Chaucer.* Ed. Larry D. Benson et al. Boston: Houghton Mifflin, 1987. Based on *The Works of Geoffrey Chaucer.* Ed. F.N. Robinson. 2nd ed. Boston: Houghton Mifflin, 1957.

Cheney, Donald. *Spenser's Image of Nature: Wild Man and Shepherd in "The Faerie Queene."* New Haven: Yale UP, 1966.

Cheney, Patrick. *Marlowe's Counterfeit Profession: Ovid, Spenser, Counter-Nationhood.* Toronto: U of Toronto P, 1997.

———. *Spenser's Famous Flight: A Renaissance Idea of a Literary Career.* Toronto: U of Toronto P, 1993.

———. "Spenser's Completion of *The Squire's Tale:* Love, Magic, and Heroic Action in the Legend of Cambell and Triamond." *Journal of Medieval and Renaissance Studies* 15 (1985): 135–55.

Child, Francis James. *The English and Scottish Popular Ballads.* 1882. New York: Folklore, 1956.

Cleland, James. *The Institution of a Young Nobleman.* Oxford, 1607.

Cohen, Gustave. *Ronsard: Sa vie et son oeuvre.* Paris: Gallimard, 1956.

Cohn, Norman. *The Pursuit of the Millennium: Revolutionary Millenarians and Mystical Anarchists of the Middle Ages.* 1957. Oxford: Oxford UP, 1974.

Coleridge, Samuel Taylor. *Coleridge's Miscellaneous Criticism.* Ed. T.M. Raysor. Cambridge: Harvard UP, 1936.

Colón, Hernando. *Historia del Almirante.* Ed. Luis Arranz. Trans. Alfonso Ulloa. Madrid: Historia 16, 1984.

Conley, Tom. *The Self-Made Map: Cartographic Writing in Early Modern France.* Minneapolis: U of Minnesota P, 1996.

Cooper, Thomas. *Thesaurus linguae romanae et britannicae.* London, 1565.

Cooper, Carolyn. *Noises in the Blood: Orality, Gender and the "Vulgar" Body of Jamaican Culture.* Durham, NC: Duke UP, 1995.

Cotgrave, Randle. *A Dictionarie of the French and English Tongues.* London, 1611.

Covarrubias, Sebastián de. *Tesoro de la lengua castellana o española.* Ed. Martín de Riquer. Lengua y literatura 3. Barcelona: Alta Fulla, 1989.

Crane, Mary Thomas. *Framing Authority: Sayings, Self, and Society in Sixteenth-Century England.* Princeton: Princeton UP, 1993.

Crawford, Jon G. *Anglicizing the Government of Ireland: The Irish Privy Council and the Expansion of Tudor Rule, 1556–78.* Dublin: Irish Academic P in association with the Irish Legal History Society, 1993.

Cummings, R.M., ed. *Spenser: The Critical Heritage.* New York: Barnes and Noble, 1971.

Curtius, Ernst Robert. *European Literature and the Latin Middle Ages.* Trans. Willard R. Trask. Bollingen Series 36. Princeton: Princeton UP, 1953.

Damasio, Antonio. *Descartes' Error: Emotion, Reason, and the Human Brain.* New York: Putnam, 1994.

Daniel, Samuel. *The Collection of the Historie of England.* London, 1618.

———. *Poems and a Defence of Ryme.* Ed. Arthur Colby Sprague. Cambridge: Harvard UP, 1930.

———. *The Queenes Arcadia.* London, 1606.

Dasenbrock, Reed Way. *Imitating the Italians.* Baltimore: Johns Hopkins UP, 1991.

Dassonville, Michel. *Ronsard: Etude historique et littéraire V: Un brasier sous la cendre (1565–1575).* Geneva: Droz, 1990.

D'Aubigné, Agrippa. *Oeuvres.* Ed. Henri Weber. Paris: Gallimard, 1969.

De Grazia, Margreta. *Shakespeare Verbatim: The Reproduction of Authenticity and the 1790 Apparatus.* Oxford: Clarendon, 1991.

Degh, Linda. *Folktales and Society: Story-Telling in a Hungarian Peasant Community.* Trans. Emily M. Schossberger. Bloomington: Indiana UP, 1969.

Dekker, Thomas. *The Whore of Babylon.* Ed. Marianne Gateson Riely. New York: Garland, 1980.

Deleuze, Gilles, and Félix Guattari. *Anti-Oedipus: Capitalism and Schizophrenia.* Trans. Robert Hurley, Mark Seem, and Helen R. Lane. Minneapolis: U of Minnesota P, 1983.

Dent, R.W. *Proverbial Language in English Drama Exclusive of Shakespeare, 1495–1616.* Berkeley: U of California P, 1984.

———. *Shakespeare's Proverbial Language.* Berkeley: U of California P, 1981.

Dictionary of National Biography. Ed. Leslie Stephen and Sidney Lee. 66 vols. London, 1885–1901.

Digby, Sir Kenelm. "A Discourse Concerning Edmund Spenser (1628)." *Spenser: The Critical Heritage.* Ed. Cummings. 148–49.

Dillon, Myles, and Nora K. Chadwick. *The Celtic Realms.* London: Weidenfeld and Nicolson, 1967.

Dirlik, Arif. "The Postcolonial Aura: Third World Criticism in the Age of Global Capitalism." *Critical Inquiry* 20 (1994): 328–56.

A Discourse upon the Exposicion & Understanding of Statutes, with Sir Thomas Egerton's Additions. Ed. Samuel E. Thorne. San Marino, CA: Huntington Library, 1942.

Doe, Norman. *Fundamental Authority in the Late Medieval English Law.* Cambridge: Cambridge UP, 1990.

Dolan, Frances E. *Dangerous Familiars: Representations of Domestic Crime in England, 1550–1700.* Ithaca, NY: Cornell UP, 1994.

———. "Taking the Pencil Out of God's Hand: Art, Nature, and the Face-Painting Debate in Early Modern England." *PMLA* 108 (1993): 224–38.

Donne, John. *Poems.* Ed. Herbert J.C. Grierson. 2 vols. Oxford: Clarendon, 1912.

Drayton, Michael. *Works.* Ed. J. William Hebel. 5 vols. Oxford: Basil Blackwell, 1932–42.

Dubrow, Heather. "The Message from Marcade: Parental Death in Tudor and Stuart England." *Attending to Women in Early Modern England.* Ed. Betty S. Travitsky and Adele F. Seeff. Newark: U of Delaware P and Associated UP, 1994. 147–67.

———. *Shakespeare and Domestic Loss.* Cambridge Studies in Renaissance Literature. Cambridge: Cambridge UP, 1999.

———. "'In thievish ways': Tropes and Robbers in Shakespeare's Sonnets and

Early Modern England." *Journal of English and Germanic Philology* 96 (1997): 514–44.

Duffy, Maureen. "Renaissance: Sex and Violence." *The Erotic World of Faery.* London: Hodder and Stoughton, 1972. 127–36.

Eberly, Susan. "Fairies and the Folklore of Disability: Changelings, Hybrids, and the Solitary Fairy." *The Good People: New Fairylore Essays.* Ed. Peter Narvaez. New York: Garland, 1991. 227–50.

Eggert, Katherine. "'Changing all that forme of common weale': Genre and the Repeal of Queenship in *The Faerie Queene,* Book V." *English Literary Renaissance* 26 (1996): 259–90.

Ellis, Steven G. "Henry VIII, Rebellion and the Rule of Law." *Historical Journal* 24 (1981): 513–31.

———. "'Not Mere English': The British Perspective 1400–1650." *History Today* 39 (1988): 41–48.

———. *Tudor Ireland: Crown, Community and the Conflict of Cultures, 1470–1603.* London: Longman, 1985.

Ellis, Steven G., and Sarah Barber, eds. *Conquest and Union: Fashioning a British State 1485–1725.* London: Longman, 1995.

Elshtain, Jean. *Public Man, Private Woman.* Princeton: Princeton UP, 1981.

Erasmus, Desiderius. *Apophthegmes.* Trans. Nicholas Udall. London, 1564.

———. *Copia: Foundations of the Abundant Style.* Trans. Betty I. Knott. Ed. Craig R. Thompson. Vol. 24 of *Collected Works of Erasmus.* Toronto: U of Toronto P, 1978.

———. *De pueris instituendis. Desiderius Erasmus Concerning the Aim and Method of Education.* Ed. William Harrison Woodward. New York: Columbia U Teacher's College, 1964.

———. *Erasmus on His Times: A Shortened Version of the Adages of Erasmus.* Trans. Margaret Mann Phillips. London: Cambridge UP, 1967.

The Faerie Leveller, Or King Charles his Leveller descried and deciphered in Queene Elizabeths dayes. By her Poet Laureat Edmond Spenser, in his unpareld Poeme, entituled, The Faerie Queene. A lively representation of our times. London, 1648.

Fallon, Jean M. *Voice and Vision in Ronsard's "Les Sonnets pour Helene."* New York: Peter Lang, 1992.

Falls, Cyril. *Elizabeth's Irish Wars.* London, Methuen, 1950.

Finucci, Valeria. *The Lady Vanishes.* Stanford: Stanford UP, 1992.

Firth, Katharine R. *The Apocalyptic Tradition in Reformation Britain, 1530–1645.* Oxford: Oxford UP, 1979.

Fixler, Michael. *Milton and the Kingdom of God.* Evanston, IL: Northwestern UP, 1964.

Fleming, Juliet. "The Ladies' Man and the Age of Elizabeth." *Sexuality and Gender in Early Modern Europe.* Ed. James Grantham Turner. Cambridge: Cambridge UP, 1993. 158–81.

Fletcher, Angus. *The Prophetic Moment: An Essay on Spenser.* Chicago: U of Chicago P, 1971.

Fletcher, Anthony. *Gender, Sex, and Subordination in England: 1500–1800.* New Haven: Yale UP, 1995.

Florio, John. *Queen Anna's New World of Words.* London, 1611.

Fogarty, Anne. "The Colonization of Language: Narrative Strategy in *A View of the Present State of Ireland* and *The Faerie Queene,* Book VI." *Spenser and Ireland: An Interdisciplinary Perspective.* Ed. Patricia Coughlan. Cork, Ireland: Cork UP, 1989. 75–108.

Foucault, Michel. *The History of Sexuality.* 3 vols. Trans. Robert Hurley. New York: Pantheon, 1978–86.

Fowler, Alastair. "The River Guyon." *MLN* 75 (1960): 289–92.

Fowler, Earle Broadus. *Spenser and the Courts of Love.* Menasha, WI: George Banta, 1921.

Fowler, Elizabeth. "The Failure of Moral Philosophy in the Work of Edmund Spenser." *Representations* 51 (1995): 47–76.

Foxe, John. *Acts and Monuments of John Foxe.* Ed. Josiah Pratt. 8 vols. London, 1877.

Fraser, Russell. *The War against Poetry.* Princeton: Princeton UP, 1970.

Freud, Sigmund. *The Standard Edition of the Complete Psychological Works.* Trans. James Strachey. 24 vols. London: Hogarth, 1953–74.

Fried, Debra. "Spenser's Caesura." *English Literary Renaissance* 11 (1981): 261–80.

Frye, Susan. *Elizabeth I: The Competition for Representation.* New York: Oxford UP, 1993.

G.H. *Mirrour of Maiestie.* London, 1618.

Galyon, Linda R. "Scudamore Family." *Spenser Encyclopedia* 634–35.

Garcilaso de la Vega, El Inca. *Comentarios reales de los Incas.* Ed. Aurelio Miró Quesada. 2 vols. Biblioteca Ayacucho 5–6. Caracas: Biblioteca Ayacucho, 1976.

———. *Royal Commentaries of the Incas and General History of Peru, Part One.* Trans. Harold V. Livermore. Austin: U of Texas P, 1966.

Gasper, Julia. *The Dragon and the Dove: The Plays of Thomas Dekker.* Oxford: Clarendon, 1990.

Gebauer, Gunter, and Christoph Wulf. *Mimesis: Culture—Art—Society.* Trans. Don Reneau. Berkeley and Los Angeles: U of California P, 1995.

The Geneva Bible: A Facsimile Edition. Ed. Lloyd E. Berry. Madison: U of Wisconsin P, 1969.

Giamatti, A. Bartlett. *Exile and Change in Renaissance Literature.* New Haven: Yale UP, 1984.

———. *Play of Double Senses: Spenser's "Faerie Queene."* Englewood Cliffs, NJ: Prentice, 1975.

Giddens, Anthony. *The Constitution of Society.* Cambridge, England: Polity, 1984.

———. *Modernity and Self-Identity: Self and Society in the Late Modern Age.* Stanford: Stanford UP, 1991.

Gless, Darryl J. *Interpretation and Theology in Spenser.* Cambridge: Cambridge UP, 1994.

Goldberg, Jonathan. *Endlesse Worke: Spenser and the Structures of Discourse.* Baltimore: Johns Hopkins UP, 1981.

Gomme, Andor, ed. *The Roaring Girl.* By Thomas Middleton and Thomas Dekker. London: Ernest Benn, 1976.

Goodman, Godfrey. *The Fall of Man.* London, 1615.

———. *The Fall of Man.* London, 1616.

Goodman, Nelson. *Ways of Worldmaking.* Indianapolis: Hackett, 1978.

Grafton, Anthony. *Defenders of the Text.* Cambridge: Harvard UP, 1991.

Grant, Alexander, and Keith J. Stringer. *Uniting the Kingdom? The Making of British History.* London: Routledge, 1995.

Greenblatt, Stephen. *Renaissance Self-Fashioning: From More to Shakespeare.* Chicago: U of Chicago P, 1980.

———. *Sir Walter Ralegh: The Renaissance Man and His Roles.* New Haven: Yale UP, 1973.

Greene, Roland. "Fictions of Immanence, Fictions of Embassy." *The Project of Prose in Early Modern Europe and the New World.* Ed. Elizabeth Fowler and Roland Greene. Cambridge Studies in Renaissance Literature and Culture 16. Cambridge: Cambridge UP, 1997. 176–202.

Greene, Thomas M. *The Light in Troy: Imitation and Discovery in Renaissance Poetry.* New Haven: Yale UP, 1982.

Greenlaw, Edwin. "Spenser's Fairy Mythology." *Modern Philology* 15 (1918): 105–22.

Grendler, Paul. *Schooling in Renaissance Italy.* Baltimore: Johns Hopkins UP, 1989.

Grenfell, Morton, ed. *Elizabethan Ireland.* London: Longman, 1971.

Guillory, John. *Poetic Authority: Spenser, Milton, and Literary History.* New York: Columbia UP, 1983.

Hackett, Helen. *Virgin Mother, Maiden Queene: Queen Elizabeth I and the Cult of the Virgin Mary.* London: Macmillan, 1995.

———. "'Yet Tell Me Some Such Fiction': Lady Mary Wroth's *Urania* and the 'Femininity' of Romance." *Women, Texts, and Histories, 1575–1760.* Ed. Clare Brant and Diane Purkiss. London: Routledge, 1992. 39–68.

Hadfield, Andrew. *Edmund Spenser's Irish Experience: Wilde Fruit and Salvage Soyl.* Oxford: Clarendon, 1997.

———. "Spenser and Republicanism." Talk given at the Spenser Society Luncheon, Toronto, 1997.

————. "Who Is Speaking in Spenser's *View of the Present State of Ireland*? A Response to John Breen." *Connotations* 4 (1994–95): 232–41.

Halliwell-Phillips, James. "Mr. Fox." *The Book of Days: A Miscellany of Popular Antiquities.* Ed. R. Chambers. London: W. and R. Chambers, n.d. 1: 291.

Hallowell, Robert E. *Ronsard and the Conventional Roman Elegy.* Urbana: U of Illinois P, Illinois Studies in Language and Literature, 1954.

Halpern, Richard. "The Great Instauration: Imaginary Narratives in Milton's 'Nativity Ode.'" *Re-Membering Milton: Essays on Texts and Traditions.* Ed. Mary Nyquist and Margaret Ferguson. New York: Methuen, 1987.

Hamilton, A.C., ed. *The Faerie Queene.* 1977. London: Longman, 1980.

Hankins, John Erskine. "Spenser and the Revelation of St. John." *PMLA* 60 (1945): 364–81.

Hannay, Margaret, ed. Introduction to *Silent But for the Word: Tudor Women as Patrons, Translators, and Writers of Religious Works.* Kent, Ohio: Kent State UP, 1985.

Haraway, Donna J. *Modest_Witness@Second Millennium. FemaleMan©_Meets_OncoMouse™: Feminism and Technoscience.* New York: Routledge, 1997.

————. "Situated Knowledges: The Science Question in Feminism as a Site of Discourse on the Privilege of Partial Perspective." *Feminist Studies* 14 (1988): 575–99.

Hartland, Sidney. *English Fairy and Other Folk Tales.* London, 1890.

Harvey, Gabriel. "A New Letter of Notable Contents, 1593." *The Works of Gabriel Harvey.* Ed. Alexander B. Grosart. 3 vols. 1884–85. New York: AMS, 1996.

Hauser, Arnold. *The Social History of Art.* Trans. Stanley Godman. 4 vols. New York: Vintage, 1957.

Hayes, Tom. *The Birth of Popular Culture: Ben Jonson, Maid Marian and Robin Hood.* Pittsburgh: Duquesne UP, 1992.

Heal, Felicity, and Clive Holmes. *The Gentry in England and Wales, 1500–1700.* Stanford: Stanford UP, 1994.

Healy, Thomas. *New Latitudes: Theory and English Renaissance Literature.* London: Edward Arnold, 1992.

Heberle, Mark. "Pagans and Saracens in Spenser's *The Faerie Queene.*" *Comparative Literature East and West: Traditions and Trends.* Ed. Cornelia N. Moore and Raymond A. Moody. Honolulu: U of Hawaii College of Languages, Linguistics, and Literature, 1989. 81–87.

Hebreo, León. *Diálogos de Amor.* Ed. Eduardo Juliá Martínez. Trans. Garcilaso de la Vega, El Inca. 2 vols. Madrid: Librería General Victoriano Suárez, 1949.

Helgerson, Richard. *The Elizabethan Prodigals.* Berkeley: U of California P, 1976.

————. *Forms of Nationhood: The Elizabethan Writing of England.* Chicago: U of Chicago P, 1992.

―――. *Self-Crowned Laureates: Spenser, Jonson, Milton and the Literary System.* Berkeley: U of California P, 1983.

Hendricks, Margo. "'Obscured by dreams': Race, Empire, and Shakespeare's *A Midsummer Night's Dream.*" *Shakespeare Quarterly* 47 (1996): 37–60.

Herman, Peter C. *Squitter-Wits and Muse-Haters: Sidney, Spenser, Milton, and Renaissance Antipoetic Sentiment.* Detroit: Wayne State UP, 1996.

Herrup, Cynthia B. *The Common Peace: Participation and the Criminal Law in Seventeenth-Century England.* Cambridge: Cambridge UP, 1987.

Hexter, Ralph J. *Ovid and Medieval Schooling.* Munich: Arbeo, 1986.

Hieatt, A. Kent. *Chaucer, Spenser, Milton.* Montreal: McGill-Queen's UP, 1975.

Hill, Christopher. *The World Turned Upside Down: Radical Ideas during the English Revolution.* 1972. Harmondsworth: Penguin, 1975.

Hirst, Derek. "The English Republic and the Meaning of Britain." *Journal of Modern History* 66 (1994): 451–86.

Holland, Eugene W. "Schizoanalysis and Baudelaire: Some Illustrations of Decoding at Work." *Deleuze: A Critical Reader.* Ed. Paul Patton. Oxford: Blackwell, 1996. 240–56.

Hooker, Richard. *The Laws of Ecclesiastical Polity.* 2 vols. London: Dent, 1907.

Hoskyns, John. *Direccions for Speech and Style. The Life, Letters, and Writings of John Hoskyns, 1566–1638.* Ed. Louise Brown Osborn. New Haven: Yale UP, 1937. 103–66.

Howard, Donald R. *Chaucer: His Life, His Works, His World.* New York: Dutton, 1987.

Huarte, Juan. *The Examination of Mens Wits.* 1594. Trans. Richard Carew. Ed. Carmen Rogers. Scholars' Facsimiles and Reprints, 1959.

Hull, Suzanne W. *Chaste, Silent and Obedient: English Books for Women, 1475–1640.* San Marino, CA: Huntington Library, 1982.

Hume, Anthea. *Edmund Spenser: Protestant Poet.* Cambridge: Cambridge UP, 1984.

Hunter, William B., Jr., ed. *The English Spenserians.* Salt Lake City: U of Utah P, 1977.

Hurstfield, Joel. *The Queen's Wards: Wardship and Marriage under Elizabeth I.* 2nd ed. London: Frank Cass, 1973.

Irwin, Terence. *Classical Thought.* New York: Oxford UP, 1989.

Jacobs, Joseph. *English Fairy Tales.* New York: Grosset and Dunlap, 1985.

James VI of Scotland (later I of England). *Daemonologie.* Edinburgh, 1597.

Javitch, Daniel. *Proclaiming a Classic.* Princeton: Princeton UP, 1991.

Jenkins, Raymond. "Spenser and the Clerkship in Munster." *PMLA* 47 (1932): 109–21.

―――. "Spenser: The Uncertain Years 1584–1589." *PMLA* 53 (1938): 350–61.

Johnson, Francis R. *A Critical Bibliography of the Works of Edmund Spenser Printed before 1700.* Baltimore: Johns Hopkins UP, 1933.

Jones, Ann Rosalind. *The Currency of Eros: Women's Love Lyric in Europe, 1540–1620*. Bloomington: Indiana UP, 1990.

Jordan, Constance. "Household and State: Transformations in the Representation of an Analogy from Aristotle to James I." *Modern Language Quarterly* 54 (1993): 307–26.

Kahn, Victoria. *Rhetoric, Prudence, and Skepticism in the Renaissance*. Ithaca, NY: Cornell UP, 1985.

Kaske, Carol V. "The Audiences of *The Faerie Queene*." *Literature and History* 3 (1994): 15–35.

———. "Spenser's Pluralistic Universe: The View from the Mount of Contemplation (F.Q. I.X)." *Contemporary Thought on Edmund Spenser: With a Bibliography of Criticism of "The Faerie Queene," 1900–1970*. Ed. Richard C. Frushell and Bernard J. Vondersmith. Carbondale: Southern Illinois UP,1975. 121–49, 230–33.

Kaske, Robert E. "The Knight's Interruption of the *Monk's Tale*." *ELH* 24 (1957): 249–68.

Kermode, Frank. *Shakespeare, Spenser, Donne: Renaissance Essays*. London: Routledge and Kegan Paul, 1971.

———, ed. *The Tempest*. By William Shakespeare. Arden Shakespeare Paperbacks. London: Methuen, 1964.

Kerrigan, William. "The Articulation of Ego in the English Renaissance." *The Literary Freud: Mechanisms of Defence and the Poetic Will*. Ed. Joseph H. Smith. New Haven: Yale UP, 1980. 261–307.

———. *The Sacred Complex: On the Psychogenesis of "Paradise Lost."* Cambridge: Harvard UP, 1983.

King, John N. *English Reformation Literature: The Tudor Origins of the Protestant Tradition*. Princeton: Princeton UP, 1982.

———. "Queen Elizabeth I: Representations of the Virgin Queen." *Renaissance Quarterly* 43 (1990): 30–73.

———. *Spenser's Poetry and the Reformation Tradition*. Princeton: Princeton UP, 1990.

Kinney, Clare Regan. *Strategies of Poetic Narrative: Chaucer, Spenser, Milton, Eliot*. Cambridge: Cambridge UP, 1992.

Kintgen, Eugene R. *Reading in Tudor England*. Pittsburgh: U of Pittsburgh P, 1996.

Knapp, Jeffrey. *An Empire Nowhere: England, America and Literature from "Utopia" to "The Tempest."* Berkeley: U of California P, 1992.

Kocher, Paul H. *Science and Religion in Elizabethan England*. San Marino, CA: Huntington Library, 1953.

Krier, Theresa M. *Gazing on Secret Sights: Spenser, Classical Imitation, and the Decorums of Vision*. Ithaca, NY: Cornell UP, 1990.

Labriola, Albert C. "Milton's Eve and the Cult of Elizabeth I." *Journal of English and Germanic Philology* 95 (1996): 38–51.

Lamb, Mary Ellen. "Apologizing for Pleasure in Sidney's *Apology for Poetry:* The Nurse of Abuse Meets the Tudor Grammar School." *Criticism* 36 (1994): 499–519.

———. *Gender and Authorship in the Sidney Circle.* Madison: U of Wisconsin P, 1990.

———. "Women Readers in Mary Wroth's *Urania.*" *Reading Mary Wroth.* Ed. Naomi Miller and Gary Waller. Knoxville: U of Tennessee P, 1991. 210–27.

Lane, John. *An Elegie vpon the death of the high and renowned Princesse, our late Souerayne Elizabeth.* London, 1603.

———. *John Lane's Continuation of Chaucer's Squire's Tale.* Ed. Frederick J. Furnivall. London, 1888.

———. "Tritons Trumpet to the twelve monethes." British Library MS. Reg. 17. B. xv.

Lanyer, Aemilia. *The Poems of Aemilia Lanyer: "Salve Deus Rex Judaeorum."* Ed. Susanne Woods. New York: Oxford UP, 1993.

Laqueur, Thomas. *Making Sex: Body and Gender from the Greeks to Freud.* Cambridge: Harvard UP, 1990.

Latham, Minor White. *The Elizabethan Fairies.* New York: Columbia UP, 1930.

Laurentius, M. Andreas. *A Discourse of the Preservation of the Sight: of Melancholike Diseases; of Rheumes, and of Old Age.* 1599. Trans. Richard Surphlet. Ed. Sanford Larkey. Shakespeare Association Facsimiles no. 15. London, Oxford UP, 1938.

Le Comte, Edward, and John Shawcross. "An Exchange of Letters: By Sex Obsessed." *Midwest Quarterly* 8 (1974): 55–57.

Leicester, H. Marshall. *The Disenchanted Self: Representing the Subject in "The Canterbury Tales."* Berkeley: U of California P, 1990.

Lerer, Seth. *Chaucer and His Readers.* Princeton: Princeton UP, 1993.

Leslie, Bruce R. *Ronsard's Successful Epic Venture: The Epyllion.* French Forum monographs, no. 11. Lexington, KY: French Forum Publishers, 1979.

Leontis, Artemis. *Topographies of Hellenism: Mapping the Homeland.* Ithaca, NY: Cornell UP, 1995.

Levine, Laura. *Men in Women's Clothing: Anti-theatriality and Effeminization 1579–1642.* Cambridge: Cambridge UP, 1994.

Lewalski, Barbara K. "*Samson Agonistes* and the 'Tragedy' of the Apocalypse." *PMLA* 85 (1970): 1050–62.

———. *Writing Women in Jacobean England.* Cambridge: Harvard UP, 1993.

Lewis, C.S. *The Allegory of Love: A Study in Medieval Tradition.* New York: Oxford UP, 1936.

Lloyd, Lodowick. *The Choyce of Jewels.* London, 1607.

Low, Anthony. *The Georgic Revolution.* Princeton: Princeton UP, 1985.

Lupton, Julia Reinhard. "Home-Making in Ireland: Virgil's Eclogue I and Book VI of *The Faerie Queene.*" *Spenser Studies* 8 (1987): 119–45.

Lyly, John. *The Complete Works of John Lyly.* Ed. R. Warwick Bond. Vols. 2–3. 1902. Oxford: Clarendon, 1967.

Macfarlane, Alan. *Witchcraft in Tudor and Stuart England: A Regional and Comparative Study.* London: Routledge and Kegan Paul, 1970.

MacNeill, J.G. Swift. *The Constitutional and Parliamentary History of Ireland till the Union.* 1917. Port Washington, NY: Kennikat, 1970.

Maley, Willy. Rev. of *The British Problem, c. 1534–1707: State Formation in the Atlantic Archipelago.* Ed. Brendan Bradshaw and John Morrill; *Uniting the Kingdom? The Making of British History.* Ed. Alexander Grant and Keith J. Stringer; *Religion and Political Culture in Britain and Ireland: From the Glorious Revolution to the Decline of Europe.* By David Hempton. *History Ireland* 4 (1996): 53–55.

———. *Salvaging Spenser: Colonialism, Culture and Identity.* London: Macmillan, 1997.

———. "Spenser and Scotland: The *View* and the Limits of Anglo-Irish Identity." *Prose Studies* 19 (1996): 1–18.

Malynes, Gerard de. *Consuetudo, vel Lex Mercatoria: or, The Ancient Law-Merchant.* 1622. Amsterdam: Theatrum Orbis Terrarum, 1979.

Manley, Lawrence. *Literature and Culture in Early Modern London.* Cambridge: Cambridge UP, 1995.

Marcus, Leah S. *Childhood and Cultural Despair.* Pittsburgh: U of Pittsburgh P, 1978.

———. "Shakespeare's Comic Heroines, Elizabeth I, and the Political Uses of Androgyny." *Women in the Middle Ages and the Renaissance: Literary and Historical Perspectives.* Ed. Mary Beth Rose. Syracuse, NY: Syracuse UP, 1986.

———. *Unediting the Renaissance: Shakespeare, Marlowe, Milton.* New York: Routledge, 1996.

Marotti, Arthur. "Patronage, Poetry, and Print." *Patronage, Politics, and Literary Traditions in England, 1558–1658.* Ed. Cedric C. Brown. Detroit: Wayne State UP, 1993. 21-46.

Maus, Katharine Eisaman. *Inwardness and Theater in the English Renaissance.* Chicago: U of Chicago P, 1995.

Maxwell, James. *Carolanna: A Poem in Honor of Our King.* London, 1619.

Mazzola, Elizabeth. "Apocryphal Texts and Epic Amnesia: The Ends of History in *The Faerie Queene.*" *Soundings* 78 (1995): 131–42.

McCabe, Richard A. *Incest, Drama, and Nature's Law 1550–1700.* Cambridge: Cambridge UP, 1993.

McClintock, Anne. "The Angel of Progress: Pitfalls of the Term 'Post-Colonialism.'" *Social Text* 31–32 (1992): 84–98.

McGinn, Bernard. *Visions of the End: Apocalyptic Traditions in the Middle Ages.* New York: Columbia UP, 1979.

McLeod, Randall. "'The very names of the Persons': Editing and the Invention of Dramatick Character." *Staging the Renaissance: Reinterpretations of Elizabethan and Jacobean Drama.* Ed. David Scott Kastan and Peter Stallybrass. New York: Routledge, 1991. 89–96.

Melbancke, Brian. *Philotimus: The Warre betwixt Nature and Fortune.* London, 1583.

Middleton, T., and T. Dekker. *The Roaring Girl.* 1611. Ed. John S. Farmer. Amersham: Tudor Facsimile Texts, 1914.

Mignolo, Walter D. *The Darker Side of the Renaissance: Literacy, Territoriality, and Colonization.* Ann Arbor: U of Michigan P, 1995.

Miller, David Lee. *The Poem's Two Bodies: The Poetics of the 1590 "Faerie Queene."* Princeton: Princeton UP, 1988.

———. "Spenser and the Gaze of Glory." *Edmund Spenser's Poetry.* Ed. Hugh Maclean and Anne Lake Prescott. 3rd ed. New York: Norton, 1993. 756-64.

———. "Spenser's Vocation, Spenser's Career." *ELH* 50 (1983): 197–231.

Miller, Fred D., Jr. *Nature, Justice, and Rights in Aristotle's "Politics."* Oxford: Clarendon, 1995.

Miller, Naomi. *Changing the Subject: Mary Wroth and the Figurations of Gender.* Lexington: UP of Kentucky, 1996.

———. "Engendering Discourse: Women's Voices in Wroth's *Urania* and Shakespeare's Plays." *Reading Mary Wroth.* Ed. Naomi Miller and Gary Waller. Knoxville: U of Tennessee P, 1991. 154–72.

———. "'Not much to be marked': Narrative of the Woman's Part in Lady Mary Wroth's *Urania.*" *Studies in English Literature* 29 (1989): 121–38.

Milton, John. *Complete Prose Works of John Milton.* Ed. Don M. Wolfe et al. 8 vols. New Haven: Yale UP, 1953–82.

———. *John Milton: Complete Poems and Major Prose.* Ed. Merritt Y. Hughes. Indianapolis: Odyssey, 1957.

———. *The Poems of John Milton.* Ed. John Carey and Alastair Fowler. London: Longman, 1968.

Miskimin, Alice. *The Renaissance Chaucer.* New Haven: Yale UP, 1975.

Montrose, Louis. "The Elizabethan Subject and the Spenserian Text." *Literary Theory/Renaissance Texts.* Ed. Patricia Parker and David Quint. Baltimore: Johns Hopkins UP, 1986. 303–40.

———. "'Shaping Fantasies': Figurations of Gender and Power in Elizabethan Culture." *Representations* 2 (1983): 1–29. Rpt. in *Representing the English Renaissance.* Ed. Stephen Greenblatt. Berkeley: U of California P, 1988. 31–64.

———. "Spenser's Domestic Domain: Poetry, Property, and the Early Modern Subject." *Subject and Object in Renaissance Culture.* Ed. Margreta de

Grazia, Maureen Quilligan, and Peter Stallybrass. Cambridge: Cambridge UP, 1996. 83–130.

Mulcaster, Richard. *In mortem serenissimae reginae Elizabethae* and *The translation of certaine latine verses written vppon her majesties death called a comforting complaint.* London, 1603.

Mulholland, Paul A., ed. *The Roaring Girl.* By Thomas Middleton and Thomas Dekker. Manchester: Manchester UP, 1987.

de Muret, Marc-Antoine. *Commentaires au premier livre des Amours de Ronsard.* Ed. Jacques Chomarat, Marie-Madeleine Fragonard, and Gisèle Mathieu-Castellani. Geneva: Droz, 1985.

———. "Hélène avant Surgères: pour une lecture humaniste des *Sonnets pour Hélène.*" *Sur des vers de Ronsard: 1585–1985.* Ed. Marcel Tetel. Paris: Amateurs de livres, 1990. 127–43.

Murrin, Michael. *The Allegorical Epic: Essays in Its Rise and Decline.* Chicago: U of Chicago P, 1980.

Nashe, Thomas. *The Works of Thomas Nashe.* Ed. Ronald B. McKerrow. 5 vols. Rpt. with corrections and supplementary notes by F.P. Wilson, 1958; rpt. Oxford: Basil Blackwell, 1966.

Niccols, Richard. *The Mirrour for Magistrates, as a Winter Night's Vision.* Ed. Joseph Haslewood. London, 1815.

Nicolson, Marjorie Hope. *A World in the Moon: A Study of the Changing Attitude toward the Moon in the Seventeenth and Eighteenth Centuries.* Smith College Studies in Modern Languages 17.2. Northampton, MA: Smith College, 1936.

Nohrnberg, James. *The Analogy of "The Faerie Queene."* Princeton: Princeton UP, 1976.

Norbrook, David. *Poetry and Politics in the English Renaissance.* London: Routledge and Kegan Paul, 1984.

———. "The Politics of Milton's Early Poetry." *John Milton.* Ed. Annabel Patterson. London: Longman, 1992.

Norton, Mary Beth. *Founding Mothers and Fathers.* New York: Alfred Knopf, 1996.

O'Connell, Michael. *Mirror and Veil: The Historical Dimension of Spenser's "Faerie Queene."* Chapel Hill: U of North Carolina P, 1977.

Okin, Susan Moller. *Justice, Gender, and the Family.* New York: Basic Books, 1989.

O'Leary, Stephen D. *Arguing the Apocalypse: A Theory of Millennial Rhetoric.* New York: Oxford UP, 1994.

Ong, Walter. "Latin Language Study as a Renaissance Puberty Rite." *Studies in Philology* 56 (1959): 103–24.

Orgel, Stephen. "Margins of Truth." *The Renaissance Text: Theory, Editing, Textuality.* Ed. Andrew Murphy. Manchester: Manchester UP. Forthcoming.

———. "'Nobody's Perfect: Or Why Did the English Stage Take Boys for Women?" *South Atlantic Quarterly* 88 (1989): 7–29.

Osborn, James M. *Young Philip Sidney, 1572–1577.* New Haven: Yale UP, 1972.

Ovid. *Metamorphoses.* 2nd ed. Trans. Frank Justus Miller; rev. G.P. Gould. Loeb Classical Library. 6 vols. Cambridge: Harvard UP, 1984.

———. *Ovid's Metamorphoses Englished, Mythologized, and Represented in Figures.* Trans. George Sandys. Oxford, 1632.

———. *P. Ouidii Metamorphosis seu fabvlae poeticae: earvm que interpretatio ethica, physica et historica Georgii Sabini.* Frankfort, 1589.

The Oxford Dictionary of English Etymology. Ed. C.T. Onions. Oxford: Clarendon, 1966.

The Oxford Dictionary of English Proverbs. 3rd ed. Revised F.P. Wilson. Oxford: Clarendon, 1970.

Parker, Patricia A. *Inescapable Romance: Studies in the Poetics of a Mode.* Princeton: Princeton UP, 1979.

———. *Literary Fat Ladies: Rhetoric, Gender, Property.* London: Methuen, 1987.

Pateman, Carole. *The Sexual Contract.* Stanford: Stanford UP, 1988.

Patrides, C.A. "'Something like Prophetick strain': Apocalyptic Configurations in Milton." Patrides and Wittreich 207–37.

Patrides, C.A., and Joseph Wittreich, eds. *The Apocalypse in English Renaissance Thought and Literature.* Ithaca, NY: Cornell UP, 1984.

Patterson, Annabel. *Pastoral and Ideology: Virgil to Valèry.* Berkeley: U of California P, 1987.

———. *Reading between the Lines.* Madison: U of Wisconsin P, 1993.

Patterson, Lee. *Chaucer and the Subject of History.* Madison: U of Wisconsin P, 1991.

———. "'What Man Artow?': Authorial Self-Definition in *The Tale of Sir Thopas* and *The Tale of Melibee.*" *Studies in the Age of Chaucer* 11 (1989): 117–75.

Pavlock, Barbara. *Eros, Imitation, and the Epic Tradition.* Ithaca, NY: Cornell UP, 1990.

Pearsall, Derek. *The Life of Geoffrey Chaucer.* Oxford: Blackwell, 1992.

———. "The Squire as Story-Teller." *University of Tennessee Quarterly* 34 (1964): 82–92.

Peele, George. "The Old Wives Tale." *Dramatic Works of George Peele.* Ed. Frank S. Hook. New Haven: Yale UP, 1970. 385–421.

Perry, Curtis. "The Citizen Politics of Nostalgia: Queen Elizabeth in Early Jacobean London." *Journal of Medieval and Renaissance Studies* 23 (1993): 89–111.

Pocock, J.G.A. "British History: A Plea for a New Subject." *Journal of Modern History* 47 (1975): 601–28.

———. "Conclusion: Contingency, Identity, Sovereignty." Grant and Stringer 292–302.

———. "The Limits and Divisions of British History: In Search of the Unknown Subject." *American Historical Review* 87 (1982): 311–36.

Prescott, Anne Lake. *French Poets and the English Renaissance: Studies in Fame and Transformation.* New Haven: Yale UP, 1978.

———. "Spenser (Re)Reading du Bellay: Chronology and Literary Response." *Spenser's Life and the Subject of Biography.* Ed. Judith H. Anderson, Donald Cheney, and David R. Richardson. Amherst: U of Massachusetts P, 1996. 131–45.

———. "Titans." *Spenser Encyclopedia* 691.

Puttenham, George. *The Arte of English Poesie.* Ed. Gladys Doidge Willcock and Alice Walker. Cambridge: Cambridge UP, 1936.

Quilligan, Maureen. "The Constant Subject: Instability and Authority in Wroth's *Urania* Poems." *Soliciting Interpretation: Literary Theory and Seventeenth-Century English Poetry.* Ed. Elizabeth D. Harvey and Katharine Eisaman Maus. Chicago: U of Chicago P, 1990.

———. "Lady Mary Wroth: Female Authority and the Family Romance." *Unfolded Tales: Essays on Renaissance Romance.* Ed. George M. Logan and Gordon Teskey. Ithaca, NY: Cornell UP, 1989. 257–80.

———. *Milton's Spenser: The Politics of Reading.* Ithaca, NY: Cornell UP, 1983.

Quint, David. "Bragging Rights: Honor and Courtesy in Shakespeare and Spenser." *Creative Imitation: New Essays on Renaissance Literature in Honor of Thomas M. Greene.* Ed. David Quint et al. Binghamton, NY: Medieval and Renaissance Texts and Studies, 1992. 391–430.

———. *Epic and Empire: Politics and Generic Form from Virgil to Milton.* Princeton: Princeton UP, 1993.

Rackin, Phyllis. "Foreign Country: The Place of Women and Sexuality in Shakespeare's Historical World." *Enclosure Acts: Sexuality, Property, and Culture in Early Modern England.* Ed. Richard Burt and John Michael Archer. Ithaca, NY: Cornell UP, 1994. 68–95.

Rambuss, Richard. "Spenser's Lives, Spenser's Careers." *Spenser and the Subject of Biography.* Ed. Judith H. Anderson, Donald Cheney, and David A. Richardson. Amherst: U of Massachusetts P, 1996. 1–17.

———. *Spenser's Secret Career.* Cambridge: Cambridge UP, 1993.

Rathborne, Isabel E. *The Meaning of Spenser's Fairyland.* New York: Columbia UP, 1937.

Rawson, Maud Stepney. *Bess of Hardwick and Her Circle.* New York: John Lane, 1910.

Raynes, Harold E. *A History of British Insurance.* Rev. ed. London: Sir Isaac Pitman and Sons, 1950.

The Resurrection of Our Lord. Malone Society Reprints. Oxford: Oxford UP, 1912.

Richardson, Alan, and Mary Thomas Crane. "Literary Studies and Cognitive Science: Toward a New Interdisciplinarity." *Mosaic.* Forthcoming.

Richardson, Brian. *Print Culture in Vernacular Italy.* Cambridge: Cambridge UP, 1994.

Rigolot, François. "Homer's Virgilian Authority: Ronsard's Counterfeit Epic Theory." *Discourses of Authority in Medieval and Renaissance Literature.* Ed. Kevin Brownlee and Walter Stephens. Hanover, NH: UP of New England, 1989. 63–75.

Roberts, Josephine. "Labyrinths of Desire: Lady Mary Wroth's Reconstruction of Romance." *Women's Studies* 19 (1991): 183–92.

———. "Radigund Revisited: Perspectives on Women Rulers in Lady Mary Wroth's *Urania.*" *The Renaissance Englishwoman in Print.* Ed. Anne Haselkorn and Betty Travitsky. Amherst: U of Massachusetts P, 1990. 187–207.

Roche, Thomas P., Jr. *The Kindly Flame: A Study of the Third and Fourth Books of Spenser's "Faerie Queene."* Princeton: Princeton UP, 1964.

Ronsard, Pierre de. *Amours de Cassandre.* Muret, 1553.

———. *Oeuvres complètes.* Ed. Paul Laumonier. Rev. and completed by Isidor Silver and Raymond Lebèque. 20 vols. Paris: Hachette, 1914–75.

———. *Oeuvres complètes de Ronsard.* Ed. Gustave Cohen. Paris: Gallimard, 1950.

Rose, Mark. *Heroic Love.* Cambridge: Harvard UP, 1968.

Rumrich, John. "Milton's God and the Matter of Chaos." *PMLA* 110 (1995): 1035–46.

Sadler, Florence. "*The Faerie Queene:* An Elizabethan Apocalypse." Patrides and Wittreich, *The Apocalypse in English Renaissance Thought and Literature.* 148–74.

Saint German, Christopher. *Doctor and Student.* Southwarke, 1529–31.

———. *The Secunde dyaloge in Englysshe bytwene a doctour of dyuyntye and a student in the lawes of Englande.* Southwarke, 1530.

Samaha, Joel. *Law and Order in Historical Perspective: The Case of Elizabethan Essex.* New York: Academic, 1974.

Satterthwaite, A.W. *Spenser, Ronsard, and DuBellay: A Renaissance Comparison.* Princeton: Princeton UP, 1960.

Sawday, Jonathan. *The Body Emblazoned: Dissection and the Human Body in Renaissance Culture.* London: Routledge, 1995.

Schochet, Gordon J. *The Authoritarian Family and Political Attitudes in Seventeenth-Century England.* Oxford: Blackwell, 1975.

Schoenfeldt, Michael. "Fables of the Belly in Early Modern England." *The Body in Parts.* Ed. David Hillman and Carla Mazzio. New York: Routledge, 1997. 243–61.

Scot, Reginald. *The Discoverie of Witchcraft.* London, 1584.

Seshadri-Crooks, Kalpana. "At the Margins of Postcolonial Studies." *Ariel* 26 (1995): 47–71.

Shakespeare, William. *The Riverside Shakespeare.* Ed. G. Blakemore Evans et al. 2nd ed. Boston: Houghton Mifflin, 1997.

Shanley, Mary Lyndon. "Marriage Contract and Social Contract in Seventeenth-Century English Political Thought." *Western Political Quarterly* 32 (1979): 79–91.

Sharpe, J.A. "The History of Crime in Late Medieval and Early Modern England: A Review of the Field." *Social History* 7 (1982): 187–203.

Sharpe, Jenny. "Is the United States Postcolonial? Transnationalism, Immigration, and Race." *Diaspora* 4 (1995): 181–99.

Sharpe, Kevin. *Politics and Ideas in Early Stuart England.* London: Pinter, 1989.

Shaver, Anne. "A New Woman of Romance." *Modern Language Studies* 21 (1991): 63–77.

Sherman, Nancy. *The Fabric of Character: Aristotle's Theory of Virtue.* Oxford: Clarendon, 1989.

Shohat, Ella. "Notes on the 'Post-Colonial.'" *Social Text* 31–32 (1992): 99–113.

Shroeder, John W. "Spenser's Erotic Drama: The Orgoglio Episode." *ELH* 29 (1962): 140–59.

Shuger, Debora Kuller. *The Renaissance Bible: Scholarship, Sacrifice, and Subjectivity.* Berkeley: U of California P, 1994.

Sidney, Sir Philip. *The Poems of Sir Philip Sidney.* Ed. William A. Ringler, Jr. Oxford: Clarendon, 1962.

———. *A Defence of Poetry. Miscellaneous Prose.* Ed. Katherine Duncan-Jones and Jan van Dorsten. Oxford: Clarendon, 1973.

Silberman, Lauren. *Transforming Desire: Erotic Knowledge in Books III and IV of "The Faerie Queene."* Berkeley: U of California P, 1995.

Spelman, Elizabeth. *Inessential Woman.* Boston: Beacon, 1988.

Spelman, Sir John. *The Reports of Sir John Spelman.* Ed. J.H. Baker. 2 vols. London: Selden Society, 1977–78.

Spenser, Edmund. *The Faerie Queene.* Ed. A.C. Hamilton. London: Longman, 1977.

———. *The Faerie Queene.* Ed. Thomas P. Roche, Jr. 1978. New Haven: Yale UP, 1981.

———. *The Poetical Works of Edmund Spenser.* Ed. J.C. Smith and Ernest de Sélincourt. 3 vols. Oxford: Clarendon, 1909–10.

———. *The Yale Edition of the Shorter Poems of Edmund Spenser.* Ed. William Oram et al. New Haven: Yale UP, 1989.

———. *A View of the Present State of Ireland.* Ed. W.L. Renwick. Oxford: Clarendon, 1970.

———. *The Works of Edmund Spenser: A Variorum Edition.* Ed. Edwin Greenlaw, Charles Grosvenor Osgood, and Frederick Morgan Padelford. 11 vols. Baltimore: Johns Hopkins UP, 1932–57.

The Spenser Encyclopedia. Ed. A.C. Hamilton et al. Toronto: U of Toronto P; London: Routledge, 1990.

Spikes, Judith Doolin. "The Jacobean History Play and the Myth of the Elect Nation." *Renaissance Drama* 8 (1977): 117–49.

Spivak, Gayatri. "Scattered Speculations on the Question of Cultural Studies." *Outside in the Teaching Machine.* New York: Routledge, 1993.

The Statutes of Ireland. Dublin, 1621.

Statutes of the Realm. London, 1810–22.

Stephanus, Carolus [Charles Estienne]. *Dictionarium historicum geographicum poeticarum.* Oxford, 1670.

Stern, Virginia F. *Gabriel Harvey: His Life, Marginalia and Library.* Oxford: Clarendon, 1979.

Stillman, Robert E. "Spenserian Autonomy and the Trial of New Historicism: Book VI of *The Faerie Queene.*" *English Literary Renaissance* 22 (1992): 299–314.

Stone, Lawrence. *The Family, Sex, and Marriage in England 1500–1800.* New York: Harper and Row, 1977.

Strohm, Paul. *Social Chaucer.* Cambridge: Harvard UP, 1989.

Suleri, Sara. *The Rhetoric of English India.* Chicago: U of Chicago P, 1992.

———. "Woman Skin Deep: Feminism and the Postcolonial Condition." *Critical Inquiry* 18 (1992): 756–69.

Suzuki, Mihoko. *Metamorphoses of Helen: Authority and Difference in Homer, Virgil, Spenser, and Shakespeare.* Ithaca, NY: Cornell UP, 1989.

Swanson, Judith A. *The Public and the Private in Aristotle's Political Philosophy.* Ithaca, NY: Cornell UP, 1992.

Swift, Carolyn Ruth. "Feminine Identity in Lady Mary Wroth's Romance *Urania.*" *English Literary Renaissance* 14 (1984): 328–46.

Tanner, Marie. *The Last Descendant of Aeneas: The Hapsburgs and the Mythic Image of the Emperor.* New Haven: Yale UP, 1993.

Tasso, Torquato. *Jerusalem Delivered.* Ed. John Charles Nelson. Trans. Edward Fairfax. New York: Capricorn-Putnam, 1963.

———. *Gerusalemme liberata.* Ed. Lanfranco Caretti. Turin: Einaudi, 1971.

Taylor, Karla. "Proverbs and the Authentication of Convention in *Troilus and Criseyde.*" *Chaucer's Troilus: Essays in Criticism.* Ed. Stephen A. Barney. Hamden, CT: Archon, 1980. 277–95.

Thomas, Keith. *Rule and Misrule in the Schools of Early Modern England.* Reading: U of Reading P, 1976.

Thompson, Edward. *Sir Walter Ralegh.* New Haven: Yale UP, 1936.

Tierney, Brian. "Aristotle and the American Indians—Again." *Cristianesimo nella storia* 12 (1991): 295–304, 315–22.

———. "Origins of Natural Rights Language: Texts and Contexts, 1150–1250." *History of Political Thought* 10 (1989): 615–46.

Tilley, Morris Palmer. *A Dictionary of the Proverbs in England in the Sixteenth and Seventeenth Centuries.* 1950. Ann Arbor: U of Michigan P, 1966.

Tonkin, Humphrey. *Spenser's Courteous Pastoral: Book Six of "The Faerie Queene."* Oxford: Clarendon, 1972.

Tuana, Nancy. "Aristotle and the Politics of Reproduction." *Engendering Origins: Critical Feminist Readings in Plato and Aristotle.* Albany: State U of New York P, 1994. 189–206.

Tuve, Rosamund. *Allegorical Imagery: Some Mediaeval Books and Their Posterity.* Princeton: Princeton UP, 1966.

———. *Images and Themes in Five Poems by Milton.* Oxford: Clarendon, 1957.

Van Dorsten, Jan. *The Radical Arts.* Leiden: Leiden UP, 1973.

Vaughan, William. *Directions for Health, Naturall and Artificiall.* London, 1626.

Virgil. *Opera virgiliana cvm decem commentis . . . et Badii Ascensii elucidatione.* Lyon, 1529.

———. *Works.* Ed. H. Rushton Fairclough. Loeb Classical Library. 2 vols. Cambridge: Harvard UP, 1916.

Walker, Julia M. "Bones of Contention: Posthumous Images of Elizabeth and Stuart Politics." *Dissing Elizabeth: Negative Representations of Gloriana.* Durham, NC: Duke UP, 1998. 252–76.

———. "Reading the Tombs of Elizabeth I." *English Literary Renaissance* 26 (1996): 510–30.

———. "Spenser's Elizabeth Portrait and the Fiction of Dynastic Epic." *Modern Philology* 90 (1992): 172–99.

Wall, Wendy. *The Imprint of Gender: Authorship and Publication in the English Renaissance.* Ithaca, NY: Cornell UP, 1993.

Waller, Gary. *The Sidney Family Romance.* Detroit: Wayne State UP, 1993.

Warner, Marina. *From the Beast to the Blonde: On Fairy Tales and Their Tellers.* New York: Farrar, Straus, and Giroux, 1994.

Waters, D. Douglas. *Duessa as Theological Satire.* Columbus: U of Missouri P, 1970.

Watkins, John. *The Specter of Dido: Spenser and Virgilian Epic.* New Haven: Yale UP, 1995.

Weinberg, Florence. "Double Dido: Patterns of Passion in Ronsard's *Franciade.*" *Lapidary Inscriptions: Renaissance Essays for Donald A. Stone, Jr.* Ed. Barbara C. Bowen and Jerry C. Nash. French Forum monographs, no. 74. Lexington, KY: French Forum Publishers, 1991. 73–85.

White, Stephen D. *Sir Edward Coke and "The Grievances of the Commonwealth," 1621–28.* Chapel Hill: U of North Carolina P, 1979.

Whitman, Jon. *Allegory: The Dynamics of an Ancient and Medieval Technique.* Cambridge: Harvard UP, 1987.

Wilkes, Kathleen V. "The Good Man and the Good for Man." *Essays on Aristotle's Ethics.* Ed. Amélie Rorty. Berkeley: U of California P, 1980. 341–57.

Willet, Andrew. *Joy of the English Church for the Coronation of a Prince*. London, 1603.

Williams, Kathleen. *Spenser's World of Glass: A Reading of "The Faerie Queene."* Berkeley and Los Angeles: U of California P, 1966.

Willson, David. *James VI and I*. Oxford: Oxford UP, 1956.

Wilson, Thomas. *A Discourse Uppon Usurye*. 1572. Rpt. as *A Discourse upon Usury*. Ed. R. H. Tawney. London: G. Bell and Sons, 1925.

Wilson, Violet A. *Queen Elizabeth's Maids of Honour*. New York: Dutton, 1923.

Wimberly, Lowry. *Folklore in the English and Scottish Ballads*. 1928. New York: Frederick Ungar, 1959.

Wittreich, Joseph. *Feminist Milton*. Ithaca, NY: Cornell UP, 1987.

Wofford, Susanne Lindgren. *The Choice of Achilles: The Ideology of Figure in the Epic*. Stanford: Stanford UP, 1992.

———. "Gendering Allegory: Spenser's Bold Reader and the Emergence of Character in *The Faerie Queene III*." *Criticism* 30 (1988): 1–21.

Woodbridge, Linda. "Amoret and Belphoebe: Fairy Tale and Myth." *Notes and Queries* 33 (1986): 340–42.

———. *The Scythe of Saturn: Shakespeare and Magical Thinking*. Urbana: U of Illinois P, 1994.

Wooden, Warren W. *Children's Literature of the English Renaissance*. Ed. Jeanie Watson. Lexington: UP of Kentucky, 1986.

Woods, Susanne. Introduction. *The Poems of Aemilia Lanyer: "Salve Deus Rex Judaeorum."* New York: Oxford UP, 1993.

———. "Vocation and Authority in Aemilia Lanyer." *Aemilia Lanyer: Gender, Genre and the Canon*. Ed. Marshall Grossman. Lexington: UP of Kentucky, 1997. 83–98.

Woolf, D.R. "Two Elizabeths? James I and the Late Queen's Famous Memory." *Canadian Journal of History* 20 (1985): 167–91.

Wright, Thomas. *The Passions of the Minde*. London, 1621.

Wroth, Mary. *The First Part of The Countess of Montgomery's Urania*. Ed. Josephine Roberts. Binghamton, NY: Medieval and Renaissance Texts and Studies, 1995.

Wurtsbaugh, Jewel. *Two Centuries of Spenserian Scholarship*. Baltimore: Johns Hopkins UP, 1936.

CONTRIBUTORS

Judith H. Anderson, professor of English at Indiana University, has written numerous articles and a book on Spenser, *The Growth of a Personal Voice: Piers Plowman and* The Faerie Queene (Yale, 1976). She is also an editor of *Spenser's Life and the Subject of Biography* (Massachusetts, 1996) and of Donaldson's translation of *Piers Plowman* (Norton, 1990), and she is author of *Biographical Truth: The Representation of Historical Persons in Tudor-Stuart Writing* (Yale, 1984) and *Words That Matter: Linguistic Perception in Renaissance English* (Stanford, 1996).

David J. Baker is associate professor of English at the University of Hawaii. He is the author of *Between Nations: Shakespeare, Spenser, Marvell, and the Question of Britain* (Stanford, 1997), and co-editor, with Willy Maley, of *An Uncertain Union: The British Problem in Renaissance Literature* (forthcoming).

Elizabeth Jane Bellamy is an associate professor of English and Critical Theory at the University of New Hampshire. She is the author of *Translations of Power: Narcissism and the Unconscious in Epic History* (Cornell, 1992) and *Affective Genealogies: Psychoanalysis, Postmodernism, and the "Jewish Question" After Auschwitz* (Nebraska, 1997).

Patrick Cheney is a professor of English and Comparative Literature at Pennsylvania State University. He is the author of *Spenser's Famous Flight: A Renaissance Idea of Literary Career* (Toronto, 1993) and of *Marlowe's Counterfeit Profession: Ovid, Spenser, Counter-Nationhood* (Toronto, 1997) as well as co-editor (with Anne Lake Prescott) of *Approaches to Teaching Shorter Elizabethan Poetry* (MLA, 2000). A past chair of "Spenser at Kalamazoo," he is currently president of the International Spenser Society.

Heather Dubrow is Tighe-Evans Professor (and John Bascom Professor) at the University of Wisconsin-Madison. She is the author of five books, of which the most recent is *Shakespeare and Domestic Loss: Forms of Deprivation, Mourning, and Recuperation* (Cambridge, 1999). Her other publications include a co-edited collection of essays, a chapbook of poetry, and articles on teaching.

Roland Greene is the author of *Unrequited Conquests: Love and Empire in the Colonial Americas* (Chicago, 1999) and *Post-Petrarchism: Origins and Innovations of the Western Lyric Sequence* (Princeton, 1991), and the editor, with Elizabeth Fowler, of *The Project of Prose in Early Modern Europe and the New World* (Cambridge, 1997). He is at work on a book about early modern worldmaking.

William J. Kennedy is professor of Comparative Literature at Cornell University. He has written *Rhetorical Norms in Renaissance Literature* (Yale, 1978), *Jacopo Sannazaro and the Uses of Pastoral* (New England, 1983), and *Authorizing Petrarch* (Cornell, 1994). He is currently completing *The Site of Petrarchism*, a study of early modern national sentiment in European poetry.

John N. King is professor of English at Ohio State University. His books include *English Reformation Literature: The Tudor Origins of the Protestant Tradition* (1982), *Tudor Royal Iconography: Literature and Art in an Age of Religious Crisis* (1989), and *Spenser's Poetry and the Reformation Tradition* (1990), all published by Princeton University Press. He serves as co-editor of *Literature & History*, literature editor of *Reformation*, and advisory board member for the British Academy project to edit *John Foxe's Acts and Monuments of the Christian Martyrs*.

Mary Ellen Lamb is a professor at Southern Illinois University, Carbondale. She is the author of *Gender and Authorship in the Sidney Circle* (Wisconsin, 1990), as well as numerous essays on early modern women and Shakespeare in such journals as *English Literary Renaissance, Criticism, Shakespeare Studies, and Shakespeare Survey*.

David Lee Miller is professor of English and associate dean of Arts and Sciences at the University of Kentucky. He is the author of *The Poem's Two Bodies: The Poetics of the 1590* Faerie Queene (Princeton, 1988), and co-editor, with Alexander Dunlop, of the MLA volume *Approaches to Teaching Spenser's* Faerie Queene (MLA, 1994). He is currently working on a study of filial sacrifice in Virgil, Shakespeare, and other writers.

Jacqueline T. Miller is associate professor of English at Rutgers University. She is the author of *Poetic License: Authority and Authorship in Medieval and Renaissance Contexts* (Oxford, 1986), and articles on Spenser, Sidney, and other Renaissance subjects. Her current work focuses on the gendered discourses of linguistic power and linguistic nationalism in the early modern period.

Shannon Miller is currently an assistant professor at Temple University. She is the author of *Invested with Meaning: The Raleigh Circle in the New World* (Penn, 1998) and is working on a book-length project entitled *Voicing Violence: Textual and Social Violence in Early Modern Women Writers.*

Anne Lake Presscott is Helen Goodhart Altschul Professor of English at Barnard College. The author of *French Poets and the English Renaissance* (Yale, 1978) and *Imagining Rabelais in Renaissance England* (Yale, 1998), she is co-editor, with Thomas P. Roche, of *Spenser Studies* and, with Hugh Maclean, of the Norton edition of Spenser's poetry.

David Quint is professor of English and Comparative Literature at Yale University. He is the author of *Epic and Empire* (Princeton, 1993) and *Montaigne and the Quality of Mercy* (Princeton, 1998).

Michael Schoenfeldt is professor of English at the University of Michigan. He is the author of *Prayer and Power: George Herbert and Renaissance Courtship* (Chicago, 1991), and of *Bodies and Selves in Early Modern England: Physiology and Inwardness in Spenser, Shakespeare, Herbert, and Milton* (Cambridge, 1999).

Lauren Silberman is the author of *Transforming Desire: Erotic Knowledge in Books III and IV of* The Faerie Queene (California, 1995), as well as articles on Spenser, Jonson, and Medieval and Renaissance mythography. She has been president of the International Spenser Society and program chair for "Spenser at Kalamazoo."

John Watkins is associate professor of English and Medieval Studies at the University of Minnesota, Twin Cities. He is the author of *The Specter of Dido: Spenser and Virgilian Epic* (Yale, 1995) and numerous articles on medieval and early modern literature. He is currently finishing a book manuscript entitled '*In Queene Elizabeth's Dayes': History and Sovereignty in Early Modern England, 1603–1714.*

Susanne Woods is the author of *Natural Emphasis: English Versification from Chaucer to Dryden* (Huntington, 1985) and *Lanyer: A Renaissance Woman Poet* (Oxford, 1999) and is co-editor, with Elizabeth H. Hageman, of the Oxford University Press series *Woman Writers in English, 1350–1850*. She has taught at the University of Hawaii, at Brown University, where she founded the Brown University Women Writers Project in 1988, and at Franklin and Marshall College. She is currently provost of Wheaton College in Massachusetts.

INDEX

Bale, John, 149, 158
ballads: fairy queens in, 82, 92–93
beastliness, 239–40
Beilin, Elaine, 140
Belman of London (Dekker), 210
Belphoebe, 32, 34, 35, 36, 37, 38, 39, 40, 88
Belsey, Catherine, 143
Bennett, Josephine, 32
Bentley, Gerald, 244–45
Berger, Harry, 19, 21, 30, 215, 246
Berry, Craig, 89
Bess of Hardwick, 41n. 11
"Better a mischief than an inconvenience": contexts found in, 221–26; in *A View of the Present State of Ireland,* 219–20, 221, 226–29
Binet, Charles, 68
"blent," 19–20
Bocage (Ronsard), 67
Bodin, Jean, 220
body: allegory of self and, 234–43
Bononome, Gioseffo, 55
Book of Martyrs (Foxe), 158, 159
books; in Wroth's *Urania,* 121–22
Bower of Bliss: Acrasia in, 90–91, 93–94; destruction of, 16–17, 25–26, 29–31, 240–41; figure of "Genius" and, 26–27; gates of, 235; gender perspective in, 94–95; geographic imagining of, 184, 185; Guyon and, 16–17, 21, 24–25; Spenserian worldmaking and, 24–25, 27–31
Boyle, Elizabeth, 38
Braggadocchio, 35
bride, ownership of. *See* sexual ownership
Brideling, 87
Bridges, John, 224
brigands: as thieves, 205–8
Britannia (Camden), 195
Britishness: modern debate in, 193–95, 200–201; *A View of the Present State of Ireland* and, 193–95
Britomart, 97, 99, 102, 123, 139–40, 159
Brown, Keith, 194
Browne, William, 163
Buchanan, George, 205
Bullen, Anne, 131
Burbon, 228

Burghley, Lord. *See* Cecil, William
burglary, 209–10. *See also* thievery
Burke, Peter, 83
Burleigh, Lord. *See* Cecil, William
Burton, Robert, 234–35, 238
Busirane. *See* House of Busirane

Cain, Thomas, 184
Calidore, 38, 82, 103, 157, 205–6, 207–8
Cambell, 49, 50
Camden, William, 195
Camões, Luíz Vaz de, 181, 185
Canacee, 49, 50
Canny, Nicholas, 194–95, 200, 202
Canterbury's Pilgrimage (Laud), 153
Canterbury Tales (Chaucer): issues of textual ownership and, 49–50, 51–52; Spenser's Squire of Dames and, 47, 49–50
Capp, Bernard, 158
careers, poetic. *See* poetic careers
Carey, John, 169
Carlo, 181–82
Carolanna (Maxwell), 146n. 9
Cary, Henry, 107
Castle of Alma, 234–43
Castle of Health (Elyot), 239
catachresis, 191n. 2
Catherine de' Medici, 68, 71, 76n. 19
Catholicism: New World and, 182, 186–87; satire of, 148–55; thievery and, 214
Cavanagh, Sheila, 200
Cecil, William, 77n. 20; 102, 138
Celts, 211
Cerberus, 149
Cervantes, Saavedra, 18
Chaos, 152
Charlemagne, 183, 187
Charles (prince of England), 134
Charles I (king of England), 168, 171
Charles II (king of England), 154, 157
Charles V (Holy Roman Emperor), 181
Charles IX (king of France), 68
Chaucer, Geoffrey: Spenser's Squire of Dames and, 45–46, 47, 49–50, 51–52, 55, 58, 59; *Canterbury Tales,* 47, 49–50, 51–52; *The Tale of Sir Thopas,* 45, 46, 49, 99n. 5; *Troilus,* 58